Pasts Beyond Memory

A follow-up and complementary volume to *The Birth of the Museum*, *Pasts Beyond Memory* examines the relations between evolutionary theory, political thought and museums in Britain, the United States and Australia in the late nineteenth and early twentieth centuries. Drawing on recent developments in social theory, science studies and visual culture studies, it creates significant new frameworks for understanding the relations between museums and society.

Tony Bennett explores the evolutionary museum in relation to the earlier Enlightenment museum and cabinets of curiosity, illuminating the distinctive forms of visual knowledge associated with archaeological, ethnological, geological and natural history evolutionary displays. He also considers the new forms of social authority that evolutionary scientists aimed for in pitting their ability to read the lessons of prehistoric times against the text-based authority of the humanities.

The new ideas of what a person was that evolutionary thought created became the basis for new forms of cultural governance, which the book examines in the context of British and American new liberalism, and the colonial administration of early twentieth-century Australia.

Both a historical investigation and a contribution to current debates, *Pasts Beyond Memory* will help all museums seeking to shed the legacy of evolutionary conceptions and colonial science, so that they can contribute to the development and management of cultural diversity more effectively.

Tony Bennett is Professor of Sociology at the Open University, UK and a Director of the ESRC Research Centre on Socio-cultural Change. His current interests focus on the sociology of culture, the history and theory of museums, and cultural policy. His recent publications include *The Birth of the Museum: History, Theory, Politics* (Routledge 1995) and *Culture: A Reformer's Science* (1998).

Museum Meanings

Series editors

Eilean Hooper-Greenhill

Flora Kaplan

The museum has been constructed as a symbol in Western society since the Renaissance. This symbol is both complex and multi-layered, acting as a sign for domination and liberation, learning and leisure. As sites for exposition, through their collections, displays and buildings, museums mediate many of society's basic values. But these mediations are subject to contestation, and the museum can also be seen as a site for cultural politics. In post-colonial societies, museums have changed radically, reinventing themselves under pressure from many forces, which include new roles and functions for museums, economic rationalism and moves towards greater democratic access.

Museum Meanings analyses and explores the relationships between museums and their publics. 'Museums' are understood very broadly, to include art galleries, historic sites and historic houses. 'Relationships with publics' is also understood very broadly, including interactions with artefacts, exhibitions and architecture, which may be analysed from a range of theoretical perspectives. These include material culture studies, mass communication and media studies, learning theories and cultural studies. The analysis of the relationship of the museum to its publics shifts the emphasis from the museum as text, to studies grounded in the relationships of bodies and sites, identities and communities.

Pasts Beyond Memory

Evolution, Museums, Colonialism

Tony Bennett

 Routledge
Taylor & Francis Group

LONDON AND NEW YORK

First published 2004
by Routledge
11 New Fetter Lane, London EC4P 4EE

Simultaneously published in the USA and Canada
by Routledge
29 West 35th Street, New York, NY 10001

Routledge is an imprint of the Taylor & Francis Group

Typeset in Sabon by
Keystroke, Jacaranda Lodge, Wolverhampton
Printed and bound in Great Britain by
TJ International Ltd, Padstow, Cornwall

British Library Cataloguing in Publication Data
A catalogue record for this book is available from the British Library

Library of Congress Cataloging in Publication Data
Bennett, Tony.
Pasts beyond memory: evolution museums colonialism / Tony Bennett.
p. cm. — (Museum meanings)
Includes bibliographical references and index.
1. Museums–Philosophy. 2. Museums–Historiography. 3. Museum
techniques–Historiography. 4. Museum exhibits–Technological
innovations. 5. Evolution–History–19th century.
6. Evolution–History–20th century. 7. Science–History–19th century.
8. Science–History–20th century. 9. Colonies–History–19th century.
10. Colonies–History–20th century. I. Title. II. Series.
AM7.B385 2004
069′.01—dc22
2003024482

ISBN 0–415–24746–2 (hbk)
ISBN 0–415–24747–0 (pbk)

To the memory of my mother

Contents

List of figures

Acknowledgements

This book has, it turns out, been ten years in the making. Not that it's the only thing I've done over that period; but it has, all the same, been on my mind pretty constantly so that, let the world treat it as it will, it is good to be bringing the work that has gone into it to at least an interim sense of closure. And good, too, to be able to thank those who have helped, in various ways, along the way.

Of these, pride of place must go the Australian Research Council for supporting the project through its Research Grants programme. Without that support, the research that has been required for an undertaking of this kind would not have been possible. I am, then, most grateful to the Australian Research Council, and all the more so for the fact that its support made it possible for Robin Trotter to assist me throughout the early stages of the inquiry. Robin's contribution to the research was of inestimable significance: her thoroughness, determination to leave no archival stone unturned, and sheer commitment to the project greatly enriched the research resource that I was able to draw on in writing the book, and provided a continuing momentum for the project when other more pressing commitments distracted my attention from it. I am greatly in her debt.

I owe a debt, too, to the many library staff and archivists who have helped this project, either through their advice to me directly or in the assistance they lent to Robin. I am therefore pleased to record my thanks to the staff of the libraries at the American Museum of Natural History, the Australian Museum in Sydney, the British Museum (Natural History), the Horniman Museum and Library in south London, the National Museum of Victoria, the Pitt Rivers Museum at Oxford University, and the Queensland Museum in Brisbane. Special thanks, too, to Louise Tythacott for her generous assistance, when Curator of Ethnology at the National Museums and Galleries on Merseyside, in guiding me to and through archival materials relating to the early history of the Liverpool Museums. I am similarly indebted to Michael Hanlon, the Director of the Pitt Rivers Museum.

I owe a debt, too, to the many friends and colleagues with whom I have discussed the issues this book grapples with at various stages in its development. I have benefited greatly from several discussions with Ivan Karp and Corinne Kratz from the Center for Public Scholarship at Emory University, and especially appreciated their invitation to visit that Center early in 2003 when my work in drafting this book was at a critical stage. The opportunity, on a number of occasions, to share ideas with Barry Hindess and Christine Helliwell from the Australian National University, is one I have valued, especially for helping me to address issues concerning the limitations placed on liberal forms of government in colonial contexts. To Barry, too, a special thanks for putting me right on some of the more arcane aspects of conjectural history.

My interest in many of the issues this book engages with was first stimulated by Anne Coombes's work. It has, then, been good to have the benefit of discussing my work with Anne on a number of occasions. I have especially appreciated her open-minded encouragement for some of the lines of inquiry I wished to develop, even though they pointed in a somewhat different direction from her own work. Such colleagues are rare. But not that rare, for the same is true of Mary Bouquet who, when we met at a conference in Denmark, was instantly generous in sharing with me her extensive knowledge of late-nineteenth-century ethnology museums. I learned a good deal from this, as I did from several discussions with Tom Mitchell whose researches for his *The Last Dinosaur Book* ran in directions similar to my own. And my thanks to Ruth Phillips of Carleton University in Ottawa for the strong encouragement she gave me, when she was Director of the Museum of Anthropology at the University of British Columbia, at a stage when my ideas about the form this book should take were only just beginning to take shape.

During the period I have worked on this book, I have supervised some exceptional students whose own researches into different aspects of museum history and theory have helped to illuminate my own inquiries. I must mention Robin Trotter here again and Donna McAlear, whose thesis on Australian and Canadian museum approaches to indigenous cultures both obliged and enabled me to engage with complex, albeit distressing, histories that have been central to my concerns. I also thank Masaaki Morishita, whose work on Japanese art museums has proved instructive for the light it has thrown on the complex ways in which museum practices have been shaped in the context of varied histories of cross-culture contact.

I have been fortunate in being able to present my research at various stages in its development at a number of conferences and seminars where, as is usually the case, I learned far more from my interlocutors than I fear they will have learned from me. My thanks, then, to the following institutions for inviting me to present my work at the events indicated: the Institute for Liberal Arts, Emory University, Atlanta, for my participation in the 1995 *Race, Identity, and Public Culture* conference; to the Pavis Centre at the Open University for inviting me to take part in its *Museums as Contact Zones* conference in 1996; to the organisers of the *Objects and Others* conference at the Centre for Inter-communal Studies, University of Western Sydney, and to the Consortium of Humanities Institutes and Centres, for inviting me to present a public lecture in association with its 1997 meeting at the University of California, Santa Barbara, on issues relating to chapter 7. Thanks also to the Museum of Anthropology at the University of British Columbia, the organisers of the Ultimo seminar series at the University of Technology Sydney, and to the School of Humanities at Griffith University, the Department of English, Critical Theory and Philosophy, University of Wales, Cardiff, and the Department of Sociology at the University of Manchester for the opportunity to rehearse early versions of the arguments that are presented here as chapter 2. I am similarly grateful to the organisers of the 1999 *Frontiers of Memory* conference at the University of East London, to the *Museums as Mirrors* conference held at the National Museum of Denmark in Copenhagen in 2000, to the Humanities Research Centre at the Australian National University, and to the British Sociological Association's Museums and Society Study Group for the opportunity to present and debate raw versions of the arguments that are central to my concerns in chapter 4. I owe a similar debt to the organisers of the *Exhibiting Culture/Displaying Race* conference organised on behalf of the Interdisciplinary Nineteenth-Century Studies Association at the University of Oregon in 2001.

I am grateful, too, for my involvement in the Rockefeller Foundation's *Museums and Global Public Spheres* programme and for the opportunity this gave me to present work in progress for this book at the *Museums, Local Knowledge and Performance in an Age of Globalisation* workshop organised by University of the West Cape in 2002. Both this and my participation in a later symposium at the Rockefeller conference centre in Bellagio allowed me to benefit from extended discussions with Martin Hall, Barbara Kirshenblatt-Gimblett, Fred Myers, Ciraj Rassool and Leslie Witz. My thanks, then, to Ivan Karp and Corinne Kratz, as the programme convenors, for inviting me to participate in the programme, and to Tomás Ybarra-Frausto, Lynn Szwaja and Jennifer Adair from the Rockefeller Foundation for making that participation both possible and enjoyable.

Many of the arguments in chapter 7 were given their first dress rehearsal at the 2002 symposium *Metropolis and Primitivism* at the International Research Centre for Cultural Studies in Vienna. I am, then, grateful to Klaus Muller-Richter, Robert Matthias Erdbeer, Kristin Kopp and Daniela Schmeiser, the organisers of that symposium, for inviting me to contribute to this occasion which I found invaluable for what it taught me regarding the specificity of the intellectual formation of *fin-de-siècle* British anthropology when compared to its German counterpart. I am also grateful to Peter Hamilton and Roger Hargreaves for the opportunity to present related work at *The Beautiful and the Damned* symposium that was held at the National Portrait Gallery, London, in 2002. And special thanks to Bryan Turner for some probing questions which made me rethink some key issues.

In some of the chapters that follow I draw on earlier formulations of related issues in a range of publication venues. While, almost invariably, the particulars of the arguments presented here have changed considerably from their initial outings, it is appropriate to record my appreciation to the journals and publishers concerned for both giving this work its first airings and permitting its revised appearance in this book. The general aspects of my argument were first presented in Bennett (1997) 'Regulated restlessness: museums, liberal government and the historical sciences', *Economy and Society*, vol. 26, no. 2. Some aspects of chapters

1 and 2 were first presented in Bennett (2002) 'Archaeological autopsy: objectifying time and cultural governance', *Cultural Values*, vol. 6, nos 1 and 2. Bennett (2001) 'Pasts beyond memories: the evolutionary museum, liberal government and the politics of prehistory', *Folk: Journal of the Danish Ethnographic Society*, no. 43 (autumn) offers an earlier version of chapter 4. I also draw in chapter 4 on Bennett (2003) 'Stored virtue: memory, the body and the evolutionary museum', in S. Radstone and K. Hodgin (eds) *Regimes of Memory*, London and New York: Routledge. Finally, Bennett (1998) 'Pedagogic objects, clean eyes and popular instruction: on sensory regimes and museum didactics', *Configurations: A Journal of Literature, Science and Technology*, vol. 6, no. 3, was my first attempt to address the specific structures of vision associated with evolutionary collections. Some of its arguments appear, extended and revised, in chapter 7.

I also owe a debt to the various people who, either as editors or colleagues, commented on the work presented in these contexts. Special thanks in these regards to Christel Braae, Michael Dillon, Paul du Gay, Paula Findlen, Michael Harsbmeier, David McCallum, Susanna Radstone, Inger Sjórslev and Deborah Tyler.

When I first started work on the research for this book, I worked at Griffith University where the early stages of my work benefited considerably from the invigorating intellectual ethos of the Faculty of Humanities, and especially the commitment to the interdisciplinary pooling of ideas and expertise. The general theoretical arguments informing my approach to the relationships between evolutionary museums and liberal government in what follows owe a good deal to conversations with Jennifer Craik, Mark Finnane, Ian Hunter, Colin Mercer, Denise Meredyth, Jeffrey Minson and David Saunders. They owe even more, though, to John Frow – then at the University of Queensland – who, in an intellectual collaboration that now extends over many years, has been unstinting in his friendship and support.

I am also the beneficiary of Griffith University's commitment to the virtues of good administration, especially in the staff with whom it was my pleasure to work while Director of the Australian Key Centre for Cultural and Media Policy. My thanks, then, to Glenda Donovan, Bev Jeppeson and Karen Perkins for their expert support, without which I should never have been able to complete this project. The same goes for the equally excellent support I have enjoyed since returning to the Open University in the UK from the secretarial and administrative staff of the Sociology Discipline and of the Pavis Centre for Social and Cultural Research. My thanks, then, to Molly Freeman, Karen Ho, Denise Janes and Pam Walker, but most especially to Margaret Marchant for her highly professional support in finalising the manuscript. And thanks to John Hunt for his help with the illustrations.

If my work for this book has stretched over nearly a decade, it has also spanned two continents and a period of dramatic change in my personal and family life. When I started work on the book, I lived in Brisbane with a full household of young adults who were destined, over the coming years, to leave the family nest to start their own lives and careers. We none of us then envisaged how far apart we would all come to be – or, in spite of that, how close we would remain. My thanks, then, to Tanya, Oliver and James for pursuing their own lives with a vigorous confidence and independence, and yet always working to overcome the 'tyranny of distance' that is the downside of global dispersion. And to Sue – for still being with me, a pillar of strength and unfailing source of encouragement and commitment.

But I dedicate the book to the memory of my mother who died shortly before it was completed, after a long and cruel illness which made her passing a mercy. But a wrenching one, all the same – and so I am pleased to have this opportunity, in a book that is about memory, to record that the debt I owe her will never escape mine.

Tony Bennett
Kidlington, Oxfordshire
September 2003

Introduction

I take my title, *Pasts Beyond Memory*, from the moment in Joseph Conrad's *Heart of Darkness* when, as he nears his journey's end, Marlow, surprised by the whirl of black limbs on the river bank, evokes the scene of savagery as one beyond the reach of effective memory:

> The prehistoric man was cursing us, praying to us, welcoming us – who could tell? We were cut off from the comprehension of our surroundings; we glided past like phantoms, wondering and secretly appalled, as sane men would be before an enthusiastic outbreak in a madhouse. We could not understand, because we were too far and could not remember, because we were travelling in the night of first ages, of those ages that are gone, leaving hardly a sign – and no memories.
>
> (Conrad [1902], 1995: 62)

All of the aspects of what Johannes Fabian calls the 'denial of coevalness' (Fabian, 1983: 31) that characterised the colonial structure of anthropological discourse are present here: the placing of the Other in a time different from that of the observer, and the equation of distance from Europe with travelling backwards in time. 'Going up that river,' Marlow recalls, 'was like travelling back to the earliest beginnings of the world, when vegetation rioted on the earth and the big trees were kings' (Conrad, 1995: 59). In this way, the scene of prehistoric savagery is connected to – emerges out of – the untold ages of geological and natural history.

These 'pasts beyond memory' were still, when *Heart of Darkness* was first published in 1902, relatively new pasts: the term 'prehistory', like 'the dinosaur', made its first appearance in the 1840s.[1] They had not always existed. As such, they were and remain the products of a distinctive set of intellectual labours in the related fields of geology, palaeontology, natural history, prehistoric archaeology and anthropology. The techniques that these disciplines developed for reading rock formations, fossilised remains, ruins, tools, technologies and ornaments as the remnants of long past epochs progressively severed the connection that had previously limited the known past to a remembered past that had been transmitted to the present through the storage systems of writing or oral tradition. Limitless vistas of pasts going back beyond human existence, let alone memory, came rapidly into view as the once mute traces they had left behind were made eloquent through the application of new methods of analysis and interpretation.

The evolutionary principles of classification and exhibition developed in the new museums of natural history, ethnology and geology which flourished in the closing decades of the nineteenth century played a key role in making these pasts visible and knowable. There were, however, two aspects to this role. The first concerns the respects in which such museums functioned as the 'laboratories' for these disciplines, providing the contexts in which the new pasts they organised could become thinkable and perceptible as new realities in the fields of thought and vision. The second concerns the part played by the exhibition practices of those museums in translating these pasts into a significant component of late-nineteenth-century public culture, enlisting them in service of new strategies of cultural governance. In both regards, these museums served as the incubators for broader developments affecting the very grammar of the artefactual field by providing new rules for the classification and combination of objects. This had repercussions throughout the museum sector, challenging the practices of art museums as well as those of museums centred on classical archaeological collections, for example.

While these developments both affected and involved museums internationally, their initial influence was greatest in Britain. This is partly because developments within and across geology, natural history, palaeontology, prehistoric archaeology and anthropology were forged into a distinctive intellectual synthesis in Britain: one that proved to be a potent influence on late Victorian public culture. However, it was also partly because the champions of these sciences – which I shall call the historical sciences for reasons I shall explain in chapter 2 – were particularly effective in urging the need for state investment in evolutionary museums and in then exercising effective patronage over their key appointees. The circumstances in France and Germany were quite different and relatively unaffected by the developments in Britain. However, British museums were a significant point of reference for museum practices throughout the English-speaking world, especially, after the 1880s, through the influence of the London-based Museums Association. While there is a broader picture here that still needs to be examined, I have limited my comparative concerns to contemporary developments in Australia and the United States – not because these are essentially similar, nor because, in either case, what has to be reckoned with are derivatives of British developments. On the contrary, my interest is in how these three national contexts provide a set of contrapuntal perspectives on the relationships between post-Darwinian developments in the historical sciences, the functioning of evolutionary museums as a new kind of memory machine, the changing practices and priorities of liberal forms of government, and the quite different connections that were forged between the historical sciences and practices of government in colonial relationships between occupying and indigenous populations.

Mary Poovey's perspective on the relationship between the development of markets and civil society and the emergence of liberal forms of government provides a useful point of departure from which to broach these concerns. In place of earlier absolutist strategies of rule, which aimed to make the population knowable through abstract and impersonal forms of calculation monopolised by the sovereign authority, and in place of government by decree and a reliance on coercive means of securing obedience, the forms of personal autonomy associated with the eighteenth-century development of markets and civil society both assumed and required new forms of self-regulation. The discourses of aesthetics – crystallising into an identifiably distinctive formation at about this time – played a significant role in developing new forms of self-government that could meet this need, laying out the self in the form of a set of divisions which allowed new forms of action of self on self to emerge. It was thus to aesthetics that Anthony Ashley Cooper, Earl of Shaftesbury, looked as a model for the development of forms of moral government that allowed the self to act surgically on itself through, in Poovey's words, 'a kind of introspection that "multiplies" the self by dividing it into segments that can act independently' (Poovey, 1998: 177). While originally forming a part of a renovated culture of civic humanism and, as such, restricted to the cultivation of virtue on the part of the landed and mercantile classes, this aesthetic technology of a multiply divided self was subsequently grafted on to forms of self-governance with – at least in aspiration – a broader social reach and circulation. It was an active component in the eighteenth-century culture of taste (Brewer, 1995) and played a major role in the subsequent development of the art museum, providing the discursive ground on which it was to discharge its obligations as a reformatory of public morals and manners (Bennett, 1995b).

In the latter part of the nineteenth century, however, the historical sciences provided the basis for the development of a different and, as it proved, rival structure of the self which depended on the introduction of a historical split into the organisation of the person. This had its roots in eighteenth-century conjectural history – a term coined by Dugald Stewart in 1790 – which, as it happens, Poovey also discusses. So called because it relied on retrospective reasoning in which the past was deduced from the known principles of human nature rather than on experience or eye-witness accounts, conjectural history was essentially concerned with 'how "rude" societies became "civilised"' (Poovey, 1998: 215). This was a project which necessarily relied on conjecture given that, as Poovey puts it, 'one could not see, or read accounts of anyone who had seen, the transition from hunter-gatherer to agricultural society' (221). At odds with the forms of authority that had been painfully constructed for the experimental sciences with their reliance on verification by authoritative witnesses (Shapin and Schaffer, 1985; Shapin, 1994; Eamon, 1994), conjectural history fell out of favour in the early nineteenth century. It was, however, revived in the latter part of the century, mainly owing to the influence of evolutionary theory (McGregor, 1997). This was, however, more than simply a revival. The conjectural paradigm now operated in a much broader intellectual context as a set of procedures that were applied across the historical sciences – to account not merely for the transition from rude to civilised societies but also for the history of the earth and of life on earth. Questions concerning the origins of society were, as a consequence, relocated by being placed in the contexts of these longer histories. The conjectural paradigm was also able to claim a new authority, one closer to that which had earlier been claimed for the experimental sciences, in the respect that, once re-read in the light of evolutionary theory, the rock formations, the flora and fauna, and the human inhabitants of colonised territories did indeed seem to embody the possibility that the past might be reconstructed on the basis of eye-witness accounts of its continuing existence within the present. The transition from hunter-gatherer to agricultural society was, to the colonial eye, only too readily perceptible. This ability to read the past directly from the evidence of things themselves – rocks, fossils, bodies, tools, pottery – was also the basis of a challenge to the intellectual authority of the humanities, whose claims to know the past were based on the indirect evidence of its textual mediations and were, in any case, limited to a mere few thousand years.

The implications of these developments for questions of governance were most evident in the mutation in the conception of the person that was produced when the newly excavated deep pasts of prehistory were viewed in the light of theories of evolutionary inheritance.[2] For these 'pasts beyond memory' were regarded as being active and effective within the present through their functioning as a layer in the formation of the modern person whose make-up was increasingly visualised archaeologically as so many strata superimposed one on top of the other. This is clear in *Physics and Politics*, where Walter Bagehot, more widely known for his work as a legal and constitutional theorist, explored the implications of Darwin's work, and of evolutionary thought more generally, for the manner in which the activity of government should be conducted and the ends towards which it should be directed. An archaeological conception of the person is evident from the opening pages:

> If we wanted to describe one of the most marked results, perhaps the most marked result, of late thought, we should say that by it everything is made 'an antiquity'. When, in former times, our ancestors thought of an antiquarian, they described him as occupied with coins, and medals, and Druids' stones; these were then the characteristic records of the decipherable past, and it was with these that decipherers busied themselves. But now there are other relics; indeed, all matter is become such. Science tries to find in each bit of earth the record of the causes which made it precisely what it is; those forces have left their trace, she knows, as much as the tact and hand of the artist left their mark on a classical gem. . . . But what here concerns me is that man himself has, to the eye of science, become 'an antiquity.' She tries to read, is beginning to read, knows she ought to read, in the frame of each man the result of a whole history of all his life, of what he is and what makes him so, – of all his forefathers, of what they were and of what made them so.
>
> (Bagehot, 1873: 2–3)

My initial interests concern the role that was played by this conception of the person in the transition, in Britain, from the classical liberalism of the mid-century period, with its parsimonious assessment of the good that government could do, to the more active moral and educative role that was proposed for government in the formulations of *fin de siècle* new liberalism.[3] More particularly, it concerns the role that was envisaged for evolutionary museums in translating the newly produced 'pasts beyond memory' into distinctive memory machines. As 'evolutionary accumulators', museums were envisaged as a means for acting developmentally on the social by productively activating the tension between the modern and archaic layers of the self provided by the archaeological structure of the person so as to give this a progressive momentum.[4] I go on to show, however, how this developmental effect of evolutionary museums was targeted at socially restricted groups – in essence, the white male members of metropolitan powers – in ways which entailed that, for other persons in other contexts, the operation of museums as evolutionary accumulators had to be conceived differently in response to the social logics of different local circumstances. This was especially true of colonial contexts where, cast in the role of the primitive, indigenous populations were axiomatically denied the historical depth required for an archaeological layering of the self and were, therefore, just as axiomatically placed entirely outside the liberal reform strategies of evolutionary museums. The connections between museums, the historical sciences and practices of governance in such contexts have to be sought elsewhere, in the form of colonial administration developed for regulating the arrangement of bodies in social space.

The theoretical framework from which I approach these questions is that provided by Michel Foucault's perspective of governmentality (Foucault, 1991) and the considerable literature that has been developed in its wake examining the role played by various forms of knowledge and expertise in organising differentiated fields of social management in which social conduct is subjected to diverse strategies of regulation. My chief interests here lie in identifying the implications of what Mitchell Dean calls an 'analytics of government' for the study of museums in contrast to those accounts of museums which rely on earlier theories of the state and ideology (Dean, 1999). The main differences can be briefly stated. Where museums have been examined from the perspective of ideology, the emphasis has fallen on examining their role in reproducing and legitimating forms of power which are said to have their origins in some pre-existing set of social relations, whether they be those of class domination (as in theories of the capitalist state) or those of gender domination (associated with accounts of the patriarchal state). The role of museums, or that of other cultural institutions, is then viewed as secondary – as a role of relay and reinforcement – in relation to these relations of power. An analytics of government, by contrast, focuses on how distinctive relations of power are constituted in and by the exercise of specific forms of knowledge and expertise, and on the ways in which these give rise to specific mechanisms, techniques and technologies for shaping thought, feelings, perceptions and behaviour. Instead of looking *through* the mechanisms that are produced when particular forms of knowledge and expertise are translated into practical, technical and institutionalised forms to decipher the modes of power that *lie behind* them, the perspective of governmentality typically looks *at* those mechanisms, focusing on their mundane details and particularities to identify how particular forms of power are constituted *there*, within those mechanisms, rather than outside or behind them. This does not negate the need to then look at the connections between the forms of power that are exercised through these mechanisms and the organisation of relationships of class, gender and ethnicity;

but it does change significantly how the orders of these connection might be construed and accounted for.

It is in this light that I approach the relations between the historical sciences and museums, paying particular attention to the technical forms – different systems of classification and exhibition arrangements, for example – through which the forms of knowledge and expertise associated with those sciences became practically effective in evolutionary museums. Yet, if the impetus of Foucauldian and post-Foucauldian scholarship has encouraged the development of an analytic gaze which looks closely at the 'microphysics of power' – in which power exists in and through the technical forms in which it is exercised – it has often proved less adept at undertaking such detailed, close-up inspection than other intellectual traditions which share a sense of the importance of the mundane particularities of technical arrangements and processes. This is especially true of the now extensive body of work defined by the confluence of interests and procedures between science studies, techno-science and actor-network theory. The work of Bruno Latour, in particular, has had an evident influence on recent approaches to museums, especially those that aim to engage with the new relations of action and effect that are produced by their distinctive forms of classification and exhibition. It is, accordingly, to this literature that I look when zooming in on particular aspects of museum practice to identify the mechanisms that are at work within them and the new entities they shape and produce.

These, then, albeit briefly delineated, are the issues with which this study engages and the perspectives it adopts. I shall be equally brief in outlining the order in which the book's main arguments are developed. I begin, in chapter 1, by relativising evolutionary museums, placing them in a historical perspective as a means of highlighting their distinctive properties. I also look a little more closely at the 'historical sciences', outlining the respects in which the stratification of time these produced gave rise to a new archaeological conception of the person and new ways of laying out the self as a zone for management. The first chapter is also where I review the literature on governmentality, especially its concern with the forms of self-rule through which liberal forms of government typically work, and articulate the relevance of these concerns to the study of museums. This provides the basis for a brief examination of the different interpretations of new liberalism in late-nineteenth-century Britain, Australia and the United States, and of the developing relations between museums, adult education and mass schooling which, in all three countries, provided crucial new interfaces through which the action of museums on the social was organised.

Chapter 2 is where I look in detail at the intellectual developments in the fields of geology, palaeontology, natural history, archaeology and anthropology which provided, in the late-nineteenth-century synthesis of the historical sciences, the distinctive forms of knowledge that both informed, and were informed by, the practices of evolutionary museums. Reviewing the earlier paradigm of conjectural history – and sometimes drawing a longer bow – I trace the development, across each of these disciplines, of an 'archaeological gaze' in which the relations between past and present are envisaged as so many sequential accumulations, carried over from one period to another so that each layer of development can be read to identify the pasts that have been deposited within it. I then turn to the equally distinctive procedures through which the pasts produced by these different disciplines were strung together to provide an account of the history of the earth, of life on earth, and of human culture and civilisation as an integrated and seamless progression. In doing so, I show how the archaeological gaze operated across and between the historical sciences and how, when viewed in the context of colonial relations, it operated as a system for ranking races hierarchically according to the different degrees of historical depth that were accorded to racialised bodies and cultures.

I then turn, in chapter 3, to examine the varied technical developments through which the new entities produced by the historical sciences were translated into the practices of evolutionary museums. I draw here on the perspectives of actor-network theory and science studies to examine the role that evolutionary museums played in stabilising the entities produced by the historical sciences and organising the relations between them into intelligible sequences. I place special emphasis here on the role of the typological method which imposed an evolutionary re-training on artefacts in providing for, in McGrane's economical summary, 'the linear and serial museum arrangement of rock, stone axe, flint knife, iron knife, bow and arrow, rifle, cannon, and atomic missile' (McGrane, 1989: 102). This is not to say that the typological method was the only technical form in which evolutionary histories were made museologically visible and perceptible. Far from it. Yet, or so I shall argue, the typological method provided the main technical device of evolutionary museums. Even when not directly used, its organising principles often underpinned other evolutionary arrangements. It provided new principles of substitutability regulating the exchange of objects between museums and, thereby, exerted a significant influence on the organisation of the entire artefactual field: it proved crucial, for example, in enabling local museums with small collections to arrange evolutionary exhibits and thus played an important role in the development of new capillary relations between central and local collections. I conclude this chapter by considering the sharply contrasting tendencies that characterised the relationships between anthropology and museums in late-nineteenth-century Germany. While here, too, the object-based sciences challenged the authority of the humanities, that challenge was differently articulated owing to the negligible influence of evolutionary thought on German museum practices at this time. This contrast serves, contrapuntally, to foreground the distinctive forms of historicisation associated with the typological method.

Chapter 4 pulls together the perspectives developed in the first three chapters by bringing them to bear on the role of evolutionary museums in the reform strategies of post-Darwinian liberalism in Britain. The discussion here focuses on the relationships between museums as evolutionary accumulators and the archaeological structure of the person produced by the historical sciences. It connects these to contemporary concerns regarding the role of habit in the transmission of the inheritance of one generation to the next and the fear that, while necessary for evolutionary advancement, habit could also become a blockage to progress and, in certain circumstances, a cause of degeneration. These concerns were most fully rehearsed in relation to the distinctive dynamics of colonial governance where, in assessments of Asian despotism like that offered by John Stuart Mill in relation to India, the enforcement of habit by traditional forms of rule meant that subject populations were viewed as lacking the capacity for those forms of autonomous and dynamic self-development that liberal forms of government presupposed (Helliwell and Hindess, 2002). Domestically, the extension of the suffrage to include the working classes occasioned similar anxieties, posing for the reforming wing of post-Darwinian liberalism a delicate task as to how to organise and act on the subjectivity of the working man so as install there a regulated capacity for evolutionary self-development. The deployment of museums as evolutionary accumulators was, I argue, one response to this difficulty, albeit one that, in the main, excluded women and children from – or placed them in a different relation to – the developmental dynamic it sought to establish.

Questions concerning the relationships between museums and the child are very much to the fore in chapter 5, where the centre of attention moves to the United States, and particularly the American Museum of Natural History in New York. I am interested in this as a compelling example of an institution which, although privately funded, was thoroughly governmental in its understanding of its civic role. It therefore offers a useful opportunity to emphasise – as Foucault did – that governmentality is not to be confused with, or limited to, the actions of the state or even publicly funded organisations, but rather concerns a much broader orientation to the regulation of conduct which spans public–private relations of ownership and state/civil society distinctions. These issues are explored through a discussion of the relations between American interpretations of the new liberalism and their relationship to the currency of 'the new museum idea' in the United States. The influence of this 'idea' on the American Museum of Natural History was most evident in the relationships it developed with New York's public school system in order to respond to what it regarded as its most urgent civic task: reaching migrant children to involve them, and their families, in the dynamics of American citizenship. Yet this involved a completely different set of strategies from those which, in the Museum's most famous galleries, connected an unqualified 'nature red in tooth and claw' interpretation of Darwinism to the unbridled capitalist ethos of America's post-bellum bourgeoisie and led, in the early twentieth century, to a eugenic conception of the Museum's tasks which stood in direct contrast to the Huxleyan view of the relations between evolution and liberalism which allegedly served as its model. My interests here focus on Henry Fairfield Osborn, especially on his reformulation of the museum's role in relation to the social dynamics of habit, evolutionary inheritance and accumulation. This centred on his conception of the museum as a distinctive kind of memory machine, promoting an unconscious mnemonics through which the race plasm of white Americans was to be renewed and reinvigorated.

The vicissitudes of the relations between the historical sciences, evolutionary thought and new liberalism are also the subject of chapter 6, where the focus shifts to Australia, particularly the Australian Museum in Sydney and the National Museum of Victoria in Melbourne. Throughout the latter part of the nineteenth century, Australia played a key role in the development of evolutionary thought and, especially in Britain, its colonial inflection. It seemed, almost providentially, to confirm the equation of distance from Europe with the notion of travelling back in time. Located at the furthest possible distance from London, it boasted the oldest rock formations, and, in its flora, fauna and Aboriginal inhabitants, what were interpreted as the most primitive life forms and culture.[5] A survival of the past in the present, Australia typically served as a ground zero for evolutionary narratives, a concrete location for the beginning of things. The networks of colonial science that organised the early relations between British and Australian museums also played a key role in supplying the artefacts which, in European and North American museums, were used to represent the beginnings of sequences of evolutionary development: the Aboriginal throwing sticks which commenced Henry Pitt Rivers's displays of weaponry, for example. Yet evolutionary thought made relatively little headway in Australia's main museums until the 1890s. There were a number of reasons for this. Local scientific elites, representing pre-Darwinian schools of scientific thought, proved successful in dominating the governing bodies of the major museums and appointing curators who would favour their points of view. This tended to insulate Australian museums from the reforming impetus of the new liberalism which, in any case, articulated with class relations in Australia in ways that differed from both the British and American cases. However, I argue that account also needs to be taken of the legacy – by no means dormant – of a frontier history in which racial violence was a common occurrence.[6] In the context of post-Darwinian reform liberalism in Britain, evolutionary museums were typically committed to gradualist displays, carrying the message that, just as 'nature makes no jumps', so progress in society and culture could only come about slowly. Yet to read nature as a template for society in this way posed obvious problems in a colonial context where the dynamics of occupation more typically required a belief in an unbridgeable gap in the relations between the occupying and indigenous populations.

One way in which this manifested itself was in the denial of any autonomous historicity to Australia's Aboriginal peoples, in much the same way that, in the period after the Indian Wars, Native Americans were de-historicised. This had, in both contexts, significant consequences for the early development of both anthropology and archaeology in their commitment to remain, by and large, 'surface grazers', content with what might be found on the ground or just beneath the surface rather than, on the model of European prehistoric archaeology, excavating progressively longer pasts by digging more deeply. In the Australian case, this was in good measure a consequence of the equation of distance from Europe with the past. If early Australian archaeologists tended to be 'spade shy', this was, as Tom Griffiths has shown, mainly because they believed that prehistory was still a living presence, readily observable in the stone tools and human remains that could be obtained by shallow excavations (Griffiths, 1996a). In the American case, the politics of the past were complicated by the relations between the remains of Native and Mezzo Americans. But in both contexts, this reluctance to excavate deep histories, combined with the sense that colonists and colonised were separated from each other by an unbridgeable gap, militated against the influence of evolutionary displays or tended in favour of displays that stressed discontinuities in the relations between the occupying and indigenous populations.

In examining these issues I draw again on the distinction between liberal and colonial forms of governmentality and the ways in which the historical sciences were deployed between the two. In metropolitan contexts, the historical sciences provided a template for the development of new forms of self-management which provided an alternative response to the social imperatives of evolution from that represented by the statist programmes of eugenics. In colonial contexts, however, these knowledges operated differently, as components of what Nicholas Dirks (2000) calls the ethnological state which, far from encouraging a dialectic of self-development that would foster a break with habit, converted ethnological categories into administrative instruments designed to keep subject populations at the level of the archaic. What most distinguished the deployment of the historical sciences in these contexts was their use in administrative procedures that categorised indigenous populations *as if* they were museum specimens and managed their location in social space *as if* this were a matter of assigning them to appropriate places within evolutionary museum displays. I am especially interested here in Baldwin Spencer and his role – moving from the Pitt Rivers Museum, to the National Museum of Victoria and, later, to the Northern Territory as Chief Protector of Aborigines – in translating museum knowledges into colonial forms of administration.

I come, finally, in chapter 7 to a question that occurs in all three countries concerning the relations between evolution and the politics of vision in museum displays. I take my bearings here from the differences between the Enlightenment museum, based on Linnaean principles of classification, and the linear sequencing of forms of life produced by evolutionary arrangements. This displaced the problem of the *monstrous* – an exile from the order of things in Linnaean classification – into that of the *mutant*, who threatens to undermine the rationality of evolutionary orderings of nature by jumping over the stages of development which allow forms of life to be arranged in unilinear sequences. There is also the added difficulty that the processes of evolution are, in Darwin's construction, so slow and gradual as to be imperceptible while also generating no stable vantage point from which their direction might be discerned. This concern is echoed, in evolutionary museum displays, in the remarkable significance that was invested in how to arrange the relations between objects in sequences so that the pace and direction of their development might be properly discerned. I place this discussion in a broader context by showing how these concerns were exacerbated by fears that the popular eye might be led astray by the misleading influence of popular entertainments, both old (magic lantern shows) and new (the cinema), as well as by the lingering influence of the culture of curiosity and the 'quack' science of phrenology. One response to this need to guide the eye in order that it might correctly interpret museum arrangements consisted in the multiplication of descriptive and explanatory labels, resulting in a highly textualised museum environment – a paradoxical outcome given the insistence of the object-based historical sciences that the truth of things was to be observed directly in things themselves, unaided by textual mediation.

This leads me to a final note of qualification. Governmentality theory, Mitchell Dean suggests, is characteristically concerned to provide a 'thick' description of the practices of government (Dean, 2002: 121). This often means that it adopts what Dean calls the 'programmer's view' in seeking to reconstruct the logic underlying particular programmes of government, and the specific articulation of means, ends and objects of government that this effects. Matters invariably become more complex, however, when account is taken of the relationships between such programmes and the social relations and practices they seek to manage. The balance of my concerns in this study tilts more towards reconstructing such a 'programmer's view' in the account it offers of the relations between the historical sciences, evolutionary museums and both metropolitan liberal and colonial forms of government. This does not, however, reflect any diminished sense of the importance of the different considerations that have to be taken into account if analysis is to comprehend the more disparate and contended histories that are generated by the interfaces between governmental programmes and the fractious organisation of the social they seek to regulate. To the contrary, I have sought to show how this generated a host of torsions and contradictions within the programmes that evolutionary showmen proposed for regulating conduct within the new horizons of historical time opened up by the discovery of 'pasts beyond memory'.

While the Postscript does not engage adequately with these issues, it does map out some directions which might prove fruitful for future exploration. It does so by outlining the respects in which the 'pasts beyond memory' produced by evolutionary museums came to function as an integral component in the organisation and make-up of the social as a result of the ways in which they were mobilised across a wide range of programmes of social management. Their role in thus constituting the social in the form of a 'slow modernity' is offered as a counterweight to those accounts of modernity which construe its discourses and practices as necessarily ruptural.

1

Dead circuses
Expertise, exhibition, government

Towards the end of his career, George Sherwood, Chief Curator in the Department of Education at the American Museum of Natural History, recounted the story of a little boy who, after a school trip to his local museum, rushed home to tell his mother that he had had a great day at 'the *dead* circus' (Sherwood, 1927: 267). A more telling description of evolutionary museums would be hard to come by. For such museums were dedicated, almost exclusively, to the exhibition of dead things: the reconstructed remains of extinct forms of life; fossils; the stuffed and preserved carcasses of dead animals; mummified corpses rescued from the sepulchral vaults of pyramids and other burial sites; and no end of skulls, skeletons and body parts. And in ethnological collections, the metaphorically and the literally dead confusingly collided as the artefacts of colonised peoples, contextualised as the remnants of dead or dying peoples, were displayed side-by-side with their physical remains.[1]

The arrangements of such museums were also dependent on new practices of classification and exhibition which allowed dead things to be represented, con-textualised and exchanged in new and increasingly complex ways. Developments in the field of taxidermy allowed the dead to be resurrected in increasingly lifelike forms.[2] The dug-up past – the past of fossils, extinct species and of ancient civilisations – became larger and more precisely calibrated as increasingly refined techniques of stratigraphical analysis allowed the times of nature and culture to find a common measure in the master clock of geological time. Sacred sites were plundered in the name of science as museums accumulated their stockpiles of dead 'primitives', circulating these between themselves through new principles for the exchange of prehistoric equivalents in which a cast of the skull of the 'last Tasmanian' could be swapped for a cast of the skull and jaws of a tyrannosaurus.[3] Collecting and hunting merged as closely related activities, speeding the passage of both humans and animals – Australian Aborigines were commonly referred to as 'black game' or 'black vermin' (Kingston, 1988: 192) – from the realm of the living to that of the dead in order that they might become parts of museum instal-lations.[4] So common was the traffic that, in 1907, a South African journalist was able to propose, in racist jest, that 'the scientific world would be truly grate-ful' if a docile Bushman might be found who 'could be induced to pack himself in formalin and ship himself to Europe for the purpose of ornamenting a dust-proof show case, side by side with the mummies of Egypt' (Legassick and Rassool, 2000: 4).

There was, of course, nothing particularly new about this association between museums and death. The Renaissance conception of museums as places for 'immortals cadavers' (Findlen, 2000: 173) was further developed, most famously by Quatremère de Quincy ([1815] 1989), in the late-eighteenth and early-nineteenth-century conception of the art museum as (in Adorno's later phrase) 'mausoleums for works of art' (Adorno, 1967: 175). This imagery was also central to Balzac's evocation of the museum as, in Didier Maleuvre's telling summary, a 'place of conflict between the domineering dead and the beleaguered living' (Maleuvre, 1999: 268). What was new, however, was the form taken by this association. In 1890, R. P. Cameron, writing to support the reform of museums in accordance with evolutionary principles, complained that the popular idea of a museum was still that of 'a sort of charnel house for dead animals, skeletons and skulls; that it was a dungeon-like place, dark, dusty and dreary' (Cameron, 1890: 83). Yet, however much evolutionary museums sought to dissociate themselves from the second part of this accusation – a historical echo of the criticisms that had been levelled against the collections of the *ancien régime* during the French Revolution (Poulot, 1997) – their endeavours to translate evolutionary principles into an effective form of public pedagogy served only to multiply their charnel house associations. In the process, however, death was significantly re-contextualised in being historicised as both existing and new classes of objects were grouped into new configurations brought under the influence of new relations of expertise and exhibition.

The expert as showman

When called to task for the slow rate of labelling the Pitt Rivers collection in its new home at the University of Oxford, Henry Balfour replied, somewhat tartly, that such work took time and admonished that he knew of no museum in the world that could dispense with 'the company of an expert as showman'.[5] What this view of expertise meant for the organisation of the museum space, and for the roles of the expert and of the public within that space, is graphically clear in Thomas Huxley's proposals for the contexts in which natural history specimens would best be displayed:

> The cases in which these specimens are exhibited must present a transparent but hermetically closed face, one side accessible to the public, while on the opposite side they are as constantly accessible to the Curator by means of doors opening into a portion of the Museum to which the public has no access.
>
> (Huxley, 1896a: 128)

On the one side, the expert, like the impresario of a dead Punch-and-Judy show, lays out his specimens in accordance with the principles of evolutionary science; on the other side of the hermetically sealed glass divide is the public, denied access to the back-stage area in which the expert organises the *mise-en-scène* for his specimens and determines what roles – of narrative and representation – to accord them (Figure 1.1). The curator here is the source of an absolute authority and the museum the site of a monologic discourse in which the curator's view of the world, translated into exhibition form, is to be relayed to a public which is denied any active role in the museum except that of looking and learning, absorbing the lessons that have been laid out before it.

This reflected the fact that, if the museum was a dead circus, it was also, in David Goodman's telling phrase, organised in 'fear of circuses'. The case Goodman has in mind is the part that was played, in the debates leading to the foundation of Melbourne's National Museum of Victoria in 1854, by the wish to combat the influence of the visiting circus and its accompanying menagerie which, every year, brought into the city a living nature that was showy and flashy, a nature that still pulsed to the culture of curiosity (Goodman, 1990). In opposition to this, Frederick McCoy, the Museum's first Director, saw his role as ringmaster of 'a classifying house' in which the dead and mute specimens of natural history were arranged in a rigorous taxonomy in testimony both to the power of reason to organise and classify as well as to nature's own inherent rationality. However, the point has a more general validity. In the late nineteenth century, the principles of the circus – which developed into an imperialised form for the exhibition of strange and marvellous representatives of both the animal and human kingdoms – had spilled over into the popular entertainment zones of the international exhibitions. Here, too, the museum took issue with the circus. In the US context, the living curiosities of a colonial imagination stalked the midway zones of the world's fairs in living villages of peoples from 'remote' parts of the world, reconstructions of how the west was won in the face of Indian savagery, and the caged display of wild animals and 'primitives' as semiotic equivalents. In the

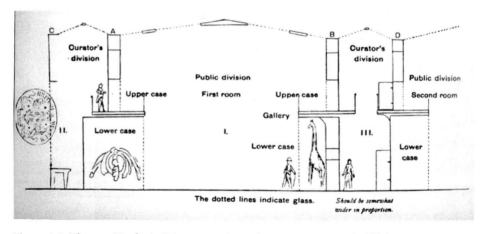

Figure 1.1 Thomas Huxley's 'Diagrammatic section across museum', 1896.

Source: Thomas H. Huxley (1896a) 'Suggestions for a proposed natural history museum in Manchester'. Report of the Museums Association.

14

official exhibition zones, however, the new forms of expertise associated with evolutionary forms of natural history and ethnology sought to arrange a different kind of show through the studied manipulation of bones, skulls, teeth, carcasses, fossils and artefacts, representing what were believed to be the dead or dying customs and practices of colonised peoples.[6] The value of dead primitives over living ones is clarified by Andrew Zimmerman who notes how, in the German context, anthropologists distrusted live displays because of the opportunity they afforded for active forms of self-presentation which – like those of the 'trouser nigger' – would disavow the primitivism they were meant to represent (Zimmerman, 2001: 37). Only the peeling away of custom, clothing, skin and flesh to reveal the skeletal truth of the body beneath could provide an ultimate basis for the 'objective' scientific demonstration of racial difference. And whatever the national context, the expert as showman pitted his authority against that of visual tricksters – like P. T. Barnum – whose hoaxes at the American Museum brought museums generally into disrepute while also serving as a constant reminder of the principles of curiosity from which, in a painful history of a century and more, the museum had sought to detach itself.

There was, of course, and had been for some time, a good deal of traffic between these live and dead circuses.[7] More than one living representative of primitiveness in the midway zones of the world's fairs ended their careers, quite involuntarily, as dead exhibits in a museum; and, in some cases, this was a journey from one part of a museum to another.[8] Many circus animals suffered the same fate: the natural history collections of the Liverpool Museum benefited substantially from donations of dead animals from Barnum and Bailey's Circus. There was also – and P. T. Barnum played a key role here too – a good deal of systematic interaction between the hunting expeditions through which circuses acquired their animals and the acquisition of specimens for museums (Betts, 1959). The world of the circus also sometimes spilled over into the museum, although rarely without occasioning controversy. Henry Fairfield Osborn's attempts to animate the past by exhibiting extinct species in active, lifelike postures at the American Museum of Natural History was thus condemned by George Brown Goode, of the Smithsonian Institution, as smacking too much of the showman (Rainger, 1991: 89–90).[9] Baldwin Spencer, McCoy's successor at the National Museum of Victoria, was equally prepared to blur the lines between museum and circus in his public lectures (Figure 1.2). Culturally, however, fairs and circuses on the one hand, and museums on the other, belonged, if not to separate spheres – for there remained a good deal of permeability between the two (Ritvo, 1997: 21) – to spheres that were in a state of increasing tension with each other.

The programme of evolutionary museums was, in this sense, continuous with the rational programme through which the Enlightenment museum had earlier struggled to detach itself from the baroque principles of display that had characterised cabinets of curiosity (Stafford, 1994). However, this protracted process of differentiation was not just a matter of a once-and-for-all break with the past. To the contrary, it was a break that had to be constantly repeated as the museum, alongside various rational and improving forms of spectacle and entertainment, sought, by claiming the authority of reason, to distinguish itself from, and to act

Figure 1.2 Cover of Savage Club 'Smoke Night' programme, featuring Professor Baldwin Spencer's lecture on 'Aboriginal Life in Central Australia', 1902.

as a counterweight to, the continuing influence of the illusionist trickery of fairground entertainers, prestidigitators, sleight-of-hand conjurers and popular showmen. The anxieties generated by these popular shows clustered around the concern that their audiences would have their powers of perception so dulled by conjurers and tricksters that they would be unable to understand the object lessons that the expert as showman would put before them.

Jonathan Crary addresses a related set of issues in his discussion of Georges Seurat's *Parade de cirque* (1887–8) and gives them a distinctive late-nineteenth-century context in noting how Seurat's depiction of the circus crowd suggests both 'the regressive immobility of trance' and 'the machinic uncanniness of automatic behaviour' (Crary, 2001: 229). These negative perceptions of the crowd drew a good deal of their force from the apprehensions that gathered around the role of habit in evolutionary thought. These focused on whether the working and popular classes were so ensnared in automatic forms of perception and response that they might be unable to develop the critical forms of reflexive self-monitoring required by liberal forms of self-rule. As we shall see, these concerns about the role of habit played a significant role in debates concerning the didactics that were best suited to carry the message of evolutionary displays to working-class visitors. This took place, however, in the context of a significantly reorganised museum environment in which it was not, as in the Enlightenment museum, the rationality of nature's order that was exhibited but the sequence, direction and temporality of its development.

A brief contrast between two different principles for the exhibition of natural history specimens will help make my point here. The first comprises the geometrical principles that William Sharp Macleay developed for the arrangement of natural history specimens in his Sydney cabinet. Strongly influenced by Georges Cuvier and motivated by a wish to counter what he viewed as the pernicious influence of the French Revolution, the basic principle of Macleay's arrangement – the so-called Quinary system (Figure 1.3) – was circular, with classes, orders and species being joined together through interconnecting circles which linked all forms of life, binding them into relations of permanent circular repetition (Stanbury and Holland, 1988: 20–1; Fletcher, 1920). 'One plan', as Macleay put it, 'extends throughout the universe, and this plan is founded on the principle of a series of affinities returning into themselves, and forming as it were circles' (cited in Mozley, 1967: 414). The system was partly developed to provide a greater flexibility in the arrangement of the relations between different forms of life than those permitted by earlier visualisations of nature's order based on linear principles: the tree of life, for example, in its portrayal of life's many branches spreading from a common root and origin, and John Hunter's anatomical displays in which the hierarchical organisation of the Great Chain of Being was made visible as 'individual organs, rather than entire beings, were displayed in parallel linear sequences – independent hierarchies, for example, of stomachs, genitalia, and lungs' (Ritvo, 1997: 29).

In contrast to such rigid linear schemas, the Quinary system was intended to function as a more flexible combinatory, allowing a wide range of affinities and analogic bonds to be established through the arrangement of circles within circles, and the overlapping of these onto one another. The more directly political target Macleay had in view was Jean Baptiste Lamarck, whose evolutionism, in allowing for the unrestricted transformation of lower forms of life into higher ones, provided a template for radical thought in suggesting that the untrammelled ascent of individuals through existing social hierarchies and, indeed, the overthrow of such hierarchies, might be possible. Macleay's arrangement, in bending the

17

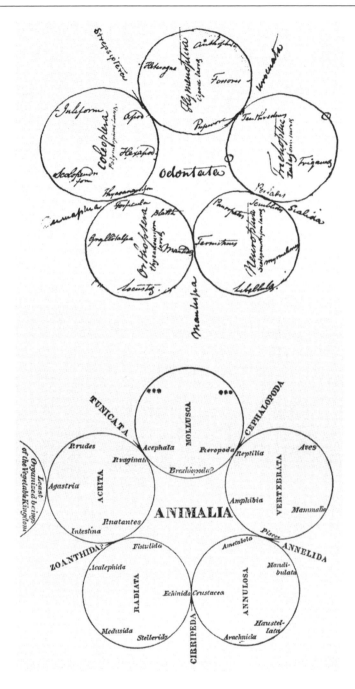

Figure 1.3 Diagrams illustrating William Sharp Macleay's Quinary system. The upper figure is in Macleay's hand from the MSS of *Horae Entomologicae* (1819–21); the lower figure is in the same plan printed by the Linnaean Society of London.

Source: Peter Stanbury and Julian Holland (eds) (1988) *Mr Macleay's Celebrated Cabinet*, Sydney: Macleay Museum, University of Sydney.

ascending lines of Lamarck's evolutionary streams into self-enclosing circles, both destroyed the political force of Lamarck's 'upward-moving nature . . . while leaving the idea of continuity intact' (Desmond, 1994: 90).

Although it had a lingering influence,[10] the popularity of the Quinary system peaked in the 1830s. Charles Darwin had never liked its 'vicious circles' and 'rig-maroles' (cited in Ritvo, 1997: 33), but Thomas Huxley was a temporary convert. When he visited Australia in 1848, Huxley had extensive discussions with Macleay – whose influence on Sydney's fledgling scientific culture was considerable. On his return to England, Huxley advocated the virtues of Macleay's 'circular system', whose economy he greatly admired. Yet, in his display of the evolution of the horse at the Royal Institution in 1871, Huxley departed from the Quinary system in every significant respect in arranging fossils and bones in an uninterrupted and single line of development (see Figure 1.4) to tell the story of the horse as, in Desmond's terms, 'a history of streamlined growth and toe-reduction, the making of society's "exquisite running engine"' (Desmond, 1997: 19).[11] There are connections between these two systems: both retained faith with the principle, derived from Buffon, that nature makes no jumps. But, in Huxley's case, it did progress and in a manner which gave its continuity a different meaning. The key difference between the two systems in this respect consisted in the different ways in which they related to time: in the first case, as a measure of repetition and recurrence; in the second, as a measure of unrepeatable events organised into developmental sequences. It was as a consequence of this shift that dead things, in evolutionary museums, assumed an added semantic horizon as, in being inserted in new relations of time, they were resituated as the present's prehistory.

Bernard McGrane's discussion of the nineteenth-century development of anthropology as a 'necrology practiced on the living' (McGrane, 1989: 111) in its production of primitives as living dead – the ghosts of our ancestors – points in a similar direction. In historicising difference by applying the Darwinian principle that classification is genealogical to the relations between peoples, anthropology transformed relationships of simultaneous space into linear time by back-projecting colonised peoples into the prehistoric past, a point of origin for the organisation of genealogical chains of descent that were made visible in museums through the exhibition of linear sequences of skulls, skeletons, tools and pottery. Here, as in natural history museums, the artefactual domain was rearranged as objects were located in new relations of space and time and, in the process, connected to new practices of government and self-government.

Time and space in the museum

One of the central arguments of Bruno Latour's *Science in Action* is that each science works through 'a cycle of accumulation that allows a point to become a *centre* by acting at a distance on many other points' (Latour, 1987: 222). This contention has significantly influenced recent approaches to early-nineteenth-century European natural history museums in which the objects of natural history,

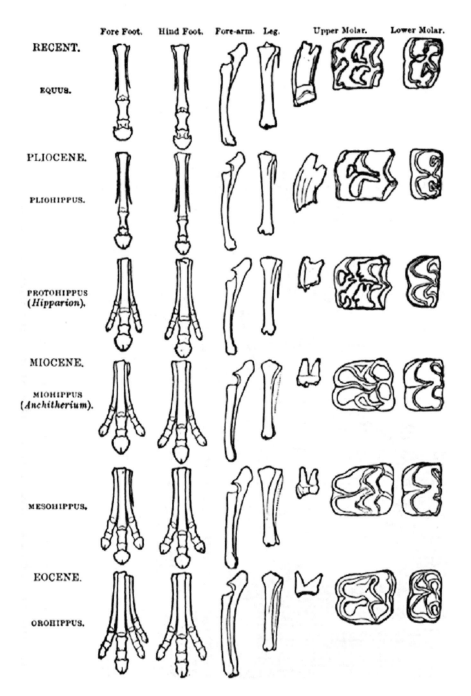

Figure 1.4 O. C. Marsh's table of fossil horses prepared to illustrate Thomas Huxley's public lectures.

Source: Thomas H. Huxley (1893–4) *Collected Essays*, vol. 4, London: Macmillan and Co.

20

increasingly disconnected from the collecting practices of the gentlemanly virtuoso, were reassembled in new and more systematic configurations as parts of colonial networks of science and government (Gascoigne, 1994; Miller and Reill, 1996). The accumulation in one place of the flora and fauna from a variety of distant places and their assembly in new contexts and combinations permitted the development of abstract and totalising frameworks of knowledge because of the new relations they made perceptible. As Latour puts it:

> The zoologists in their Natural History museums, without travelling more than a few hundred metres and opening more than a few dozen drawers, travel through all the continents, climates and periods . . . Many common features that could not be visible between dangerous animals far away in space and time can easily appear between one case and the next! The zoologists *see* new things, since this is the first time that so many creatures are drawn together in front of someone's eyes.
>
> (Latour, 1987: 225)

This capacity to make global systems of relations visible and knowable enabled metropolitan museums to function as 'centres of calculation' that were able to 'act at a distance' on a variety of peripheral locations, providing the intellectual frameworks within which the activities conducted there could be organised. To the extent that museums in peripheral locations lacked the means of accumulating natural history specimens from other points in order to themselves become centres of calculation, their place in the emerging networks of science and government was a subordinate one. The paradox here – and it is one writ large in the history of geology, too[12] – is that centres of calculation devalue the knowledge that is produced at the sites of collection where objects are found by making a knowledge of such objects dependent on an appreciation of their place within systems of relationships which are only visible from those centres.

Georges Cuvier's elevation of the sedentary naturalist over the field naturalist exemplifies the logic at work here. The field naturalist, he wrote in 1807, reviewing a report of Alexander von Humboldt, may observe objects and living things 'in their natural surroundings, in relationship to their environment, and in the full vigour of life and activity', but he lacks the means of drawing comparisons between them with the result that his observations are 'broken and fleeting' (Cuvier, cited in Outram, 1996: 259–61). The sedentary naturalist may labour under the disadvantage that his knowledge of 'living beings from distant countries' is secondary and mediated so that a 'thousand little things escape him . . . which would have struck him if he had been on the spot' (260). But there are compensating advantages:

> If the sedentary naturalist does not see nature in action, he can yet survey all her products spread before him. He can compare them with each other as often as is necessary to reach reliable conclusions. . . . He can bring together the relevant facts from anywhere he needs to. The traveller can only travel one road; it is only really in one's study (*cabinet*) that one can roam freely throughout the universe, and for that, a different sort of courage is needed . . . which does not allow its possessor to leave a subject

21

until, by observation, by a wide range of knowledge, and connected thought, he has illuminated it with every ray of light possible in a given state of knowledge.

(Cuvier, cited in Outram, 1996: 261–2)

The Muséum National d'Histoire Naturelle, under Cuvier's direction, performed an analogous function for the public: it provided for the public witnessing of nature's order by, as Dorinda Outram puts it, bringing together 'in one place the whole range of the natural order, which, in the "real world", would never be found together in one space' (256). However, this also meant 'that the visitor to the Muséum could see not only the denizens of many different parts of the earth's surface together in one spot, but also the products of many different eras of the earth's history' (256). This perspective is crucial if we are to understand how, by accumulating objects from different places, evolutionary museums were able to make new relations of *time* perceptible. This is not to press the case for the temporal organisation of evolutionary museums at the expense of their spatial co-ordinates. It is, to the contrary, both the spatial and the temporal aspects of the discourses organising their exhibits – and the relations between these – that have to be attended to. It is true of all museums that what Frederick Bohrer calls 'the presentness of the artefact' (Bohrer, 1994: 199) strives to overcome both temporal and spatial distance, rendering present that which is absent because it occurred long ago or is located far away. In the 'strategies of presence' organising evolutionary museum exhibits, the 'long ago' and the 'far away' were super-imposed on one another through the network of assumptions which equated what was distant from Europe with its prehistory. This manoeuvre applied to geology and natural history just as much as to anthropology. It was evident in the expectation that the maritime exploration of the Pacific would allow Europeans to overcome both space and time in bringing back the past – the living past of forms of life that were extinct in Europe – from far away. Perhaps the most famous and economical example of how the colonial structure of natural and human times overlapped is John Lubbock's contention that 'the Van Diemaner and South African are to the antiquary, what the opossum and the sloth are to the geologist' (Lubbock, 1865: 336). However, we can also see this structure at work in the system of equivalences that was established between the fossils found lying on the surface in the 'far away' of Australia with those excavated, through coal-mining, from the deep past of Europe (Desmond, 1982: 14–15, 148–9).

It is, however, the lamination on top of one another of the spatio-temporal co-ordinates produced by the different historical sciences that interests me most here. At a later point in *Science in Action*, Latour suggests that to suppose 'that it is possible to draw together in a synthesis the times of astronomy, geology, biology, primatology and anthropology has about as much meaning as making a synthesis between the pipes or cables of water, gas, electricity, telephone and television' (Latour, 1987: 229). From the perspective of contemporary science, this is no doubt correct. However, the closing decades of the nineteenth century were characterised by precisely such a synthesis in which these sciences – whose development had hitherto proceeded along more separate lines – were compacted, temporarily, into a close and cohesive unity. Thomas Huxley, defining anthropology as a branch of biology, thus referred to the closely integrated roles played by anthropological, geological, biological and archaeological investigations in demonstrating 'the antiquity of the human species' (Huxley, 1893: 119). Henry Pitt Rivers, echoing this assessment, argued that the result was 'a band of union between the physical and cultural sciences which can never be broken' in which 'history' is 'but another term for evolution' (cited in Thompson, 1977: 40).

Michel de Certeau identifies the distinctive properties of this intellectual formation:

> One hundred years ago, history represented society as a collection and recollection of its entire development. It is true that history was fragmented into a plurality of histories (biological, economic, linguistic, and so on). But among these scattered positivities, as among the different cycles that characterised each of them, historical knowledge restored the same through their common ground of an *evolution*. It sewed all of these discontinuities together by running through them as if they were the successive or coexisting figures of a same meaning – that is, of an orientation – and by evincing in a more or less teleological writing the interior unity of a direction or a development.
>
> (de Certeau, 1988: 83)

De Certeau also sees the connection between museums and death in the analogies he draws in exploring the properties of historical writing in which the dead are calmed in 'scriptural tombs'.[13] For 'what proliferates in historical discourse', de Certeau argues, 'are elements "below which nothing more can be done except display," and through which *saying* reaches its limit, as near as possible to *showing*' (100). The discourse which organises these elements – proper names, localities, coins are the examples he gives – has what de Certeau calls a '"gallery" structure' which, like any history gallery, 'represents the dead along a narrative itinerary' (100).

It was only in the context of late-nineteenth-century evolutionary thought that this gallery structure was translated into a regulative principle that was at work within each of the histories organised by a range of disciplinary museums, and across the relations between them. Dead things had not, of course, been absent from earlier museum contexts. The Muséum National d'Histoire Naturelle under Cuvier's direction was, like the natural history collections of the British Museum under Richard Owen, Hunter's earlier anatomical collections, and William Macleay's 'vicious circles', full of dead things. These were not, however, arranged in accordance with a narrative itinerary. At the Muséum National d'Histoire Naturelle, death was splayed open – 'murdered to dissect' (Brown, 1997: 80) – in order to reveal, in the exploded interiors of different forms of life, the functional interrelations of their organs and, thereby, the principles of their relation to the conditions of their existence and their place within the abstract scheme of classification. 'Cuvier's galleries', as Outram puts it, 'were full of objects to be looked not *at*, but *into*' (Outram, 1984: 176). Just as important, Cuvier's comparative anatomy exhibits did not include fossils, thus providing no opportunity for tracing narrative connections between extinct and existing forms of life (Sloan,

1997). At the Hunterian Museum, similarly, the anatomised human body yielded its secrets to the dissecting and highly sexualised gaze of surgical medicine (see Jordanova, 1985). In neither case, however, were these dead things historicised.

It would be a mistake, though, to view the historicisation of museum displays as entirely a nineteenth-century matter. Horst Bredekamp has convincingly demonstrated the 'training of the historicising eye' (Bredekamp, 1995) that was associated with the history of the *Kunstkammer* from the sixteenth through to the eighteenth centuries, when it gave way to the new forms of historicisation associated with the post-Winckelmann programme for the art museum. This was, however, a historicising eye which operated largely in the relations between broad categories – *naturalia, artificialia, scientifica* – rather than within each of them. It was also characterised by the 'freeze-frame' form of time-lapse photography in which time runs jerkily rather than in the flowing form of connected developmental sequences. It was, by contrast, only in the last forty years or so of the nineteenth century that dead things were narrativised across a range of museum disciplines and, just as important, the relations between them. By the end of the century, an international network of museums had been established which, basing their practices on the post-Darwinian synthesis of the historical sciences, made a new set of interconnecting times publicly perceptible. The telling of each time in the form of a unilinear developmental sequence provided the conditions for their amalgamation in a totalising narrative, in which the history of the earth supplied the master time which calibrated the histories of life on earth, and those of human civilisations, cultures and technologies.

Evolution as temporal conscience

What connections might there be between these new forms of publicly perceptible time and the concerns of governance? Norbert Elias provides a route into this question in his assessment of the role of different systems and devices for measuring time in serving 'human beings as means of orienting themselves within the succession of social, biological and physical processes in which they find themselves placed [and] as a way of regulating their behaviour in relation to each other and themselves' (Elias, 1987: 2). A little later in the same essay, Elias proposes the concept of 'temporal conscience' to describe how particular social institutions of time are translated from an external compulsion into 'a pattern of self-constraint embracing the whole life of an individual' (11). This is precisely what E. P. Thompson (1967) was concerned with in his classic essay on the emergence of time–work discipline in the clocked time of the factory and whose central insights Graeme Davison extends in his perception that 'the clock on the wall or in the waistcoat pocket is but the metronome for a soul already singing to the music of modernity' (Davison, 1993: 6). But how is the temporal conscience of daily or calendar time connected to the horizons of epochal or deep time? How is the temporal coherence that is placed on the ordering of an individual life related to the temporal frameworks which organise the sequencing of generations? And how is the sequencing of generations related to the deeper structures of geological and cosmic time? These questions were raised with an increasing urgency and insistence in the second half of the nineteenth century as discoveries across the full range of the historical sciences had dissolved the foreshortened time of the mosaic calendar into the infinitely receding structures of the deep time, which the dreaded clinking of the geologists' hammers had brought into view.[14]

Anne McClintock gets at some of the issues that were involved in these concerns in her account of the relations between what she calls panoptical time and anachronistic space in late Victorian culture. Taking her cue from Fabian, she argues that the chief legacy of Darwinism was to map human and natural times onto each other in a new global and secularised time that was also spatialised in its anachronistic construction of colonial peripheries as the past in the present. In characterising this as panoptical time, McClintock's concern is with the respects in which the evolutionary narratives of the period organised time so that the full sweep of global history might be 'consumed – at a glance – in a single spectacle from a point of privileged invisibility' through visual forms (like evolutionary trees) which displayed 'evolutionary progress as a measurable spectacle' (McClintock, 1995: 37). Taken together, McClintock suggests, panoptical time and ana-chronistic space functioned as an administrative and regulatory technology whose principal mechanism was, paradoxically, one of freezing history by denying the agency of those subjects whose political perspectives threatened to make the bourgeois, male and imperial culture of the late Victorian era merely a stage in history rather than its end or telos. Women, the working classes and the colonised: the agency of all of these, in McClintock's perspective, was 'disavowed and projected onto anachronistic space: prehistoric, atavistic and irrational, inherently out of place in the historical time of modernity' (40).

If Victorians were obsessively concerned with the representation of progress, then, this was solely with a view to bring progress to a halt with the present. It is from this perspective that McClintock assesses the role of museums in the organisa-tion of panoptical time. The Victorian 'fixation with origins, with genesis narratives, with archaeology, skulls, skeletons and fossils – the imperial bric-à-brac of the archaic', she argues, was most clearly evident in the museum which, as 'the modern fetish-house of the archaic', became 'the exemplary institution for embodying the Victorian narrative of progress' (40). But its effect was to stop time in its tracks by making history appear 'static, fixed, covered in dust' – with the paradoxical effect that 'in the act of turning time into a commodity, historical change – and especially the *labour* of changing history – tends to disappear' (40).

There are a number of worrying aspects to this account. Although ostensibly concerned with post-Darwinian tendencies in Victorian Britain, McClintock draws her examples indiscriminately from the French Enlightenment, Hegel, late-nineteenth-century German anthropology and early-nineteenth-century exhibition practices. As a consequence, significant differences between what were historically distinctive forms of evolutionary thought are dissolved into a vast and un-differentiated soup of social evolutionism. It is, however, the more general aspects of her argument concerning the relations between museums and the split time of modernity that concern me here. These echo Latour's assessment of the 'temporal conscience' of modernity as one which depends on establishing a radical break with the past:

> The moderns have a peculiar propensity for understanding time that passes as if it were really abolishing the past behind it. . . . They do not feel that they are removed from the Middle Ages by a certain number of centuries, but that they are separated by Copernican revolutions, epistemological breaks, epistemic ruptures so radical that nothing of that past survives in them – nothing of that past ought to survive in them.
>
> (Latour, 1993: 68)

The difficulty here is that precisely the opposite was true of the way in which the past was constructed in the historical sciences, and of how the concerns this gave rise to were refracted in debates concerning the role of museums in organising a new temporal conscience. Far from positing a radical separation of the present from the past, late-nineteenth-century social and political theorists were centrally preoccupied with the implications of the ways in which the mechanisms of habit and inheritance translated the 'pasts beyond memory' produced by these sciences into a potent force within the present.

While, then, I think McClintock is right in the significance she accords questions of time, she treats these as solely ideological questions in which representations of time are assessed in relation to ideologies of class, race and gender. What this misses are the respects in which the new horizons of the past opened up by the excavations of the historical sciences posed quite new ways of thinking about the tasks of social management. This is especially true of the role that the historical sciences played in revising and adapting the strategies of liberalism in the last quarter of the nineteenth century. For it was in the context of a distinctive articulation of the relationships between the new forms of expertise produced by these sciences, the principles of liberal government and the need to extend these to new populations that the practices of late-nineteenth-century museums were reorganised. As we shall see, this did not result in any simple unity of museum philosophy or method. What is clear, though, is that the current of scientific thought and opinion which constituted the cutting-edge of museum practice throughout this period was one which, far from seeking to stop history in its tracks, was concerned that the mechanisms of progress – duly and properly regulated – should be kept on the go in ways which, contrary to the statist implications of eugenic programmes, respected the freedom and autonomy of individuals. This was to be accomplished by translating the particular ways of 'acting upon time' (Osborne, 1998: 157) associated with the expertise of the historical sciences into ways of acting on and managing the self within the framework of a new temporal conscience. And it is here, within the architecture of the self that this temporal conscience produces, that the relations between questions of time and those of race, class and gender that McLintock is rightly concerned with will find a more productive setting.

Expertise, exhibition, government and new liberalism

Questions concerning the relations between expertise and government have come to occupy a new prominence within the humanities and social sciences in the wake of Foucault's work on the relationships between knowledge and power and his influential account of governmentality.[15] Not all of this work points in the same direction: Foucault's earlier writings on knowledge and power still imply the possibility of a general concept of power, a view questioned by those who have sought to quarry the implications of his later work on governmentality which stresses the range, variety and dispersal of the mechanisms that have been developed for organising and regulating social conduct.[16] However, both of these aspects of the Foucauldian legacy stress the importance of the roles played by different forms of knowledge and expertise in organising specific strategies, techniques and mechanisms for shaping and regulating human conduct in the context of differentiated fields of social management which, while not unconnected, do not derive an ultimate and unifying coherence from some supra source of power located in a class or state. They also both stress the need to take account of the ways in which such strategies of governing seek to enrol the governed as active agents in their own governance, implanting the objectives of government into the dynamics of selfhood so that they become self-acting imperatives for the individuals concerned.

This requires that attention focus on the history of the varied technical devices through which particular knowledges are translated into distinctive practically operable forms and diffused through everyday social and cultural practice. Nikolas Rose, borrowing from Gaston Bachelard's notion of 'phenomotech-nology', thus stresses the distinctive role played by expertise in the processes through which a science provides a means for acting on the objects it constructs via the instruments in which its theories are materialised. Applying this perception to psychology, Rose defines psychological expertise as follows:

> By expertise is meant the capacity of psychology to provide a corps of trained and credentialed persons claiming special competence in the administration of persons and interpersonal relations, and a body of techniques and procedures claiming to make possible the rational and human management of human resources in industry, the military, and social life more generally.
>
> (Rose, 1998: 11)

It is through the deployment of particular forms of expertise in particular relations of government that particular ways of speaking the truth and making it practical are connected to particular ways of acting on persons – and of inducing them to act upon themselves – which, in their turn, form particular ways of acting on the social.

The literature exploring these questions is now considerable, with a notable emphasis on the distinctive forms of rule and self-rule associated with liberal forms of government which, in positing the freedom and autonomy of the person, stress the need to recruit the voluntary and active participation of individuals in their own governance.[17] Two issues have been somewhat neglected in these debates. The first concerns the forms of expertise that are associated specifically with the cultural sphere and the role that these play in organising cultural resources into means of governing. This is surprising in view of the widespread recognition of the role played by aesthetics in the early development of liberal forms of self-government. What tends to be missing from such accounts, though, is a focus on the 'phenomeno-technological' processes through which aesthetic conceptions are translated into particular technical forms which are then brought to bear on the regulation of social conduct.

Late-nineteenth-century museum practices provide a good historical context in which to engage with issues. Peter Hoffenberg touches on some of the reasons why, in describing the commissioners for the international exhibitions that flourished in this period as the first generation of cultural bureaucrats – a new clerisy – whose 'expertise produced that strange beast known as "culture"' (Hoffenberg, 2001: xviii). In truth, this formulation over-unifies the situation somewhat, as museums and exhibitions provided the context for contending forms of expertise which, when translated into the museum environment, produced a number of different versions of culture rather than just the one. However, what Hoffenberg gets to is the crucial role of museum curators, directors, education officers, exhibition commissioners, etc., in mediating the relations between specific knowledges (anthropology, archaeology and natural history, for example, as well as theories of perception) and the technical forms of their institutional deployment in ways that were calculated to involve individuals in their own self-governance and self-development. It is this perspective that I seek to develop.

The second area of neglect concerns the tendency, within the historical periodisation of liberal forms of government, to skip right over the new liberalism of the late nineteenth century which, as I have already noted, played an important role in the development of modern forms of cultural governance. This is true of Nikolas Rose, whose periodisation of liberalism neglects it entirely in running directly from the classical *laissez-faire* liberalism of the early to mid-nineteenth century through to what he calls the forms of 'social government' based on the principles of collective welfare and social insurance that were developed in the early twentieth century (Rose, 1996).[18] Yet the new liberalism was distinctive, especially in expanding the social reach of cultural forms of governance. This point is perhaps best made by means of a contrast with the earlier period of classical liberalism which, Poovey suggests, was split, in its strategies and tactics, along class lines. Poovey accounts for this in terms of the influence of Adam Smith's *Theory of Moral Sentiments*, which argued that the cultivation of virtue was fuelled by the mechanism of a specular morality in which individuals became self-governing by adjusting their conduct in response to the moralising gaze of others. In Smith's analysis, this self-developing moral capacity was denied to the urban working classes who, sunk 'in obscurity and darkness' in the large towns and cities, were beyond the reach of the moralising gaze of the middle classes. The working poor had therefore to be 'treated differently from those individuals capable of specular morality: because their literal bodies could no longer be seen, the former had to be conceptualised as an aggregate; because they could not govern themselves, they had to be governed from above' (Poovey, 1995: 34). As a consequence, the strategies of the first generation of liberal reformers – Edwin Chadwick and James Kay Shuttleworth, for example – aimed to develop an 'efficient morality' which, rather than working via the interiorised forms of specular morality which characterised the middle classes, subjected the poor to state-directed forms of visual control in arranging for the 'surveillance and ocular penetration of poor neighbourhoods' (35).

This strategy did not entirely disappear with the new liberalism. But it was no longer thought sufficient in view of the increasing perception of the need to cultivate capacities for self-monitoring, self-government and self-development throughout all classes and, in some formulations, to extend these to women and children as well as to the male head of household. It was the latter who had formed the privileged and, in some contexts, the only point of application for earlier strategies of government.[19] It is in this light that we can best understand the distinctive signature of the new liberalism which differed from its predecessor in licensing state action in the cultural and moral sphere. It did so, however, less with a view to directly promoting moral goodness than to helping free individuals from the hindrances which might impede their ability to develop their moral potentialities themselves by providing the contexts and resources that would assist in this (Richter, 1964: 283–9). Huxley's work was important here. Drawing on the discoveries of natural history and the anthropological evidence of 'archaic' societies, Huxley took issue with the 'fictitious history' of social contract theory whose influence he castigated as tending to lead either to 'anarchy', by refusing to 'acknowledge the right of any government except the government of the individual by himself' (Huxley, 1890b: 860), or to 'regimentation', be it in the form of Rousseau's general will or in the statist orientations of contemporary socialist or eugenic thought to which he was equally opposed. His purpose in doing so was to defend a moral, cultural and educative role for the state as a means of mediating between these false extremes of 'no government' and 'intrusive government' in view of the role it could play in shaping and directing individual self-government.[20] In his critique of anarchy and its 'persistence in letting alone as a definition of the whole duty of the statesman' (856), Huxley was thus careful to note that this meant that 'state education goes, as a matter of course, and with it all state-aided museums, libraries, galleries or art, parks, and pleasure grounds' (859).

The relationship between new liberalism and the new education movement is important here. For in its criticisms of earlier disciplinary forms of schooling in which morality was to be acquired through the rote repetition of mechanical actions complemented by panoptic mechanisms of surveillance, and in its commitment to cultivating an independent, questioning and self-activated approach to learning and moral development, the new education movement echoed the break that new liberalism aimed to make with classical liberalism.[21] Again, Huxley is a key figure here. Attacking both the state elementary school and the public school for, in different ways and for different classes, approaching learning and morality as matters of repetition and mechanical obedience, Huxley counterposes to these the principles of liberal education as ones aiming to produce an adult who would be, in all capacities, capable of self-direction:

> That man, I think, has had a liberal education who has been so trained in youth that his body is the ready servant of his will, and does with ease and pleasure all the work that, as a mechanism, it is capable of; whose intellect is a clear, cold, logic engine, with all its parts of equal strength, and in smooth working order; ready, like a steam engine, to be turned to any kind of work, and spin the gossamers as well as forge the anchors of the mind; whose mind is stored with a knowledge of the great and fundamental truths of nature and of the laws of her operations; one who, no stunted ascetic, is full of life and fire, but whose passions are trained to come to heel by a vigorous will, the servant of a tender conscience; who has learned to love all beauty, whether of nature or of art, to hate all vileness, and to respect others as himself.
>
> (Huxley, 1868: 370)

That Huxley expected a lot from this capacity of self-direction is clear when he goes on to note that its value would be tested in proving to the workman 'once for all, that it is better for his own people, better for himself, better for future generations, that he should starve than steal' (371). He was also clear that this capacity could not be developed without a radical revision of the prevailing methods of teaching. This is evident in the comparison he draws between instruction in the classics – a negative model, for Huxley, of rote, repetitive and pointless learning – and the lingering influence of outmoded teaching practices in the field of palaeontology. Were he to look for a parallel to 'verse-making and essay-writing in the dead languages', he says, then he would do what the palaeontology instructor presently does:

> In the first place I could get up an osteological primer so arid, so pedantic in its terminology, so altogether distasteful to the youthful mind, as to beat the recent famous production of the headmasters out of the field in all these excellences. Next, I could exercise my boys upon easy fossils, and bring out all their powers of memory and all their ingenuity in the application of my osteo-grammatical rules to the interpretation, or construing, of those fragments. To those who had reached the higher classes I might give odd bones to be built up into animals, giving great honour and regard to him who succeeded in fabricating monsters most entirely with the rules.
>
> (Huxley, 1868: 375)

The root of Huxley's objection here is to the influence of classics in substituting, via arid primers and misleading grammars, a textually mediated relationship to the object for the experience of a direct encounter with the object itself. He makes the same point, perhaps more emphatically, in an earlier essay in which he extols the pedagogic virtues of chalk over and above the whole canon of the humanities:

> I weigh my words well . . . when I assert, that the man who should know the true history of the bit of chalk which every carpenter carries about in his breeches-pocket, though ignorant of all other history, is likely, if he will

think his knowledge out to its ultimate results, to have a truer, and therefore a better, conception of this wonderful universe, and of man's relation to it, than the most learned student who is deep-read in the records of humanity and ignorant of those of Nature.

(Huxley, 1896b: 4)

The reasons for this stress on the value of teaching from objects rather than from texts are numerous. In part a reflection of the ethos of the historical sciences in contesting the cultural authority of the classics and humanities, it also reflected the revival of interest in the theories of Johan Heinrich Pestalozzi – for whom the first rule was 'to teach always by *things* rather than by *words*' (cited in Selleck, 1968: 203) – prompted by the active learning orientation of the new education. Whatever its causes, however, it meant that museums were placed on the front line in the educational agendas of the period. This was evident in the increasingly close connections between museums and the development of compulsory public schooling, and in the stress that was placed on the value of museums as instruments of adult education.[22]

This stress on adult education as not just a worthwhile activity for voluntary, benevolent and self-help organisations, as had been true of mid-century liberalism, but also as a legitimate activity of government was a distinctive characteristic of new liberalism: indeed, both the new universities of the period and museums emerged as important sites for extension activities directed at the working classes. This was, therefore, an important area of activity for intellectuals schooled in the historical sciences and, once again, none more than Huxley who, at different stages in his career, gave public lectures for the working classes in a variety of contexts: as part of his employment at the Government School of Mines from 1854; developing his own programme of Sunday Evenings for the People in 1866 in secular opposition to the power of the pulpit; and, in 1868, as Principal of the South London Working Men's College, which numbered John Lubbock among its Council members.[23]

The new liberalism, new education, and adult education: these provided the political contexts in which, in late-nineteenth-century Britain, developments in the historical sciences and their implications for practical affairs were debated by the leading liberal intellectuals of the period. This was especially true of the Lubbock Circle, so-called because its members, all liberal evolutionists, initially focused their work around John Lubbock's term of office – commencing in 1863 – as President of the Ethnological Society whose title reflected a specifically British legacy.[24] Entering into English usage only in the 1830s, the terms 'ethnology' and 'ethnological' included a consideration of the civil or cultural as well as physical and climatic causes of racial variation (Bravo, 1996: 339–41). As such, and in view also of its monogenetic premises, ethnology was initially championed by middle-class Quaker philanthropists as a means, at least in theory, of including all peoples in the developmental dynamic of civilisation. This legacy remained active in the period of the Lubbock Circle. Thomas Huxley, who succeeded Lubbock as President in 1868, Charles Darwin, Lubbock himself, Edward Tylor, Henry Pitt Rivers, Henry Flower and Augustus Franks are among the key names here. Between them, they spanned natural history, geology, archaeology and anthropology, each of which was concerned with reconstructing lost pasts on the basis of the traces or survivals they had deposited in the present. This was a provisional intellectual synthesis that was to fall apart in the early twentieth century as each of these sciences became more specialised as their research bases moved away from museums to the developing university sector. The increased mathematisation of biology and geology also meant that the conditions that had made for a dialogue between the physical and the humanistic sciences no longer obtained. It was also a nationally specific synthesis. In France, under the influence of Paul Broca, the leading school of anthropological thought had a distinctively more physicalist cast owing to its close associations with craniometry.[25] It was, accordingly, of a markedly more racist hue that was much closer to that of the disciplinary ensemble of biology, anatomy, chemistry, natural philosophy and physiology that anthropology was connected to in the work of the Anthropological Society which, in Britain, was outmanoeuvred and intellectually discredited as (in Huxley's phrase) a 'scientific mob' by the Lubbock Circle through its domination of the rival Ethnological Society.[26]

Equally, though, the influence of the intellectual synthesis associated with the Lubbock Circle was by no means confined to Britain. On the contrary, its international influence was extensive in view of London's role as the main metropolitan centre of Anglophone international scientific networks. There is broad agreement that Australia remained at the first of the three-stage model of colonial science proposed by Basalla (1967) until the 1880s, with colonial scientists and scientific organisations confined largely to the role of collecting 'raw' scientific data and then sending it to the metropolitan centres of Europe, and especially, London for authoritative analysis and interpretation.[27] The fact that the first three recipients of the Clarke medal, awarded for meritorious contributions to the geology, mineralogy or natural history of Australia, were Richard Owen, Thomas Huxley and George Bentham of the Royal Gardens at Kew is a good measure of the extent of this colonial dependency (Inkster, 1985). However, Inkster suggests that, by the 1880s, Australia had moved into the second stage of Basalla's model in which the colonial scientist is still trained in metropolitan centres but, forgoing the subservient role of data provision, aims to achieve recognition in those centres for independent work conducted in the colonial context. The relations between the United States and British science cannot be told in the same terms. There had been a strong tradition of home-grown American science which, since the late eighteenth century, had challenged the Eurocentric assumptions of both natural history and anthropology, and especially Buffon's account of America as a land of environmental degeneration (Orosz, 1990). By the late nineteenth century, the United States was a fully independent metropolitan centre of science in its own right. Be that as it may, the late-nineteenth-century English synthesis of the historical sciences enjoyed considerable cultural authority and influence in America.

International networks and the new museum idea

One of the main routes through which this influence travelled was that of the increasingly internationalised network of museums. The spread of this, at root, European form was initially limited to white settler societies in the Americas, India, Australia and South Africa and to British colonial territories in Asia (Prosler, 1996). The resulting institutions were, however, usually quite modest in scope, often just the collecting wings of scientific or philosophical societies, and, in functioning mainly as places of assembly and intellectual exchange for colonial scientific and social elites, initially quite limited in their public reach.[28] In Australia, for example, it was not until the 1870s to 1890s that colonial governments in each of the states committed to support the development of major public museums (see Kohlstedt, 1983). While, in some cases, these were generalised collections including art and social history materials, their primary focus was on geology, natural history, and, increasingly towards the end of the century, ethnological collections. It was also during this period that the museum became a more widespread international form with, according to Prosler, museums opening in Bangkok (1874), Japan (1871), China (1905) and Korea (1908).

At the same time, in the metropolitan centres of Europe and America, two related developments should be noted. The first concerns the tendency towards increased disciplinary specialisation and differentiation compared with the earlier *omnium gatherum* structure of collections at institutions like the Smithsonian Institution and the British Museum.[29] The second is the significant increase in the rate of establishment of new museums of natural history, ethnology and geology. Simon Knell (1996) notes the increasing prominence of geological, zoological, botanical and archaeological collections in local museums over the period 1888–1914 and, in particular, the severance of their earlier association with literary and philosophical societies. David van Keuren has similarly estimated that, of the 71 new museum collections established in Britain over the 1870s to 1890s, 28 were natural history collections and 5 ethnological collections (van Keuren, 1982: 155). By 1900, the USA had 200 natural history museums and Britain 250 (Jenkins, 1994). Susan Sheets-Pyenson (1987) similarly comments on the strong natural history focus of colonial museums established in the second half of the nineteenth century and notes their significant popularity in this period with annual visitation rates frequently in excess of 100,000.

It was, then, this increasingly internationalised network of museums and a denser network of capillary relations between national and local museums that supplied one of the primary institutional sites for the activities of the Lubbock Circle as they sought to harness the historical sciences to the purposes of governing, taking issue with the role of humanistic disciplines in a conscious and articulate alliance with the theory and practice of the new liberalism. Huxley was constantly active in the museum world from his period at the School of Mines to his role in securing Richard Owen's succession at the British Museum (Natural History) for the Darwinian Henry Flower.[30] Pitt Rivers was equally active in arranging and rearranging his ethnological collections – at Bethnal Green, the South Kensington Museum and, finally, the University of Oxford – in accordance with the principles of his typological method.[31] Tylor was a source of constant advice to Henry Balfour during the period that Balfour was first curator of the Pitt Rivers collection in its Oxford installation.[32] And finally, as King (1997) shows, it was Franks who pushed and prodded the British Museum into expanding its ethnological collections and displaying them in accordance with evolutionary principles. Through a variety of routes, the ideas developed in these contexts began to spread abroad and, just as important, to feed back into British debates as multiple lines of communication began to develop between the different components of this international network.

In America, Henry Fairfield Osborn viewed his mission at the American Museum of Natural History as that of putting into effect Huxley's educational principles and evolutionary philosophy while, at the Smithsonian, Otis Mason – as Rydell (1984) has shown – played a crucial role in internationalising the typological method and, in the process, adapting it to new purposes.[33] Although blocked for a while in Australia by anti-evolutionary scientific establishments in both Sydney and Melbourne, McCoy's replacement as Director of the National Museum of Victoria in 1899 by Baldwin Spencer – who had been well schooled in evolutionary natural history and anthropology while at Oxford, where he had become a devotee of the typological method, retaining an active association with Tylor and Fraser throughout his career – signalled a significant extension of the Lubbock Circle's influence into the southern hemisphere.[34] At the same time, to avoid the impression that this network had only a single hub, by the 1890s the American Museum of Natural History was beginning to emerge as a major point of reference for Australian museums while it was also George Brown Goode at the US National Museum at the Smithsonian who emerged as the most articulate and influential advocate of 'the new museum idea'.[35]

Like most ideas of the same kind, 'the new museum idea' was, in fact, many ideas in one, encompassing the new importance that was placed on museums as instruments of adult education and the need to develop closer links with the new systems of state-provided schooling which began to develop in this period in Britain, Australia and the United States. I shall look more closely at the currency of this idea in chapter 5. For now, though, three points will suffice. The first is the new focus on natural history and ethnology museums rather than art museums as the most fitting conduit for propagating the ethos of the 'new museum idea'. This was a departure from the 'museum idea' of the 1850s, as advocated by Henry Cole, which envisaged for itself a particular role in reforming the working man. The second concerns the role that was played by 'the new museum idea' as the credo of a distinctive phase in the professionalisation of museum practice and administration. There are a number of aspects to this: the emergence of new forms of curatorial specialism; the development of a professional career structure in the increasingly well-trodden route from curator to director; and the emergence of new professional roles, including those of docent and specialist education officers. The one I shall be most concerned with, however, concerns the role of professional organisations in providing a context for the sharing and spread of a common culture of museum philosophy and administration. The role of the British Museums Association was crucial here. Holding its inaugural meeting in 1889, this association had been established as the result of the agitations of liberal reformers closely attached to the Lubbock Circle and – along with the British Association for the Advancement of Science – it remained an important focus for their work into the early twentieth century.[36] It was also an important vehicle for the internationalisation of museum practice, especially in terms of its influence on museums in British colonial contexts, and served as a significant forum for debate for both American and Australian museum workers until those countries established their own professional museum associations in the early twentieth century.

My third point concerns the broader discursive setting for 'the new museum idea'. The earlier museum idea had formed part of a series of related ideas – 'the statistical idea', 'the education idea' and 'the sanitary idea' – which had helped to disseminate more disciplinary forms of self-governance which characterised the earlier phase of liberalism. 'The new museum idea', by contrast, had its setting in the midst of the new liberalism and the new education movement at a time when all three of these new 'ideas' and their intersections had an international, albeit variable, currency. This setting was also one in which, in lieu of the earlier 'sanitation idea', eugenic conceptions of population – whose influence ran across the spectrum of political opinion – became increasingly important. This had markedly anti-liberal implications for the strategies and tactics of governing, whose logic became evident in the relations that were developed between museums, the historical sciences and both immigrant and indigenous populations in the early twentieth century. Before I examine this though, I want to look more closely at the procedures of the historical sciences with especial regard to their constructions of the relations between the pasts of deep time and the present, the challenge to the humanities that was articulated through their object-centredness, and the distinctiveness of their synthesis in the British context.

2

The archaeological gaze of the historical sciences

In the midst of discussing how 'history, in its traditional form . . . transforms *documents* into *monuments*', Foucault adds, as an aside, that there 'was a time when archaeology, as a discipline devoted to silent monuments, inert traces, objects without context, and things left by the past, aspired to the condition of history, and attained meaning only through the restitution of a historical discourse' (Foucault, 1972: 7; emphasis in original). He might have added, had he had the British context in mind, that the same was true of geology, natural history and ethnology, all of which, in their nineteenth-century formation, aimed at the restitution of a historical discourse, albeit one that was to be arrived at via the application of scientific method. William Whewell's work was important here in providing a broadened ambit for the methods of conjectural history derived, most immediately, from the Scottish Enlightenment.[1] This was the service performed by his conception of the 'palaetiological sciences' as including all 'those researches in which the object is, to ascend from the present state of things to a more ancient condition, from which the present is derived by intelligible causes' (Whewell, 1837: 481). The combination of historical reasoning and – as a counter to the hypothetical deductions of conjectural reasoning – scientific method is made clearer when Whewell goes on to define palaetiology as describing 'those speculations which thus refer to actual past events, but attempt to explain them by laws of causation' (481–2). These methods were to be applied to *artificialia* just as much as to *naturalia*, thereby overcoming the division between natural and human history:

> Such speculations are not confined to the world of inert matter; we have examples of them in inquiries concerning the monuments of the art and labour of distant ages; in examinations into the origin and early progress of states and cities, customs and languages; as well as in researches concerning the causes and formations of mountains and rocks, the imbedding of fossils in strata, and their elevation from the bottom of the ocean. All these speculations are connected by this bond, – that they endeavour to ascend to a past of things, by the aid of the evidence of the present. In asserting, with Cuvier, that 'The geologist is an antiquary of a new order,' we do not mark a fanciful and superficial resemblance of employment merely, but a real and philosophical connexion of the principles of investigation. The

organic fossils which occur in the rock, and the medals which we find in the ruins of ancient cities, are to be studied in a similar spirit and for a similar purpose.

(Whewell, 1837: 482)

Whewell goes on to articulate what can perhaps best be characterised as an 'archaeological gaze' in suggesting how the present might be read to identify the pasts that have been sedimented within it as the remnants of one historical period are carried over and compressed into the next one, preserving a record of time's passage in the sequential layering of its accumulations. 'The relics and ruins of the earlier states', as he puts it, 'are preserved, mutilated and dead, in the products of later times' so that it is 'more than a mere fanciful description, to say that in languages, customs, forms of society, political institutions, we see a number of formations superimposed upon one another, each of which is, for the most part, an assemblage of fragments and results of the preceding condition' (484). We can see this archaeological gaze at work some thirty years later when, in a lecture he gave to the working men of Norwich in 1868, Thomas Huxley metaphorically places an imaginary bit of chalk under a microscope to reveal the successive layers of history that have been stored up with it:

Thus there is a writing upon the wall of cliffs at Cromer, and whoso runs may read it. It tells us, with an authority which cannot be impeached, that the ancient sea-bed of the chalk sea was raised up, and remained dry land, until it was covered with forest, stocked with the great game the spoils of which have rejoiced your geologists. How long it remained in that condition cannot be said; but 'the whirligig of time brought its revenges' in those days as in these. That dry land, with the bones and teeth of generations of long-lived elephants, hidden away among the gnarled roots and dry leaves of its ancient trees, sank gradually to the bottom of the icy sea, which covered it with huge masses of drift and boulder clay. Sea-beasts, such as the walrus, now restricted to the extreme north, paddled about where birds had twittered among the topmost twigs of the fir trees. How long this state of things endured we know not, but at length it came to an end. The upheaved glacial mud hardened into the soil of modern Norfolk. Forests grew once more, the wolf and the beaver replaced the reindeer and the elephant; and at length what we call the history of England dawned.

(Huxley, 1896b: 27)

Huxley returned to the same theme a year later in his essay 'Geological reform', where he aimed to free Whewell's palaetiological sciences – and geology in particular – from the restrictions which the leading geologist of the Scottish Enlightenment, James Hutton, had placed on them. In his commitment to a rigorous 'presentism' – that is, to the belief that 'the present order of things', the actual constitution of the earth as it is now, provided geology with its only reliable data – Hutton committed geology to the methods of retrospective deduction by obliging it to take things as they are at present and, from these, to 'reason with regard to that which must have been' (Hutton, cited in Huxley, 1896b: 310). This led Hutton to conclude, in his *Theory of the Earth* (1795), that an inquiry based on such principles yielded 'no vestige of a beginning, – no prospect of an end' (310). It was this that Huxley took issue with, objecting not to Hutton's presentism but to the artificial limitation which he thought both Hutton and, later, Charles Lyell had placed on the procedures of retrospective deduction by arguing that the oldest fossiliferous rock strata constituted a veil beyond which it was impossible to see further. While prepared to accept that, in their existing state, the palaetiological sciences might have difficulty in penetrating this veil, Huxley saw no reason why it should forever remain impenetrable. He therefore looked to Kant's account of speculative geology which, accepting no limits to the capacity of retrospective deduction ('Give me matter,' Kant said, 'and I will build the world' (320)), offered the basis for a universal theory of evolution in which the findings of all the historical sciences – from astronomy, through geology, biology and archaeology – might be synthesised. This is not to suggest that Kant's thought was evolutionary in a proto-Darwinian sense. To the contrary, he opposed any suggestion of a genealogical connection between species. However, his *General History of Nature and Theory of the Heavens* (1755) played a key role in historicising both nature and the earth in its conception of both as still incomplete, still in the process of coming into existence, thereby extending the duration of both the past and the future beyond the limited compass of their earlier biblical conception (Toulmin and Goodfield, 1977: 129–39). For Huxley, Kant's attraction was that – until actual science caught up – he provided a way of by-passing Hutton's scrupulous 'presentism' that would allow the accounts of the past produced by the different historical sciences to be dovetailed into a totalising history: 'He [Kant] knows no bounds to geological speculation but those of the intellect. He reasons back to a beginning of the present state of things; he admits the possibility of an end' (323).

In short, Huxley looked to Kant for a means of providing an unrestricted narrativisation of the historical sciences, to tell the story of things – *naturalia* and *artificialia* – from their beginning to their end in order to provide the basis for a new scientific world view, based on new vistas of time, that might take the place of natural theology. That it was possible to enunciate such a view at the end of the 1860s was due to the coming together of a number of conditions which allowed a variety of dug-up things to be interpreted as prehistorical. This newly produced zone of the past, moreover, was placed in a distinctive relationship to history and to the present to the degree that the relations between past and present events were understood to be governed by even and constant principles of succession marked by uniform principles of time and action. Huxley once again provides a convenient illustration of the seamless quality of this archaeological gaze in which the past is piled up into the present in an uninterrupted sequence of development:

> There can be no doubt that the existing Fauna and Flora is but the last term of a long series of equally numerous contemporary species, which have succeeded one another, by the slow and gradual substitution of species for species, in the vast interval of time which has elapsed between the deposition of the earliest fossiliferous strata and the present day.
>
> (Huxley, 1893: 125)

It was as a result of these new intellectual procedures that the objects collected within museums came to be moved around on an unprecedented scale as their relationships to one another were reconfigured as a result of the new narrativisations of the relationships between *naturalia* and *artificialia* to which they gave rise. In the process, those objects acquired a new depth structure requiring new practices of vision which, rather than looking *at* or *into objects*, were directed along *the relations between* them to discern how the pasts that had been accumulated and sedimented within them from earlier phases of development were carried over into, and built on by, the next phase of development. It will therefore repay our attention to look a little more closely at the mid- to late-nineteenth-century developments through which the procedures of archaeology, geology, natural history and anthropology were historicised in new and distinctive ways which situated their concerns within a shared understanding of time as a continuous unfolding of the past into the present.

The odds and ends of history

In describing his excavations at Cranbourne Chase, Henry Pitt Rivers argued that, though some might find it tedious

> to dwell on the discovery of odds and ends, that have, no doubt, been thrown away by their owners as rubbish, . . . yet it is by the study of such trivial details that Archaeology is mainly dependent for determining the dates of earthworks.
>
> (Cited in Hudson, 1982)

The reference to 'trivial details' here establishes a connection between the procedures of archaeology and those other sciences, which rose to prominence in the same period, in which the interpretation of apparently insignificant details was accorded pride of place. In art history, from its origins in the detection of forgeries, through Johann Winckelmann to Giovanni Morelli, it was the insignificant details of a composition – the way ear-lobes or noses were painted – whose 'little insights', as Winckelmann called them (cited in Preziosi, 1989: 92), provided the key to the painter's identity and so, also, to the correct placement of a work historically. In Freud's psychoanalytic practice, it was the seemingly irrelevant minutiae of the dreamwork or verbal slips that provided the analyst with his means for bringing buried pasts to light. In medicine, finally, the interpretation of symptoms provided the basis for diagnostic connections between morbidities and their invisible causes arising out of processes that lay hidden in the depths of the body. These are the three conjectural sciences that Carlo Ginzburg (1980) discusses in outlining the relationship of conjectural methodologies to the procedures of Sir Arthur Conan Doyle's Sherlock Holmes, whose ability to solve a crime by reconstructing the past on the basis of the fragments – cigarette ash, for example – it had deposited in the present was, and remains, legendary. But then so were the reconstructive feats performed by those other conjectural sciences whose field was explicitly historical – archaeology, geology and palaeontology – which, although only mentioned in passing by Ginzberg, occupied the centre of Huxley's attention in his discussion of the conjectural method (Huxley, 1882).[2]

Cuvier and, later, Richard Owen dazzled their contemporaries by reconstructing extinct forms of life (the moa, dinosaurs) on the basis of their fragmentary remains and exhibiting them – lest they be taken for magicians – with all the authority that the expert-as-showman could muster (see Figure 2.1). The result was a proliferation of newly discovered pasts – Conan Doyle's lost worlds[3] – as prehistoric forms of life were resurrected through the application of techniques of retrospective deduction which allowed past causes to be inferred from their present effects and wholes to be deduced from their parts. Related developments in archaeology brought its excavations into close theoretical contact with those of palaeontology. The emergence of prehistoric archaeology and the increasing importance accorded its concerns in the last thirty years or so of the nineteenth century, when it temporarily eclipsed classical archaeology, is particularly important here.[4] This is especially so when prehistoric archaeology, which focused mainly on Europe, is considered in its relation to the parallel inquiries of prehistoric anthropology (or paleoanthropology). If prehistoric archaeology established a new zone of human prehistory, then prehistoric anthropology construed the current practices of colonised peoples as its semiotic equivalent. In thus establishing a symbolic exchange of equilavents between Europe's deep past and its remote colonial outposts, these two sciences comprised the human-centred nucleus of that wider disciplinary ensemble, which also included geology, natural history and palaeontology, comprising the historical sciences.

Two factors played a crucial role in the development of each of these historical disciplines, and the relationships between them, over the late eighteenth and nineteenth centuries. The first consisted in the conceptual reorientations and techniques that allowed dug-up and found artefacts – the odds and ends of the past that Pitt Rivers refers to – to be historicised and located within an increasingly finely calibrated past that was conceived as a sequence of interconnecting developmental series. The second consisted in the development of techniques for reading these pasts which freed the historical sciences from their tutelage to philology and other text-based methods of interpretation, thus providing a methodological basis for the claims of new forms of expertise that were pitted against the philological disciplines.

Alain Schnapp's account of the history of archaeology combines these two perspectives in connecting developments in archaeology to those in related disciplinary fields. Although periodisations of human history had proliferated in both the classical and medieval worlds, none of these had historicised the earth or what was found within it. They therefore did not establish a distinctive artefactual realm relating to a time preceding that of written records. As a consequence, objects that were dug up from the earth or found on its surface – whether minerals, fossils, ammonites, urns, pots, vases or coins – were not interpreted historically as either a source of evidence for extinct forms of animal life or as remnants of earlier ways of human life.[5] Nor, indeed, were such objects clearly distinguished from one another as belonging to the separate realms of natural and human

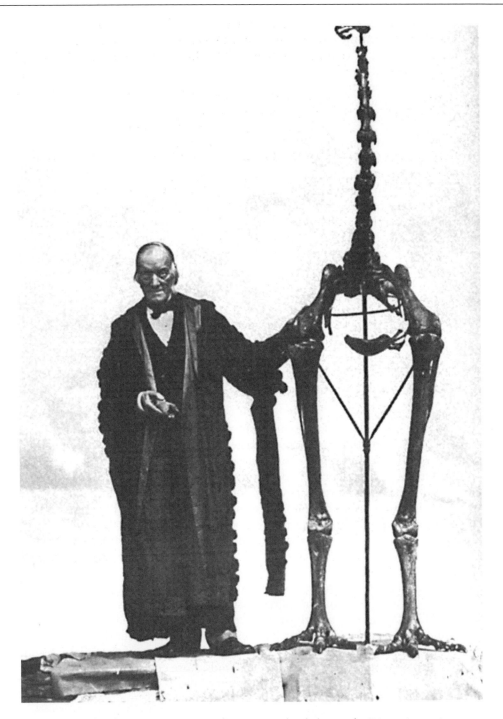

Figure 2.1 Richard Owen c. 1877, standing next to the skeleton of a *Dinornis maximus*.

Source: Richard Owen (1879) *Memoirs of the Extinct Wingless Birds of New Zealand*, vol. 2, London, plate 97.

history. Rather, they were viewed as the products of, variously, ahistorical processes at work in the earth; of alchemic processes which converted rock into minerals or fossils; or of the subterranean labours of dwarf potters. Thus interpreted, dug-up and found objects functioned as more or less accidental irruptions of the past into the present: 'if a consciousness of the antiquity of remains was awakened, it is always in a fortuitous fashion, like a rupture of the impervious barrier which separates the present from the past' (Schnapp, 1996: 97).

Given that the earth was not seen as a potential source of history, the location of objects within it – the depth at which they were found, the relations between one site of excavation and another – played little role in their interpretation. This depended on literary methods of exegesis in which it was the ingenuity of the construction – the ability to locate the object within a literary tradition – that mattered. That artefacts might themselves be interpreted as direct sources of evidence of earlier historical periods was unthinkable until well into the early modern period. Schnapp, reflecting on the fifteenth-century excavations of ancient Rome which provided the initial incubus for modern European antiquarian practices, underlines the respects in which what was unearthed was not historically marked:

> The antiquaries of Rome were so quick to proclaim the quality of the things they found, and to boast of their historical and mythological merits, that they neglected the value of the objects themselves as a source of knowledge. Excavation was like exploiting a quarry, and interpretation depended solely upon the availability of written sources to identify the monument.
>
> (Schnapp, 1996: 125)

The first step in establishing human prehistory as a separate realm and archaeology as its legitimate interpreter consisted in the challenge to literary-based methods of historical interpretation that originated in the work of seventeenth-century antiquaries in their development of what Schnapp calls 'archaeological "autopsy"' (181).[6] This was a new way of reading which, relying more on the senses of sight and touch than on the principles of philological analysis, would help to form a new language of history whose signs comprised the visible marks on the buried remains which provided the material evidence for pasts beyond writing. It was through this method of 'archaeological "autopsy"', Schnapp argues, that 'archaeology won its independence – by delivering a text of another nature than that of the literary tradition' (181), thus yielding a 'vision of the earth not just as a potential treasure-chest but as a repository of interpretable traces' (213). The second and third steps constructed a grammar for this past by providing the basic principles for its decipherment. Seventeenth-century antiquarians had developed a rhetoric in praise of the primacy of the object, seeing in coins and inscriptions on archaeological finds more enduring, less corruptible and more direct forms of evidence than literary ones. They consequently spoke, in John Aubrey's formulation, of the need for 'an algebraic method to make the stones give evidence for themselves' (193).

However, it was not until the early eighteenth century that the rudiments of a systematic method for reading the past on the basis of the physical qualities of its artefactual remains were developed. These comprised early versions of what would later come to be known as the typological or comparative method – 'the ancestor', as Schnapp describes it, 'of all archaeological reasoning' (241) – which provided a grammar for spatialising and temporalising the past. It accomplished the former by proposing ways of reading the design traits common to objects found within a particular territory that established a distinctive provenance for them within that territory while simultaneously allowing objects not exhibiting those traits to be excluded as foreign. This allowed cultures to be territorialised on the basis of their artefactual remains. Their historicisation followed from the development of techniques designed to detect the progress of design traits through time within the same territorial culture.

This aspect of archaeology's temporal grammar depended on the use of principles of stratigraphical analysis, borrowed from geology, which made possible a layered approach to the excavation and management of archaeological sites. This, in its turn, allowed the past itself to be thought of as a series of layers superimposed, in an irreversible sequence, one on top of the other. If Cuvier's use of stratigraphical techniques in his palaeontological excavations had provided the basis for a systematic chronology, rooted in geological time, then the key developments that enabled a connection to be made between the history of the earth, natural history and human prehistory are attributable, first, to the work of Christian Jürgen Thomsen, the leading figure in early-nineteenth-century Scandinavian archaeology, and, subsequently, to that of Boucher de Perthes in France.

Thomsen's main innovation was to produce a universal and generalisable method for reading the human past by suggesting that similar technologies might be read as evidence of comparable levels of cultural development. Translated into the basis of the three-age model (the stone, iron and bronze ages) which he developed for his museum displays, Thomsen's method differed from the previous three-, four- or five-age systems that had been common since classical times by providing a means for organising increasingly large clusters of objects into their respective stages within a chronological system that was both universalisable and empirically verifiable.[7] Rendering the artefactual domain readable in new ways, this allowed human prehistory to be made publicly manifest in the form of a narrative in which the now readable testimony of hitherto mute artefacts connected human pasts to the present in a common and irreversible sequence. In 1847, Boucher de Perthes developed a means of integrating the sequential ordering of human technologies with the techniques of stratigraphical analysis developed in the sphere of palaeontology. This proved crucial in establishing human antiquity – finally achieved through the discovery of human remains at Brixham Cave a little more than a decade later – by providing a common chronology for flora, fauna and human artefacts which, equating depth with age, overcame the objections that had earlier prevented human remains found in the same strata as extinct species from serving as proofs of human antiquity.[8]

Schnapp indicates how, once human antiquity had been established, the typological principles of archaeological reasoning which had made this possible continued to be developed, in the second half of the nineteenth century, in a manner that related these developments in archaeology to collateral developments in other historical sciences:

> Typology freed archaeology from the tutelage of text; technology liberated it from the nature/culture dilemma; and stratigraphy from the local/universal paradox. Typology places the object in an identifiable time-frame and renders it useful as historical evidence. Attention to technological features, by establishing the 'natural' and 'cultural' components of each product, allows each object to be assigned its particular function. Stratigraphy adds another dimension: the object was buried by the action of depositional phenomena at the same time local and universal. Every object and every monument is destined to find its place in a general process of stratification which is linked to the history of the planet.
>
> (Schnapp, 1996: 321)

The disciplinary synthesis that resulted from these developments was given a distinctive 'twist' in England. Bruce Trigger thus notes that, while the work of Thomsen and Scandinavian archaeology more generally had influenced the earlier work of Daniel Wilson in Scotland, the late-nineteenth-century blossoming of prehistoric archaeology south of the border tended to proceed independently of these earlier developments and to head in a different direction (Trigger, 1989: 73–100). This reflected the increasing influence of Darwinian thought which, Trigger suggests, meant that prehistoric archaeology looked increasingly to natural history for its methodological paradigms. One consequence of this was to reduce the autonomy that Thomsen had won for archaeology by proposing, through the combination of stratigraphical analysis and seriation, techniques for dating archaeological materials that were specific to those materials. By contrast, the synthesis of archaeology, geology and palaeontology proposed by John Lubbock (1865) subordinated archaeology to dating techniques derived from geology, thus equating, in effect, archaeological types with index fossils. Similarly, Pitt Rivers's typological method – while undoubtedly influenced by Thomsen's earlier work – also drew on the classificatory principles of contemporary natural history displays as a model. It is, then, to the relations between geology and natural history that we must look to unravel the distinctive qualities of the discursive field in which late-nineteenth-century prehistoric archaeology and anthropology found their broader intellectual settings and defined their place in relation to each other.

Reading the rocks

In the preface to his 1858 text *The Story of a Boulder*, Archibald Geikie, a key figure in the relationships between English and Scottish geology,[9] recommends the virtues of studying nature at first hand rather than relying on its textual mediation in books or even the objects in museums. 'He who would know what physical science really is,' he writes, 'must go out into the fields and learn it for himself', for he then 'sees the objects of his study with his own eyes, and not through "the spectacles of books;" facts come home to him with a vividness and reality they never can possess in the closet' (Geikie, 1858: viii). Yet Geikie immediately proceeds, in his first chapter, to place a particular textual grid over the rocks which, as a geologist, are his primary concern. This involves a double movement which, by laying the rocks bare, stripping them of the authority of the classical and literary texts through which, in the Renaissance, their study had been mediated, simultaneously constructs them as texts of an altogether different sort. When introducing the boulder that is to serve as the pretext for the history of the earth which follows in later chapters, Geikie initially evokes the language and associations of the picturesque by placing the boulder in a ravine – 'not many hundred yards from the sequestered village of Colinton' – which he describes as 'one of the most picturesque nooks in the county' (1). There then follows an extended description of the boulder – of the shape and texture of its surface, of the lichen that clings to it – in which, through the currency of the picturesque, it becomes indistinguishable from all that surrounds it, melting into a scene of verdant beauty whose aesthetic qualities are underlined by quotations from Horace.

Geikie's purpose in placing the boulder within this essentially literary and aesthetic system of meaning is to cut through it to reach another level of meaning, one that depends on penetrating the boulder's surfaces to reveal the traces of the anonymous geological processes that are hidden within its depths. Hammer in hand, Geikie, no longer adopting the distanced perspective of the picturesque but seated, now, on the boulder, begins to chip away at its surface, and 'after a little labour', he opens up a different horizon of truth as, digging deeper, he finds 'well-marked traces of at least two widely-separated ages' (4–5). Rather than being read through the filter of other books, the rock progressively reveals its true and deeper meaning by being read as itself a book in which the script of time has been made legible:

> The surface striation bore undoubted evidence of the glacial period, the embedded plants as plainly indicated the far more ancient era of the coal-measures, while the pebbles of the base pointed, though dimly, to some still more primeval age. I had here, as it were, a quaint, old, black-letter volume of the middle ages, giving an account of events that were taking place at the time it was written, and containing on its earlier pages numerous quotations from the authors of antiquity.
>
> (Geikie, 1858: 5)

At the end of the book, Geikie, much like Huxley with his piece of chalk, summarises the succession of layered pasts that he has unearthed by reading 'the memorials of bygone ages, traced in clear and legible characters on the boulder' (258) to evoke a scene of endlessly receding deep pasts until, evoking a primal volcanic scene, a 'dark night comes down in which we can detect no ray of light and beyond which we cannot go' (260). In doing so, he makes clear the work he has performed in detaching the boulder from one system of reading to install it in another:

> But it rests there as the memorial of far earlier centuries, and of an older creation; and though now surrounded with all that is lovely or picturesque – the twinkling flowers on every side, the wide arch of boughs overhead,

and the murmuring streamlet in the dell below – and though forming itself no unimpressive object in the scene, the boulder looks out upon us unconnected with anything around. Like a sculptured obelisk transported from the plains of Assyria to the streets of London, it offers no link of association with the order of things around it; its inscriptions are written in hieroglyphics long since extinct, but of which the key yet remains to show us that the rocks of our planet are not masses of dead, shapeless matter, but chronicles of the past; and that all the varied beauty of green wood and waving wood is but a thin veil of gossamer spread over the countless monuments of the dead.

(Geikie, 1858: 258)

Geikie's text represents a rough summation of the point that geology had reached by the mid-nineteenth century. Nicolaas Rupke summarises the main achievements of geology to this date as consisting in, first, extending the earth's history 'back immeasurably before the appearance of man'; second, establishing that the period of prehuman history 'had not been a single period of continuity, but a concentration of successive worlds . . . each characterised by a particular extinct flora and fauna'; and, third, that 'the nature of the historical succession had been progressive; that successive worlds increasingly resembled our present world, both with respect to its inhabitants and to the environmental conditions under which they lived' (Rupke, 1983: 3). Rupke attributes these accomplishments to the effects on geology of developments in two areas of study: the role of chemistry in the mineralogical classification of rock formations, and the use of techniques derived from comparative anatomy in reading the fossil record. Although quite separate from each other, these developments combined to undermine the classical *episteme* as well as the lingering effects of the Renaissance *episteme*.

These effects were much the same as those traced by Foucault in the field of natural history. Within the Renaissance *episteme*, minerals, 'occupying the same conceptual domain as plants and animals . . . were studied and described according to the same system of knowledge' (Albury and Oldroyd, 1977: 189) so that their description always included a compilation of their use and representation in literature, history, religion and myth.[10] While later, within Linnaean classification, the cultural detritus of Renaissance description had been swept away to focus on the observable similarities and differences in the characteristics of minerals, this was still an analytical gaze which scarcely bothered to look beneath the realm of visible appearances to concern itself with the internal chemical composition of mineral substances. It was R. J. Hauy who, by establishing a connection between the external form of crystals and their internal geometric structures, paved the way for a system of classification based on the invisible and internal properties of the mineral world and the chemical laws governing their combination and transformation.

This event was akin to Cuvier's anatomical dissections of living beings and the principles of classification to which these gave rise, as forms of life were grouped into classes on the basis of a new set of relations between their inner structure as living beings and their visible external characteristics in which the latter were read as the surface effects of the former. The interiorised gazes of chemistry and anatomy thus brought minerals and living beings together in a new regime of classification in which, to cite Foucault's classic discussion, classification no longer aimed 'to refer the visible back to itself, while allotting one of its elements the task of representing the other' but sought rather 'to relate the visible to the invisible, to its deeper causes, as it were, then to rise upwards once more from that hidden architecture towards the more obvious signs displayed on the surface of bodies' (Foucault, 1970: 229). This opening up of an inner space within living beings created the possibility for a history of life that would trace its development as a series of adaptations of inner structures to changing conditions of life, with the external features assigned the role of mediating the transactions between the inner organisation of organic life and the external conditions of the environment.

The synchronisation of these perspectives in mineralogy and natural history made possible the project of geology as an empirical history of the earth that displaced both the purely empirical tasks of geognosy, committed solely to the structural description of rock formations and their relations to one another, and speculative histories of the earth like Hutton's *Theory of the Earth*. Rejecting the conjectural basis of the latter, Cuvier distinguished his concerns from those of geognosy in the respect that, while concurring that the historicity of geological events had first to be established before analysis could proceed to their probable causation, he defined the latter as the true task of geology.[11] This aspect of his work was instrumental in transforming a whole new set of objects from, to recall Foucault's terms, 'documents into monuments' of pasts beyond memory. The perception that *'fossil bones are almost always different from those of the animals that live on the ground that conceals them'* (Cuvier [1800] in Rudwick, 1997: 51) was central to the interpretive procedures involved in Cuvier's comparison of the geologist with antiquarians:

> the former will have to go and search among the ruins of the globe for the remains of organisms that lived at its surface, just as the latter dig in the ruins of cities in order to unearth the monuments of the taste, the genius, and the customs of the men who lived there. These antiquities of nature, if they may be so termed, will provide the physical history of the globe with monuments as useful and as reliable as ordinary antiquities provide for the political and moral history of nations.
>
> (Cuvier [1798] in Rudwick, 1997: 35)

These monuments also needed to be read in a particular way if their meaning – for Cuvier, that of the punctuation of the earth's history by a series of sudden and violent catastrophes – were to be correctly deciphered. 'These great and terrible events', as Cuvier put it, 'are clearly imprinted everywhere, for the eye that knows how to read history in their monuments' (Cuvier [1826] in Rudwick, 1997: 190).

It was by means of these intellectual moves that Cuvier opened up the perspective of prehistory *avant la lettre*. Might there not be, he asked, 'some glory for man to know how to burst the limits of time, and, by some observations, to recover the history of the world, and the succession of events that preceded the birth of the human species?' (185). It was surely, he argued in another context, now man's glory to be able to reconstruct 'the history of the thousands of centuries that preceded his existence, and of the thousands of beings that have not been his contemporaries!' (Cuvier, [1812] in Rudwick, 1997: 252). In *The Wild Ass's Skin* [*La Peau de Chagrin*; first published 1831], Balzac describes Cuvier's universe as one in which 'dead things live anew and lost worlds are unfolded before us' (Balzac, [1831] 1977: 41).[12] And the sense of this deep past as a stratified one is evident in Balzac's invocation of the 'Cuvier effect':

> As one penetrates from seam to seam, from stratum to stratum and discovers, under the quarries of Montmartre or in the schists of the Urals, those animals whose fossilised remains belong to antediluvian civilisations, the mind is startled to catch a vista of the milliards of years and the millions of peoples which the feeble memory of man and an indestructible divine tradition have forgotten and whose ashes heaped on the surface of our globe, form the two feet of earth which furnish us with bread and flowers.
>
> (Balzac, [1831] 1977: 40–1)

Yet stratification here is not accumulation. The dead worlds that Cuvier conjured up by establishing that some species had become extinct did not relate to one another in a continuous developmental sequence. To the contrary, his commitment to catastrophism led to a history of life on earth which was a case of either a hop, a skip and a jump, or a hop, a skip and a dead end, within time scales which, if no longer mosaic, were still too short to allow for the long evolutionary sequences required for one class to evolve into another.[13]

A geological basis for longer and continuous histories of life and of the earth, and for interactions between the two, was provided by the eventual ascendancy of A. G. Werner's geognosic findings over Hutton's more speculative, steady-state account of the earth as a circular process of repetition.[14] Werner provided a method for discriminating minerals and their compounds in the order of their succession together with a means of generalising this such that the same order of succession might 'be found in all parts of the globe, thus allowing the correlation of similar strata in different regions according to a single historical time-scale' (Albury and Oldroyd, 1977: 202). The consequences of this were similar to those of the typological method in archaeology. Werner's criteria for establishing distinct geological formations and their identity from place to place – the extent of a deposit, the structure and texture of its mineral composition, and its relative position in the stratigraphical column – thus constituted, in the words of a contemporary, a means for 'assembling, analysing, relating and comparing a large number of distant facts which do not have the slightest apparent relation to one another' (203).

However, account has also to be taken of Lyell's role in bringing to geology a self-conscious awareness of its relationship to historical methodology. Cuvier's accomplishments were always limited in this regard. Martin Rudwick likens Cuvier's reconstructions of past forms of life to antiquarian reconstructions of classical buildings, and argues that both lacked any 'consistent attempt to turn such isolated "antiquarian" reconstructions into a truly historical *sequence* of reconstructions in continual flux' (Rudwick, 1979: 70). Frank Bourdier similarly notes that Cuvier's retrospective deductions aimed at the reconstruction of species archetypes that regulated the existence of species in ways that were unmarked by time's passage (Bourdier, 1969: 44). Yet if Cuvier did not provide a model for historical reasoning, neither did the Neptunists who, as heirs of the Renaissance *episteme*, insisted on the continuing relevance of literary forms of evidence to complement and interpret geological findings. It was precisely in order to free the earth's history from the burden of superimposed textualisations of this kind that Lyell looked to contemporary historiography and philology for methodological paradigms with which to combat their influence. Drawing on these, he proposed a direct and immanent textualisation of geological phenomena according to which the depositions of the earth's development were to be regarded as so many 'documents', 'inscriptions' or 'monuments' which 'had to be "read" in a language that had to be learned' in order to be able to decipher the correct sequence of events (Rudwick, 1979: 72).[15]

These, then, are among the intellectual contexts against which Geikie's programme of reading the rocks needs to be understood. However, account has also to be taken of William Buckland and the English school of historical geology, which – in spite of its name – restrained the application of historical principles of analysis by requiring that they be reconciled with natural theology.[16] This meant that, however much historical methods might illuminate the detailed steps taken on the way, they could not throw any essential light on the path of the earth's development since this assumed the form of a divine plan governing the earth from its original conception and throughout its subsequent unfolding through time. Geikie thus concludes *The Story of a Boulder* in a gesture which bends the knee of geology before the demands of natural theology:

> Geology lifts off for us the veil that shrouds the past, and lays bare the monuments of successive creations that had come and gone long ere the human race began. She traces out the plan of the Divine working during a vast cycle of ages, and points out how the past dovetails with the present, and how the existing condition of things comes in as but the last and archetypal economy in a long progressive series.
>
> (Geikie, 1858: 262)

Geikie's reading of the rocks also offers a history from which man is absent, or to which he is introduced only as a single and culminating event located in a present representing an undifferentiated qualitative leap in relation to the deep time preceding it.[17] Published in 1858, *The Story of a Boulder* thus did not register the effects of the establishment, in the same year, of human antiquity and the consequent requirement that the development of humanity itself be treated as a gradual and continuist process. Nor did it anticipate the challenge that would be presented a year later when the publication of Darwin's *Origin* opened up the prospect that the histories of the earth and of life on earth had to be read as directionless, dependent wholly on natural mechanisms and admitting of no jumps with respect to the development of animal – including human – life.

Filling in time

In his assessment of the Lamarckian and Darwinian accounts of evolution, Georges Canguilhem argues that they are most significantly distinct in the role they accord time. In Lamarck, time is credited with 'the power to produce the continuous and progressive if somewhat irregular series of organised life forms, "from the most imperfect to the most perfect"' (Canguilhem, 1988: 108). This was also true of those who, reading Darwin through Lamarckian spectacles, converted time's passage into a law of progress. Darwin, however, was clear that the mere lapse of time itself did nothing. Instead, he thought of time 'not as a power but as a factor whose effects could be perceived directly in distinct but complementary forms: fossils, embryos, and rudimentary organs', and in which the fossil represented 'petrified time; the embryo, operative time; the rudimentary organ, retarded time' (108–9). The passage Canguilhem has in mind occurs towards the end of the *Origin* where Darwin, predicting that one of the consequences of the theory of natural selection would be that 'classifications will come to be, as far as they can be so made, genealogies' (Darwin, [1859] 1968: 456), distinguishes the three main sources of evidence from which such genealogies will be constructed:

> Rudimentary organs will speak infallibly with respect to the nature of long-lost structures. Species and groups of species, which are called aberrant, and which may fancifully be called living fossils, will aid us in forming a picture of ancient forms of life. Embryology will reveal to us the structure, in some degree obscured, of the prototypes of each class.
>
> (Darwin, [1859] 1968: 457)

Cast in this light, nature's wonders, far from being exiles from scientific rationality, become crucial keys to its construction. Stephen Jay Gould thus argues that imperfections are the key to narrative and history, and thus also to genealogical classifications, in Darwin's work. Gould makes the point in discussing James Hutton's account of the earth as an endlessly recurring, three-stage cycle of decay, deposition and uplift in which each stage automatically generates the next. In portraying the earth as a perfect, self-regulating machine destined to reprocess itself endlessly through the repetition of these three stages, Hutton was obliged to avoid 'all metaphors implying sequence and direction' because of the taint of imperfection which these implied: 'for if things improve in time, then the world machine was not made perfect, and if they decline, then the earth is not perfect now' (Gould, 1987: 85). For Darwin, by contrast, nature's oddities and imperfections facilitate the introduction of narrative into natural history. It is, as we have already seen, aberrant species which serve him as the key to 'forming a picture of ancient forms of life' while, as others have noted (Gould, 1987: 43, 84; Desmond and Moore, 1992: 172, 590), Darwin relied just as much as Morrelli or Freud on apparently insignificant but anomalous details in his reconstructions of lines of descent and inheritance.

Imperfections, oddities, anomalous details: if these were the raw materials of Darwin's historical method, the end to which that method aspired was to fill up time with continuities, with sequences of lineal descent in which – since 'species are produced and exterminated by slowly acting and still existing causes, and not by miraculous acts of creation and by catastrophes' (Darwin, [1859] 1968: 457) – every form of life would find its place and explanation in the orders of historical succession within which it was located, without the need for vain searches after species essences. All of this would come about, Darwin suggests,

> when we regard every production of nature as one which has had a history; when we contemplate every complex structure and instinct as the summing up of many contrivances, each useful to the possessor, nearly in the same way as when we look at any great mechanical invention as the summing up of the labour, the experience, the reason, and even the blunders of numerous workmen.
>
> (Darwin, [1859] 1968: 456)

This underlines the stress on storage and accumulation which informs the narrative structure of the *Origin*. There is, however, a difficulty here arising from the incompleteness of the geological record:

> The noble science of Geology loses glory from the extreme imperfection of the record. The crust of the earth with its embedded remains must not be looked at as a well-filled museum, but as a poor collection made at hazard and at rare intervals.
>
> (Darwin, [1859] 1968: 457)

By 'well-filled' here, Darwin had in mind the museum's capacity to arrange rock formations and fossil remains into sequences conveying the impression of continuity. That Darwin is aware of the contrived nature of this continuity is clear from an earlier passage in which the museum's reconstructions of evolutionary history are viewed as hopelessly inadequate:

> The number of specimens in all our museums is absolutely as nothing as compared with the countless generations of countless species which certainly have existed. We should not be able to recognise a species as the parent of any one or more species if we were to examine them ever so closely, unless we likewise possessed many of the intermediate links between their past or parent and present states; and these many links we could hardly ever expect to discover, owing to the imperfection of the geological record.
>
> (Darwin, [1859] 1968: 439)

For Charles Lyell, the imperfection of the geological record had served as a barrier to the construction of 'any kind of global narrative' (Secord, 1997: xix). Darwin also accepted this incompleteness as something that future researches might compensate for but never entirely overcome. Since it is just as much a fact of the earth's history that traces of past forms of life have been erased by the processes of its formation as it is that such traces have also been selectively preserved, the filling-in of gaps in the fossil record could never be completed. Equally, though, the course of future scientific work (and, as we shall see, that of the curator) is mapped out as an endeavour to fill in those gaps as far as possible while recognising that some lost pasts might prove unrecoverable. The most that can be expected is an increasing accumulation of connecting lines of descent as palae-ontological investigations convert what might seem to have been evolutionary dead ends into stages in evolutionary sequences.

The relationship between dead ends and evolutionary stages was accordingly one of the two main 'bones of contention' at issue in both the pre- and post-Darwinian controversies of the mid-century period. The second – given that, by the early 1850s, most schools of scientific thought subscribed to some form of evolutionary theory[18] – centred on the mechanisms of evolution and the degree to which these applied indiscriminately to men and animals. The main public contestants in both controversies were Owen and Huxley in the contending positions they adopted on, respectively, the most significant public icon of prehistory – the dinosaur – and on the relations of man to the higher primates. It will be worth looking briefly at each of these in turn.

Originally coined by Owen in the 1840s, the term 'dinosaur' referred to a new order he had constructed from the remains of the megalosaur and iguanodon as a prehistoric fabrication fashioned with specific political purposes in view. In making dinosaurs stand erect, thereby separating them from the lesser, crawl-ing reptiles and placing them next to mammals on life's scale, Owen made them the central figures in a narrative of degeneration (the ancestors of today's lizards) that had as its target Lamarck's conception of life's untrammelled ascent through ever higher and more advanced forms of life in view of the role this had played in the evolutionary rhetorics of British radicalism (Desmond, 1982: 115–19). Although Huxley's earlier position on the need to establish a continuity of evolution within the fossil record was patchy and inconsistent,[19] his later contributions to the dinosaur controversy, in the late 1860s, were motivated by the need to topple Owen's dinosaur in favour of one that could serve as the public emblem of an uninterrupted story of lineal descent. In his famous reconstruction of the archaeopteryx as a link between birds and reptiles, Huxley refashioned dinosaurs as the ancestors of birds, thus restoring an upward continuity to life while also establishing that one class could transmute into another (121–9).[20]

Huxley's interventions at the other end of the evolutionary scale were motivated by similar concerns. Although Owen had conceded the ground to evolution, his main concern, in the 1850s and 1860s, was to provide an alternative, non-materialist account of the mechanism of evolution in order to reconcile it with the ultimately theistic conceptions on which his work rested. Drawing on German Romantic transcendentalism, he fashioned, in his theory of archetypes, an idealist and teleological account of evolution in which the development of each species followed the path of a foreordained divine plan. This was meant to serve as a bulwark against the materialist and directionless implications of natural selection. As a part of this, Owen read the osteological evidence relating to the relation-ships between man and the apes in a manner calculated to place an absolute divide between the two. Man, for Owen, was 'the sole species of his Genus, the sole representative of his Order' (Rupke, 1994: 266). Placed, as Rupke puts it, on 'an elevated taxonomic pedestal', man was kept 'out of the reach of any known evolutionary hypothesis' (268) through the divine gift of intellectual and moral faculties which lifted him as far above the animal kingdom as the faculties of motion and sensation raised animals above plants.

In his 1861 essay 'On the relations of man to the lower animals', Huxley set out to knock man off the pedestal on which Owen had so carefully placed him. This discrowning of *homo sapiens* involved three components. First, Huxley re-read the osteological evidence in order to demonstrate that, no matter how great the chasm separating man from the gorilla with regard to the structure of the foot, skull or pelvis, it was no larger – and sometimes smaller – than that separating the gorilla from the orang or the orang from the gibbon. This confronted head-on Owen's contention that man constituted an order separate from the apes and unique to himself. 'The structural differences between Man and the Man-like apes', Huxley writes, 'certainly justify our regarding him as constituting a family apart from them; though inasmuch as he differs less from them than they do from other families of the same order, there can be no justification for placing him in a distinct order' (Huxley, [1896c] 1968: 145). This being so, there can, Huxley argued, be no basis for quarantining man from the mechanisms of evolutionary development which apply throughout the rest of the animal world:

> But if Man be separated by no greater structural barrier from the brutes than they are from one another – then it seems to follow that if any process of physical causation can be discovered by which the genera and families of ordinary animals have been produced, that process of causation is amply sufficient to account for the origin of Man.
>
> (Huxley, [1896c] 1968: 147)

These two aspects of Huxley's argument are carried as much by means of a distinctive visual rhetoric as they are by Huxley's accounts of his anatomical dissections. When Owen had contrasted human skulls with those of apes, he reinforced his point visually by means of a bipolar juxtaposition which stressed the significance of the differences between human skulls and those of apes compared with those differences which might be discerned within each of these two sets (see Figure 2.2). The rhetorical force of Huxley's illustrations, by contrast, works to undermine this bipolar logic by arranging the human skull as part of a sequence in which the difference separating it from that of the ape type selected for the purpose of closest comparison (the chrysothrix) is not greater than that separating two sets of paired ape skulls (see Figure 2.3). The same is true of the representation of the relations of the human skeleton to those of the major ape types, except that here – in what was to become the basic grammar of natural history museum displays – no pairs are privileged in the placing of man within a sequence which is animated, from left to right, by the unstated but implied effects of time which mark the spaces between each stage in the sequence (Figure 2.4).[21] The consequences of this arrangement are evident when contrasted with Owen's comparison of the skeleton of a human with that of a gorilla which, in its simple bipolarity, stresses their incommensurability while the manner of their juxtaposition implies no order of lineal descent connecting the two (Figure 2.5).

In the third aspect of his argument, Huxley provides for a different kind of historicisation. However much he wishes to argue that man is 'in substance and in

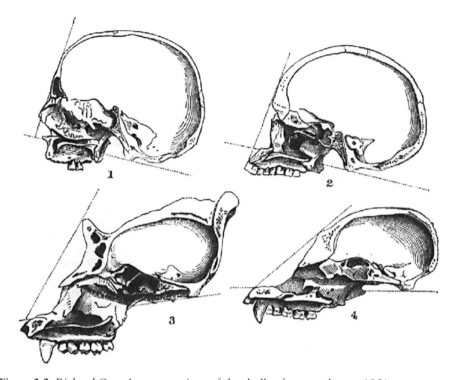

Figure 2.2 Richard Owen's cross sections of the skulls of men and apes, 1851.

Source: 'Proceedings of the societies. Zoological Society', *The Literary Gazette and Journal of Science and Art*, no. 1817.

structure, one with the brutes' (155), he is at equal pains to make it clear that, in all other respects, man is qualitatively distinct from 'the brutes'. In his case, however, this is not – as Owen had it – because the divine gift of moral and intellectual faculties established an essential and unbridgeable distinction between the human and animal worlds. Rather, for Huxley, it is the contingent acquisition of language that establishes a distinction based on naturalistic premises but pointing, ultimately, in a different direction. Inviting his reader to view man as 'that great Alps and Andes of the living world', and remarking the disbelief of the awe-struck voyager when confronted with the geologist's claims that alpine peaks are but 'the hardened mud of primeval seas, or the cooled slag of subterranean furnaces' (155), Huxley also images human history as a set of processes through which the past is accumulated as a set of sedimented effects deposited within the present. It is by virtue of 'the marvellous endowment of speech' (155), he argues, that, man

> has slowly accumulated and organised the experience which is almost wholly lost with the cessation of every individual life in other animals; so that, now, he stands raised upon it as on a mountain top, far above the level of his humble fellows, and transfigured from his grosser nature by reflecting, here and there, a ray from the infinite source of truth.
>
> (Huxley, [1896c] 1968: 156)

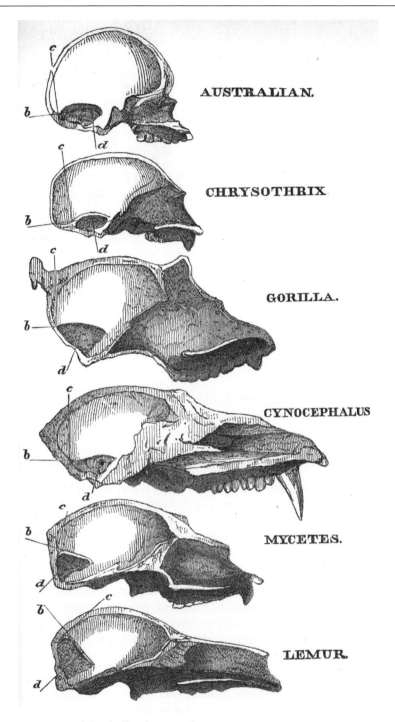

Figure 2.3 Sections of the skulls of man and various apes, 1896.

Source: Thomas H. Huxley [1896c] (1968), *Man's Place in Nature, and Other Anthropological Essays*, New York: Greenwood Press.

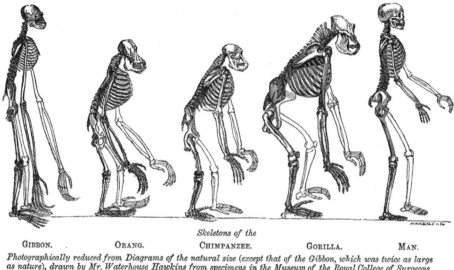

Skeletons of the

GIBBON. ORANG. CHIMPANZEE. GORILLA. MAN.

Photographically reduced from Diagrams of the natural size (except that of the Gibbon, which was twice as large as nature), drawn by Mr. Waterhouse Hawkins from specimens in the Museum of the Royal College of Surgeons.

Figure 2.4 Drawing by Waterhouse Hawkins reduced and arranged in sequence, 1896.

Source: Thomas H. Huxley [1896c] (1968), *Man's Place in Nature, and Other Anthropological Essays*, New York: Greenwood Press.

The gesture towards religion in the final phrase is evident. However, my interest here is with the respects in which Huxley's formulation opened the way to an understanding of the course of human history and culture as an additional set of evolutionary processes through which the present structures of human societies could be read as the outcomes of the pasts that had been stored up within them.

As we have seen, Huxley was impatient with the limits which Hutton and Lyell had placed on geological speculation. He evinced a similar frustration with the restrictions which Cuvier had placed on the reach of conjectural reasoning, suggesting that subsequent advances in morphology opened up the prospect of reasoning back beyond the facts of the geological record to deduce the orders of succession for pasts for which no evidence remains:

> The same method of reasoning which enables us, when furnished with a fragment of an extinct animal, to prophesy the character which the whole organism exhibited, will, sooner or later, enable us, when we know a few of the later terms of the genealogical series, to predict the nature of the earlier terms.

> In no very distant future, the method of Zadig, applied to a greater body of facts than the present generation is fortunate enough to handle, will enable the biologist to reconstruct the scheme of life from its beginning, and to speak as confidently of the character of long extinct living beings, no trace of which has been preserved.

> (Huxley, 1882: 148)

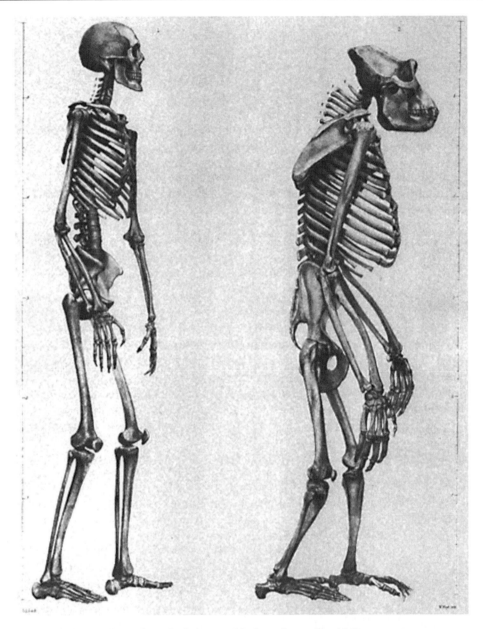

Figure 2.5 Comparison of man's skeleton with that of a gorilla, 1862.

Source: Richard Owen (1862) 'Osteological contributions to the natural history of the anthropoid apes, No. VII. Comparison of the bones of the limbs of the *Troglodytes gorilla*, *Troglodytes niger*, and of different varieties of the human race; and on the general characters of the skeleton of the gorilla', *Transactions of the Zoological Society*, vol. 5, part 1, plate 13.

The task Huxley envisaged for ethnology in his 1865 essay 'On the methods and results of ethnology' was the essentially similar one of back-filling the past of human development by identifying its concerns as being with 'the persistent modifications of mankind' and 'the distribution of those modifications in present and past times' (Huxley, 1968: 209). Reviewing the evidence that the ethnologist has to work with, Huxley passes quickly over the recorded past which is the field of history proper and 'the unrecorded remains of man's works' which comprise the field of archaeology, suggesting that 'when the question arises as to what was the condition of mankind more than a paltry two or three thousand years ago, history and archaeology are, for the most part, mere dumb dogs' (211, 212). He recommends instead that the ethnologist should look to zoology as his highest court of appeal in reconstructing the history of mankind. Yet what Huxley then offers under the guise of a quick zoological sketch of the distribution of human types is not that at all; or not only that, since it is accompanied by an equally brief description of their technologies. The result is an account in which physical traits and available technologies merge in measuring what Huxley calls the 'ethnological intervals' which separate different human types which are, at the same time, stages of civilisation.

It is easy to see here the influence of the disciplinary synthesis of natural history, ethnology and archaeology in Huxley's putative construction of a universal historical narrative. However, it is equally important to note that this narrative takes the form of a journey – starting in Australia and Tasmania and moving thence to New Zealand and the Americas before working his way back through Asia and the Middle East, to Africa, Europe and the Mediterranean – through which Huxley converts movement through space into movement through evolutionary time. The 'brief voyage' (225) from Tasmania to New Zealand brings about a change from the 'long and narrow' skulls of the Australian Aborigines (still little changed from 'the dawn of history') (212), and their 'dark, usually chocolate-coloured skins; fine dark wavy hair, dark eyes, overhung by beetle brows; coarse, projecting jaws' (222–3) to the long skull, wavy-to-straight hair and brown skin of the Maori, for example. Cross to the Americas and (except for the Fuegians and Esquimaux) skulls become wide and high, the hair is straight, and the skin 'various shades of reddish or yellowish brown' (226).

But each step in this journey is also one of technological and cultural progress – from the absence of cultivation, metals, pottery, fabrics, bow and arrows and anything more sophisticated than bark canoes among the 'Australian tribes' to the Maoris, Polynesians and Micronesians who 'cultivate the ground, construct houses, and skilfully build and manage outrigger, or double canoes; while, almost everywhere, they use some kind of fabric for clothing' (226), and thence to the sometimes 'remarkable degree of civilisation' (227) in the Americas with animal husbandry, pottery, textiles, and metals all in evidence – with, at the other end of the scale, the 'two great stocks' of the Xanthrocoi (mainly the Chinese) and the Melanochroi (mainly west Europeans) who have 'originated everything that is highest in science, in art, in law, in politics, and in mechanical inventions' (232). These formulations were to prove highly influential in developing the procedures through which – by combining physical traits and technological accomplishments to establish 'ethnological intervals', and depicting colonised peoples as an arrested stage of development – late-nineteenth-century Victorian anthropology measured the progress of cultures and civilisations.[22]

History in motion

In the appendix to his 1870 text *The Origin of Civilisation and the Primitive Condition of Man*, Lubbock seeks to establish that all peoples, even the most savage, share a capacity for development, either through their own efforts or by responding to the helping hand of more developed civilisations. The low condition of the Aborigines, he argues, is no proof that they could not raise themselves but merely that they have lacked the requisite means of improvement through which to initiate a civilising process with its own momentum and dynamic. As for the degenerationist view that such peoples are moving backward into deeper and deeper levels of savagery, Lubbock accounts for this as an optical illusion produced by the historical mobility of western civilisation:

> The delusion is natural, and like that which everyone must have sometimes experienced in looking out of a train in motion, when the woods and fields seem to be flying from us, whereas we know that in reality we are moving and they are stationary.
>
> (Lubbock, [1870] 1978: 328)

A more telling visualisation of the respects in which modernist conceptions of western societies as a form of history in motion have depended on the construction of colonised peoples as static would be hard to come by. Although this equation of spatially distant places with remote pasts has a longer history, it was significantly reshaped by the contrasting patterns of response of different schools of archaeology to the discovery of human antiquity in 1858. This evoked little response from the more established traditions of archaeology in Britain. The official associations – the Society of Antiquaries, the British Archaeological Association, and the Archaeological Institute – continued, by and large, to ignore the fact that the reach of the human past had been significantly extended. Still committed to the methods of historical archaeology, their domestic horizons rarely extended back beyond the Saxon or Roman periods and, when they did dig the barrows from the Celtic or pre-Celtic periods, they proved unable or unwilling to adapt their historical methods to interpret the new forms of prehistoric artefactual evidence they unearthed. This was left to those whom Bowdein van Riper calls 'the geological archaeologists' (van Riper, 1993: 192): that is those who, like Lubbock, Pitt Rivers and William Boyd Dawkins, echoing Huxley's criticisms of the limitations of the existing methods of archaeology, looked to extend its concerns back beyond the written and recorded past by developing methods, akin to those of geology and palaeontology, that would allow the anonymous remnants of hitherto unknown and undecipherable pasts to become readable as parts of narratives of human development that could connect with the narratives being established for the histories of the earth and of life on earth. In this intellectual formation, prehistoric archaeology and anthropology were distinguishable mainly in terms of their spatial distribution (the one was applied 'over here' to the prehistory of Europe, the other 'over there' to the interpretation of the prehistoric 'past within the present' represented by colonised peoples) and the fact that one was concerned with depths and the other with surfaces.

I shall come back to this last point shortly. First, though, I want to highlight the change of focus which these intersecting developments entailed. In an essay he wrote in 1862 reviewing the excavations of Boucher de Perthes in the Somme Valley, Lubbock expressed their significance in the following terms:

> While we have been straining our eyes to the East, and eagerly watching investigations in Egypt and Assyria, suddenly a new light has arisen in the midst of us; and the oldest relics yet discovered, have occurred, not among the ruins of Nineveh or Heliopolis, not in the sandy plains of the Nile or the Euphrates, but in the pleasant valleys of England and France, along the banks of the Seine and the Somme, the Thames and the Waveney.
>
> (Lubbock, cited in Poulter, 1980: 34)

This displacement of questions concerning human antiquity and the origins of civilisation from their association with debates concerning the lines of historical succession and influence between Indian, Egyptian, Mesopotamian and Graeco-Roman culture and their reterritorialisation in the more homely soils of France and Britain eventually obliged the classics, as one contemporary put it, to turn 'in their long sleep' (Levine, 1986: 170). An important focus for debate in early- to mid-nineteenth-century classics scholarship had been the competing accounts of the origins of western civilisation offered by what Martin Bernal has (controversially) called the Ancient and the Aryan models. In the Ancient model, which had been dominant in the eighteenth century, Egypt was viewed as the precursor of, and the main progenitor for, Greek culture. In the Aryan model, this connection was denied in the construction of a lineage for western civilisation which, by attributing the foundations of Greek culture to the invasion of the Indo-European speaking Hellenes, traced its roots to Asiatic sources.

The main point at issue in these debates was race: cutting the earlier Egyptian–Greek lineage was, as Bernal puts it, essential in order 'to keep black Africans as far as possible from European civilisation' (Bernal, 1991: 30). Since Egypt was a part of Africa, then it could not be regarded as the font of Greek civilisation without, in accordance with the logic of nineteenth-century Hellenism, placing the whole subsequent history of European civilisation on African foundations. Egyptian artefacts were subjected to a similar reclassification: as Bernal records, Wilhelm von Humboldt's 1833 plan for a new national museum in Berlin excluded Egyptian artefacts from the category of *Kunst*, reserved exclusively for Greek and Roman antiquities and Renaissance art, since their role could only be that of testimonies to a long-dead culture rather than as models to be harnessed to a programme of public education (Bernal, 1991: 254). Cuvier took a different tack. When examining the crania of Egyptian mummies, he maintained that the Egyptians were not – could not have been – black: 'no race of Negro', he wrote, 'produced that celebrated people who gave birth to the celebrated civilisation of ancient Egypt, and from whom the whole world has inherited the principles of its laws, sciences, and perhaps also religion' (Cuvier, cited in Schiebinger, 1993: 188).

The forms of reasoning deployed in these debates depended on the compressed time horizons which, prior to the 1850s, still governed the dominant conceptions of human history. William Bynum stresses the extent to which these conflated species time with the time of civilisation:

> There is no hint that any extended period might have elapsed between the appearance of Homo sapiens as a biological species and Homo sapiens as a civilised being with well-developed languages, written records, traditions, and the trappings of civilisation. Civilisation and its institutions had developed from relatively simple to more highly complex forms. Early man was simpler than his descendants of the nineteenth century. But certain crucial human characteristics – language, use of tools, social instincts – were aboriginal, with the result that man and early civilisation were virtually coexistent.
>
> (Bynum, 1974: 273)

These conceptions played an important role in organising the terms of debates between the advocates of monogenetic conceptions of human development and those favouring polygenetic lineages. For the latter made good use of the principles of mosaic time combined with the two to three thousand years of recorded history to argue that these could not, when put together, accommodate the long sequences required if the existing differences of human types were to be accounted for as emerging from a single source. Here, again, as Donald Grayson (1983: 159–62) shows, Egyptian remains were at the centre of contention. In his 1844 study *Crania Aegyptica*, Samuel Morton went over the same craniological ground that Cuvier had earlier covered, while also drawing on the evidence of Egyptian monuments to demonstrate that the existing distinctions between 'Caucasians' and 'Negroes' were clearly evident two millennia before Christ. This was too early for their differentiation to be accommodated within the thousand years since the flood which conventional biblical chronology allowed. Just as important, it suggested that the racial differentiation of humankind had not been significantly marked by time over the intervening period.

The establishment of human antiquity called the terms of these debates into question by opening up a new domain of 'pasts beyond memory', thereby providing for 'a period of extended but indefinite time during which early man gradually developed the social and cultural attributes which characterise the earliest times for which written records exist' (Bynum, 1974: 386). It also provided the durations of time that were necessary if human physical differences were to be accounted for as evolutionary developments from a single source. These elongated time scales did not, in themselves, guarantee the ascendancy of monogenetic conceptions; indeed, in the USA, Morton's advocacy of polygenesis, alongside that of Louis Agassiz, remained influential up to and beyond the post-bellum abolition of slavery. In the British context, however, they played a significant role in marginalising the virulently racist polygeneticism of James Hutton and the Anthropological Society. They also placed the development of

61

human culture and civilisation in a longer perspective, decentring the question of Egyptian–Greek relationships which, from the longer perspectives of human prehistory, could no longer bear the singular weight that earlier debates had placed on them. They were also, finally, crucially important to the synchronisation of methods across the fields of natural history, anthropology and archaeology which characterised the late-nineteenth-century development of the typological method. For when viewed through the Darwinian lens, Thomsen's approach to the evolution of artefacts and design traits was increasingly recast in terms of an analogy with the evolution of species. Construing the type, as manifested in a particular design trait for example, as a kind of information that was transmitted across generations through copying, changes in design were interpreted as the outcome of minor, unconscious and directionless variations. These variations, in being copied and then subjected to more random variations, to be copied in their turn, provided a mechanism which, working not through single acts of individual creativity but through a combination of chance and habit on the part of large numbers of anonymous cultural producers, could account for how one design trait might – through a succession of tiny changes, imperceptible in themselves, but carried out over immensely long periods – eventually be transformed into an entirely different one.[23]

That said, a marked asymmetry characterised the application of these investigative procedures in metropolitan and colonial contexts. As we have seen, the symbolic production of colonial space in the late Victorian era was anachronistic in the sense that it constituted a far away that did double service as the distant past. This manoeuvre was not unprecedented: Stocking attributes its first distinctive modern variant to the role of Turgot's work in temporalising the differences between peoples which, in Montesquieu, had been represented solely in spatial terms (Stocking, 1987: 14). What was new in the late Victorian period was the role played by a new set of relationships between surfaces and depths through which – to recall Anne McClintock's terms – panoptical time and anachronistic space were superimposed one on the other. For if the far away could now be equated with the distant pasts which had been excavated in Europe, this was only because of a structural disparity between the forms of evidence which such equations brought into comparison. Where the spades of the geological archaeologists dug deeper and deeper into the soils of France and England in order first to establish and then to extend the reach of human antiquity, the surfaces of North America and Australia were, for a long time, barely scratched or, where excavations did take place, were governed by highly strategic calculations linked to the politics of land in the context of highly fraught colonial frontiers. It was thus the measurable similarities, especially cranial ones, between the dug-up remains of prehistoric humans and the 'found' remains of 'living primitives' which served to establish a new system of equivalences for different human types – racially theorised – to be distributed sequentially through evolutionary time. It was, similarly, precisely by *not* digging deeper, by limiting their attention to the stone tools which could easily be found on the surface and drawing these into relationships of semiotic equivalence with the excavated stone-age tools of Europe, that early Australian archaeologists helped to sustain the conceptions of Europe's armchair theorists that colonised peoples could be represented as primitive but not ancient, as living relics of the European past but without any history of their own.[24] In the context of colonial relations, the effects of the archaeological gaze of the historical sciences were literally petrifying: for A. P. Elkin, writing in the 1930s, the legacy of evolutionary anthropology in relation to Australia's Aborigines was 'to think of that people archaeologically, as though they were as their stones' (Elkin, cited in McGregor, 1997: 214).

This archaeological structure of evolutionary thought received its most influential theoretical elaboration in the work of Edward Tylor, for whom 'the institutions of man' were 'as stratified as the earth on which he lives' (McGrane, 1989: 90). However, Tylor's more distinctive accomplishment, Bernard McGrane argues, was to reconstruct 'the surface of non-European differences' across a 'stratification of time' so that 'differences residing in geographical space' were turned into 'differences residing in developmental historical time', thereby transforming 'a *comparative table of differences into a genealogical scale of development*' (94). However, McGrane goes on to suggest, that it is crucial to see this operation as aiming at new forms of modern self-knowledge if its consequences are to be properly understood. While representations of wild and savage peoples at the world's edge had long been a part of western constructions of the Other, these did not integrate those Others into the dynamics of western civilisation or the modern self. By contrast, the transformation of peoples distant from Europe into primitives representing moments of prehistory relocated them as ancestors evoking – in a new and distinctive mnemonics – memories of the long distant past but one which still survived as the bottom-most layer in the archaeological make-up of modern man.

It was this conception of man that provided the discursive framework from which evolutionary museums derived their rationality as distinctive memory machines operating within the anxieties about progress and its relations to habit that this archaeological construction of the person gave rise to. Before exploring their functioning in this respect more fully, however, their technical organisation merits closer attention.

3

Reassembling the museum

In proposing the concept of 'time's arrow' as a way of imaging linear and directional time, Stephen Jay Gould summarises its effect as that of representing history as 'an irreversible sequence of unrepeatable events' within which each moment 'occupies its own distinct position in a temporal series, and all moments, considered in proper sequence, tell a story of linked events moving in a direction' (Gould, 1987: 11). Bruno Latour, in considering the temporal strategies of modernism, suggests that the belief that the past from which the modern differentiates itself has passed irreversibly is the result of a set of procedures through which otherwise disparate elements are cohered into temporally marked sets whose succession generates the appearance of time's passage as a continuous flow. Time's arrow is, in this interpretation, a fabrication:

> Entities have to be made contemporary by moving in step and have to be replaced by other things equally well aligned if time is to become a flow. Modern temporality is the result of a retraining imposed on entities which would pertain to all sorts of times and possess all sorts of ontological statuses without this harsh disciplining.

> (Latour, 1993: 72)

In the case of the temporal sequencing associated with the historical sciences, this harsh disciplining was chiefly the work of the typological method, whose ordering of objects into the relations between geological, natural and human time made those sequences thinkable while at the same time giving them a material form. The role of museums, as the centres of calculation within which objects from diverse locations were collected and arranged into these sequences, was thus a constitutive one. It is not, that is to say, a matter of seeing typological museum displays as simply a means of representing the new orderings of time emerging from the historical sciences. Rather, playing a role in relation to those sciences analogous to that played by the laboratory in relation to the experimental sciences, the museum played a key role in the operations through which the historical sciences measured and partitioned time, and distributed human and non-human actors across it. Yet the typological method was also central to the public pedagogy of the evolutionary museum just as it was the lynchpin of the new system for managing objects and the relations between them which made it possible for earlier collections to be disassembled and reassembled in new configurations.

The key figure here was Pitt Rivers. When Otis Mason travelled to Europe in 1889, he wrote of his excitement at witnessing Pitt Rivers's typological method at first hand, marvelling at its economy as 'the only one in which every piece has a *raison d'être*' (Mason, cited in Hinsley, 1981: 109). The curator of the museum at the Royal College of Surgeons was similarly moved, at the opening ceremony for the Wellcome Historical Medical Museum, to suggest that 'we who have to do with the administration of museums will do well to adopt Pitt Rivers as our Patron Saint', singling out three aspects of Pitt Rivers's work for particular praise:

> It was Pitt Rivers who demonstrated how reliable human history could be built up, bit by bit, in the shelves and show-cases of a museum; it was he who made the spade an instrument of exact history in the hands of a trained observer; it was he who pressed home the study of living primitive peoples as a clue to the customs, myths and beliefs of our long dead ancestors.
>
> (Keith, 1913: 103–4)

The first and second of these attributes were extensions of the principles that had already been developed by Christian Jürgen Thomsen in the sphere of archaeology; the last reflected the distinctive properties of the late-nineteenth-century synthesis of the historical sciences. Perhaps Pitt Rivers's more decisive innovation, however, was to recast the principles of typological reasoning by modelling them on the procedures of the natural sciences.

> The more we examine into the culture of the primitive inhabitants of the globe, the more we perceive it to have expanded and developed upon a plan analogous to that which has been observed in the development of species, and the more evident it becomes that the method of investigating these memorials should be the same systematic method which we employ for investigating the phenomena of the animal and vegetable kingdoms.
>
> (Pitt Rivers, cited in M. W. Thompson, 1977: 34)

And this entailed similar principles of classification.

> Human ideas, as represented by the various products of human industry, are capable of classification into genera, species and varieties, in the same manner as the products of the vegetable and animal kingdoms, and in their development from the homogeneous to the heterogeneous they obey the same laws.
>
> (Pitt Rivers, 1875: 307)[1]

This had two main consequences. First, it made it theoretically possible for all museum collections to be reassembled in accordance with the same principles through the operation of a common grammar across all museum types. The combination of lithological, stratigraphical and topographical characteristics found in geological collections;[2] the linear sequencing of developmental stages within and between species; the ordering of human types into evolutionary sequences; the arrangement of tools, weapons and pottery into sequences: the whole of the material world could be lined up and placed before the eyes in a manner which allowed each display to tell its own story, seemingly without the need for textual mediation. It promised a means of making each object auto-intelligible through the place that was arranged for it within an evolutionary sequencing of things that was – to come to the second point – cumulative. For, in Pitt Rivers's interpretation, the ordering of culture was not simply like that of nature; it also followed on from it so that each sequencing of things would – like each object in every display – eventually find its place within a larger sequencing of sequences.

Yet, as has often been noted, the arrangement of entire collections in accordance with the principles Pitt Rivers advocated – detaching artefacts from their originating contexts and arranging them in long and purportedly universal evolutionary sequences, from the simple to the complex – was a relatively rare occurrence (Bouquet, 2000; Coombes, 1994: 117). Geographical displays were more common, as were displays in which typological principles were deployed within differentiated regional contexts but not across them so as to construct universal developmental sequences. Be this as it may, the typological method played a decisive role in rearranging the artefactual field owing to the respects in which – as a method spanning the divide between *naturalia* and *artificialia* – it provided a putatively universal grammar of things. For it was this grammar that provided the leading edge of the programmes for reforming museum collections advocated by pro-Darwinist curators. This was because of the role it eventually attained as a 'black box' for evolutionary thought, a mechanism which, by securing a fit between the evolution of species and cultures and its own operations as a working instrument,[3] was able to function as a more or less taken-for-granted means of organising and producing evolutionary knowledge through the network of relations between human and non-human actors it organised. It is, however, only by considering the differences between the circumstances in which this method was deployed in metropolitan and colonial contexts that the distinctive forms of closure characterising the typological method, and their effects, can be fully appreciated.

Black-boxing evolution

In his discussion of the relations between fieldwork and the laboratory in the soil sciences, Latour argues that one advantage of the latter is that it enables objects from different locations and times to become contemporaries of one another, occupying the same time and space where they can be subjected to 'the same unifying gaze' (Latour, 1999: 38). It also allows the researcher to 'shift the position of specimens and substitute one for another as if shuffling cards' as the specimens, once detached from their original location, 'become as mobile and recombinable as the lead monotype characters of a printing press' (38). This last characteristic, Latour goes on to argue, plays a crucial role in the production of new knowledge owing to the opportunity it affords of arranging things in shifting combinations so as to make new relations and affinities perceptible. It is through the distancing and abstracting effects of movements of this kind, rather than from contemplating the entanglements of things in the field, that new actors – defined in terms of what they can do, the performances they are capable of – are produced and, where the movements that sustain such actors are repeated, stabilised.

The processes involved here are best illuminated in terms of the two main defining principles of actor-network theory which, as John Law defines them, are those of *relational materiality* and *performativity*. The first applies the semiotic principle of the relationality of entities to all materials rather than only to those that are linguistic. If this principle entails that entities acquire their reality from the relations within which they are located, this also means that 'they are *performed* in, by, and through those relations' with the consequence that 'everything is uncertain and reversible, at least in principle . . . never given in the order of things' (Law, 1999: 4; emphasis in original). The principle of *performativity*, accordingly, is concerned with how, in practice 'things get performed (and perform themselves) into relations that are relatively stable and stay in place' (4). This is pre-eminently the work of institutions which, in co-ordinating the relations between human and non-humans, 'provide all the mediations necessary for an actor to maintain a durable and sustainable substance' (Latour, 1999: 307).

While the principles of actor-network theory are now widely applied to museums,[4] David Jenkins's discussion of the relations between fieldwork, classification and labelling comes closest to describing the role played by museum practices in fabricating, stabilising and administering new entities. The labelling of objects at the site of collection, effecting their archival inscription from the outset; the translation of objects into a two-dimensional visual grammar through the drawings that are made of them as they are accessioned; and their translation into a classified inventory recording the provenance of each object: these processes, Jenkins contends, have two main consequences. The first consists in 'a reduction of the empirical world to new, more easily manageable objects that are, in Latour's phrase, "mobile immutable, presentable, readable and combinable with one another"' (Jenkins, 1994: 254). And the second arises from the relations between these different stages in the processing of the museum object. 'Each step – field collection, proper labelling, archival systematisation, and museum display – was,' Jenkins argues, 'apparently linked to the prior step, ensuring the authenticity and stabilising the meanings of ethnographic collections' (255). But within this sequence, he notes, citing the expenditure priorities of the evolutionary collections of the Field Columbian Museum of Natural History in Chicago as an example, 'the archival systematisation of ethnographic artefacts' was often 'more important than field expeditions' (255).

I have already touched on these issues when noting how Henry Balfour was berated for his failure to label the Pitt Rivers collection quickly enough, and will have more to say on this subject when considering the role of labelling in relation to the politics of vision posed by evolutionary collections. For now, though, the point I want to make concerns the part played by the processes Jenkins calls attention to in organising the distinctive role of nineteenth-century museums as sites of what Jan Golinski calls 'visible knowledge' where knowledge is constructed 'in the very process of display itself, without that display making reference back to some anterior location or previous occasion of private experimental work' (Golinski, 1998: 95). John Pickstone (1994) sees museums as having played a key role in this regard in furnishing the basis for a distinctively museological mode of scientific reasoning whose procedures, essentially comparative and classificatory, depended on the ability to make observations across, and thence analytical abstractions from, large bodies of material of the kind that, at that time, could only be provided by museums. This rings true of the phase of armchair anthropology in its dependence on the perception of relations of difference and similarity across large classes of objects that museums made possible.[5] The role played by the typological method here can be seen from the summary offered by Henry Balfour, perhaps Pitt Rivers's most faithful disciple.

> Suffice it to say that, in classifying his ethnological material, he adopted a *principal* system of groups into which objects of like form or function from all over the world were associated to form series, each of which illustrated as completely as possible the varieties under which a given art, industry, or appliance occurred. Within these main groups objects belonging to the same region were usually associated together in *local* sub-groups. And wherever amongst the objects or other implements exhibited in a given series there seemed to be suggested a *sequence of ideas*, shedding light upon the probable stages in the evolution of this particular class, these objects were specially brought into juxtaposition. This special grouping to illustrate sequence was particularly applied to objects from the same region as being, from their local relationships, calculated better to illustrate an actual continuity. As far as possible the seemingly more primitive and generalised forms – those simple types which usually approach most nearly to *natural* forms, or whose use is associated with primitive ideas – were placed at the beginning of each series, and the more complex and specialised forms were arranged towards the end.

> The primary object of this method of classification by series was to demonstrate, either actually or hypothetically, the origin, development, and continuity of the material arts, and to illustrate the variations whereby the more complex and specialised forms belonging to the higher conditions of culture have been evolved by successive slight improvements from the simple, rudimentary, and generalised form of a primitive culture.
>
> (Balfour, 1904b: 692; emphasis in original)

There are a few key points to note here. The first concerns the adaptability of the method with regard to its ability to effect different articulations of relations of space and time according to whether objects are assembled in trans-regional universal series, or in series within regions. There is also the added possibility that these, too, might be arranged developmentally or, as an ideal that Pitt Rivers posited and that was extensively discussed in subsequent debates, with regional and typological principles of display interacting so that artefacts might be codified along both axes simultaneously.[6] The second point concerns the interaction between the two principles of analogy and continuity which inform Pitt Rivers's conception of the relationships between ethnological and natural series. Philip Steadman highlights the first of these principles in his discussion of the role of 'the Darwinian analogy' in the accounts of the evolution of design developed by Pitt Rivers (1906), Henry Balfour (1893) and Alfred Haddon (1895). The key to this consists in the role accorded innumerable minor variations to account for the evolution of design – whether of tools, weapons or design motifs – as, like that of natural species, the unintended outcome of anonymous and directionless processes whose central mechanism is essentially that of '"unconscious variation" through accidental inexact copying' (Steadman, 1979: 106). Since this is a mechanism which places the relations between heredity and habit, remembering and forgetfulness, at its heart, it will repay closer attention.

The problem posed by the series that evolutionary showmen assembled, Steadman argues, was that they might 'begin and end with examples so widely different that, unless the intermediate links were known, it would not be imagined that they were in any way related' (103). Pitt Rivers's series of New Ireland paddle design is a case in point (Figure 3.1). No one, he says, who compared the last figure in this series to the first 'without the explanation afforded by the intermediate links, would believe that it represented the nose of a human face' (Pitt Rivers, 1906: 42). But it is the nature of the explanation offered by those intermediate links that matters here. For these are not the result of deliberate and conscious changes by individual cultural producers. Rather, since the form of cultural production that is involved here is that of craft production, in which large numbers of such designs are produced by anonymous producers imitating templates passed down by tradition, such transitions are the result of inexact copying in which minor, unintended variations are – in being copied in their turn – amplified so as to become, eventually, a new design template. There is thus both an accumulation of the past and a departure from its legacy at work here; evolution, we might say, is a matter of bad habit in which both the perpetuation of habit, and the breach of habit, are necessary to introduce sequence.

This account of cultural evolution is not merely analogous to the Darwinian account of natural evolution; it is also continuous with it, emerging from it – through the connecting link of habit – as an extension of natural evolution. As Steadman notes, Pitt Rivers's series always began with 'those objects and tools which most closely resembled natural forms, from which they might have been derived' (Steadman, 1979: 91). The history of Australian weapons, Pitt Rivers thus contended, 'can be traced by their connecting links to the simple stick, such as might have been used by an ape or elephant before mankind appeared upon this earth' (Pitt Rivers, 1875: 302). Once the process of evolution acquires a degree of momentum, then both its mechanisms and tempo are themselves subject to development as the ratio between what he calls the *intellectual mind*, capable of reasoning on unfamiliar occurrences and of making conscious adjustments in response, and the *automaton mind*, governed by quasi-instinctual forms of habit, changes in favour of the former. However, as Balfour astutely notes (Balfour, 1904b: 692), the focus of Pitt Rivers's theoretical attention was on the early stages of cultural evolution, when human behaviour was believed to be regulated by what Pitt Rivers called a 'persistent conservatism' (Pitt Rivers, 1875: 300).

But then, and by the same token, Pitt Rivers's typological displays were also characterised by a 'persistent conservatism' owing to the degree to which they depicted evolution as a process which depended on the accumulated weight of the past being carried on into the innovations that break with it. Nélia Dias

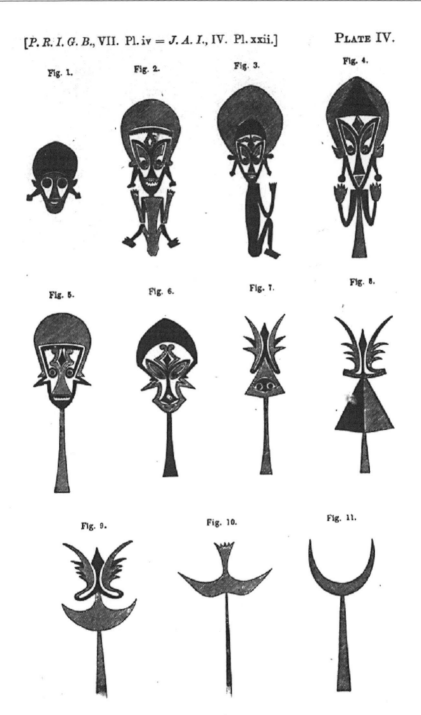

[*P. R. I. G. B.*, VII. Pl. iv = *J. A. I.*, IV. Pl. xxii.]　　PLATE IV.

Figure 3.1 Ornamentation of New Ireland paddles, showing the transition of form.

Source: A. H. Lane-Fox Pitt Rivers (1906) *The Evolution of Culture, and Other Essays*, Oxford: The Clarendon Press, plate IV.

makes a similar point when noting the respects in which the typological method constitutes a distinctive mnemonics, functioning 'as an *aide-mémoire*, allowing for the recall of information that has already been stored', making possible 'the memorisation of things in a certain order' (Dias, 1994: 166–7). The organisation of the gaze that is involved here is archaeological: seeing is a matter of seeing how, in the succession of ideas which typological arrangements make visible, the inheritance of the past continues to exist as a layer within the make-up of each step in evolutionary development.

It is, finally, crucial that this message is carried by things. Pitt Rivers had no need of actor-network theory to be fully aware of the similarities between the relational properties of the typological method and those of language. 'Every form', he wrote, 'marks its own place in sequence by its relative complexity or affinity to other allied forms, in the same manner that every word in the science of language has a place assigned to it in the order of development or phonetic decay' (Pitt Rivers, 1875: 303). The role of the typological method, however, is to step in precisely where the analysis of language fails owing to its ability to provide evidence of pasts beyond writing. It is here, echoing the object-centred rhetoric of the historical sciences, that the scientific study of the material arts comes into its own. It is 'in approaching prehistoric times, or in studying modern savages who represent prehistoric man', Pitt Rivers argues, that 'language loses its persistency, or fails us altogether' while the value of 'ideas embodied in material forms increases in stability and permanence' (303).

This assessment of the value of material over textual evidence applied just as much to the body of the savage as something that could be scraped clean of the detritus of culture to reveal, in skulls and skeletons and the measures that might be taken of them, the anatomical bedrock of racially differentiated types which might also be arranged in evolutionary sequence. This is not something that solely concerns the arrangements of human remains within the museum, however. To the contrary – and this is central to how evolution comes to be black-boxed – once typological reasoning is translated from the metropolitan contexts of armchair anthropology into colonial contexts, it becomes an instrument of colonial rule in view of its ability to classify and order subject populations *as if* they were museum collections.

I draw here on the work of Nicholas Dirks and Peter Pels who, discussing the increasing significance of caste as the conduit for the more despotic and authoritarian forms of colonial rule that were developed in India in the wake of the 1857 rebellion, note the declining significance of an orientalist archive based on knowledge of India's religious and antiquarian texts in favour of an 'ethnological articulation of knowledge on bodies' (Pels, 2000: 83) in providing a new administrative basis for colonial rule. Focusing on the debates leading to the authorisation of an ethnographical survey of India in 1901, Dirks notes its role as 'an imperial laboratory' (Dirks, 2000: 163) in which the speculative sequences of racial evolution proposed by Europe's armchair anthropologists could be put to the test of actual observation, both visual and craniometrical. The stratifications of caste provided, in the words of H. H. Risley, the Director of Ethnography for

India, '"a vast storehouse of social and physical data" which had only to be recorded to resolve the problems of racial sequencing that Europeans, given the '"less trustworthy evidence"' they had to work with, could not be expected to master (Risley, cited in Dirks, 2000: 163). But this encounter with the real was, of course, entirely pre-coded by the assumptions of European anthropological thought. This meant that, by being disconnected from their earlier orientalist textualisation and relocated within the field of knowledge as corporeally differentiated racial types, the colonised were shifted out of history – and thereby out of the dynamics of modern state formation – through their construction as prehistoric.

Edgar Thurston, the Superintendent of the Madras Museum between 1885 and 1908, recorded that that his anthropometric fieldwork in the Wynaad region was often frustrated by the Paniyan women who, 'when I appeared in their midst, ran away, believing that I was going to have the finest specimens among them stuffed for the museum' (Thurston, cited in Dirks, 2000: 165). While stories of colonial collecting are full of reminiscences of this kind, they occlude the more significant point that what matters most about the relations between museum anthropology and indigenous populations in colonial contexts is that the latter are subjected to forms of administration in which they are treated *as if they were in a museum already*. As David Jenkins (1994: 263) notes, the effects of typological arrangements were bureaucratic as well as taxonomic; indeed, they were bureaucratic *because* taxonomic, offering a means of reducing complexity to manageable proportions – a significant advantage when compared, for example, with genealogical trees with their proliferating branches. I shall return, in chapter 7, to show how these bureaucratic virtues were adapted to the purpose of colonial administration in late-nineteenth- and early-twentieth-century Australia. More immediately relevant to my current purpose, however, is the role that typological principles played as a means of reforming museum collections, reassembling them on a new basis and providing new principles for their administration.

Bureaucratising the past

Shortly after taking up office in 1894, Henry Forbes, the Director of Liverpool's Free Public Museums, outlined the principles which he believed ought to guide the rearrangement of the biological collections in the Lord Derby Museum:

> The exhibition should also be such as to attract those who have no object beyond amusement or relaxation; they should find the Museum a book with its pages open and its narrative so clearly set out, that they are unawares following a connected story, unfolded from room to room before their eyes, which may excite their interest and further attention. . . . A Biological Museum should, therefore, be as it were a Book of animals and plants, explained in words understandable of all persons of ordinary education, commencing with the description of the simpler forms, and leading step by step to the higher and more complex. This scientific and only intelligible method the Director desires to adopt, therefore, is as to present to the visitor

the lowest forms of life in the Animal and Vegetable Kingdoms on his entrance, gradually, introducing him from room to room to those of nearest affinity, in ascending order till the highest are reached.

(Forbes, 1901: 5)

From this point of view, Forbes concluded, the Liverpool Free Public Museums were 'far from being as well constructed for the purposes of a Museum as they might be' (5) as visitors were obliged to constantly retrace their steps and visit galleries out of sequence if they were to follow the ascending orders of nature's continuity. Nor was it alone in this regard. While, Forbes argues, 'there is no biologist but admits that [evolutionary principles] are not only the ideal, but the only true and intelligible principles on which a Museum should be arranged, and who does not on every opportunity advocate their adoption in all new Museums', he also concludes that 'there is not (surprising as it may appear) in this country a single museum arranged on these principles' (5).

Henry Flower, Director of the British Museum (Natural History) would have shared this assessment. There was concern that his appointment to this role in 1884 represented the growing influence of 'State-Darwinism' and that his rearrangement of the Index Museum had transformed it into a place where 'little children run in and out, and without the knowledge or desire of their parents or guardians, grow up Evolutionists' (*Jus*, 9 December 1887). Yet, as Flower soon discovered, his ability to rearrange the Museum's exhibition areas in accordance with evolutionary principles was seriously limited. Whereas Richard Owen, as Superintendent of the Natural History Departments of the British Museum, had enjoyed substantial control over the curatorial direction of those departments, the new position of Director to which Flower was appointed carried no specific responsibility for exhibition policy. This remained with the Keepers of the different departments, many of whom were agnostic with regard to evolutionary theory and disinclined to rearrange their exhibits in accordance with its requirements (Stearn, 1981: 72). Not until Albert Gunther, the Keeper of Zoology, retired in 1895 was Flower able to exert direct control over the exhibitions of a specific department. Indeed, it was the lack of a curatorial power base that had earlier obliged Flower to concentrate on the Index Museum – the portion of the collection, exhibited in the main hall, that Owen had planned to serve as an abbreviated introduction to the whole collection – as the only space available to him to experiment with evolutionary ideas.

Flower also had a hostile architectural environment to reckon with. This is not just a matter of the Romanesque associations that Alfred Waterhouse incorporated into his design in order that the Museum might meet Owen's purpose of serving as a 'cathedral of science'.[7] The internal layout of the Museum proved a more serious impediment, frustrating the exhibition of evolutionary continuities, as Owen had planned (Owen, 1862), by placing the main hall between the two major exhibition areas. The effect of this, Flower (1888) noted in his first guide to the collections, was to separate the Departments of Geology and Zoology from each other in a manner which, while perfectly suited to the exhibition of Owen's Platonic archetypes, inhibited the exhibition of evolutionary connections between extinct and continuing forms of life. The Museum was also considered just too showy for proper scientific exhibitions. For Robert Kerr it reflected too much the principles of the Bazaar, producing an environment in which 'specimens lose scale and importance, the casual visitor is bewildered, the student is interrupted, and the display sinks from the character of science to that of show' (Kerr, cited in Yanni, 1999: 111).

Evolutionary displays resting on typological principles were thus far from carrying all before them; but they were the cutting edge in a programme of museum reform, which aimed to rearrange collections both within museums and across the relations between them. The ethos of this programme was aptly summarised by W. Boyd Dawkins – the Professor of Geology at Owen's College and Curator of the Manchester Museum[8] – who, regretting the lack of order that he saw in England's local and provincial museums, urged the need for the Museums Association to develop a co-ordinated approach to museum reform. 'In very many museums,' he complained, 'art is not separated from natural history, nor from ethnology, and the eye of the beholder takes in at a glance the picture of a local worthy, a big fossil, a few cups and saucers, a piece of cloth from the South Seas, a war club or two, and very possibly a mummy.' This inclusion 'of articles which have no sort of relationship with the rest,' he concluded, 'converted the whole into rubbish, using the word in the Palmerstonian sense of being "matter in the wrong place"' (Dawkins, 1892: 17).

Yet if the essential tasks of museum reform centred on converting rubbish into well-ordered displays, this was less a matter of putting matter back into place than of putting it into the new places provided by evolutionary principles of classification and display. This involved an extensive programme of rearrangement, through which the artefactual domain was subjected to new principles of order as objects were disconnected from the assemblages in which they had earlier been exhibited and then reassembled in new configurations. It is important to be clear, however, that these changes did not involve adding *new kinds* of objects to the artefactual domain; the historical sciences provided a new grammar of exhibition, not a new set of exhibitionary morphemes and phonemes. The generative structure of this grammar consisted in the relations between two organising principles. The first sorted objects into the differentiated fields established by the disciplinary divisions characterising the historical sciences. The second assembled objects into temporally organised sequential relations constructed within, or spanning the relations between, these sciences.

Disciplinary differentiation was produced by a number of means. These included the establishment of museums which, from the outset, focused on one or more of the historical sciences. A second, and usually more protracted process, consisted in the reorganisation of earlier multi- or pre-disciplinary collections to provide the materials for a number of different museums with clearly differentiated disciplinary foci. A third consisted in the introduction of more clearly demarcated disciplinary divisions within existing museums that retained the multi-disciplinary focus of their earlier collections.

Examples of the first kind of differentiation include Chicago's Field Columbian Museum of Natural History which, drawing on the materials exhibited at the

World's Columbian Exhibition of 1893, had a dual natural history and ethnology focus from the outset. The American Museum of Natural History (AMNH) is another case in point. However, although the AMNH was incorporated in 1868, it was not until the establishment of a Department of Anthropology in the late 1890s that its ethnological collections were given serious attention. The Smithsonian Institution is an example of the second process, with the establishment, in 1881, of the US National Museum and the development, within it, of separate divisions of archaeology and ethnology.[9] The drawn-out process through which the British Museum's natural history collections were eventually detached from the British Museum's Bloomsbury collection to establish the British Museum (Natural History) at South Kensington in 1881, and the equally protracted separation of the Museum's ethnological collections from the Department of British and Medieval Antiquities and Ethnography where they remained until 1921 (having been placed there in 1866) are also important examples.[10]

Changes in the exhibition practices relating to classical archaeological collections were, considered from the perspective of the museum system as a whole, particularly significant in making it possible for the development of human cultures and civilisations to be portrayed in unilinear progressive sequences. This had been inhibited, in the late eighteenth and early nineteenth centuries, by the severance of the relations of historical filiation that had earlier been recognised between Greek and Egyptian culture. This view, which was most influentially translated into museum practice by Johann Winckelmann, provided the main principles governing archaeological exhibits at the British Museum where they held sway until the 1850s. Thereafter, a number of forces conspired to overturn these principles of display. These, in Ian Jenkins's account (1992), included the influence of two parliamentary inquiries appointed to explore the relative merits of historical and aesthetic principles for exhibiting archaeological materials, and the favour that the former found with parliamentarians on the grounds of their greater public intelligibility. The challenge posed by the Museum's mid-century Assyrian acquisitions was also relevant in view of the role these played in restoring to Egyptian culture the progressive momentum that Winckelmann had denied it, thereby facilitating the construction of an Egyptian–Assyrian–Greek lineage. The increasing influence of emerging evolutionary conceptions of natural history on archaeological practice was, however, more crucial in shifting the focus of attention away from an aesthetic stress on the object's singularity to emphasise its historically representative qualities. This brought classical archaeology more into line with the findings of prehistoric archaeology and anthropology in a manner that allowed it to contribute to the organisation of unidirectional and cumulative accounts of the development of human culture.

There are many examples of the third kind of process in which existing museums retained a multi-disciplinary focus but were rationalised by differentiating disciplines more clearly and supplying, through the application of typological principles of display, a common grammar between them. This was very common in provincial or local museums which played a key role in the development of new distributive relations through which the artefactual field was hitched up to the apparatuses of adult education and popular schooling.[11]

The Horniman Museum in London is a case in point. Initially established as a private museum, but one with a strong commitment to serve all social classes, the Horniman Museum's collections were originally arranged as an assemblage of national and colonial curios reflecting the personal interests of its owner, the tea-merchant Frederick Horniman (Levell, 1997). As such, it was, as Anne Coombes puts it, 'a colourful illustration of the eclectic display policy' (Coombes, 1994: 115) that the Museums Association took issue with. Once the Museum passed into the ownership of London County Council in 1901, it was subjected to an extended programme of rationalisation in order to transform its collections into evolutionary displays with both an ethnological and a natural history focus.[12] The description, in the 1908 Annual Report, of the rearrangement of the relations between the Museum's departments gives some idea of the extent to which its collections were rearranged:

> The most important change in this department during the year has been the removal of the Egyptian collection from its former position in the Natural History Hall. The mummies are now conveniently placed in the South Corridor, and most of the other Egyptian antiquities are in the section of Magic and Religion, to which they properly belong. The space left vacant by the Egyptian collection is being filled up with the specimens upon which the future section of Physical Anthropology will in part be based. In this section it is proposed to illustrate the zoological affinities of man by means of specimens and preparations of allied animals (apes and monkeys), and to give the outlines of the more important external and skeletal differences that exist between the various races of man.
>
> (*Seventh Annual Report of the Horniman Museum and Library*, 1908: 6)

The Museum's collections of musical instruments and tools were rearranged and labelled in accordance with similar principles, reflecting the Museum's commitment to replicate, as far as possible, Pitt Rivers's typological method and 'to avoid overcrowding, and ensure the visibility of all specimens and the legibility of all labels' (*Annual Report of the Horniman Museum and Library*, 1913: 7).

One consequence of this was to introduce a programmatic approach to acquisitions and exhibition planning of a kind that had not previously been possible. This was because the commitment to arranging evolutionary series allowed gaps to be identified where, in a collection philosophy that stressed the singularity of the object, none had previously existed. Equally, and Shelton (2000: 170–1) makes the same point, those gaps could then be filled by judicious acquisitions in which it was not the individuality of the object that mattered but its ability to be fitted in the place prepared for it. This aspect of the typological method is made especially clear in a report prepared by Henry Balfour in 1890 in which he advised, in connection with his work on the Pitt Rivers collection, that 'it has been and would be in the future possible to greatly improve the existing series by filling up gaps in their continuity, or to add a new series, and so to advance greatly the educational value of this unique collection' (Pitt Rivers Museum, *Foundation and Early History*, folio 38, Report, p. iii). Balfour returns to this theme in later correspondence with Pitt Rivers, from whom Balfour had sought permission to publish an article on the series in the collection illustrating evolution in ornamental art. Pitt Rivers withheld his permission, asserting an authorial principle in relation to the original collection in regarding this as having a unity and integrity rooted in his own intentions. Balfour, writing in reply on 28 November 1890, understands the implications of the typological method much more clearly in stressing how collections based on its principles can be endlessly progressively augmented and improved:

> In undertaking the work of rearranging and adapting the collection in its new home, I did not dream that it would be intended that the collection, as it existed at S. Kensington, complete though many of the series were, was to be considered complete and its arrangement final. I gathered from reading your papers, as I have since been further led to suppose by your own statements, that the collection was to be progressive, even as it illustrates progress; that all endeavours were to be made to render it as complete as possible, and to increase its educational value, that it should always maintain itself among museums as one of particular importance.
>
> (Pitt Rivers Museum, *Foundation and Early History*, Folios 83–4)

Lee Rust Brown notes the operation of a similar principle in the late-eighteenth-century arrangement of the Muséum National d'Histoire Naturelle, in which Enlightenment classification allowed a space to be reserved for everything as yet awaiting discovery to complete its microcosmic assembly of the world. 'The Museum', as he puts it, 'could afford to welcome all new facts precisely because it was sure that every new fact would disappear into one *lacune* or another, and bring its encyclopedic representation of the world a step closer to perfection' (Brown, 1997: 103). The typological method operated with a different set of relations between objects and spaces in which the latter were to be filled by the former only to the degree that they could connect two points in a line of evolutionary development. But the principle remained the same.

What it is at issue here is a transformation in the object's status across the whole artefactual field, in which it was no longer its singularity or uniqueness that counted but its substitutability – that is, its ability to stand for other objects of the same type representing a stage within a developmental sequence. It was this transformation that allowed the museum object, in being both movable and repeatable, to perform its new function as part of an expanded distributive system. By according objects, no matter what their cultural provenance, the role of representing stages within universal evolutionary sequences, the typological method established a system of equivalences between objects which allowed them to circulate between collections and, by filling in the gaps to make up complete evolutionary series, to make good the deficiencies that would otherwise occur, in the same way that was possible in natural history or geology collections.

Occasionally, the evolutionary showman would lose nerve and put a case for retaining earlier exhibition practices. This was not true of Pitt Rivers, who remained intransigently critical of displays 'calculated rather to display the several articles to advantage, on the principle of shop windows, than to facilitate the deductions of science' (cited in Petch, 2001: 243). Balfour, however, argued that the odd gruesome or sensational exhibit 'did good by arresting the attention of the visitor' (cited in Rudler, 1897: 62). More important than such occasional losses of nerve, however, the processes I have outlined ran up against other histories which, in particular contexts, proved the more effective. This was true, for example, of the skirmishes which saw Gerard Kreft and, with him, evolutionary science kept outside the doors of the Australian Museum.[13] The continuing popularity, among colonial elites, of collections that functioned as trophies of conquest is another case in point,[14] as is the limited headway made by evolutionary principles at Harvard's Museum of Comparative Geology.[15] Typological principles also had only a partial impact on the ethnological and archaeological displays of the British Museum, occasioning Pitt Rivers to describe the Museum as being in 'a molluscous and invertebrate condition of development' producing 'nothing but confusion in the minds of those who wander through its long galleries with but little knowledge of the periods to which the objects relate' (cited in Mack, 1997: 46). There were also rival systems of knowledge and expertise working to limit the sphere of influence of the evolutionary showmen to particular regions of the artefactual domain. Developments in the historical sciences did not greatly influence collections focused on art and design, where the assumptions of orientalism held greater sway.[16] The currency of the primitive within art collections governed by aesthetic principles was also quite different from the one I have described, deriving its logic more from its relationship to aesthetic modernism rather than to developments in prehistoric archaeology and anthropology.[17] Finally, the influential exhibitions organised by missionary organisations, while often adopting evolutionary principles, were just as likely to be governed by salvationist principles which stressed the common, and therefore redeemable, humanity of 'primitive' peoples.[18]

When all of these qualifications are made, however, the application of typological principles played a key role in pressing a new set of claims to scientific authority during a period when the management of museums was becoming increasingly professionalised and attached to nascent public education systems.[19] This was partly a matter, in Britain, of a marked increase in the number of museums passing into, or established under, public ownership. This was especially true at the local and provincial levels where, from the 1870s, local authorities became significantly involved in the establishment and management of museums as 'statements of a new civic order' (Kavanagh, 1994: 15), which reflected the increased stress placed on the moral and educative responsibilities of government associated with the new liberalism. In view of this, national institutions located in London assumed new functions as the centres of newly formed public networks with an increasingly national scope.

The picture was different in Australia, and different again in the United States. While, in Australia, local literary, scientific and philosophical societies had often provided the initial spur prompting the establishment of museums, these were closely related to the State governments of the different colonies. Rather than originating in an autonomous and pre-existing realm of civil society, Australia's first museums were thus envisaged as among the means through which such a society was to be formed and they called, with notable success, on the aid of government to assist in this process.[20] Even so, there was often a good deal of tension between the political wing of government and the scientific intelligentsia, with the result that the conduct of museum affairs was often out of step with the political orientations of the different State parliaments responsible for the legislative and financial aspects of their administration. This gap tended to be closed in the 1880s and 1890s as, in each State, the major museums were brought more clearly under the control of parliamentary governments. These were, however, essentially State-based institutions in which each major State museum – the National Museum of Victoria, the Queensland Museum, the Australian Museum and the South Australian Museum, for example – formed the centre of a State-based network comprising a handful of provincial museums and the mechanics' institutes and societies of arts that were scattered through their rural hinterlands.

The United States, as Kohlstedt (1986) notes, similarly lacked an institution capable of playing a central and co-ordinating role on a national scale. The influence of the Smithsonian Institution certainly grew during this period, especially through the prominent advisory role that the curatorial staff of the US National Museum played in connection with several major international exhibitions and the permanent collections to which these gave rise.[21] Even so, it did not match that of many city or State-based museums and, perhaps more important, was the exception to the rule in being publicly owned. Established, usually, as the result of voluntary and private initiative, most American natural history museums remained under private ownership and direction. However, the new importance that was attributed to museums as a means of civic education made them the beneficiaries of philanthropic funding on a scale that allowed them to match, and sometimes to exceed, the scope and size of state-funded institutions in Europe. There remained, however, the significant difference that even the most important of these museums – like the American Museum of Natural History – functioned more as the centres of State- or city-based networks than of national networks.

The typological method played a key role in the organisation of these networks. Henry Balfour was clear on its virtues in this regard when comparing the relative advantages of geographical versus typological principles of display for ethnological collections. While the former might serve best for large museums with extensive collections relating to particular localities, Balfour stressed the value of the typological method for smaller collections. By allowing objects not regionally connected to be placed in the same sequence to illustrate evolution, it allowed museums to draw on objects from unrelated collections in order to assemble the prehistoric past and illustrate its evolutionary momentum. Nor was he in any doubt as to the virtues of the typological method from the point of view of the development of a national museum system. It provided new principles of exchange to govern the circulation of objects between museums to the degree that one museum might buy or borrow objects from another to fill up gaps in its evolutionary sequences, just as another museum might be willing to part with such objects to the degree that it already possessed a surfeit of objects which (however dissimilar they might be in other respects) were, typologically speaking,

79

substitutable. His reasoning was, in these respects, tellingly similar to those deployed by museum geologists in their concern to reform local collections so that they might provide educational series whose gaps would be filled by drawing on central repositories (see Knell, 1996).

These same qualities played a similarly enabling role in relation to the tendency, shared in all three countries, for museums to become more closely aligned with the two most distinctive moral and civic machineries of late-nineteenth-century liberal government: adult education and popular schooling. There were few museums that had not, by the 1880s and 1890s, developed extensive programmes of public lectures through which the object lessons of things were to be relayed far beyond the museum's walls through the connections that such programmes established with university extension classes and 'outreach' activities more generally.[22] The connections that were developed with the emerging state-based systems of popular schooling were arguably of greater significance. These were many and varied in form. The inclusion of school visits to museums as formal elements in school curricula,[23] special lecture programmes, and museum games designed to focus the child's attention on the museum as a learning environment are all examples of this new relationship.[24] A more distinctive innovation consisted in the construction of specially designed specimen boxes for natural history, geology and ethnological collections – all resting, in the works of one critic, on the 'insignificant individuality' of the object[25] – so that the lessons of both nature and culture might be circulated throughout the schooling system and be taken right into the classroom.[26] The net effect of these developments was to make the child – newly conceived as a future citizen – an object of the museum's most active and anxious attention whereas, previously, children had been either benignly neglected or, sometimes, openly disparaged by museum administrators.[27]

At the same time that they were inscribed within these new capillary machineries of adult education and popular schooling, museums of ethnology and natural history formed parts of increasingly internationalised museum networks.[28] These networks facilitated the exchange of objects (usually flowing from periphery to centre) and of knowledge and techniques (usually flowing in the reverse direction).[29] There was, as a consequence, a tendency for the terms in which debates regarding the civic and educational functions of museums were posed to be part of a shared lexicon that exhibited a number of distinctive characteristics. The first consisted in a marked stress on the distributive functions of museums in which each museum was approached from the point of view of both its relations to other museums and its connections to other distributive mechanisms. There had, in Britain, been plenty of inquiries into the purposes and management of museums in the mid-century period, and many of these had proposed far-reaching reforms to make museums more accessible to the public and better able to manage large numbers of visitors. However, these had focused mainly on museums in the capital city, sometimes in relation to one another, but seldom in relation to a national network of museums.[30] The first inquiry to adopt such a perspective was initiated by the British Association for the Advancement of Science when, as a part of the campaign that would eventually lead to the establishment of the Museums

Association, it established a Committee on Provincial Museums and charged it with the task of surveying all boroughs in the United Kingdom regarding the management of provincial museums and the state of their collections. In concluding that too many of 'these institutions have hitherto been but toys and hobbies, and require complete re-organisation' (Lewis, 1989: 6), the Committee espoused the reformist ideology that would come to characterise the Museums Association as it fixed its attention on the relations between museums as parts of a national distributive mechanism that was to connect with adult education and popular schooling. This focus was evident in the functions that were proposed for museums at the inaugural meeting of the Association in 1889. These included: the development of means for the interchange of duplicate and surplus specimens and of means for securing models, casts and reproductions; the introduction of a scheme capable of providing for a general supply of labels, illustrations and information; a uniform method for arranging natural history collections; the promotion of museum lectures to working men; and the preparation of small educational loan collections for circulation among schools. Similar concerns characterised the deliberations of the Committee that was appointed by the Australian Association for the Advancement of Science in 1890 to consider the Improvement of Museums as a Means of Popular Education.[31] They were also evident in the debates within the American Association for the Advancement of Science that prepared the ground for the establishment of the American Museums Association in 1906.[32]

Here too, then, in facilitating an expanded international network, the virtues of the typological method were evident; it allowed things to travel a long way and yet remain in the same place. Much like the disciplinary effects of Jeremy Bentham's panopticon in claiming to reform morals, preserve health, invigorate industry, diffuse instruction and lighten public burdens 'all by a simple idea in architecture' (Bentham, 1843: 39), the typological method – relatively simple in itself – effected a disciplining of objects which had manifold effects. These included a distinctive status of objecthood whose properties can be thrown into relief by briefly considering the contrasting developments which characterised late-nineteenth-century German museums.

Archaeological objects

It is noticeable, if we go back for a moment to Henry Forbes, how extensively he draws on textual images and metaphors in describing his ideal museum. Visitors, he says, should 'find the Museum a book with its pages open and its narrative so clearly set out, that they are unawares following a connected story, unfolded from room to room before their eyes', or, in another formulation, 'a Book of animals and plants, explained in words understandable of all persons of ordinary education' (Forbes, 1901: 5). This stands somewhat at odds with the claims of the historical sciences to find, in the evidence of things themselves, a new set of truths whose elucidation would require other methods than those of textual interpretation. It also stands at odds with their claim to make the lesson of things visible by so arranging them before the eye that their meaning would be transparent, unaided by the supplement of words. Yet Forbes's formulations are no exception in these regards. To the contrary, this contradiction between, on the one hand, an object-centred rhetoric, and, on the other, the organisation of a museum environment in which, ultimately, words prevailed over things, was a systemic one within Anglophone museum practices.

Its currency was not, however, universal. German anthropological museums of the same period, Andrew Zimmerman notes, rigorously excluded any textual supplements such as explanatory labels or guidebooks. They were also, with the odd exception, opposed to evolutionary arrangements as offering, in the words of one anthropologist, 'merely a doctrinaire interpretation (*Auffasung*), but no real understanding through viewing (*Anschauung*)' (Zimmerman, 2001: 185). This was not because of a fetishistic commitment to the value of single things in isolation from one another. On the contrary, the museum arrangements favoured by German anthropologists were intended to promote a syncretic practice of vision which 'forced the eye to leap from thing to thing', inhibiting undue focus on 'any single artifact' as 'all were forcibly combined into a totality' (181). This was, however, to be the work of the eye, unaided by the kinds of pre-interpretation that narrative frameworks inevitably provide.

This more radical ocular-centrism reflects the lack of any developed connections between German anthropology museums and popular schooling. Nor were those museums conceived as significant instruments of adult education. Behind these differences, however, lay some more fundamental ones concerning anthropology's relations to other disciplines in Germany and Britain. One aspect of this concerned the antagonistic relationship anthropology took up in relation to the programme of *Bildung* that comprised the main legacy of post-Kantian humanism. As a textually mediated process of historical self-shaping, *Bildung* excluded from its purview of humanity and culture all those peoples without written records. Since these were, by definition, regarded as being outside history, so they were also judged incapable of participating in a process of cultural development which depended on the self attaining progressively higher levels of self-consciousness through the forms of self-communion that were made possible via a constantly accumulating textual archive. This resulted in a correspondingly low estimation of the value of object-based disciplines, like anthropology, as concerning themselves with archaeological bric-à-brac of no historical value. The value of a humanistic practice that thus depended on the exclusion of the majority of humanity was, Zimmerman argues, called increasingly into question in the 1880s and 1890s as Germany, in the context of increasing competition between European powers to extend their spheres of colonial influence, acquired its own colonies. In taking issue with *Bildung*, German anthropology sought the basis for a new humanism in the study of the colonised who, cast in the mould not of the primitive but that of the *Naturvölker*, were to provide evidence of a common substratum of human nature 'unobscured by the masks of culture and the complications of historical development' (3).

Eschewing the subjectivism of historicist forms of textual interpretation, anthropology thus 'focused not on canonical texts of celebrated cultural peoples but on the bodies and the everyday objects of the colonised' (4). It was this determination to peel away the superficial accretions of civilisation and lay bare the truths to be found beneath which explains why the human skull became the ultimate anthropological object:

> The absence of flesh . . . meant for anthropologists a human body without the subjective history of tissue, whose thickness depends in part on eating habits and other behaviours. More than any ethnographic artifact, the skull presented anthropologists with an object that could be studied in a way fundamentally different from the interpretative methods of the humanities.
>
> (Zimmerman, 2001: 86)

The claims of German anthropology in these regards played an important role in the relations between late-nineteenth-century German science and liberalism. The idea that truth should be produced through observable facts subject to democratic verification within the limits of a given scientific community was contrasted with what was viewed as an authoritarian practice of the truth associated with the philosopher's claim to a privileged interpretation of a body of texts. More important, the programme of cultural modernisation, or *Kulturkampf*, that anthropologists proposed represented modernity as a break with the past to be forged via the application of science. This involved a significant break with the tradition of *Bildung*, which presupposed a model of time in which past and present were connected in a continuum. It also constituted the basis for a rejection of those moves, most notably represented by Tylor, through which, in British anthropology, the colonised-as-primitive were represented as the first stages in evolutionary narratives which culminated in the European present as both their outcome and the vantage point from which the sequencing human cultures could be interpreted and made intelligible. The suggestion that the development of cultures might be placed in longer narratives, including natural and geological times, was similarly rejected. The fusion, via Haeckel, of Darwinism with Goethean *Naturphilosophie* and cell embryology, did provide for a historicisation that could account for the evolution of the human species from a single ancestor (Weindling, 1989: 43–7). However, German anthropologists eschewed this as a model for their work, preferring contemporary tendencies in botany which, still largely Kantian in orientation, remained stoutly anti-evolutionist. The continuing legacy of the German distinction between geognosie and geology, and the devaluation of the narrative orientation of the latter, also contrasted with the situation in Britain, where the theological cast of early-nineteenth-century geology provided a narrative system which later Darwinian accounts transformed into secular narratives.

These arguments raise some difficulties for Suzanne Marchand's account of the role of German museums as the incubators for new forms of knowledge that were to prove crucial in the eventual victory of an anthropological view of culture over an older, more aristocratic view. Marchand characterises these new knowledges (her list is historical geography, ethnology, art history, folklore studies, prehistory, archaeology and palaeontology) as 'the ethnological sciences' on the grounds that they 'all aspired, in one way or another, to convert material evidence into historical narratives, and usually expended their energies on the study of more or less exotic societies and eras with little in the way of written records' (Marchand, 2000: 181).[33] Her contention, like Zimmerman's, is that the increasing prominence of these sciences contributed to a relative decline in the cultural authority of German humanism. Acting like a Trojan horse, they undermined the principles of classification that had underlain museums centred on the classics owing to the stress that they placed on the typical – that is, on traits shared by large numbers of artefacts – over the beautiful, or the uniquely distinguishing qualities of singular aesthetic objects. As a consequence, the older notion of culture as 'acquired refinements' gave way before the ascending influence of the anthropological view of 'culture as a complex of traits and styles' (181).

While there is much to value in this account, there are reasons for doubting that this group of knowledges functioned in quite so integrated a manner as Marchand suggests. It is not merely the markedly anti-historical orientation of German anthropology that is at issue here. There is also the further consequence to which this gives rise of the disconnection between natural history and human history, and the ruptural accounts of modernity that German anthropology fashioned on this basis. While this conforms to Latour's general characterisation of modernism as effecting a ruptural divide between the modern and its pre-history, exactly the opposite is true of the account of modernity proposed by the late-nineteenth-century Anglophone synthesis of the historical sciences. This depended on a fusion of different time perspectives into an integrated narrative in which the legacy of each period is carried over into the one that succeeds it, depositing the past as a constantly active force in the present. The archaeological structure of this distinctive form of historical reasoning is realised in typological displays in which each stage of development is imprinted with the legacy of that which preceded it. Each object is thus inherently archaeological in its organisation; it represents a distinctive moment in saving up the past and passing it on. This organisation of material culture both presupposed and worked to produce a self quite differently constituted from that which Latour imagines, a self organised in terms of a division between its archaic and modern components which, in the specific combination of restraining and progressive influences it effected, made possible a distinctive dialectic of self-development as an accumulative process. And this required, in turn, as an operative technology, that the museum should also function as an evolutionary accumulator.

4

The connective tissue of civilisation

The virtue of Nietzsche's concept of 'mnemotechnics', Nikolas Rose argues, is that, rather than seeing memory as 'something immediate, natural, a universal psychological capacity', it draws attention to the varied technical devices through which the past is 'burned' into the present 'as a warning, a comfort, a bargaining device, a weapon, or a wound' (Rose, 1998: 179). It is from this perspective that Didier Maleuvre (1999) claims a distinctive productivity for the art museum, viewing this as a technology of memory which, by rendering a number of different and disconnected pasts simultaneously present, involves them in an active and inescapably political process of re-memorisation.[1] He does so by reading the episode in Balzac's *The Wild Ass's Skin* [*La Peau de Chagrin*; 1st edn 1831] in which Raphaël visits 'the old curiosity shop' (Balzac, 1977: 33) as a critical commentary on the formative rationality of the modern museum that was under development, just across the river, at the Louvre. The art museum, on this interpretation, manifests the new, rootless historical consciousness of modernity. In place of 'the image of the past as a homogeneous continuum rolling into the present', it relentlessly prises objects away from their originating locales and assembles them together so that all pasts are synchronically aligned, assembled in the same place and time, producing a 'flash of remembrance in which all historical layers exist simultaneously' (Maleuvre, 1999: 278).

Yet there is also a proto-evolutionary logic at work in Balzac's commentary on the museum. While the collection initially strikes him as 'a chaotic medley of human and divine works' in which the 'beginnings of creation and the events of yesterday were paired off with grotesque good humour' (Balzac, 1997: 34), Raphaël's route through the galleries subjects this apparently random miscellany to a disciplinary ordering. His glance – subject, initially, to an archaeological and art-historical organisation – at first takes in the whole of the ancient world, and is led from there, through a series of stages (Moses and the Hebrews, imperial and Christian Rome, the medieval period, the dawn of Indian and Chinese civilisation) to culminate in the Renaissance. His gaze then becomes anthropological-cum-historical as, prompted by objects recalling past ways of life (of Flemish workers, Cherokee hunters and medieval châtelaines), he 'made all the formulas of existence his own' (38). But it is only in being subjected to a geological organisation that Raphaël's gaze is stretched beyond the cultural realm to encompass the immense reaches of time that had been newly installed in the museum – not at the Louvre but at the Muséum National d'Histoire Naturelle – as a result of Georges Cuvier's palaeontological reconstructions of extinct forms of life. As a consequence, 'the flash of remembrance in which all historical layers exist simultaneously' (Maleuvre, 1999: 278) is extended back beyond the time of human memory to

> catch a vista of the milliards of years and the millions of peoples which the feeble memory of man and an indestructible divine tradition have forgotten and whose ashes heaped on the surface of our globe, form the two feet of earth which furnish us with bread and flowers.
>
> (Balzac, 1997: 40–1)

This effect is duplicated by the master who, as the keeper of the collection, bears the impress of its organisation in his person to the degree that he has himself become a storehouse of all that it contains:

> Since my mind has inherited all the forces which I have not misused, this head of mine is still better furnished than my showrooms are. 'Here,' he said, tapping his forehead, 'here are the riches that matter. I spend beatific days letting my intelligence dwell on the past; I can summon to mind whole countries, vistas of beauty, views of the ocean, the faces that history has transfigured. . . . how could one prefer all the disasters of frustrated desires to the superb faculty of summoning the whole universe to the bar of one's mind?
>
> (Balzac, 1997: 53)

However, the organisation of memory that is evident here is, finally, only proto-evolutionary. Evoking a simultaneity of pasts within a stadial conception of time, the logic connecting the different layers of the past is one of succession and replacement rather than one of development and accumulation. The past that is summoned to the bar of the mind in evolutionary museums, by contrast, is both stratified and accumulating, comprising part of a mnemotechnics in which – just as important – the mind exhibits the same, archaeological characteristics. For it is in the symmetry that is evident between the organisation of the evolutionary collection and that of the person as storehouses in which the past accumulates that a distinctive practice of memory is organised and, in the literature of the period, connected to a distinctive set of concerns concerning the role of habit in social life and its implications for the practices of liberal government.

Accumulating pasts: habit, memory and self-government

Laura Otis provides a useful means of entry into these questions in her account of what she calls 'organic memory', a pervasive late-nineteenth-century meta-phorical construction of the relations between body and memory which 'placed the past *in* the individual, *in* the body, *in* the nervous system' (Otis, 1994: 3; original emphasis). In this conception, the past is viewed as a force that has deposited itself in the body, leaving a set of residues or traces there, so that the individual is a summation of the whole history that had preceded him or her. This conception was most coherently developed in those schools of evolutionary thought where Jean Baptiste Lamarck's law of the inheritance of acquired characteristics was viewed in conjunction with Ernst Haeckel's law that ontogeny recapitulates phylogeny. If the former provided a means whereby changes induced in the organism as a result of its adaptation to its changing environment could be transmitted to the next generation, the latter contended that all of the changes which had thus been stored in the body were recapitulated in the history of the single organism as it progresses from egg cell to full maturity. That said, these arguments had a much broader currency: Darwin's concept of pangenesis, for example, provided a toe-hold within Darwinism for an account of the trans-generational transmission of acquired characteristics that was to prove influential in many applications of Darwinism to the social and political fields.

It was as a result of conceptions of this kind that the new pasts that had been fabricated within the recently constructed horizons of prehistory were able to enter into the field of memory. No longer limited to what had been passed down through oral tradition, writing or other storage and retrieval systems, the reach of memory was stretched backwards in time to encompass the much deeper pasts that had been written into the body. This entailed that the body, too, was conceived in a new light as itself a storage and retrieval device in which the past was 'remembered', albeit that the memories coded into the body needed to be deciphered by the evolutionary scientist if this bodily mnemonics were to be translated into a practice of conscious recollection. Alternatively, this decipher-ment could be undertaken by the cultural anthropologist or the psychoanalyst for, as Otis shows, this conception of the body as a laminated entity was extended, metaphorically, to other fields of thought, with the result that the archaeological construction of the person as an entity comprised of successive layers took a number of different forms depending on how the constitution of those layers was construed – sometimes as corporeal, sometimes as cultural, sometimes as psychological, and sometimes as all three at once. It also provided a template, in anthropology, for an understanding of culture as itself a storage and retrieval system, and, in psychoanalysis, for a layered conception of the organisation of the psyche in which the mind of each individual bore the impress of the whole historical development of the species and, in some formulations, of pre-human evolution. By 1895, Otis argues, Miguel Unamuna's metaphor of a lake bottom for culture, describing a process through which layers of cultural development had been progressively sedimented one on top of the other, had acquired an almost universal currency, albeit that the mechanisms of transmission from one period of development to the next were sometimes conceived biologically, sometimes in terms of the cumulative momentum of tradition, and sometimes in terms of institutional mechanisms. For Freud, similarly, the memory traces left by the archaic heritage of biological evolution were a means of bridging the gap between individual and group psychology, enjoining the psychoanalyst to bring to the surface of conscious recollection both the heritage of ancestral impressions and the individual experience that had been added to this heritage.

This new conception of memory was closely associated with the new depth structure of vision associated with the development of the archaeological gaze of the historical sciences. Kate Flint throws useful light on this in her discussion of the ways in which the relationships between the past and present associated with such accounts of organic memory were expressed in terms of 'a vocabulary of surface and depth, of the hidden and revealed, of dark and of light' (Flint, 2000: 140). As we saw in chapter 2, this new depth structure for the organisation of vision derived from the practices of archaeology and geology which, in their concern to make the hidden visible, developed new principles of legibility as reading became a matter of deciphering the relationships between the successive layers of meaning which lie behind the visible surface of the present. As Flint notes, however, similar principles were applied to the social body in its new archaeological conception as a series of layers, of surfaces and depths, within which the past survived as an atavistic presence in the lower classes, resulting in a good deal of anxious 'archaeological pathologising' (162) in attempts to peel back the surface veneer of the urban fabric to penetrate to the hidden life of the primitive strata beneath.

It is, however, in the increasingly prevalent understanding of human memory as a palimpsest that these new ways of thinking and visualising the past and its relations to the present are most clearly brought together. Flint takes as her prompt here Freud's account, in *Civilisation and its Discontents*, of the preservation in each successive archaeological layer in the development of Rome of elements from the preceding layers. Freud interprets this as a metaphor for a view of mental life in which 'the primitive is . . . commonly preserved along-side of the transformed version which has arisen from it' and in which 'nothing which has once been formed can perish' (Freud, 1969: 5–6). However, this way of visualising the organisation of the mind depended on a revised understanding of the palimpsest that had been undertaken earlier in the century, principally, according to Josephine McDonagh, in the work of Thomas de Quincey. Conceived initially as 'a piece of vellum whose surface had been erased of inscription for re-use', it was only late-eighteenth-century developments in chemistry which, by enabling the recovery of former inscriptions, transformed the palimpsest from its earlier conception as – once scraped – a *tabula rasa*, into that of an archaeologically layered entity, capable of generating practices of reading in which 'ancient texts, formerly considered lost, were excavated from the forgotten depths of these manuscripts' (McDonagh, 1987: 210). McDonagh goes on to indicate how, under the influence of evolutionary thought, the imagery of the palimpsest was subsequently extended to provide a means of visualising the person as a storage system in which all that had gone before was retained for retrieval in the present:

> Just as contemporary scientific developments enabled former inscriptions to be recalled, thereby giving the palimpsest a history it had never before had, so too did contemporary evolutionary sciences give people a history, a past from which they had evolved as physiological, psychological and social beings. And the palimpsest offered a convenient way of figuring such a process, for as the surface is always wiped clean, successive generations might make new inscriptions which would always be retained and joined together by the retentive function of the palimpsest.
>
> (McDonagh, 1987: 212)

The relationship between this new imagery of the palimpsest and new under-standings of the person as an evolutionary storehouse is clear in the concept of 'stored virtue' that Walter Bagehot's proposes in *Physics and Politics* as a summary of his account of the means – partly moral and cultural, partly natural and biological – through which the skills and aptitudes acquired in one generation are carried through to the next, to be deposited there as a cumulative inheritance which, in turn, awaits further development and cultivation. The lynchpin of this account is Bagehot's concept of 'the connective tissue of civilisation', through which skills acquired through repetition and social training are imprinted on the nervous system and, thereby, transmuted into a physical inheritance that is transmitted – via an inherited nerve element – from one generation to the next. For this provides 'a physical cause of improvement from generation to generation . . . which enables each to begin with some improvement on the last' (Bagehot, 1873: 8). If, as Bagehot argues, the 'body of the accomplished man has thus become by training different from what it once was, and different from that of the rude man', this is because it has become 'charged with stored virtue' (6). Lodged in the body, this stored virtue is carried forward to the next generation, via a practice of bodily mnemonics, as an inheritance that is simultaneously biological, cultural and social.

In formulations of this kind – by no means unique to Bagehot – the person is installed in a new dialectic of remembering and forgetting, leading to a new assessment of the significance of character within the specular morality that had characterised classical liberalism. One consequence of this is that Smith's 'man within' comes to be redeployed, and refashioned, in the context of this archae-ological organisation of the person. The arguments of Stefan Collini (1979, 1991) are important here in showing how the tendency to place questions of character, and character development, in the new relations of time that had been constructed by the historical sciences facilitated the transition from classical *laissez-faire* liberalism to the greater stress on the cultural and moral role of the state that characterised the new liberalism. Whereas the stress on self-reliance promoted by the former had earlier been a reason for opposing state action of any kind, the historicisation of character – and, thereby, the transformation of the essential task from that of cultivating self-reliance to one of developing and enhancing the capacities of the self through time – became a reason for urging state action in the cultural and moral sphere in view of the obstacles that it was believed impeded the formation of a such a developmental relationship to the self.

The manner in which these obstacles were perceived had its roots in a distinctive set of anxieties concerning the role of habit in the development of character (Joyce, 2003: 117–19). Accorded a distinctive role in mediating between consciousness and unconsciousness, between desire and compunction, habit, a socially enforced form of learning via repetition, constituted a despotic mechanism at the heart of liberal programmes of ethical governance. It served, Mariana Valverde suggests, to cultivate a despotic relation to the self that reconciled two otherwise contra-dictory features of liberal governance: the stress on individual autonomy on the one hand, and, on the other, the average sensual man's lack of capacity for auton-omous self-government (Valverde, 1996: 361). This was, to recall my discussion of Mary Poovey's account in chapter 1, true of classical liberalism in its development of disciplinary forms of social regulation and panoptic techniques of surveillance for the urban working classes who were believed to lack the capacity for double-levelled personhood – the development of Smith's 'man within' – necessary for the mechanism of specular morality. Collini's central contention, however, is that the political concerns that were worked through in debates concerning the role of habit were significantly transformed in the context of the late nineteenth century's 'distinctive preoccupation with the shaping power of time, with the slow, sedimentary processes of development, be it of geological layers or of linguistic forms or of legal customs' (Collini, 1991: 97–8). For these were now posed as questions concerning the organisation of the relations between different levels of the person – between, in shorthand, the accumulated legacy of habit and the developmental momentum of the will – and the distribution of different articulations of these relations across different social groups and classes.

Bagehot's apprehension, for example, was that the accumulated inheritance of the past – or what he called 'the cake of custom' – would become so thick that any spur to innovation, and thereby any progressive social momentum, would be lost. This conjured up the prospect of, at best, social stasis and, at worst, degeneration – the dark side of organic memory in which the dialectic of remembering and forgetting ceased to exhibit an accumulating logic and, instead, went into reverse as individuals or societies came to resemble their ancestors more than their parents. This was not a new fear. In discussing it in his 1894 text *Evolution and Ethics*, Huxley draws attention to his own role in warning, as early as 1862, that any theory of evolution had to include the possibilities of 'indefinite persistence in the same condition' and 'retrogressive modification' alongside that of 'progressive development' (Paradis and Williams, 1989: 62). By the 1880s, however, degeneration had assumed an altogether more central significance in the crisis that it posed for classical liberalism and the role that varying formulations of the prospect of 'brutal reversion' played in distinguishing competing responses to that crisis. Edwin Ray Lankester's 1880 text *Degeneration: A Chapter in Darwinism* was centrally implicated in these debates. As the pre-eminent Darwinian zoologist of his generation, Lankester's conclusion that humankind was just as likely to degenerate as to progress served as an authoritative confirmation that the natural sciences could no longer be cited in support of those unidirectional accounts of progress that had emerged from Spencer's metaphysical individualism. The social and political crisis of the 1880s, with rising unemployment and seemingly irreversible urban decay generating the threat – and actuality – of social unrest, played an equally important role in heightening the issues at stake in the currency of degeneration.[2]

The net effect of these developments, Daniel Pick argues, was a new economic and political vocabulary which 'refused a notion of the abstract and autonomous person and focussed on the capital of physiology, racial investment, the resources and capacities of the nervous system, growth and sexual expenditure', a vocabulary in which the body 'could not be left to itself since it was a crucial racial patrimony' (Pick, 1989: 197). The politically crucial distinctions in this context came to centre on the relations between four issues: (i) scientific accounts of the body and its history; (ii) the bearing of these issues on questions of political obligation and ethics; (iii) the relative spheres of action of the state and individuals; and (iv) the means through which virtuous forms of social conduct might be accumulated and transmitted through time. In some formulations, the circuit breaker between, on the one hand, the fear of stagnation and, on the other, the need for a 'striving, self-reliant, adaptable behaviour . . . inherently tied to movement and progress, to a future which must be regarded as to some extent open-ended' was that of 'muscular liberalism' (Collini, 1991: 109). This consisted in the contention that state-aided reformations of character giving rise to a more progressive disposition of the self – organised in relations of tension between its archaic, customary components and an open-ended commitment to self-development through time – would act instinctively on future generations through a pseudo-Lamarckian mechanism of the inheritance of acquired characteristics. Yet it was the critique of this mechanism that provided the basis, in the 1890s and early years of the twentieth century, for the emergence of an understanding of the 'connective tissue of civilisation' (the phrase is Bagehot's) that would be cultural its constitution and functioning. Huxley's (1894) *Evolution and Ethics* is especially important here in view of its naturalistic premises and procedures, its advocacy of liberal principles of government over a variety of state-centred models of government, and the break it establishes with the pseudo-Lamarckian mechanisms of muscular liberalism in ways that prepared the ground for the emergence of a concept of social development whose dynamic mechanism was specifically cultural. This, in turn, provided the discursive co-ordinates for a conception of the museum as a storage vehicle which – depending on the detail of particular formulations – either displaced or complemented the bodily inheritance of habit by providing a cultural means of accumulating the lessons of 'pasts beyond memory' and bringing these to act developmentally on the social. However, it will be instructive, before discussing Huxley's formulations further, to look more closely at Bagehot's arguments in view of their influence on the social and political thought of not only Huxley but Pitt Rivers and Darwin too.[3]

Archaeologising the self and the social

My primary interest in Walter Bagehot's *Physics and Politics* (1873) is its construction of social development as a specific process, governed by its own distinctive laws rather than by those of natural selection, in which moral and cultural forces combine with natural ones to provide a progressive mechanism – but a contingent and fragile one – through which the accomplishments of one generation can be transmitted to the next. This mechanism is, in its essentials, an adaptation – via Herbert Spencer – of Lamarck's use-based account of the transmission of acquired characteristics to the acquisition and transmission of distinctive human or social skills. Just as, for Lamarck, 'the more frequent and steady use of any given organ gradually strengthens this organ, develops it, increases its size, and gives it a power proportional to the duration of this use'

(Lamarck, cited in Barthelemy-Maudaule, 1982: 75), so, for Bagehot, it is the frequent and steady use of skills acquired via the social mechanism of drill – the model, for Bagehot, for all forms of human learning – that allows those skills to become sedimented in the person. For the virtue that is acquired in this way to accumulate progressively, however, there must be a mechanism through which the skills that are acquired in one generation can be passed on to the next. Here, Bagehot conjures up an entirely speculative mechanism by hypothesising – as a moral complement to Spencer's notion that the effects of mental exercise could be inherited[4] – that the skills acquired by means of drill are deposited in the nervous system by means of a muscular mnemonics and are thence transmitted innately to the next generation as a set of acquired characteristics. It is thus, he argues, that 'the descendants of cultivated parents will have, by born nervous organisation, a greater aptitude for cultivation than the descendants of such as are not cultivated; and that this tendency augments, in some enhanced ratio, for many generations' (Bagehot, 1873: 8). The person, in this construction, thus emerges as a historical storehouse for the accumulation and transmission of automated propensities from one generation to the next, a way-station in a process of continuing advancement.

This is, however, Bagehot insists, a 'subtle materialism' (9) in which moral and natural factors alternate with one another in a developmental dialectic which, at times, 'takes place outside of the womb' (6) only to return to it through the 'transmitted nerve element'.[5] It is also a materialism in which moral factors are, ultimately, accorded the primary role. For at every stage in this accumulating dynamic, moral force – an action of will – is decisive as the necessary spur to the development of the new aptitudes that are to be stored and transmitted via the nervous system. The exercise of will always precedes the mechanisms of drill:

> it is the continual effort of the beginning that creates the hoarded energy of the end; it is the silent toil of the first generation that becomes the trans-mitted aptitude of the next. Here physical causes do not create the moral, but moral create the physical; here the beginning is by the higher energy, the conservation and propagation only by the lower.
>
> (Bagehot, 1873: 11)

It is here that Bagehot's account of social progress breaks with the analogical reasoning derived – via Spencer – from Lamarck's law of use.[6] In Lamarck's first law of transformism, the continual exercise of an organ can only enhance and strengthen that organ. It is disuse that is the problem: 'the constant failure to use such an organ imperceptibly weakens it, deteriorates it, progressively decreases its faculties and finally makes it disappear' (cited in Barthelemy-Maudaule, 1982: 75). In Bagehot's account, by contrast, perpetual use can give rise to difficulties. The continued exercise of faculties transmitted from generation to generation via 'the connective tissue of civilisation' can become a barrier to progress if, through endless repetition, those faculties get locked in on themselves. Societies that were once in motion either fossilise: his image for modern savages, following Lubbock, is that of frozen remnants of prehistoric ways of life, having no more connection with the real civilisation of the present than do 'fossils in the surrounding strata'

(Bagehot, 1873: 113). Or they may – like the hill tribes of India or the Andaman Islanders – have 'screwed themselves' (42) into odd, dreary and uncomfortable lives through the repetition of curious habits that have proved to be historical cul-de-sacs. Whichever the case, the central problem is the same: the factors that confer an evolutionary advantage on a people in the early stages of civilisation can become an impediment to progress at a later stage. Proposing a variant of Spencer's distinction between the militant and industrial phases of progress,[7] Bagehot argues that the societies that emerged victorious from the conditions of inter-tribal war that had characterised the early stages of human evolution were those that had developed a polity and were therefore governed by law. Having 'tamed themselves' so that they were able to act as a coherent and cohesive whole, societies based on law had a decidedly *unnatural* advantage over their undisciplined rivals in the early stages of evolution. But the force of habit this establishes could ossify to become a drag on progress:

> The great difficulty which history records is not that of the first step, but that of the second step. What is most evident is not the difficulty of getting a fixed law; not of cementing (as upon a former occasion I phrased it) a cake of custom, but of breaking the cake of custom; not of making the first preservative habit, but of breaking through it, and reaching something better.
> (Bagehot, 1873: 53)

This is the central problem of arrested civilisations. Progress depends in part on the tendency for descendants to be like their forebears; but it also depends on descendants breaking with past practices. The conditions that initially secure a progressive advantage for some societies can result in the authoritarian imposition of a despotism of habit that is inimical to the varied assertion of will and moral force that is the key to the next stage of progress. 'The customary discipline,' as Bagehot puts it, 'which could only be imposed on any early men by terrible sanctions, continued with those sanctions, and killed out of the whole society the propensities to variation which are the principle of progress' (57). In such circumstances, only the advent of another polity – that of democracy, defined as system of rule based on the principle of discussion – is able to break down 'the yoke of fixed custom' (161) and reintroduce a progressive momentum to social life. For 'the mere putting up of a subject to discussion, with the object of being guided by that discussion, is a clear admission that that subject is in no degree settled by established rule, and that men are free to choose in it' (161). It is thus the principle of variability, promoted by democracy, that gives societies at the higher levels of development an edge over their competitors. At the same time, however, Bagehot recommends that if the path of progress is to be steady and regular, the principle of variability needs to be regulated by that of 'animated moderation', in which the English excel, if the 'eager restlessness' and 'highly-strung nervous organisations' that are born in conditions of continuous struggle (he has America in mind) are to be avoided.

Of course, much of this is simply a reformulation of the colonial bias at the heart of nineteenth-century liberalism that has been tellingly explored in the literature on colonial governmentality. John Stuart Mill, in his essay on representative government, thus famously denied the subaltern peoples of India any capacity for self-government, or the right to take part in the institutions of representative democracy, owing to the extent to which the despotic characteristics of traditional systems of rule were said to have denied them the mental liberty and independence needed to support the specular morality (Smith's 'man within') required for liberal forms of self-government. They had not, in Bagehot's terms, arrived at the principle of discussion and so could only be led to this through the influence of British colonial rule which, in theory if not in practice, was to eventually undo the 'yoke of custom' associated with 'Asian despotism' (Helliwell and Hindess, 2002: 145–7).

Yet Bagehot brought a new aspect to these concerns by couching them in the language of the historical sciences and thus reworking the fault-lines of liberalism in terms of the historical layering of the person those sciences gave rise to. It is useful to recall here Bagehot's assertion that, having made man 'an antiquity', science was obliged 'to read, in the frame of each man the result of a whole history of all his life, of what he is and what makes him so, – of all his forefathers, of what they were and of what made them so' (Bagehot, 1873: 3). For maintaining 'the connective tissue of civilisation' and augmenting its progressive momentum required that the 'stored virtue' that had been deposited in the nervous-cum-historical constitution of modern man be distinguished from the regressive bad habits that had also been inherited from the past. This detritus of the past had to be scaled away within an internal dialectic of reform that would detach a modernising and progressive relation to the self from the prospectively degenerative momentum of a legacy that received its most potent symbol in the doctrine of survivals. According to this doctrine, the primitive, in being represented as a remnant of the prehistoric past within the present, also functioned as an archaic component in the make-up of the modern person. 'The civilised mind', as Tylor put it, 'still bears vestiges neither few nor slight, of a past condition from which savages represent the least and civilised man the greatest advance' (Tylor, 1871: 68–9). It is, however, precisely because the savage plays this role within the archaeological structure of modern man that that his own make-up must be denied this complexity.

Conrad recognised this clearly enough at that moment in *Heart of Darkness* when Marlow is forced to acknowledge his kinship with the 'wild and passionate uproar' of the savagery he encountered:

> Ugly. Yes, it was ugly enough; but if you were man enough you would admit to yourself that there was in you just the faintest trace of a response to the terrible frankness of that noise, a dim suspicion of there being a meaning in it which you – you so remote from the night of the first ages – could comprehend. And why not? The mind of man is capable of anything – because everything is in it, all the past as well as all the future.
>
> (Conrad, [1902] 1995: 63)

But it is only modern man whose constitution is archaeologically stratified in this way. The savages themselves were outside of time. As Marlow says of the native members of his crew: 'I don't think a single one of them had any clear idea of time, as we at the end of countless ages have. They still belonged to the beginnings of time – had no inherited experience to teach them, as it were' (69).

The distinction is crucial: the denial of an archaeological constitution to the savage or primitive is essential to the role it plays in the archaeological layering of the modern self by providing, in the form of an interiorised Other, a set of co-ordinates through which the self is able to act on itself so as to mobilise itself, developmentally, in progressive relations of time.[8] Gilles Deleuze's account of the functioning of 'the fold' in Foucault's account of the structure of the self will help to make my point. Deleuze's concern is with the role played by doubling – for Foucault, a process through which an outside is interiorised in the constitution of the person – in forming 'an inside which is merely the fold of the outside' (Deleuze, 1999: 97). As a result of this folding operation, the self is formed through its relation to a non-self or other that has been folded into the self as an immanent presence. This outside that is immanent within the self creates an interior space that allows an action of the self on self to take place, but always within an architecture of the self in which the self–self relation is mediated by relations of self and other. In this way, relations of power that structure the organisation of the social are translated into a principle of internal regulation in which the mastery of others is doubled – echoed and rehearsed – in a mastery of the self.

The text Deleuze has in mind here is Foucault's discussion, in *The Use of Pleasure*, of 'the "virile" character of moderation' in the sexual ethics of the freeman of classical Greece:

> In this ethics of men made for men, the development of the self as an ethical subject consisted in setting up a structure of virility that related oneself to oneself. It was by being a man with respect to oneself that one would be able to control and master the manly activity that one directed towards others in sexual practice. What one must aim for in the agonistic contest with oneself and in the struggle to control the desires was the point where the relationship with oneself would become isomorphic with the relationship of domination, hierarchy, and authority that one expected, as a man, to establish over his inferiors.
>
> (Foucault, 1985: 83)

If, as Foucault concluded, 'moderation was man's virtue' (83), this did not mean that women could not, or were not expected, to be moderate. Rather, it meant that this was a condition which they could realise only imperfectly and through subordination to their husbands. Only men could initiate *enkrateia* – the practices of self-mastery – and only men could fully achieve it. If the structure of this practice was thus essentially masculine, this entailed, Foucault argued, that its opposite – immoderation – represented a form of passivity that was viewed as essentially feminine, a self lacking the fold of an internally doubled exterior that could make the self the site of an unremitting work on the self.

We can see here readily enough the scope for analogy in understanding the role played by representations of the primitive or savage as an archaic layer within the archaeological make-up of modern man. Clearly colonial in its structure in providing for the mastery of a level within the self of the coloniser that was connected to the exercise of mastery over the colonised, it is equally clear that, for this to be so, the colonised must function as the essential antithesis of this structure. The self of the colonised, that is, must be flat, lacking in historical depth and complexity and, thereby, not affording the inner space in which a progressive dynamic might emerge from the work of self on self, in order to serve as the interiorised other through which the archaeological fold that constitutes the inner temporal structure of modern man is organised.

That said, the structure of this fold and its operation can only be properly understood if account is also taken of the ways in which, in operating across racialised colonial relationships, it was simultaneously articulated to relations of class and gender. Ann Stoler's (1995) criticisms of Foucault are helpful here. In reviewing Foucault's account of the transition from the 'symbolics of blood' governing the aristocratic body to the formation of a bourgeois class body based on the principles of 'health, hygiene, descent, and race' (Foucault, 1978), Stoler takes issue with his tendency to see the discourses of sexuality implicated in the formation of bourgeois practices of the self playing this role independently of relations of race. 'Did any of these figures', she asks of the masturbating child, the 'hysterical woman', the Malthusian couple, and the perverse adult, 'exist as objects of knowledge and discourse in the nineteenth century without a racially erotic counterpoint, without reference to the libidinal energies of the savage, the primitive, the colonised – reference points of difference, critique, and desire?' (Stoler, 1995: 6–7). In concluding that they did not, she urges the need to take a *'circuitous imperial'* route' (7) in tracing the emergence of the bourgeois body and self in order to understand how, in both colonial and metropolitan contexts, 'bourgeois bodies were constituted as racially and relationally coded from the outset' (53).

The metaphorical transposition of the languages of race and class – in comparisons of the denizens of 'darkest England' with those of 'darkest Africa' which allowed the working classes to be viewed as 'a race apart' – played a crucial connective role here. 'It captured in one sustained image', Stoler says, 'internal threats to the health and well-being of a social body where those deemed a threat lacked an ethics of "how to live" and thus the ability to govern themselves' (127). But what is most crucial here is that this incapacity is accounted for by denying the working classes, just as much as savages and women, that archaeological organisation of the self that allowed it to be viewed as a part of a cumulative, trans-generational developmental project. The forms of mastery of the self pro-duced by the archaeological constitution of modern man thus depended on, and supplied the conditions for, mastery over a set of interconnected classed, racialised and gendered others. These, in turn, provided the conditions for an archaeological construction of the social whose depths, Stoler suggests, were polyvalent:

> the sexual model of the promiscuous working-class woman in nineteenth-century, industrialising England construed her as a 'primitive relic of an earlier evolutionary period,' . . . who stood in contrast to 'the moral model of . . . middle-class sexual restraint and civility'.
>
> (Stoler, 1995: 128)[9]

Bagehot's conception of the political community rests on similar principles. It, too, is archaeologically stratified. 'Great communities', he argued, 'are like great mountains – they have in them the primary, secondary and tertiary strata of human progress; the characteristics of the lower regions resemble the life of old times rather than the present life of the higher regions' (Bagehot, 1963: 63). And late-nineteenth-century Britain was no exception. 'We have', as he put it, 'in a great community like England crowds of people scarcely more civilised than the majority of two thousand years ago; we have others, even more numerous, such as the best people were a thousand years ago' (62–3). This archaeological stratification of the political community informed Bagehot's understanding of democracy. The fact that the vast majority of the population were backward and so still governed by the 'cake of custom' entailed a limited suffrage: the conduct of government, Bagehot argued, should be limited to the 'educated ten thousand' who had reached the level of the 'age of discussion'.

Here, too, Bagehot's formulations are a reworking of earlier concerns as his rationale for limiting the suffrage both draws on, and redefines, the boundary lines that the tradition of civic humanism had earlier proposed in its definition of the political community.[10] These distinguished those whose station in life and economic independence qualified them to participate in public discussion of matters of civic importance because they could do so disinterestedly from those who, by dint of the menial nature of their occupation and their inability to rise above the level of self-interest, were excluded from such discussions. The aesthetic theories of Sir Joshua Reynolds thus drew a rigid distinction between, on the one hand, the liberal public, comprised essentially of landed and propertied men, and, on the other hand, women and those whom Reynolds called 'mechanics': members of the artisanal classes involved in manual or merely mechanical occupations. Only members of the liberal public, Reynolds argued, could become members of the republic of taste for only they possessed those capacities for abstract and disinterested reasoning required to distil from the particular details of the work of art those abstract and general moral qualities which would be of service in forming civic virtue. Women were denied this capacity for abstract thought, and they were denied it absolutely on the basis of their sex. Mechanics were also judged to lack this ability albeit that, in their case, this incapacity was viewed as a contingent one arising from the fact that the pursuit of mechanical occupations did not require the exercise of generalising intellectual abilities.

While, then, this distinction is echoed in the limitation Bagehot places on the political community, there is the important difference that, for Bagehot, the boundary line is drawn not in terms of a distinction of occupation but in terms of the different relations of different social strata to the sedimented remains of the past that had been deposited in the present. The 'connective tissue of civilisation' was, in effect, a split one, severed along the fault-line separating those still frozen in fossilised ways of life and the representatives of progress and innovation in the present. This was true for Pitt Rivers too, who also re-worked the concerns of civic humanism in the language of the historical sciences.[11] This was clear in his reference to 'the more intelligent portion of the working classes', who constituted the key target of his ambition to so arrange museum exhibits 'in which the visitors may be able to instruct themselves' so that 'those who run may read' (Pitt Rivers, 1891: 115). Biblical in origin – it has its roots in Habakkuk when the Lord, in appearing before a prophet in a vision, commanded him to 'Write the vision, and make it plain upon tables, that he may run that readeth it' (or, in the new revised standard version, 'Write the vision, make it plain on tablets, so that a runner may read it') – this reference to 'those who run' had functioned, within the discourse of civic humanism, as a coded reference for those with menial and mechanical occupations. We find it, for example, in the reference made by John Barry – a mid-century painter – who, while taking issue with Reynolds's contention that access to the arts should be restricted to the propertied and landed classes, also urged that the wish to make art more accessible should not go so far that art should be 'so brought down to the understanding of the vulgar, that they who run may read' (cited in Barrell, 1986: 188). To avoid this, Barry advocated that the public exhibition of art should be accompanied by textual supplements in which the civic value of the art displayed might be explained to those, who while they might have the eyes to see, would still be culturally blind to art's lessons.

For Pitt Rivers, by contrast, the very purpose of his ethnological displays was that their lessons should be accessible to 'those who run' *without* the aid of textual supplements. Extolling the object-centred rhetoric of the historical sciences, he thus stresses that the 'importance of the object lessons that museums are capable of teaching' consists precisely in their capacity to impress themselves on those who 'though they have but little book learning, are extremely quick in appreciating all mechanical matters, more so even than highly educated men, because they are trained up to them' (Pitt Rivers, 1891: 116). If the distinction here between those adept in mechanical matters and educated men recalls the distinctions proposed by civic humanism, it has also to be read, in the broader context of Pitt Rivers's thought, in the light of his distinction between the intellectual and automaton minds. For the relationships between these is, much as in Bagehot's concept of stored virtue, a historical one in which what is at first learned with difficulty and with the full conscious attention of the intellectual mind becomes, through constant repetition, a matter of habit, so that it can, eventually, be passed on wholly to the automaton mind, capable only of acting intuitively, leaving the intellectual mind – capable of reasoning on unfamiliar occurrences – to pass on to new things. Given that, for Pitt Rivers, both types of reason are transmitted across generations hereditarily, what is thus a historical process within the person also becomes a way of distinguishing groups within the population in accordance with the different ratios of the automaton to the intellectual minds that is their inheritance. How, he asks, can we account for innate intellectual differences 'unless by supposing it to be proportioned to the length of time during which, or the degree of intensity with which, the ancestors of the individuals have had their minds occupied in the particular branch of culture for which that capacity is shown?' (Pitt Rivers, 1875: 298). It is by means of this supposition that Reynolds's distinction between the mechanic and the landed gentry is reworked into a historical distinction within the social body between, on the one hand, those whose ancestors' mechanical occupations meant that they could pass on only a thin accumulation of historically embodied automaton skills and, on the other, those whose ancestors' more intellectual occupations means that they were able to pass on a more thickly organised cultural inheritance.

This is, of course, as effective a way of confusing the relationships between social position and cultural competence as is evident in those discourses of aesthetics, discussed by Pierre Bourdieu (1984), in which differentiated aesthetic competences arising from class differences are held to legitimate those differences by being interpreted, instead, as outcomes of a charismatic selection. Yet the conclusions that followed from this were not simply committed to the maintenance of the status quo in the sense of preserving intact the existing distinctions between those with thickly, and those with thinly, organised cultural inheritances. On the contrary, the central issue for post-Darwinian liberalism was how, and how far, to extend the reach of the 'connective tissue of civilisation' by dispersing the ability to form and develop a self that was poised in a restless tension between its archaic and progressive components. It was in the context of these concerns that the new liberalism developed a distinctive cultural armature which supported limited forms of state intervention in the cultural sphere in order to avoid the alternative solution – that of forcibly detaching the present from the archaeological remnants of past stages of evolution – that was represented by statist programmes of eugenics. Huxley's *Evolution and Ethics* was especially important in this respect in view of its advocacy of liberal principles of government over a variety of state-centred models of government, and for breaking with the pseudo-Lamarckian mechanisms of muscular liberalism in ways that, by historicising Smith's 'man within', prepared the ground for the emergence of a concept of social development whose dynamics were specifically cultural.

Evolution, culture and liberal government

At the beginning of *Heart of Darkness*, while he is still in London, Marlow, prompted by the onset of dusk, remarks that this, too, 'has been one of the dark places of the earth' (Conrad, [1902] 1995: 18). He was thinking, he goes on, 'of the very old times, when the Romans first came here' – when, that is, England was at 'the very end of the world' where some 'decent young citizen in a toga', out on his luck, would land 'in a swamp, march through the woods, and in some inland post feel the savagery, the utter savagery, had closed round him – all that mysterious life of the wilderness that stirs in the forest, in the jungles, in the hearts of wild men' (18–20). This imaginative reversal of metropolitan–periphery relations in which the present-day metropolis (London) is figured as a periphery in relation to another imperium (Rome) was a common trope of imperialist discourse. Conrad's use is anticipated by Huxley. 'It may be safely assumed', he writes in the prolegomena to *Evolution and Ethics*, 'that, two thousand years ago, before Caesar set foot in southern Britain, the whole country-side visible from the windows of the room in which I write, was in what is called "the state of nature"' (Huxley, 1894: 59). This was not, to be sure, a timeless nature. For Huxley the state of nature at any particular time 'is a temporary phase of a process of incessant change, which has been going on for innumerable ages' (63). Such change, however, is the result of the timeless laws governing what Huxley calls the 'cosmic process'. These comprise 'the struggle for existence, the competition of each with all, the result of which is the selection, that is to say, the survival of those forms which, on the whole, are best adapted to the conditions which at any period obtain' (62). There are few surprises here. The next step Huxley takes is, however, an unexpected one. For he goes on to argue that the war of all against all, while never suspended, is overriden by the development of human society and culture which, in place of the cosmic process, installs the 'ethical process' as a cultural mechanism of self-regulation that places a check on the sway of the struggle for existence.

Huxley develops this argument by means of two comparisons – with gardening and colonisation – which, in being superimposed on each other, bring together the meanings of 'to cultivate' and 'to inhabit' that were originally present in the Latin root *colore* from which both *culture* and *colony* derive (Williams, 1976). The practice of gardening is thus one that aims to modify, adapt, regulate and, in some circumstances, suspend the operation of the laws of nature in the pursuit of humanly chosen objectives: clearing a space for some plants and cultivating them in preference to their natural competitors because they are wanted or useful. In this way, the garden embodies a 'state of art' that is not only hostile but antithetic to the state of nature: if the latter is defined by 'the intense and unceasing competition of the struggle for existence', the former aspires to 'the elimination of that struggle, by the removal of the conditions which give rise to it' (Huxley, 1894: 71). Huxley then passes quickly to superimpose a colonial frame of reference on this gardening analogy by equating the state of nature not with the past – with pre-Roman Britain – but with present-day colonial territory. 'Suppose', he hypothesises, 'a shipload of English colonists sent to form a settlement, in such a country as Tasmania was in the middle of the last century' (74). What will they do when, on landing, they find themselves in the midst of a state of nature unmarked by any distinctive history of human use and adaptation? In this situation, Huxley argues, the colonist does and must act in conformity with the laws regulating the struggle for existence:

> They clear away the native vegetation, extirpate or drive out the animal population, so far as may be necessary, and take measures to defend themselves from the re-immigration of either. In their place, they introduce English grain and fruit trees; English dogs, sheep, cattle, horses; and English men; in fact, they set up a new Flora and Fauna and a new variety of mankind, within the old state of nature. Their farms and pastures represent a garden on a great scale, and themselves the gardeners who have to keep it up, in watchful antagonism to the old *regime*.

Should this watchful antagonism lapse, the consequences are clear:

> if they are slothful, stupid, and careless; or if they waste their energies in contests with one another, the chances are that the old state of nature will have the best of it. The native savage will destroy the immigrant civilised man; of the English animals and plants some will be extirpated by their indigenous rivals, others will pass into the feral state and themselves become components of the state of nature.
>
> (Huxley, 1894: 74, 75)

The colonial frontier thus separates a realm bound by distinctively human norms of sociality from a state of nature where the war-of-all-against-all still obtains, while also marking a space across which the coloniser can carry the principles of war-against-all to the colonised. The 'ethical process' that Huxley speaks of as emerging from 'the organised and personified sympathy we call conscience' (88) thus has an exclusionary mechanism at its heart. It had much in common, in this respect, with the formulations of many of Huxley's contemporaries, who shared his concern with the implications of evolutionary science for the principles of ethical conduct.[12] Where Huxley's position is distinctive, however, is in the account he offers of the emergence of conscience and its role in moral development as a historical process resting on naturalistic premises. His target here was, as he saw it, the fabulous fictions of social contract theory in their claim that the state was founded on a mythical act of renunciation on the part of freely contracting individuals.[13] Following Hume and Darwin, Huxley posits instead an intuitive source for ethical conduct in an innate capacity for sympathy with the pains and pleasures of fellow humans. Seeing in this the embryo for the emergence of conscience – in which conduct is regulated through techniques of internal self-monitoring guided by internalised social norms – Huxley founds this capacity not in the fear of the law, as in Hobbesian accounts, but in the force of public opinion and the support it lends, just as naturalistically, to acts calculated to minimise pain and maximise pleasure. He then blends this with late-nineteenth-century faculty psychology to provide a physiological basis for the development of ethical behaviour, the emergence of a social self within the individual, that was fuelled by an accumulation of experiences transmitted by the nervous system. The result, as James Paradis puts it, was 'a formidable naturalistic framework for the emergence of human ethical behaviour' (Paradis, 1989: 16) that served also to account for the emergence of a polity that depended not on the conjectural histories of social contract theory but on reasoning backwards from causes still observable in the present. Smith's 'man within' thus emerged as the historical product of a distinctive 'dialectic of morals' in which an 'artificial personality . . . is built up alongside the natural personality' to act as 'the watchman of society, charged to restrain the anti-social tendencies of the natural man within the limits required by social welfare' (Huxley, 1894: 88).

The ethical process that was established on these premises was inscribed within a systematic dualism, in the sense that it placed ethical behaviour at the centre of a 'cultural dynamic that both depended upon physical and biological circumstances and sought to break free of them' (Paradis, 1989: 8). This provided the basis for Huxley's critique of the statist conceptions of, variously, Comtism, scientific and reform eugenics, socialism and the idealism of General William Booth's Salvation Army – little more than a disguised form of socialism so far as Huxley was concerned.[14] It is, moreover, by counterposing his own reasoning to that which founds these statist projects, that he develops his own understanding of the proper tasks of liberal government. These limit the role of the state to that of providing the conditions in which – in every individual and in society – the ethical process might regulate, rather than aspire to triumph over, the cosmic process in order to bring about the 'progressive modification of civilisation' (Huxley, 1894: 95). In his extended discussion of the colonisation of Tasmania,

Huxley asks his reader to imagine that the process of colonisation had been super-intended by 'some administrative authority, as far superior in power and intelligence to men, as men are to their cattle' (75). Might not, he asks, such an administrator be tempted, once the early stages of the struggle with nature have been completed, to

> look to the establishment of an earthly paradise, a true garden of Eden . . . within which the cosmic process, the coarse struggle for existence of the state of nature, should be abolished; in which that state should be replaced by a state of art; where every plant and every lower animal should be adapted to human wants, and would perish if human supervision and protection were withdrawn; where men themselves should have been selected, with a view to their efficiency as organs for the performance of the functions of a perfected society. And this ideal polity would have been brought about, not by gradually adjusting the men to the conditions around them, but by creating artificial conditions for them; not by allowing the free play of the struggle for existence, but by excluding that struggle; and by substituting selection directed towards the administrator's ideal for the selection it exercises.
>
> (Huxley, 1894: 78)

The ultimate weakness of this 'pigeon fancier's polity' (81), Huxley argues, consists in its combination of scientific expertise with administrative despotism which, in aiming to install the state of art over that of nature by fiat, fails to attend to the conditions that are necessary to initiate and superintend an ethical process that will involve men themselves in their self-government. Even putting aside the practical difficulty of settling upon an omniscient administrator who would be able to distinguish correctly the fit from the unfit, this 'logical ideal of evolutionary regimentation' (81) is doomed to fail because it takes no account of the natural-istic roots of the ethical process in the human capacity for sympathy. Direct selection 'after the fashion of the horticulturist and the breeder' (94) neither has nor can play a significant role in the evolution of society as the application of such principles could only weaken the ties of sympathy that hold society together. The gardening analogy, Huxley thus contends, is correctly interpreted when it attends to the difficulties of enlisting men as gardeners of themselves in a project of ethical self-cultivation that is superintended by the state in the care it takes to supply the conditions that are favourable to its exercise:

> In the modern world, the gardening of men by themselves is practically restricted to the performance, not of selection, but of that other function of the gardener, the creation of conditions more favourable than those of the state of nature; to the end of facilitating the free expansion of the innate faculties of the citizen, so far as it is consistent with the general good.
>
> (Huxley, 1894: 101)

This is as concise a summary of new liberalism's legitimation of state action in the cultural and moral sphere as any in the literature. Its distinctiveness consists in the fact that the stress it places on the need to involve men actively in governing themselves does not involve any departure from the naturalistic premises of scientific method. Far from it: it is the development of conscience, naturally derived from the human capacity for sympathy, that establishes a space within the constitution of the person within which the activity of self-government can be installed. This space is lodged within the archaeological structure of the person, albeit that, in Huxley's formulations, this structure takes a distinctive form which transfers its accumulative aspects from the individual to society. The reasons for this have to do with Huxley's rejection of the concept of use inheritance, thereby ruling out the possibility that the person might be composed of so many layers of accumulated experience acquired via the mechanisms of physical inheritance. But the Huxleyan self is still a stratified one, governed by a division between two layers in which 'the innate aggressive impulses of the ancestor' are moderated by 'the acquired social restraint of the cultured being' (Paradis, 1989: 20). The deep time of the prehistoric past thus survives in the inner constitution of the modern person as the product of 'millions of years of severe training' (Huxley, 1894: 143) in direct confrontation with the socially produced 'man within', rather than, as in Bagehot's formulations, being overlaid by the successive accretions of generations of civilisation deposited in the nervous system by the mechanisms of use inheritance.

There is, then, no natural storage mechanism capable of carrying forward the virtue learned by one generation to the next and so no ongoing, dynamic and progressive modification of the natural substratum of human behaviour such as we find in Bagehot. For Huxley, primitive man, forged in the struggle for existence, reappears, in full brutish propensity, as a component in the make-up of each individual and each generation. It is precisely because this is so that Huxley, by transferring this storage mechanism from the inner constitution of each individual to the social environment, provides for a distinctive dialectic of culture and society in which it is the trans-generational accumulation of means on acting on, curbing and regulating natural instincts that provides for the 'progressive modification of civilisation' rather than an endless repetition of the same inner drama. Every 'child born into the world will still bring with him [*sic*] the instinct of unlimited self-assertion', but the circumstances in which the lessons of self-restraint and renunciation have to be mastered mean that 'man, as a "political animal," is susceptible of a vast amount of improvement, by education, by instruction, and by the application of his intelligence to the adaptation of the conditions of life to his higher needs' (102). The consequences of this relocation of the storage mechanism through which acquired virtue is transmitted through time is nicely summarised by Lloyd Morgan, formerly a close associate of Huxley's, in his 1896 text *Habit and Instinct*:

> There must be increment somewhere, otherwise evolution is impossible. In social evolution on this view, the increment is by storage in the social environment to which each new generation adapts itself, with no increased native power of adaptation. In the written record, in social traditions, in the manifold inventions which make scientific and industrial progress possible, in the products of art, and the recorded examples of noble lives, we have an environment which is at the same time the product of mental evolution, and affords the conditions of the development of each individual mind to-day.
> (Morgan, cited in Paradis, 1989: 54)

103

Huxley's accomplishment in this regard was to deploy humanistic understandings of culture and ethics within an archaeological conception of the social, thereby imbuing it with an independent developmental mechanism through which past advances, accumulated and stored in a variety of institutional and technological forms, provided the means, essentially cultural, for acting on the social so as to contribute to its ongoing cumulative development and to curb the disturbing effects of atavistic tendencies wherever these might manifest themselves. The influence of these formulations on the subsequent development of new liberalism has been well documented. This is especially true of L. T. Hobhouse – its most influential codifier – who included Huxley among his intellectual mentors and drew on his work in proposing a distinctive object for sociology in his construction of the social as an entity governed by its own laws of development (Abrams, 1968: 96). Huxley's influence is evident, for example, in the importance Hobhouse accorded the role of morals in evolution, seeing these as overriding the laws of nature once the stage of human self-consciousness had been reached.

The aspect of Huxley's understanding of the ethical process in which I am most interested, however, consists in the role it accords culture within the architecture of the self. For it is only by putting the accumulated results of culture into play within the self, and thereby equipping it in each generation with the means of advancing rapidly to the highest levels of civilisation, that social development – as a process with an ongoing and incremental logic – is made possible. As is the case with aesthetic conceptions of self-govenment, these formulations stress the place that culture must play in mediating the relations between the separate components of a divided self. The difference, however, is that the Huxleyan self is divided by the temporal co-ordinates constituted by the historical sciences rather than by the a-temporal structure of the aesthetic relations that mark the division between, for example, Arnold's better and lesser selves, or their opposing principles of Hebraism and Hellenism. Both conceptions, it is true, provide a justification for state action in the cultural sphere as the means by which the struggle that takes place within the self might be reconciled in favour of its civilised, and civilising, components. Nonetheless, the co-ordinates within which this takes place are differently organised, and they give rise to different social and political consequences just as they differ with regard to the form of culture's action on the social that they auspice.[15]

In the dialectic of the self that aesthetic conceptions of self-governance organise, the incomplete self – aspiring to the completeness represented by the work of art – undertakes a work of progressive introspection, revision and correction that aspires to a condition in which the torsions that have wracked the self are harmoniously reconciled.[16] The same mechanism, translated to society, results in a dialectic that traces the emergence – through alienation – of a historical splitting within the subject that is only overcome when the subject is restored to its lost fullness. Yet it is not to works of aesthetic culture that Huxley looks in *Evolution and Ethics* any more than the end to which he aspires is for culture to so mediate the relations between conscience and instinct as to produce a self that is, finally, at rest, reconciled to itself. Rather, the argument of *Evolution and Ethics*, as James Paradis puts it, 'gave a social and intellectual legitimacy to science, locating the man of science within the texture of history and furnishing him with an essential role in contemporary culture' (Paradis, 1989: 17). It did so by tracing the ancient roots of the schism that characterises the make-up of the modern person, seeing in this a mechanism for an endless, restless mobility which, if properly regulated, could result in a continuous process of social development whose superintendence required the diagnoses of the man of science.

At the same time, the authority of the man of science is, in these formulations, founded on a new basis owing to the departure that they involve from earlier attempts to derive an ethics directly from the laws of nature.[17] This is clear enough in the text. Huxley is explicit in his criticisms of attempts – notably Spencer's – to base an ethics on the law of the survival of the fittest. Similarly, in rebutting the intelligibility of regarding ethics as 'applied Natural History' (Huxley, 1894: 132), he took issue with the preceding tradition of natural history – as well as the natural theology of William Paley – which, for over a century, had treated the laws of nature as the ultimate basis for human ethics. In accepting the existence of a human and civic time that had distinguished itself from the state of nature through the operation of human sympathy and conscience, Huxley disqualified nature from its earlier role in serving as a template for human conduct. The laws governing nature provided no guide for the behaviour of men in society. The authority of the man of science, therefore, derives not from knowing the laws of nature and applying these directly, as models to be emulated, but from regulating the relations between the cultural, social and natural worlds in the light of his knowledge of the reach of nature's laws and their limits, of knowing where and when their force cannot be denied, and where and when different considerations can be applied.

Yet there is still, in this understanding, a legacy of the earlier position. For in his support for the view that 'nature makes no jumps', Huxley still claimed to be able to act as nature's ventriloquist, applying its laws directly as templates for human conduct. 'The theory of evolution', he writes at one point, 'encourages no millennial anticipations' (143). Nor, one might add, did it portend any impending catastrophes: the long-term prospect of degeneration would be the product of mechanisms just as smooth, gradual and regular in their functioning as those governing the laws of nature and, by extension, those of society where the 'gradual strengthening of the social bond' (93) through the ethical process is a long, slow and cumulative affair. This view – that 'nature makes no jumps' – had had a long and contested history in which it had been variably connected to conservative, radical and reformist political tendencies in its application to both the natural and social orders, and the relations between them.[18] In the period from the 1850s, however, when catastrophist conceptions were largely defeated in both natural history and geology,[19] this 'law' – when put through the Darwinian mill of natural selection – had emerged as the coda for Darwinian liberalism in the implication that natural law also dictated that social progress could only be, and must therefore aspire to be, slow and cumulative.

The attraction of this view – aptly summarised in Darwin's pithy 'evolution baffles revolution' (Desmond and Moore, 1992: 294) – is self-evident, especially in the social agitation of the 1880s and 1890s.[20] It gave an embattled liberalism a means of engaging with the increasing influence of socialist ideologies – and with evident success in view of the more or less total commitment of British schools of socialist thought to this premise of evolutionary thought from the 1890s well into the twentieth century – while at the same time providing a means of rebutting the socially static and conservative implications of Owen's theory of archetypes. It is true that, in some interpretations, it is only the conservative, restraining effects of this law that are stressed, leading to the assessment that the post-Darwinian synthesis of the historical sciences functioned solely as a conservative bulwark against the rising tide of socialism.[21] This is, however, a misleadingly one-sided reading of the law that 'nature makes no jumps' which, in its late-nineteenth-century interpretation, has always to be read in conjunction with the unstated, but implied, rider: 'but it does progress'. The whole ethos of the new liberalism and its justification for state action in the cultural sphere can only be understood in the light of this dual orientation which, just as it required that the working man be weaned from the influence of ideologists who fuelled the expectation that his lot might be suddenly and dramatically improved through revolution, also required that progress be stimulated. This, in turn, required that the inner constitution of the modern person be mapped out in terms of a set of historical co-ordinates that could provide the means of undertaking the historical work on the self that such a project required; organising a 'regulated restlessness' within the person of a kind calculated to bring about ordered, gradual and progressive social development.

Evolutionary accumulators

It is not difficult to see why, as the cultural storage mechanism *par excellence*, the museum should have figured so prominently in Huxley's own educational strategies and those of new liberalism more generally. In accumulating all past times within itself, the evolutionary museum – by providing a summation of previous development (natural, cultural, scientific and technological), pointing a way forward and providing an instructional programme that would contribute to the realisation of this dynamic – functioned as a historical technology for operating on the present. It did so by activating the historical tension within the make-up of the modern person, giving this a progressive but gradualist momentum. This was clear enough in the programme proposed for the ethnological museum which, by means of the typological method, was to function as an evolutionary accumulator, storing – by means of their survivals – a record of each painstaking step in the processes of cultural and technological evolution, and thus providing a template for future social development as an equally painstaking and gradual process. And clear enough, too, in Pitt Rivers's own advocacy of the virtues of his method which, owing to its ability to 'impress the mind with the slow growth and stability of human institutions and industries, and their dependence upon antiquity' (cited in Chapman, 1981: 515), would contribute to check revolutionary ideas. But then Pitt Rivers goes on to say that this conservative principle, while discouraging attempts 'to break directly with the past'

(515), is necessary for the present level of civilisation to be maintained *and* developed. Far from being, in Anne McClintock's terms, a 'fetish house of the archaic' (McClintock, 1995: 40), the museum accumulates the past to both retain it and initiate a movement beyond it. Sir Arthur Keith – who had claimed Pitt Rivers as the patron saint of museum administrators – clearly recognised this in his description of the Wellcome Historical Medical Museum, where typological displays of the early history of medicine recorded a past that was to be expunged:[22]

> It is possible, as you walk through the Hall of Primitive Medicine and your eye catches again the weird and uncouth equipments of native witch-doctors which cover its walls and fill its cases, that you will view these exhibits as mere flotsam and jetsam from the Dead Sea of Medicine – one which enlightened England has long since swept away. I should like to think this is so, but when I see, as I sometimes do, mascots on the motor cars of the wealthy, charms and amulets treasured by many people – both rich and poor – ignorant and educated; when I see, as I occasionally do, the quack preferred to the man who has given his life to the study of rational Medicine; and when I see learned men call in spirits to explain unusual physical phenomena; then I am not quite so certain that this part of Mr. Wellcome's Museum does represent altogether a past stage of things. In all of us there still remains more than a trace of the primitive man.
>
> (*Wellcome Historical Museum Handbook*, 1927: 107)

It is, however, in the connection that Patrick Geddes proposed between the historical sciences, museums, education, sociology and civics that the accumulative aspect of the museum was most explicitly foregrounded. Beginning his career in Huxley's laboratory (Abrams, 1968: 96), Geddes was later closely associated with Frances Galton and L. T. Hobhouse in the Sociological Society before becoming closely involved with the Chicago school of urban sociology (Mercer, 1997). Throughout his work – an unusually incoherent if fertile mix of social evolutionary conceptions, eugenics, new liberalism, statistics, sociology, urban planning and civics – he retained a strong interest in museums as both a site and metaphor for his activities. He took an active part in the programme of public lectures offered by the Horniman Museum when it was brought under the administration of London County Council. In 1905, for example, he offered a course of ten lectures on *Great Cities: Their Place in Geography, and their Relation to Human Development* which, in its form, replicated the archaeological structure of the Museum's exhibits by – for each period of urban life studied – identifying the 'persistence and continued expansion of [the] preceding elements and influences in modern cities' (Geddes, 1905: 3).

But it is in his conception of the Outlook Tower that Geddes's understanding of the museum's role as a storage device capable of accumulating a succession of pasts, synthesising their direction, and mapping out a future – and thereby, in being applied to the tasks of civic education, serving as a means of acting developmentally on the social – is most fully elaborated. Developed in the 1890s, the Outlook Tower was shaped, in part, by the early debates of the Museums

Association in which Geddes, who had strong connections with George Brown Goode at the Smithsonian, participated (Meller, 1990: 106–7). A totalising device based on a combination of geographical and historical principles, the Tower – in both its physical form in Edinburgh as well as the broader role it played in Geddes's writings as one of his 'thinking machines' – was intended as a means of focusing the visitor's attention on localised tasks of civic development by placing these in both a world and a historical setting. The visitor's itinerary was to lead from the camera obscura (Figure 4.1), providing a view of the city and its regions, and then downwards through a succession of floors which placed that urban and civic vista in successively broader contexts, each providing a summary of historical evolution, present conditions and future prospects. The logic at work here is made clear in another of Geddes's 'thinking machines' (Figure 4.2), which provided a template for applying the accumulation of the past's lessons to the task of future civic development, projecting the future, as in the Outlook Tower, as an incitement, a series of boxes to be filled in, of beckoning stages to be completed by both carrying the past forward and leaving it behind.

Yet if the evolutionary museum was thus conceived as a progressive ethical apparatus, it was governed by a split logic owing to the differential way in which it was interpreted and applied across relations of class, race and gender. As an evolutionary accumulator, its operations could only effectively take a hold on those persons whose inner organisation exhibited a similar depth structure. The organisation of the historical fold constituting the modern person entailed that such persons be white and male. While also strongly marked in class terms, the wager of the evolutionary museum was that such a fold might also be developed within the working man. Yet that this was only a wager is evident in the anxiety that was expressed in Pitt Rivers's concerns regarding the ratio of the automaton to the intellectual mind and the extent to which male members of the working classes (the only visitor Pitt Rivers imagined for his typological displays) could acquire the inner depth, the archaeologically stratified self, needed for evolutionary self-monitoring and self-development to occur. These concerns were evident, to anticipate my concerns in chapter 7, in the extreme regulation of the museum environment and the steps taken to ensure that the visitor got 'the right message'. Within the contemporary agendas of neo-liberalism, Andrew Barry argues, the interactivity associated with modern museum displays is intended to make the visitor 'a more creative, participative or active subject *without* the imposition of a direct form of control or the judgement of an expert authority' (Barry, 2001: 149). The evolutionary showmen, by contrast, were very reluctant to let their visitors off the leash of their directive control, organising a museum environment whose injunction was less that of 'Discover! You may' of the interactive display than that of 'Learn! You must!' which Barry associated with disciplinary forms of learning.

My point here, then, concerns the hesitant and cautious way in which the evolutionary museum sought to extend the reach of liberal forms of self-government to include the male working classes. The position of women and the colonised was quite different owing to the respects in which both recalled the archaic component within the make-up of modern man that had to be regulated to

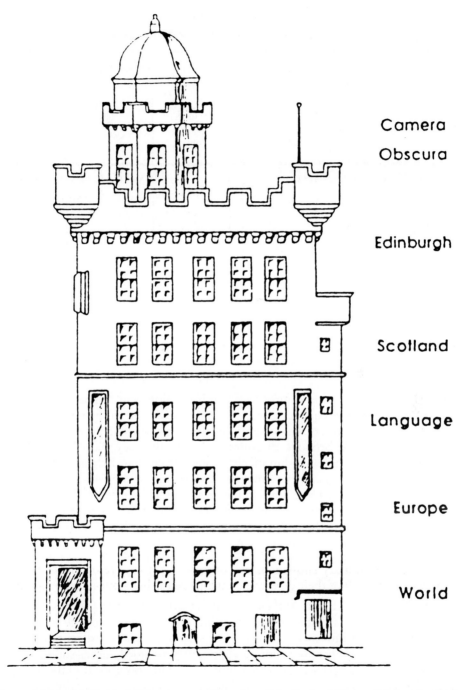

Camera
Obscura

Edinburgh

Scotland

Language

Europe

World

Figure 4.1 Patrick Geddes's *Diagrammatic Elevation of the Outlook Tower*, Edinburgh, 1915.

Source: Patrick Geddes (1915) *Cities in Evolution*, London: Williams and Norgate.

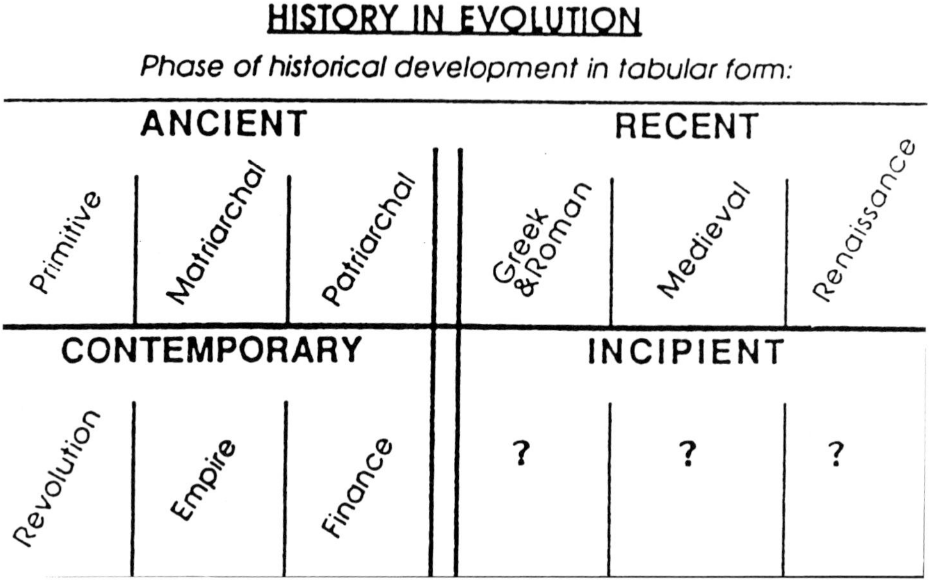

HISTORY IN EVOLUTION

Phase of historical development in tabular form:

ANCIENT				RECENT		
Primitive	Matriarchal	Patriarchal		Greek & Roman	Medieval	Renaissance
CONTEMPORARY				**INCIPIENT**		
Revolution	Empire	Finance		?	?	?

Figure 4.2 Patrick Geddes's 'History in Evolution' table, projecting the lessons of the past to future civic development.

Source: Patrick Geddes (1906) 'Cities: an applied sociology, part 2', in V. Bradford (ed.) *Sociological Papers*, London: Macmillan.

produce a person capable of progressive self-development.[23] The nature of this exclusion, and its consequences, were, however, different in the two cases. That relating to the colonised was essentially the same as that produced by their position within the broader discourse of anthropology. Bernard McGrane illuminates this interrelationship nicely in suggesting that, by transforming 'the Other into a concrete memory of the past' (McGrane, 1989: 94), anthropology's concern was not with what colonised peoples were 'in themselves' but with what – in an historicist account of the west and its origins which operated like 'a new system of mnemonics' (94) – they were for 'us'. Essentially a discourse in which non-European Others serve as a means for developing an account of the nature of western culture and its dynamics, the 'we' of anthropology, McGrane argues, was one that excluded its object, 'the primitive'. It 'speaks *of* the Other but never *to* the Other' (96). The same was true of evolutionary museum displays: the place assigned the primitive within these was designed exclusively for western eyes, for telling a story to and about a metropolitan 'we' by means of the representational roles assigned to 'them'. This exclusionary logic was most acutely evident in colonial contexts where the address of museums assumed, just as surely as their metropolitan counterparts, that 'the primitive' would only appear in the museum as an object of display and research, and never as a visitor.[24] Tom Griffiths records the long historical reach of these assumptions in recalling that, as late as the 1960s, the realisation that Aborigines might be among its visitors led one major

Australian museum to consider posting a 'health warning' to the effect that Aboriginal visitors might find the exhibits disturbing should they enter the building (Griffiths, 1996a: 95).

I shall come back to these questions. Here, however, I am primarily interested in the nature and consequences of the archaic status that was attributed to women. For it was partly through the representation of women as archaic that the authority of the male scientist, the new ventriloquist of nature's lessons, was installed in the place of that which had earlier been accorded women in their roles as domestic mediators of an altogether more benign and provident nature,[25] as well as the key positions they had been accorded within the role accorded aesthetics in earlier forms of liberal rule.[26] This, in its turn, had significant consequences for the division of labour within the museum in its articulation of differentiated gender roles on to the emerging distinction between the professional roles of the scientific expert and the responsibilities of a rapidly emerging 'voluntary sector'.

The reasons for assigning women to an archaic level of the self varied across the different schools of evolutionary thought that defined the late-nineteenth-century intellectual landscape. In the case of Darwin, the mechanisms of use inheritance combined with those of sexual selection to retain women in a state of acquiescent passivity which, by ill preparing them for the struggle for existence and obliging their dependency on the naturally more aggressive male, also deprived their psychological make-up of that dynamic tension arising out of the more complex layered self that men had developed through the ages. Those attributes where women did excel – those of intuition, imitation and perception – only confirmed their archaic status since they were, Darwin opined, 'characteristic of the lower races, and therefore of a past and lower state of civilisation' (cited in Sayers, 1982: 43). Carl Vogt, whose polygenetic interpretation of Darwin's work endeared him to the rabid racism of James Hunt's Anthropological Society, located 'woman-as-child-as-primitive' in her anatomical structure – particularly her skull size – while also attributing to her a conservative effect in the sphere of morals. Unable to catch up with man on the plane of her anatomical existence – indeed, Vogt saw the anatomical gap between the sexes increasing with the progress of civilisation – woman was also, morally and culturally, a sheet-anchor on the development of civilisation (Richards, 1983: 72–3). In Huxley's case, a *mélange* of arguments culled fairly indiscriminately from a range of sources, led him to view women as 'naturally timid, inclined to dependence, born conservative' (cited in Richards, 1983: 92) and, accordingly, destined for the greater part to 'stop in the doll stage of evolution, to be the stronghold of parsondom, the drag on civilisation, the degradation of every important pursuit with which they mix themselves' (cited in Richards, 1989: 256).

These formulations constitute a specific variant of a more general characteristic of modernist discourse through which the gendered separation of the public and private spheres was translated into differential gendered relations to time. The key question that was at issue here, Rita Felski (1999/2000) argues, was that of habit. While men, by virtue of the capacity to break with habit, vouchsafed for them by their public and economic roles outside the home, were assigned to the linear developmental time of modernity, modernist discourse has associated women, trapped into habit by virtue of their 'natural' domestic roles, with the principles of cyclical repetitive time. In doing so, it has typically deprived women of that double-levelled self that provides the space within which subjects can be mobilised, and act upon themselves progressively, within the temporal dynamics of modernity.[27] What distinguished the Darwinian version of this more general formation is the scientific validation it claimed for placing men and women differently within the dynamics of developmental time and the conclusions that followed from this regarding the place of women within the cultural and educational strategies of the new liberalism.

For women did pose a problem. The legacy of Mill's support for women could not be entirely ignored. Nor could women's place in the ethical process be neglected. While, in practice, Huxley was every bit as discriminatory as the notedly illiberal Anthropological Society in his attitudes towards women, opposing and limiting their involvement in the Ethnology Society every step of the way, he did grudgingly recognise that the case of overall social advance would be assisted through programmes of educational improvement involving women. But this was not for the sake of any contribution they might make to social progress directly. Women could contribute to 'the connective tissue of civilisation' only indirectly by becoming educated to the extent that, first, they might mute the impact of their own archaic presence within the body politic and so not act as a drag on the naturally progressive male, and second, in order that they might act as a beneficial influence on their children. Darwin had made this point many years earlier in his notebooks when he had observed: 'improve the women (double influence) and mankind must improve' (cited in Desmond and Moore, 1992: 252).

When assessing the responsibility of government for the education of women, it was their 'double influence' – their role as mothers – that carried the most weight with both Huxley and Darwin. While this might justify that women be educated to the degree necessary to perform their domestic roles in the earlier phases of child-rearing, they could see little justification for state expenditure on women in the higher levels of education that might equip them for public, professional or scientific roles. This would simply be wasteful to the degree that women's back-wardness was determined by ancient biological causes that were still operative in the present. 'What was decided among the prehistoric Protozoa', Geddes and Thompson argued in *The Evolution of Sex*, 'cannot be annulled by Act of Parliament' (cited in Richards, 1983: 93). Huxley was equally adamant that no amount of education would oblige nature to make even the tiniest of jumps in its iron-like ordering of the relations between the sexes. 'Nature's old salique law will not be repealed, and no change of dynasty will be effected' (92–3): although his later formulations on the relations between the sexes were sometimes more ameliorative, he did not shift significantly from this early assessment.[28]

The significance of these developments for the position of women within the cultural sphere becomes clearer if they are placed in a longer historical perspective. The work of Ann Shteir (1996) and others has shown how, in the earlier mid-century period, attacks on both Paleyean natural theology and the legacy of Linnaeus's binomial system – whose simplicity had helped to democratise natural history, making it especially popular with women (Koerner, 1996) – formed part of a campaign to defeminise science by establishing a 'masculine "culture of experts"' (Shteir, 1996: 159).[29] This is not to say that women passively accepted these developments any more than, in the later period, they simply rolled over and played out the 'doll's house' roles to which their stern masters of evolutionary necessity could confine them. The revisions proposed by Arabella Buckley, Charles Lyell's former secretary, to the benign narratives of earlier schools of natural history in order to take account of evolution, yet lend its support to the need for social evolution to aspire to ever higher forms of social mutuality (Merrill, 1989); Charlotte Perkins Gilman's urging the need to free women from the habitual drudgery of the domestic sphere so that they might help speed up evolution (Hayden, 1981: 183); and the more broadly based feminist campaigns against vivisection, fuelled by a sympathy for animal life that stemmed from women's classification and treatment as themselves scarcely more evolved than domestic animals: in all of these ways, the lessons of evolution were subject to a complex history of acceptance, revision, rebuttal, and derision in the writings of late-nineteenth-century feminists.[30]

There is, however, no doubt that the campaign to bring nature under the juris-diction of a 'masculine "culture of experts"' was effective in the newly emerging spheres of state education and public culture. Bernard Lightman (1997b) addresses the first of these spheres, noting the diminishing influence of popular natural history texts written by women as the introduction of natural history into the school curriculum decreased the need for home-based instruction in the subject. Their sphere of influence undermined, women's role in the schooling system was clearly subordinated to that of front-line mediators of nature's lessons as deter-mined by committees of male experts. The same was true of museums, where women made little headway in terms of influence or employment until after the First World War. Dominated, in their professional structures, almost entirely by men, women's initial roles in museums were as voluntary helpmates. This was the case at the British Museum (Natural History) with the establishment, in 1883, of the Association of Women Pioneer Lecturers to help take the Museum's message to schools, rural villages, suburban women and the members of co-operative societies as a complement to the university extension movement (British Museum (Natural History) 1893). The key point, however, is that evolu-tionary museum arrangements did not actively enlist women in any active developmental process. Teaching, rather, that their place was fixed, evolutionary museums drew on earlier exhibition rhetorics to organise their active address to women and children. This was nowhere more true than at the American Museum of Natural History where nature, subjected to a systematic dualism, was spoken in two tongues in a social and political context characterised by different imperatives.

5

Selective memory
Racial recall and civic renewal at the American Museum of Natural History

The front cover of the 1937 May Day issue of *Red Fossil*, the news-sheet of the AMNH Unit of the Communist Party of America, featured a male fist clenched in support of the clarion call of 'All Out – May First' (Figure 5.1). Inside, *Red Fossil* was preoccupied mainly with local industrial issues – protesting, for example, management's decision to fund a bust to the late Dr Sherwood by top-slicing 'voluntary contributions' from staff salaries. But, in its title and its front-page militancy, the news-sheet recalled the radical political mobilisation of deep time that had characterised the 'Red Lamarckianism' which forged evolutionary thought into such a potent force in the international labour movement of the early to mid-nineteenth century (Desmond, 1989). This late and, I suspect, short-lived historical echo of pre-Darwinian evolutionary radicalism stood in marked contrast to the ways in which 'pasts beyond memory' had been invoked at the AMNH during Henry Fairfield Osborn's presidency, which had ended the previous year.[1] Such pasts, for Osborn, figured largely as primal scenes of the struggle for existence in which – stripped of the veneer of civilisation – nature's lessons could be recalled and harnessed to the cause of civic renewal in the present. This was, however, a selective practice of memory directed primarily at *homo sapiens europaeus nordicus* – or white Americans – as part of a restorative project which aimed to renew the germ plasm which constituted the inherited bases of its racial supremacy.[2]

In developing this programme for the museum, Osborn was, in his own eyes, acting as a faithful disciple of Huxley, with whom he had trained in 1879 (Osborn, 1896). As a palaeontologist, Osborn was also well schooled in European pre-historic archaeology, citing the work of Lubbock with particular favour,[3] and he aimed, in his theory of racial selection, at a synthesis of the historical sciences of comparable scope to that which had been developed in late-nineteenth-century Britain. He did so, moreover, by staking his claims to scientific authority on the evidence for changes through time that was provided by the long series accumulated in museums at a time when the epistemological basis of the historical sciences had been largely undermined by the turn to laboratory-based experiments (Osborn, 1895: 81). Yet, although seeing himself as a spokesperson for 'Huxleyism' in America, the positions Osborn adopted differed from those of Huxley in almost every significant respect just as they differed from those of post-Darwinian reform

Figure 5.1 Front cover of *Red Fossil*, news-sheet of the American Museum of Natural History Unit of the Communist Part, vol. 7, no. 7, May Day issue 1937.

Source: Library of the American Museum of Natural History.

liberalism more generally. Huxley, as we have seen, strongly opposed the principles of state-directed social selection associated with eugenic interventions in the field of population management; Osborn, by contrast, for all that he advocated the principles of unbridled competition, was a passionate advocate of state-sponsored eugenic programmes. For Huxley, nature was, eventually, denied the role that had been accorded it within natural theology of providing a template for moral action; for Osborn, however, it was nature itself – and the more raw and uncooked the better – which provided the means of discerning correct action in accordance with the dictates of the survival of the fittest.

Yet this was, at the same time, a practice of memory, and one that involved a directly contrary relation to the 'connective tissue of civilisation' examined in the last chapter. For Osborn, the museum's task was not to augment the connective tissue of civilisation but to peel it back so as to put man back in touch with nature and, in doing so, to renew the race plasm which constituted the true source of evolutionary continuity between past and present. The race plasm formed what Brian Regal calls 'a continuous chain to the past'; as 'the hereditary basis of any species, or "race"', it comprised 'a core of foundational characters which accumulated very slowly and steadily from the deep past' (Regal, 2002: 69). Yet its force could also be obscured and dimmed by the superficial accretions of civilisation unless periodically renewed via contact with the primal scenes in which its distinctive characteristics had first been forged. The exception here was the child, especially the male child: 'the mind of the boy in the lower and higher races of mankind has not changed', Osborn argued, 'but is the same as the mind of the eolithic boy and of the cave boy' (Osborn, 1927a: 259). Still with one foot in nature, the child is already half-free of the corrupting and debilitating sheen of civilisation. The child is thus a key figure in the distinctive practice of memory Osborn proposes for the museum, providing a half-way house in a programme of recall which also required that the accumulated lessons of culture and civil-isation be put aside and forgotten if the members of *europaeus nordicus* were to be reinvigorated so as to be able to respond to the challenges of social leader-ship that were uniquely theirs. In other aspects of the AMNH's programmes, however, both before and during Osborn's presidency, the child was invoked in quite different forms. Where the migrant child was concerned – and, by extension, his or her parents – nature was more typically invoked as a palliative, a compen-sation for the urban squalor which was their lot that would also help to secure their integration into the social body, but not their leadership of it. While these differences were not necessarily contradictory, they did entail significant differences of stress and emphasis which, in their turn, reflected the different forces shaping the development of the AMNH over the late nineteenth and early twentieth centuries. It will be useful, in considering these, to look again at Donna Haraway's classic discussion of the AMNH and to probe some of the assumptions on which it rests.

Evolution, e   ...   he state

Since the reno   ...   neal and patchy affair,
Chris Healy a   ...   l entity in which the
stratified layer   ...   ly, 1997: 79). This is
a good warning   ...   the sites of a unified
discourse, fashi   ...   singular time. While
Mieke Bal (199   ...   the AMNH, Donna
Haraway (1992   ...   f the powerful conjunction of col   ...   rses informing the
development of   ...   ing Henry Fairfield
Osborn's preside   ...   Michael Schudson
(1997) alleges, b   ...   our of history and
sociology for the   ...   ment, characterise
cultural studies.   ...   n that the African
Hall might be rea   ...   course as a whole
over the 1908–36   ...   ometimes contrary
emphases that we   ...   ver this extended
period, or for the c   ...   useum's practices.
Haraway's reading   ...   ation of the relationship between   ...   MNH's activities.
Placing great stres   ...   hed as a private
institution owned   ...   pitalist families,
Haraway views the   ...   thy in their ideal
incarnation', a place   ...   s', and contrasts
this with the situatio   ...   ry were 'organs
of the state, intimate   ...   Haraway, 1992:
56). Proceeding fron   ...   expression of
the values, both class   ...   n bourgeoisie –
a reading that is fame   ...   patriarchy' and
the associations this e   ...   f the AMNH's
board of trustees and

One difficulty with th   ...   ting pressures
to which the Museum   ...   public space
of Central Park and,   ...   tments of the
city and state of New Yo   ...   hile Haraway
acknowledges these co   ...   lify her view
that the AMNH can be   ...   ing a ruling-
class ethos. Roy Rosen   ...   the mark in
suggesting that, althoug   ...   ity and state
governments and its reg   ...   ...ioners of Central Park made it 'a
hybrid institution' that served as 'a model for many future cultural establishments
in the city, under private control but public in their relative openness, non-profit
motives, and use of city and state resources' (Rosenzweig and Blackmar, 1992:
354).[4] Indeed, although it may not have been an institution of state, the AMNH
proved to be the very model of a governmental institution, understood in the

Foucauldian sense, in view of its role in pioneering new ways of using cultural resources as parts of extended programmes of civic management directed at new populations – the city child, the immigrant – that were to be widely imitated by other American museums and, indeed, in Australia and Britain. For Foucault is clear that the orientation towards population that he calls 'governmentality' is not the exclusive prerogative of state institutions; to the contrary, his thesis of the 'governmentalisation of the state' (Foucault, 1991: 103) is explicit in its expectation that governmental forms of social and cultural management first arise outside the state in a host of benevolent, philanthropic and voluntary organisations and are only later developed under the auspices of the state.

If Haraway neglects these considerations by counter-posing the AMNH to European museums along a privately owned/state-owned axis, the issues to which they point have a broader provenance. For the difference between the stress that was placed on the private versus the public ownership of museums in the United States compared to Britain proved less important than the markedly similar imperatives that arose from American interpretations of the relations between post-Darwinian tendencies in the historical sciences, the intersections of new liberalism and new education, and the organisation of a new historical nexus between museums and public schooling. That these shared imperatives were translated into different governmental forms and programmes in the US was a result of the different institutional, intellectual and political milieux shaping each of these forces and the interrelations between them.

There are a number of factors to be taken into account here, not the least being the greater heterogeneity of American science during the post-bellum years when, for a brief period, museums enjoyed parity with, and sometimes precedence over, what was still only a nascent university system (Hannah, 2000). This heterogeneity was most strongly evident in the different orientations of the Smithsonian Institution in Washington DC and the Museum of Comparative Geology at Harvard University. At the Smithsonian, for example, Otis Mason's interpretation of the typological method and Charles Rau's adaptation of the methods of prehistoric archaeology drew clearly on the models of Pitt Rivers and Charles Lubbock, albeit adapting these to new contexts and purposes. The Museum of Comparative Geology, by contrast, stood resolutely against Darwinian tendencies across all the historical sciences. Directed by Louis Agassiz, who was heir to the legacy of Cuvier both in his advocacy of catastrophist conceptions of the earth's history and in his subscription to polygenetic conceptions of separate lines of racial development, the Museum played a significant role in the development of new national scientific networks in the pre-bellum period.[5] It also proved an important training ground for the key staff of the AMNH: both Alfred Bickmore, the Museum's first President, and Osborn studied there. The social contexts in which these differences of scientific orientation were implicated were also significantly different, especially with regard to the ethnic composition of the population. The most obvious considerations here are the presence, in the United States, of a large Afro-American population, newly emancipated after the Civil War and migrating in large numbers from the southern states to the northern cities; an increasingly large immigrant population, mainly from Europe; and, from the 1860s a defeated and, in the main, dispersed population of Native Americans whose prior occupancy of the land was, nonetheless, capable of inducing a number of twists and contortions in the principles of archaeological reasoning whose application in Europe had seemed to be, literally, a straightforward matter.

Important though these differences are – and I shall return to them in due course – the development of a new generation of mainly city-based museums with collection and exhibition practices ranging across the historical sciences was prompted by an essentially similar reading of the lessons of evolutionary thought. The principal legacy of the *Origin of Species* in America, Robert Bannister (1979) argues, was the 'reform Darwinism' and the related new liberalism that flourished from the 1880s. After the fashion of Huxley's arguments in *Evolution and Ethics*, these stressed the role of intellect and culture in combating the social consequences that would ensue were natural selection and the struggle for existence allowed to have unbridled sway. The principles of the new liberalism were codified, in legal philosophy, by the work of Oliver Wendell Holmes, and, in sociology, by Lester Frank Ward in terms similar to those proposed by Hobhouse in Britain. Its philosophical underpinnings, however, were most fully developed in the new philosophy of pragmatism developed by William James, Charles Sanders Peirce and John Dewey. Accepting – indeed, embracing – the implications of a directionless nature ('the law of higgledy-piggledy'), and drawing the conclusion that nature could not therefore provide a template for moral action, the pragmatists rejected any fixed schema for conduct in favour of a more probabilistic assessment of the relations between actions and their outcomes. This provided the basis for a view of conduct as socially shaped in ways that allowed for the assertion of free will – of choice and decision with uncertain outcomes – over the inherited or natural forces of habit and repetition.[6]

The links between evolution, ethics and government that these formulations established resulted, in some cases, in direct advocacy of an expanded role for the state in the cultural sphere. This was true of George Brown Goode who, in his 1889 essay 'The museums of the future' advocating the virtues of the 'new museum idea', urged the need for the cultural and moral sphere to be viewed as an exception to Sir Robert Peel's assessment that 'the action of government is torpid at best' (Goode, [1889] 1991: 334). Only the action of government, he argued, could ensure that museums would be provided where they were most needed if their beneficial influence were to be brought to bear on the management of the social. The failure of the People's Palace movement in Britain provided a negative example of the consequences of failing to translate voluntary cultural initiatives into effective state action:

> Many of my hearers are doubtless familiar with that densely populated wilderness, the east end of London, twice as large as Brooklyn, yet with scarce an intellectual oasis in its midst. Who can say how different might have been its condition to-day if Walter Besant's apostolic labors had begun a century sooner, and if the People's Palace, that wonderful materialisation of a poet's dream, had been for three generations brightening the lives of the citizens of the Lower Hamlets and Hackney.
>
> (Goode, [1889] 1991: 334)

119

However, these connections between evolution and ethics were more typically translated into practices of government through the activities of voluntary non-state agencies rather than, as was the case in Britain, resulting in direct state investment and action in the cultural and moral sphere. One manifestation of this was the Ethical Culture movement, established by Felix Adler in New York in the 1870s, and related organisations – like the Brooklyn Ethical Association, established in 1885 – which stressed the need for the regeneration of society and the advancement of civilisation through the action of voluntary associations.[7] A second manifestation was the stress placed on the need for private philanthropy to resource the development of a public cultural sector – museums, libraries, art galleries – that would nurture the values that would provide an antidote to the brutalising effects of the struggle for existence. This paralleled the development, from the 1880s, of a favourable attitude to trusts and combinations in view of their capacity to promote order and stability in markets, thus offsetting the potentially destructive effects of unbridled competition. The net result, Bannister suggests, was an emerging formation that brought together popular schooling, philanthropic support for public culture and the defence of regulated monopoly as part of a new state–culture–industry alignment that took the place of the principles of *laissez-faire* competition that had characterised the largely Spencerian 'take' on Darwinism in the immediate post-bellum period.

All of this, then, suggests that Haraway is mistaken in positing a public museum/private museum: Europe/America contrast as the reason for reading the AMNH in purely class terms. While not suggesting that the question of public versus private ownership is inconsequential, American museum practices in the post-bellum period were shaped by the conjunctions of evolutionary thought and new liberalism as a part of a network of new governmental means for acting on the social in much the same way as their British counterparts. They were also widely perceived as models for the latter in spite of the differences in their ownership. As early as 1876, Boyd Dawkins had looked to American museums with 'feelings of envy and regret', regarding them as 'well-officered' and 'well-arranged' in comparison to the crowded jumble which he attributed to most British collections.[8] By the 1890s, however, American leadership in developing the educational functions of museums had become more or less undisputed. A sure sign of this, Sally Kohlstedt argues, was that American curators and directors began touring their own museums for models of 'best practice' rather than, as they had done earlier, looking to Europe (Kohlstedt, 1986: 167–8).[9]

This was more true of the AMNH than it was of the other city-based museums that were established in the same period (the Field Museum in Chicago and the Carnegie Museum of Natural History in Pittsburgh, for example), and more true, in some respects, than it was of the Smithsonian Institution, the only museum that could claim a fully national role. Its development, through its links with popular schooling, of new mechanisms for the capillary distribution of nature's lessons throughout the social body was widely emulated. This contributed to the leading role the AMNH played in turning the axis of the museum's social action from one conceived mainly in class terms, as was the case in Britain, to one conceived in terms of a combination of class and migrant status – a reflection of New York's distinctive position in this period of mass migration to the United States.[10] The AMNH also became one of the first major museums to manage the transition from the classic museum age of anthropology as a largely armchair practice to anchor the museum at the centre of new networks deriving from the phase of fieldwork anthropology. And in its habitat and life group displays and dioramas, the AMNH introduced new ways of organising the visual practices of visitors and of placing them in time, as well as developing new ways of dramatising museum displays that foregrounded the permeability of the relations between museums and circuses.

The AMNH was also, finally, a key site for the mixing of scientific influences from both Britain and continental Europe with more distinctively American intellectual tendencies. This had been evident, in the 1890s, in the use Franz Boas made of the anti-evolutionary legacy of German anthropology to take issue with the typological method and the anatomical reductionism this entailed when applied to the theorisation of racial types. It was also evident in Osborn's theory of evolution, in which elements of Darwin's thought – mainly the principle of the survival of the fittest – were combined with Agassiz's polygeneticism and August Weismann's germ plasm theory in a notably eclectic synthesis. This was, moreover, a synthesis which ran directly contrary to the implications of Boas's work, which had aimed to detach ways of thinking about difference from its ascription to racialised bodies by grounding it instead in culture, by attributing difference once again to racially inscribed anatomies. Yet both views of difference informed the AMNH's practices as it aimed to effect both the racial renewal of the Nordic Europeans and the cultural assimilation of immigrants. This was possible only because nature was fashioned in many different ways so that, side by side with the nature red-in-tooth-and-claw that provided the basis of the Museum's 'teddy bear patriarchy', the AMNH also continued to mobilise a discourse of nature that resembled more closely a teddy bears' picnic.

Nature's many lessons

When taking issue with the characterisation of the AMNH as a 'dead circus', George Sherwood stressed the extent to which its links with the education system had made the Museum a vital and living force throughout the city: 'the Museum messengers penetrate all boroughs of the city and deliver our visual instruction material free to any school anywhere in the Greater City' (Sherwood, 1927: 323). A similar sense of the Museum's potential as an adjunct to the school system had formed a part of its public discourse from the early years of its development. When the AMNH's cornerstone was laid in 1874, H. G. Stebbins, the President of the Department of Parks, expressed the wish that 'the museums on the Park will become valuable auxiliaries of that great free public educational system which is already the pride of our city' (5th/6th Annual Report, 1875: 42).

Yet such views had relatively little direct influence on the Museum's early years owing to the trustees' determination to insulate the AMNH as much as possible from the political controversies which characterised the affairs of the Park

Commissioners. The directions the Museum would initially follow were more clearly indicated by the speaker who followed Stebbins: Joseph Henry, the first secretary of the Smithsonian Institution, who used the occasion to advise his audience that his long struggle to limit the Smithsonian's role to the increase rather than the diffusion of knowledge looked like bearing fruit (Goode, 1897; Molella, 1983). While both of these functions had been stipulated in James Smithson's will, Henry had constantly sought to privilege the former over the latter, and was pleased to tell his audience that his efforts had born fruit in Congress's recent agreement that the Institution should 'devote its whole energies to the advance of science, the evident design of the testator' (5th/6th Annual Report, 1875: 47–8). His implication was that the AMNH should follow suit, appealing to New York's philanthropists to provide funding for 'a series of men capable not only of expounding established truths but of interrogating nature and of discovering new facts, new phenomena, and new principles' (47). The balance that was struck between the Museum's research and public education functions varied at different moments in the Museum's development.[11] Joel Orosz (1990), however, is generally correct in interpreting the AMNH's motto – 'For the people, for education, for science' – as the expression of a compromise between the stress on scientific functions that had characterised the mid-century development of American museums of natural history and the increasing requirement, as the century progressed, that museums should join in the task of public education. This shift of emphasis was partly a response to democratic criticisms of the earlier forms of social, scientific or professional exclusiveness that had formed one aspect of the American museum tradition. Just as important, however, was the increasing perception of an urgent need to enlist natural history in aid of new forms of social and civic management.

In falling in with this general trend, the AMNH gave its commitment to public educational function a distinctive organisational form through the establishment, in 1884, of the Department of Public Instruction (later to become the Department of Public Education). Established, initially, under the leadership of Alfred Bickmore – the AMNH's first Director[12] – this Department's role was initially limited to providing natural history lectures for teachers. However, it rapidly assumed a range of new functions designed to increase the Museum's social reach. These included, in 1890, the introduction of lectures for the Museum's members and their children and, in 1893, the commencement of a lecture programme for children that was supported by the New York State government (Saunders, 1956). The year 1895 saw the beginnings of a long-lasting collaboration with the Board of Education of New York City through, initially, joint sponsorship of a programme of public lectures. This led, in 1903, to the development of a system of distribution for taking nature's lessons right into the classroom through the provision of specimen boxes, whereby the lessons of nature were packed for delivery to the schools of greater New York via a fleet of specially designed trucks. These developments resulted in an increasingly close enmeshment of the Museum's concerns with those of the public education system and an increased dependency on public appropriations. This resulted, in 1909, in the State of New York amending the charter of the AMNH in order to recognise it as an educational institution

(Osborn, 1923: 1–3). Osborn recognised the implications of these developments. 'In so far as we draw on public funds,' he wrote, 'public education is our chief and final purpose; towards this all our plans tend' (Osborn, 1911: 223). But he was also an enthusiastic advocate of this conception of the museum's function. The 'new museum idea' was, in his interpretation, nothing but 'the educational idea' through which the natural history museum was to be 'animated by what may be called its ethical sense, its sense of public duty, its realisation that the general intelligence and welfare of the people are the prime reasons for its existence' (Osborn, 1927a: 246).

There were precedents for the links the AMNH developed with the school system. Charles Willson Peale was probably the first museum director to see the importance of links with schools, pioneering the practice, at his Philadelphia museum, of free admission for school teachers when accompanied by a class of scholars (Orosz, 1990: 111–15; Sellers, 1980). The circulation of natural history collections to schools had also been introduced in Liverpool as early as 1884 (Chard, 1890). However, the AMNH's approach was on a much larger scale serving, fairly quickly, as a model for the introduction of similar practices at other American museums.[13] Its example was also widely imitated overseas. Charles Hedley, visiting on behalf of the Australian Museum in 1913, aptly summarised the AMNH's impact when, in the report of his visit, he advised that on 'the side of popular education, the American Museum takes a broader view of Museum functions than does any similar institution' in extending its 'sphere of usefulness . . . beyond the galleries to the lecture hall and beyond the lecture hall to the suburban school' (Hedley, 1913: 7).

For Bruno Latour, as we have seen, the location of museums at the centre of dispersed networks of collection allows them to function as 'centres of accumulation'. Assembling together hitherto dispersed objects in ordered relationships of contiguity and difference, museums make new realities perceptible within the field of knowledge. The relationships that were developed between museums and popular schooling in the late nineteenth and early twentieth centuries placed the museum at the centre of a set of distributive networks through which the new forms of knowledge that had been made possible through its operations as a centre of accumulation could be brought to bear on the governmental task of shaping future citizens. The relations between these two networks are made graphically clear in the AMNH's Annual Reports which, from the 1890s, increasingly located the Museum as the nodal point of two sets of flows. First, the flow of objects to the AMNH through the range of scientific expeditions it organised and financed, mainly in the Americas but also in a variety of overseas locations. Second, the flow, through the capillary network of its links with the education system, of objects and messages deep into the social body of New York. The Annual Report for 1911 includes a map which indicates the places from which – through its own expeditions – new material had been accumulated in the course of that year. 'If from these localities lines were drawn to New York,' the accompanying text advises, 'they would present graphically the influx of new material and ideas for the Museum's research and exhibition.' In some annual reports, the AMNH's role as the centre of a distributive network is also illustrated by maps plotting the

123

radiating lines of influence of the Museum's extension programmes through the schools and districts of New York. In the 1911 Report, however, statistical summaries of the Museum's extension activities perform this function, advising of a significant increase in the number of pupils reached by the Museum's circulating collections (from 940,489 to 1,577,576).

It was by means of this distributive network that the AMNH was able to serve as a bridgehead into the threatening sea of potentially unassimilable difference represented by New York's immigrant population. As the main point of entry into the United States, New York had a particularly high ratio of immigrants (by 1910, 40 per cent of the population of New York City had been born overseas (Menand, 2002: 381)). This had marked consequences for the social composition of the school-age population: by 1905, 70 per cent of New York's public school children were immigrants. Although the same period saw an increase in New York's African American population, this did not present the same kind of 'problem' as that posed by this new generation of migrants, mainly from southern and Eastern Europe. Joel Kahn (2001: 88–98) suggests that this was partly because African Americans were seen as *Americans* and so similar to the 'native stock' in regard to their cultural values, and partly because the main differences between black and white Americans – at least within liberal opinion – were held to consist in the temporal lag which separated them owing to the primitivism of the African American. This was, in other words, a division that might be overcome with time. Immigrants, by contrast, were interpreted within the framework of a new discourse of cultural difference as representing an essentialised form of otherness which, moreover, they often seemed determined to maintain through exclusive social relations and cultural practices. The work of Francis Amasa Walker, first head of the US Census, was important in this regard. Viewing migrants from eastern and southern Europe as too much the product of servile and despotic cultures to be able to respond positively to the virile demands of American development, the racialised census categories he developed in the 1880s and 1890s played a major role in identifying such Europeans in the racial-cum-biological terms that Osborn later took for granted (Hannah, 2000: 176–87).

The migrant child was, accordingly, the main addressee of the programmes which the AMNH developed for distribution through the education system. This was clear from the terms in which, in his autobiographical notes, Albert Bickmore interpreted the significance of the school for the AMNH. In so doing, Bickmore underscored how this differed from the museum–school link being developed in Britain. Recording a conversation with Sir William Flower of the British Museum (Natural History) during a visit to Britain in 1893–4, Bickmore notes that 'the great minds which are moulding the destinies of the British nation' were agreed that the 'coming tempest' augured by the present 'labour troubles' would be best survived by the nation that was the best educated (Bickmore, n.d.: 121). But when Bickmore addresses the situation in New York, it is the role of the common school in combating cultural difference that he highlights, endorsing the views of the State Governor who urged the need for a close relationship between museums and schools in view of the latter's key role in transforming the migrant child from an external threat into an active and willing prop of government:

I am told that in this great city over 300,000 people can not read and write the English language. They come here because this government is an asylum for all the people of the Old World. We bid them welcome, but we ask them merely to put their children into our common schools; and no matter what their brogue is, whether it is Irish, German, Scotch, Swedish, Norwegian, Dutch, or what else it is, we ask them to put their children in the hopper of the common school, knowing that their brogue will be rubbed off in a year, and they will become able and good American citizens.

> (Cited in Bickmore, n.d.: 114–15)[14]

Natural history museums could contribute to this process, Bickmore suggested, by providing a common language of nature that would serve as an antidote to urban squalor and to the separatism of the migrant ghetto. This view represented a fairly indiscriminate amalgam of influences: the lingering legacy of natural theology in the notion of a divinely ordered and benevolent nature; the Arcadian constructions of nature that informed the post-bellum development of nature study in America (Schmitt, 1969); and the hygienic pastoralism of Central Park which, in Frederick Law Olmsted's and Calvert Vaux's Greensward conception, was envisaged both as the city's antithesis and as a means of renewing its denizens by offering them the opportunity for contact with an untouched and purifying nature (Schuyler, 1986: 77–100). In Bickmore's lectures and the notes and slides he prepared for primary and kindergarten instruction, nature is thus typically invoked as a source of wonder, health, refreshment and joy, and the countryside as a place of quiet repose for weary city folk.[15]

The migrant child continued to occupy centre-stage in the AMNH's educational activities well into the twentieth century, albeit often more from the point of view of eugenic rather than political or cultural integration. But the conceptions of nature mediating the relations between the Museum and the migrant child remained much the same. When, in 1911, the AMNH published a special issue of *The American Museum Journal* focused on the Museum's schools programmes, a teacher from Industrial School No. 5 described how the AMNH's study collections brought the lessons of nature's wonder into the migrant child's school and thence to the child's family:

> When the Museum of Natural History was brought down to Industrial School No. 5, in the shape of suitable collections in sequence for study, it was a good thing for the children of 'Little Italy of the West Side', who live so far down town, near Sullivan, MacDougal and West Houston Streets, that they have little opportunity to go to the Museum.

> The children like the birds especially and it is remarkable the aptitude with which they learn to know them. The humming bird is a great delight and the solemn owls are studied with round-eyed wonder. Three classes were taken to the Museum last term. Their experiences are always related at home to the other members of the family, and in this way the benefit is far reaching.

> (*American Museum Journal*, 1911: 259)

125

When, in 1927, Mary Knox, the Principal of Public School No. 15 in Manhatten, described the effects of the AMNH's involvement in nature study at the school, a similar set of contrasts is invoked. A school for the children of migrants on the Lower East Side, Public School No. 15, is described as an old grey building, 'surrounded by tall, dingy tenement houses, bounded by streets swarming with pushcarts and vendors of all kinds of things from second-hand kitchen utensils to fur coats, from vegetables and fruit to live fish and chickens' (Knox, 1927: 368). Nature study provides an antidote to this environment by teaching the child the value of a joyous and uncorrupted nature. Its success, Knox argues, is vouchsafed by the translation of the children's corrupted urban response to the rhythms of nature into one of spontaneous harmony. 'Putting the swing doors on the beer saloons' as a class's response to a question concerning the signs of spring is thus transformed, under the influence of nature study, into a poem to 'Daffodils dancing on the window sills'.

Osborn, espousing a dualistic conception of nature's lessons, often extolled their virtues in similar terms.[16] For while, in the struggle for the survival of the fittest, nature was a stern taskmaster, nature could also be 'gentle and beneficent' (Osborne, 1927a: 240), a source of wonder and, in serving as a model for the patriarchal family, of moral instruction. In *Man Rises to Parnassus*, Osborn thus praises all social mammals and birds for their 'comradeship, mutual helpfulness, maternal and paternal devotion to the young, the sharing of danger, and willingness to sacrifice life for offspring or for a comrade'. He goes on to merge the categories of the natural and the primitive in observing that these 'noble traits are also widely manifested among primitive human societies and especially among those who have had the least contact with western civilisations' (Osborn, 1927b: viii–ix). It was with both these aspects of nature's lessons in mind that Osborn saw, in the child, a distinctive set of pedagogic and civic possibilities. Closer to nature and to prehistory than the adult, the child, especially the boy, was more open to nature's lessons than were his elders. Representing an ideal of a direct, fresh and uncontaminated relation with nature, the child constituted a relay mechanism through which the adult, too, might be restored to the virtues of a natural schooling:

> Under these two teachers, the compelling 'Struggle for Existence' and 'Inspiring Nature,' the Eolithic boy and the cave boy attended school regularly . . . The great function of the American Museum is to bring back to life these two masters; to restore the vision and inspiration of nature, as well as the compelling force of the struggle for existence in education. This is our antitoxin for most of the educational poisons of our day. On restoration of the privileges enjoyed by the cave boy and on coming for the first time into direct vision of the wonders and beauties of nature, not only boys and girls, but men and women, young and old, feel a thrill which they may never have experienced before.
>
> (Osborn, 1927a: 260)

In developing this argument, Osborn exhibits a complexly ambivalent relation to civilisation, especially as represented by writing. The cave boys' only disadvantage, he argues, 'was the lack of the arts of writing and printing, whereby what they learned and acquired intellectually could be passed on to future generations' (259). At the same time, though, the child embodied the possibility of a perception of nature which, unlike that of the teacher, whose vision was clouded by the influence of the press, was stripped back to its natural state, freed of the accumulated, and corrupting, influence of literate civilisation. It is thus that, in restoring nature's two masters to their proper place, the museum also places books and learning back in their place as 'the handmaidens not the masters of education' (260). Similarly, in another formulation, while arguing that the museum should aim to be 'not the rival, but the helpful ally of all the spoken methods of instruction', Osborn's suspicion of writing comes through loud and clear in his characterisation of the ideal museum as 'a mute school, a speechless university, a voiceless pulpit' whose sermons are 'written in stones' and where 'every specimen, every exhibition, every well-arranged hall speaks for itself' (240).

This animosity towards book learning echoed Huxley's criticisms of the humanities when compared with the more direct forms of sensory learning afforded by the scientific analysis of the properties of things themselves. 'The great museum', Osborn claimed, 'can, however, do what neither school, college, nor even the university can; it can bring a vision of the whole world of nature, a vision which cannot be given in books, in classrooms or in laboratories', thus making it possible for the child to see 'what Darwin and Huxley put into prophecy but did not live to see' (Osborn, 1911: 224–5). It also reflected the influence of the traditions of sensory democracy that had played such a key role in the early years of the American museum movement when a number of museums broke with the hierarchical assumptions of the Enlightenment museum by appealing to the public to visit museums so that, by looking and seeing for themselves, they would become the sovereign judges of truth rather than simply trusting the judgements of experts. Aspects of this tradition survived into the mid-century period when American natural history museums were also deeply influenced by the Pestalozzian system of education in the stress it placed on the pedagogic virtues of things over words. They also had a later life, towards the end of the century, in the showmanship of P. T. Barnum who made a calculated appeal to the tradition of sensory democracy in his invitation to the public to come and see for themselves whether a mermaid or a man-monkey was a hoax or not (Harris, 1973).

The influence of these varied traditions is evident in many of Osborn's formulations.[17] He sung the praises of nature study for its ability to develop 'independent judgement', contrasting this with 'instruction from books' where 'the child is dependent on the authority of others' (Osborn and Sherwood, 1913: 4). Similarly, in a later infamous passage, warning of the danger that books can breed revolutionaries, Osborn presents the AMNH's exhibitions as being both free of interpretation ('we are scrupulously careful not to present theories or hypotheses') and yet also organised by it ('but to present facts with only a sufficient amount of opinion to make them intelligible to the visitor' (Osborn, 1923: 2)). While this anticipates a set of issues concerning the relations between words, things and vision in evolutionary museums that I look at more fully in chapter 7, I raise them here because the contradictions characterising Osborn's position on these matters are centrally implicated in his museum practice. For in spite of his anti-scriptural, pro-object bias, Osborn presided over a period in which the AMNH went to more lengths than any of its contemporaries to organise explicit narrative or dramatised contexts for its public displays. It was, indeed, this that lay behind the perceptions of curators like Goode that if – to recall Sherwood's phrase – museums were 'dead circuses', the problem with the AMNH was that its displays were not dead enough and too much like the circus. Samuel Harmsted Chubb's arrangement of a rearing horse and man (Figure 5.2), prepared under Osborn's direction and, for a while, serving as the Museum's logo (Rainger, 1991: 156), makes the point. Nature was also dramatised through murals, especially Charles Knight's depictions of prehistoric scenes, and dioramas in which – in both the African Hall and the Hall of the Age of Man – the principles of earlier habitat and life group displays were transformed into more spectacular exhibits.[18]

The place of these exhibition practices within the visual culture of the early twentieth century has been tellingly analysed by Alison Griffiths, who discusses their relations to earlier popular exhibition forms (waxwork tableaux, for example) as well as their cinematic aspects (Griffiths, 2002: 17–29). My primary interest, however, is in the distinctive practice of memory they implied, for it is one in which, far from functioning as an evolutionary accumulator, the museum acts on the stratified self of the person by stripping away the accumulated layers of civilisation to instruct, refresh and mobilise a more archaic and primal, but always racialised, plasmic self.

Renewing the race plasm: accumulation and difference

In wrestling with the implications of August Weismann's theory of heredity, which disallowed the accumulative mechanism afforded by Lamarckian accounts of the inheritance of acquired characteristics by attributing a hereditary capacity solely to what Weismann called the soma plasm, or sex cells (cells that were unaffected by any environmental influence), Osborn was fully conscious of the challenge this presented to the accounts of evolutionary accumulation proposed by the Lamarckian readings that had proved so influential in filtering the initial reception of Darwin's work in America (Stocking, 1968). The success of Weismann's ideas, he argued, would auger

> a triumph for fatalism; for, according to it, while we may definitely improve the forces of our education and surroundings, and thus civilising nurture will improve the individuals of each generation, its actual effects will not be cumulative as regards the race itself, but only as regards the environment of the race; each new generation must start *de novo*, receiving no increment of the moral and intellectual advance made during the lifetime of its predecessors.
>
> (Osborn in Rainger, 1991: 125)

To follow this argument through to its conclusion, Osborn continued, would mean that 'the only possible channel of actual improvement were in the selection of the fittest chains of the race plasm' (125).

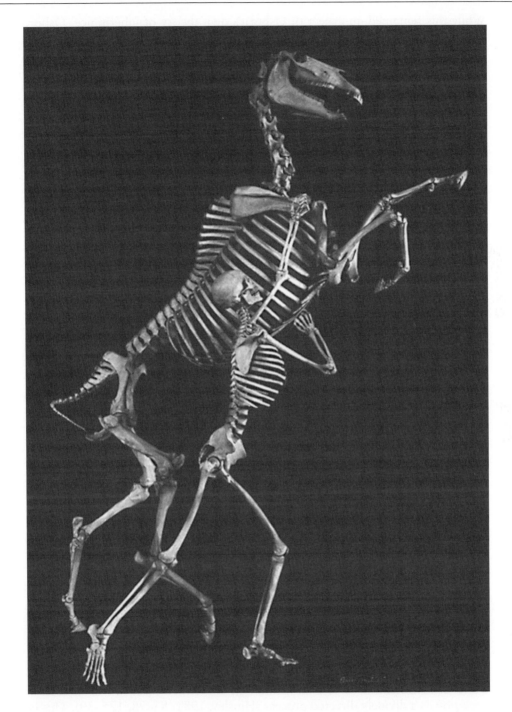

Figure 5.2 Samuel Harmsted Chubb's reconstructed skeletons of Rearing Horse and Man, which once served as the logo of the American Museum of Natural History.

Source: American Museum of Natural History.

While this remained an aspect of Osborn's own theory of inheritance, Osborn also sought to ward off the fatalist implications of Weismann's account by opening up a space for action. This space was afforded by his account of the relations between variations that were differentiated in accordance with their time of origin within the life history of the individual. While this account was variously rendered at different points in his career, its essentials remain unchanged. These are perhaps most clearly evident in one of the earliest versions of the argument, where Osborn marshals the evidence of the long series demonstrating slow and continuous evolution provided by museum collections against the emerging influence of the laboratory sciences, and where the concern to provide 'some strong progressive variational tendency in organisms to offset the strongly retrogressive principle of Repetition' (Osborn, 1895: 85) are as evident as the concern to provide an account of evolution that avoids sudden jumps or interruptions in time. So, too, is his concern to rebut the aspect of Darwin's work which he regarded as most pernicious: namely, Darwin's account of natural selection, in which evolution emerged as the directionless result of fortuitous variation. The distinctive aspect of this account consists in Osborn's construction of the relations between what he calls ontogenic and phylogenic variation: the former referring to variations from type arising from any stage in the development of an individual, and the latter comprising 'those departures from type which have become constant hereditary characters in certain phyletic series or even in a few generations' (86). While ontogenic variations introduce effects which ward off the threat of repetition, Osborn disallows the possibility that their long-term effects might be either directionless or fortuitous by arguing that only those ontogenic variations which connect with those 'definite tendencies of variation' that 'spring from certain remote ancestral causes' (95) could become phylogenic and therefore a part of the continuing development of the race. Ontogenic variation prompted by adaptations to changes in the environment could thus become of evolutionary significance only provided that they coincided with the pre-programmed, and divinely intended, path of separate development which, whether for a species or a race, was the bequest of deep time that continued to be operative within the present. The formulation thus avoids fatalism by opening up a space for the cultural action of the museum as one which, by renewing the vigour of the race plasm, can strengthen the tendency to progressive development and variation that is pre-coded into it.

'Nature can be nurtured only in so far as Nature intends' is a rough summary of the argument. As such, it was entirely in accord with the accounts of directed evolution that had proved more generally influential in the development of late-nineteenth- and early-twentieth-century American museum practices.[19] This was true, for example, at the Smithsonian where both Otis Mason, in his interpretation of Pitt Rivers's typological method, and John Wesley Powell, in developing the work of the Bureau of American Ethnology, subscribed to different versions of evolution as a divinely directed process (Hinsley, 1981: 83–98, 125–39). This is, however, of less relevance to my concerns here than the ways in which the development of the historical sciences in America was characterised by a fractured and more problematic relation to the stratification of time than was true of their

British formation. I draw here on the work of Bernard McGrane, who argues that the distinctive intellectual 'move' of Tylor's anthropology was to propose a 'stratification of time' by transforming 'the surface of non-European differences into the depth of an historical evolution' (McGrane, 1989: 94). In this formulation, what was *beyond* Europe was rearranged into a series of stages that were held to be both *before* Europe and *leading to it*. But this was true as much of the products of nature as it was of culture in an intellectual synthesis in which the whole of animate and inanimate life had been immanently historicised as parts of *one sequence*. This was less true in the United States, where the stratification of time was both more interrupted and discontinuous, and more a question of the unfolding of parallel lines of development than just the one.

There were a number of reasons for this. One of the more obvious consisted in the influence of Louis Agassiz. 'Time', Agassiz asserted in summarising his opposition to Darwin, 'does not alter organised beings' (cited in Menand, 2002: 107). Osborn's view that races, like species, follow separate pre-programmed paths thus has an important footing in Agassiz's view that separate blueprints for the development of both species and races had been established at the moment of creation. Other considerations, however, had to do with the more complex set of relations to the land, its inhabitants and the remains of earlier forms of life and civilisation contained within it that characterised the colonial contexts of 'settler societies' compared with Europe. It is the history of archaeology that is key here. In Europe, the interfaces between palaeontology and archaeology provided by the use of stratigraphical techniques of excavation and the use of principles of seriation for the classification of artefacts allowed stadial conceptions of human and cultural development to be articulated with accounts of natural evolution. Alice Kehoe (1998) argues that Daniel Wilson applied similar principles in his *Prehistoric Man*, published in 1860. As a representative of the Scottish Enlightenment, Wilson – who was well schooled in Danish archaeology – had emigrated to Canada in 1855 and, during his period in North America, made frequent visits to Native American archaeological sites in the Midwest of the USA. This had, Kehoe suggests, mixed results. On the one hand, so far as his estimation of contemporary Native Americans was concerned, Wilson was the first to suggest that they should be equated with European prehistory, thus historicising earlier conceptions of America as a natural wilderness. On the other hand, Wilson did not construe Native American civilisations as static but recognised that they, too, had gone through a developmental dynamic that was testified to by imposing earthworks and metallurgical skills.

This placed him in marked contradistinction to mid-century tendencies within US archaeology. For, in sharp contrast to late-eighteenth-century and early-nineteenth-century celebrations of the accomplishments of Native American civilisation, these repudiated any evidence of autochthonous developmental capacity on the part of Native Americans. The monumental cities that had earlier been celebrated were, as Kehoe puts it, either 'hidden in plain sight' (150) or reinterpreted as of Mesoamerican origin – an imported civilising dynamic that had been thwarted by Indian savagery.[20] This was complemented by the tendency, initiated by Samuel Morton's *American Crania* (1851), which read the record of

Native American remains so as to erect a saltational leap – an unbridgeable, anatomically grounded gap – between white and indigenous Americans. The legacy of this tradition was subsequently modified in the period from the late 1860s through to the 1890s when, mainly under the influence of Lubbock's *Prehistoric Times* (1865), American archaeology was brought under the influence of European prehistoric archaeology. While following Wilson's *Prehistoric Man* in interpreting Native American culture as evidence of Europe's own primitive prehistory, Lubbock did not follow the stress Wilson had placed on the autonomous developmental momentum of America's tribal cultures. This combination of factors, Bruce Trigger argues, meant that while a number of sites were studied both seriationally and stratigraphically from the 1870s through to the early 1900s, the evidence that these provided of change through time within those cultures was generally interpreted as of purely local significance, exceptions which did not refute the rule that such cultures were 'inherently primitive and had been static throughout prehistoric times' (Trigger, 1989: 121).

The challenge to this assumption was to come not from archaeology but from anthropology, most notably from Franz Boas, whose cultural relativism[21] challenged not only the evolutionary ranking of peoples but the basic principles of reasoning on which the historical sciences rested, including their object-centredness and their anti-philological bias. This challenge was first articulated shortly after Boas arrived in America when, in 1888, drawing on his experience at the Royal Ethnographic Museum in Berlin, he took Otis Mason to task for his use of typological principles in displaying the ethnographical materials of the US National Museum at the Smithsonian.[22] Boas took issue both with the biological analogy underlying the typological method, which Mason interpreted particularly rigidly,[23] and with the reasoning – ultimately derived from Christian Jürgen Thomsen – which allowed formally similar artefacts from widely separate areas to be assigned to the same places within evolutionary sequences on the assumption that similar circumstances would prompt similar technological inventions and adaptations. The basis of Boas's objection – which he was to develop into a wholesale critique a year after his appointment, in 1895, to the Department of Anthropology at the AMNH – was that artefacts could only be understood in the context of the particular historical and geographical culture to which they belonged and had their specific meaning and use.

To abstract artefacts from such contexts for the purposes of comparative functional analysis was, for Boas, a travesty of historical analysis. The basis for his objections in this regard came from the anti-evolutionary orientation of German anthropology which, as we have seen, was more inclined to organise peoples into the dualistic categorisation of *Kulturvölker* and *Naturvölker* – of people with and without culture in the humanistic sense of *Bildung*. While certainly evaluative, this did not result in developmental rankings and remained sensitive to the need to take account of the distinctive qualities and specific historical trajectories of different peoples (Bunzl, 1996: 43–51). Boas, however, rejected the essentialism of the *Naturvolk/Kulturvolk* distinction, insisting on the historicity of all human populations and their cultures, and, in a move that called into question the founding principles of the historical sciences, insisted also on the need to study those cultures in the context of their *actual* historical development rather than as parts of conjectural histories. This further entailed, Matti Bunzl argues, a radical break with the anti-textual premises on which the historical sciences had been founded in their critique of philology. In the stress he placed on the role of linguistics in ethnography, and in transforming Wesley Powell's collection of word lists – the linguistic equivalents of typological specimens – into the development of contextually sensitive grammars, Boas textualised ethnography's object of study. The effect of this, Bunzl argues, was to convert Native American cultures into written documents so that they might be studied on the basis of 'their equivalence to the classical object of the philological enterprise' (68) – exactly the opposite role to that played by the historical sciences in de-textualising subaltern Indian cultures in the emergence of the 'ethnographic state' in post-1857 India.

Boas translated these principles into a new visual technology in the life groups he developed for the ethnographic exhibits sponsored by the Smithsonian at the 1893 Chicago Columbian Exhibition and, subsequently, in arranging the first ethnographic displays at Chicago's Field Museum. He continued this work during his period at the AMNH which overlapped with Osborn's work, prior to becoming president, in the AMNH's department of vertebrate palaeontology. It is partly in this light that Osborn's extreme anti-scriptural bias needs to be interpreted. For where Boas proposed a culturalisation of difference, and applied this just as much to his interpretation of immigrant as of indigenous Americans,[24] Osborn countered with a re-racialisation of difference that grounded it within the hereditary histories of the different races. 'Why am I intruding in history?' he once asked. 'Because all these phenomena, all these processes, are biological processes, and all history, all human history, must be in time rewritten in terms of biology' (Osborn, 1924: 12). This was a return to conjectural history with a vengeance, lodging difference in ancestral race plasms whose origins lay somewhere in the unfathomable aeons of deep time. It was, however, the shallower slopes of this deep time that most concerned Osborn. So far as what he called the 'primary human stocks' or 'super races' were concerned – that is, *homo sapiens europaeus* or Caucasian, *homo sapiens asiaticus* or Mongolian, and *homo sapiens afer* or Negroid – their roots were so ancient that they were best regarded as quasi-zoological in nature, posing no serious threat of intermingling or racial dilution. Osborn's anxieties instead focused on the threefold set of divisions he posited within *homo sapiens europaeus* between *homo sapiens europaeus nordicus*, *homo sapiens europaeus alpinus*, and *homo sapiens europaeus mediterraneus*. These are thinly disguised racialisations of three different sources of migration to the United States which, according to Osborn, were also the sources of successive attempts to conquer and settle America – first by the Spanish (*homo sapiens europaeus mediterraneus*) who failed, then by the French (*homo sapiens europaeus alpinus*) who also failed, and then by the 'great type of northern peoples' (*homo sapiens europaeus nordicus*) whose adventurous and war-like spirit enabled them to succeed and make America in its own image. It is this racial patrimony that Osborn viewed as being under threat, not from Afro-Americans or Native Americans – too evidently, in his eyes, belonging to different primary human stocks and so posing no threat of racial dilution and enfeeblement – but from the renewed influx of the neighbouring sub-branches of *homo sapiens europaeus*. And it was this racial patrimony that was to be renewed by stripping back the veneer of civilisation to provide the opportunity for a reinvigorating contact with nature's competitive lessons.

Yet there was, paradoxically, a good deal of shared ground between the visual technologies through which these encounters with nature were organised and the life groups which Boas developed for the staging of cultural difference. Moreover, as Nélia Dias (1994) notes, both involved a visual economy that was quite different from that associated with typological displays. Typological arrangements work on the basis of the visible resemblances between the external form of the objects displayed. The message of evolution is thus carried by placing next to one another those objects that most resemble one another so that the trajectory of the viewer's eye – once cued to register that the meaning of each object depends on its relations to those on either side of it – takes in the message of evolution by simply ranging across the objects arranged before it. This involves, Dias argues, a disinterested gaze that is distanced from the scene of the exhibition. The life group, by contrast, requires 'an intervening and insisting eye' (171); it must, through the mechanism of the *coup d'oeil*, find a way of bringing the viewer into the scene of the exhibit by, initially, fixing it on a single point and thence distributing it to other points in the scene, thus organising 'a deep and penetrating look' (171). Yet, no matter how involved the eye might be in the scene, and however much it stressed the geographical and temporal specificity of the cultures on display, the life group, Dias argues, tended to freeze those cultures by presenting them 'in a static and unchanging present' (171).

Since Boas's life groups reflected the influence of earlier habitat displays designed to illustrate the variability of species in their relations to their environments (Parr, 1959, 1961), it is not surprising that a similar visual economy is found in the dioramas of the Africa Hall, where large male animals were displayed in combative tension with their habitats in order to dramatise the struggle for existence. Here is how Haraway describes their effect:

> Each diorama has at least one animal that catches the viewer's gaze and holds it in communion. The animal is vigilant, ready to sound an alarm at the intrusion of man, but ready also to hold forever the gaze of meeting, the moment of truth, the original encounter. . . . There is no impediment to this vision, no mediation. The glass front of the diorama forbids the body's entry, but the gaze invites his visual penetration. The animal is frozen in a moment of supreme life, and man is transfixed. . . . The specular commerce between man and animal at the interface of two evolutionary ages is completed. The animals in the dioramas have transcended mortal life, and hold their pose forever, with muscles tensed, noses aquiver, veins in the face and delicate ankles and folds in the supple skin all prominent. No visitor to merely physical Africa could see these animals. This is a spiritual vision made possible only by their death and literal re-presentation. Only then could the essence of their life be present. Only then could the hygiene of nature cure the sick vision of civilised man.
>
> (Haraway, 1992: 30)

However, as I have tried to show, this was by no means the only lesson on offer at the AMNH, any more than it was a lesson intended for everyone. *Homo sapiens europaeus nordicus* is the implied addressee here, stripped bare – like the child – of the overlay of culture in a scene of unconscious remembering that, in renewing the race plasm, would reinvigorate a racial stock that was threatened with dilution in the midst of a sea of unassimilable difference.

6

Evolutionary ground zero
Colonialism and the fold of memory

Towards the end of his discussion of the language and material culture of Australian Aborigines, whom he interprets as the 'lowest amongst the existing races of the world' (Pitt Rivers, 1875: 301), Pitt Rivers poses the question as to which of these affords the best evidence of prehistory. He opts in favour of material culture on the grounds that whereas 'in the earliest phases of humanity the names for things change with every generation . . . the things themselves are handed down unchanged from father to son and from tribe to tribe', continuing into the present as 'faithful records of the condition of the people by whom they were fabricated' (303–4). Pitt Rivers then goes on to project a future programme of work for colonial archaeology:

> Of the antiquity of savages we at present know little or nothing; but when archaeologists have exhausted the antiquities of civilised countries, a wide and interesting field of research will be open to them in the study of the antiquities of savages, which are doubtless to be discovered in their surface and drift deposits; and if the stability of their form has been such as we have reason to believe, we shall then be able to arrive at something like certainty in respect to the degree of slowness or rapidity, as well as the order, in which they have been developed.
>
> (Pitt Rivers, 1875: 304)

The passage was prophetic in more ways than one; indeed, if it proved an accurate prediction of the course of Australian colonial archaeology, this is precisely because of the respects in which its two main prophecies underpinned each other. For Pitt Rivers was right in conjecturing that, unlike its European counterparts, colonial archaeology would limit its attention to 'surface and drift deposits' rather than digging deeper into lower strata to find there evidence of a layered and developmental human time. And this was precisely because of what he predicted colonial anthropology would find: a stability of form in the material cultures it would unearth, suggesting an unchanging permanence of material practices, custom and stage of intellectual and cultural development. There was no need to dig deeper since the predicted evidence of what might be found was lying all around, strewn on the surface, or just below, in the recent remnants of Aboriginal life that were readily available for collection and for conjectural reconstructions of unchanging Aboriginal time lines.

This, in a nutshell, is the history of Australian archaeology in the closing decades of the nineteenth century and the opening decades of the twentieth. Indeed, in Tom Griffiths's (1996a) and other recent accounts, it is a history which lasted well into the 1930s when the stratigraphical analysis of Australian Aboriginal sites first began.[1] And its main legacy, the view of Aboriginal culture as 'primitive but not ancient', lasted a lot longer, until the 1960s, when John Mulvaney's use of carbon-dating techniques demonstrated not only the longevity of Aboriginal culture but also its change and development, thus initiating the subsequent complex, and still ongoing, negotiations of the relations between the deep time of western archaeology and that of the Aboriginal dreamtime.[2] This view of Aboriginal culture as having existed for a long time yet being unmarked by time's passage was a logical consequence of its role as an 'evolutionary ground zero' within the stratification of time that emerged from the symbiotic relations between European armchair anthropology and prehistoric archaeology. In order to serve as a point of origin, still discernible within the present, for evolutionary processes which have their culmination in the modern west, Aboriginal culture had to be placed outside of time, at its beginning. Folded into the historically split structure of the western self as a mnemonic device that allowed its lost and buried past to be recalled, Aboriginal culture was itself denied any fold of memory except in so far as this was construed as the endless recurrence of the same on a flat plane of time in which the self, denied any archaeological layering, was construed as a resolutely single-levelled, pre-modern consciousness.

In thus emptying out Aboriginal culture of any temporal dynamic of its own, this view served as an adjunct to the legal doctrine of *terra nullius* in constructing Australia as a territory that was unmarked by time prior to its European discovery and, just as important, only subsequently marked by time to the degree that it was connected to European time. Charles Long (1909) – a significant figure in the new education movement in Australia, and a strong advocate of the power of visual education – provides a convenient illustration of this in the chronological chart he proposed for teaching the timelines of Australian history (Figure 6.1). Bain Attwood offers a similar example from a 1917 school primer:

> *When people talk about 'the history of Australia' they mean the history of the white people who have lived in Australia.* There is good reason why we should not stretch the term to make it include the history of the dark-skinned wandering tribes who hurled boomerangs and ate snakes in their native land for long ages before the arrival of the first intruders from Europe . . . *for they have nothing that can be called a history.* They have dim legends, and queer fairy tales, and deep-rooted customs which have come down from long, long ago; but they have no history, as we use the word. When the white man came among them, he found them living just as their fathers and grandfathers and remote ancestors had lived before them.
>
> (Cited in Attwood, 1996b: 103; emphasis in original)

Such views resonated with those, evident from the 1840s, which interpreted Australian nature as a place where time was out of joint with itself: the 'land of living fossils', 'the palaeontological penal colony' – in these and myriad other

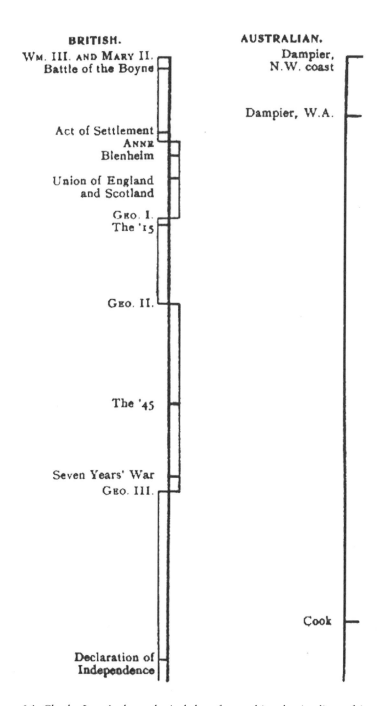

Figure 6.1 Charles Long's chronological chart for teaching the timelines of Australian history, 1909.

Source: Charles R. Long (1909) *The Aim and Method in History and Civics*, London: Macmillan and Co.

ways Australia played the role of a 'ground zero' for evolutionary accounts of nature's development.[3] As a place where backward forms of life still thrived – as Robert Chambers put it in his *Vestiges of Creation*, it was a place where 'the full time has not yet elapsed' (cited in Dugan, 1987: 83) – Australian flora and fauna provided a means by which progress might be visualised, a point of departure from which linear progression might be observed and measured.

Such general perceptions were reflected later in the century in the key role played by Australian specimens, in natural history displays, and by Aboriginal artefacts, in ethnological displays, in providing European and American museums with the starting points for their evolutionary displays. Yet although Australian museums were the main conduits through which such materials reached metropolitan museums, evolutionary arrangements made relatively little headway in Australian museums themselves until the late 1890s. There were a number of reasons for this. Some had to do with the dynamics of the colonial frontier, which meant that early collections of Aboriginal materials – and especially weaponry – were primarily trophy collections, powerful symbols of the capacity to dispossess and displace the colonised.[4] Others had to do with the fact that much of the initial headway made by Darwinism in Australia came from international networks – like those of the mechanics' institutes – linked to the labour movement, lending it strong socialistic and secular associations which found little favour among the colonial administrators and members of the 'squattocracy' who dominated museum boards of trustees (Laurent, 1994). And still others had to do with the relative weakness – both numerically, and in terms of their cultural influence – of the industrial and professional urban classes whose dissenting backgrounds and strongly meritocratic values had provided a significant aspect of the social and intellectual milieu from which, in Britain, the main champions of evolutionary thought – in geology, natural history and anthropology – were recruited (Kuklick, 1991).

While these background considerations were important, the more direct explanation has to do with the continuing operation of earlier networks which connected Australian curators and museum directors to pre- and anti-evolutionary tendencies within the international and, especially, British museum contexts. At the same time, and partly because of the strength of these networks, the success which the members of the Lubbock Circle enjoyed in placing Darwinians in positions of power and influence in British museums was not repeated in Australia where, to the contrary, such endeavours suffered some spectacular rebuffs. The literature cites a number of key episodes which symbolised this state of affairs: the largely pro-Owenist stance taken by museum-based scientists in Australia in the debates between Owen and Darwin over the classification of marsupials and monotremes; the dismissal of Gerard Krefft, once his intellectual sympathies turned too much in the direction of Darwinism, from his position of Curator at the Australian Museum in Sydney; and, perhaps most spectacularly, Frederic McCoy's publicly staged critique – complete with stuffed gorilla – of Darwin and Huxley before the Royal Society of Victoria in 1865.[5]

The turning of this anti-evolutionary tide is also usually symbolised by the appointment of Baldwin Spencer, first, in 1895, to the board and then, in 1899, as McCoy's successor, to the directorship of the National Museum of Victoria. Schooled originally in natural history, but styling himself as an evolutionary biologist, Spencer's social background was that of Mancunian industrial and nonconformist liberalism.[6] He had followed his first degree at Oxford with a stint at the University Museum where, through his involvement in installing the Pitt Rivers collection, he became acquainted with both Balfour and Tylor. An influential force in establishing evolutionary biology at the University of Melbourne after his appointment there as Professor of Biology in 1887, Spencer progressively turned his attention, like so many of his contemporaries, from natural history to anthropology. This remained the case during his term at the National Museum of Victoria which, by reactivating his networks with Darwinian curators in Britain, he transformed along evolutionary lines into an instrument of public instruction, in ways that were significantly to influence the practices of other Australian museums. Spencer also became an important figure in the history of the colonial administration of the Aboriginal population, especially during his term, in 1912, as Special Commissioner and Chief Protector of Aborigines in the Northern Territory. However, questions of 'Aboriginal administration' had concerned him before then and were to continue to do so well into the 1920s.

The period of Spencer's work in Australia coincided with a significant change in white attitudes towards the Aboriginal people of Australia: from the belief that the competition between white and black was so uneven that all that the former could do for the latter was to 'soothe the pillow' of a dying race to 'civilising' programmes which, once the continuation of Aboriginal people and culture was evident, aimed to 'lift' black into white Australia through assimilationist programmes that were epidermal as much as cultural. This represented a shift in the positioning of Aborigines within the strategies of biopolitics which, as Foucault characterises them, transformed the forms of power associated with sovereignty – the power to 'take life or let live' – into new forms for the regularisation of life that established the power to 'make live and to let die' (Foucault, 2003: 241). Yet it was also a shift which somewhat confounded the terms Foucault proposes, since it embodied an orientation to the Aboriginal population that was simultaneously one of 'let live' and 'let die': 'let live' in the sense that extinction was no longer seen as the evolutionarily ordained destiny of Aborigines, and 'let die' in the sense that their continued existence was only contemplated on the condition that – at both the cultural and epidermal levels – they were to become progressively white. This was a shift in which museum knowledges were deeply implicated, providing the templates for the classification and administration of the colonised that were to manage their movement through a social space governed by the stratification of time so as to allow their assimilation into the modern nation.

Colonial liberalism, culture and the state

If colonial liberalism is not to be interpreted as 'just one more freakish inversion of the natural order along with the duck-billed platypus and summer Yuletide',

Stuart MacIntyre (1991: 11) argues, it is necessary to consider how the principles of European liberalism were adapted and fashioned to new purposes in the context of the distinctive social relations and governmental imperatives characterising 'settler' societies like Australia in the *fin-de-siècle* period. Charles Pearson is one of the key figures in the intellectual and political lineage that MacIntyre constructs for this purpose. A leading figure in English liberal debates before settling in Australia in 1871, Pearson, who lectured in history and political economy at the University of Melbourne, became active in the liberal cause in Victoria. Writing frequently for the pro-liberal *Age*, he served for a brief period as Minister for Public Instruction in 1880–1 – when he pressed the cause of universal and compulsory secular state schooling – and, later, as a trustee of Victoria's Library, Museum and Gallery when he championed a number of proposals intended to transform that institution into a vibrant instrument of public instruction. Often defeated in practice by the weight of more traditional forces, Pearson's longer-term significance, MacIntyre argues, derived from the account of Australian liberalism he wrote on retiring from political life. For this cast a long shadow over the interpretations of new liberalism that proved so important in the political debates marking Australia's transition from being a series of separate colonial governments to a federated nation in 1901.

Published in 1894, Pearson's *National Life and Character: A Forecast* told the tale of the creative transformation of the classical English liberalism of the Manchester School into its virtual opposite on its transplantation in Australia. If, Pearson argues, the settlers of Victoria and of Australia's other colonies had carried with them the English theory of government which aimed to 'to circum-scribe the action of the State as much as possible; to free commerce and production from all legal restrictions; and to leave every man to shift for himself, with the faintest possible regard for those who fell by the way,' Australia had in fact become a place where 'the State builds railways, founds and maintains schools, tries to regulate the wages and hours of labour, protects native industry, settles the population on the land, and is beginning to organise systems of State insurance' (Pearson, 1894: 18). This was said not in apology but advocacy of Australia's role in developing new forms of government which, he predicted, would prove of increasing international relevance in the century to come when the activities of secular states would become more significant in every sphere of life – moral and cultural as well as economic. One of the reasons for this assessment, consisted in the new relations of time that followed from the weakened hold of Christian time:

> the sense of obligation, of duty to God, of living forward into eternity has disappeared. When all is said, the man who orders his life as if it were to end with the grave, or as if his thoughts and work here would not follow him beyond the grave, can scarcely fail to live more in the present than the future. . . . He will clutch with fierce avidity at power or wealth, or at the pleasures which are purchased by the possession of power and wealth.
> (Pearson, 1894: 292)

This sense of a need for new ways of regulating behaviour by organising subjects who would be capable of regulating themselves in the context of new relations

141

of secular and progressive time was broadly shared in the debates that shaped the trajectories of Australian liberalism from the 1880s through to the First World War. While echoing many aspects of new liberalism in both Britain and the United States, these debates were also shaped by the contest between free-trade liberalism, which was strongest in New South Wales, and the protectionist articulation of liberalism that was strongest in Victoria and was to become the ascendant version at the national level after the Federation of 1901. In accounting for this success of protectionist liberalism, Gregory Melleuish (1995) places particular stress on its relations with evolutionary thought and the concern that, without active state involvement, the progressive phase of European civilisation represented by the history of colonisation would come to an end as racial degeneration, leading to a final entropy, set in. Interpreting the struggle for existence as concerning more the relationships between national communities than those between individuals within the national polity, Australian new liberalism, in its protectionist articulation, denied nature the capacity to serve as a template for moral action and stressed, instead, the state's role in the provision of security as well as its role in character formation.

This stress on the moral and educative role of the state was not entirely new in the Australian context. The colonial state had, of necessity, played a strongly formative role in all aspects of Australian economic, social and cultural life from the outset: since civil society was, in essence, a creature of the state, the English liberal conception of a set of freedoms grounded in a pre-existing set of social relations ran against the grain of the process of Australian social formation (Collins, 1985; Rowse, 1978). The state was thus centrally implicated in the development of Australian schooling from the 1820s and, although the mid-century period saw its role challenged by the Anglican church, a spate of legislation in the late-century period – like the New South Wales Public Instruction Bill of 1880, denying funding to denominational schools – saw the struggle between the churches and the state settled in the latter's favour, with the significant exception of the separate and independent Catholic school system (Gascoigne, 2002: 114). It was also in this period that the remit of the state's activities in the cultural sphere was expanded to encompass museums and art galleries. This is not to say that state support for such institutions had been lacking previously; it is, rather, a matter of that support being organised on a new basis and for new purposes in comparison to the two main earlier phases of their development.

Such support had first come mainly in the form of the benevolent patronage of colonial governors, who sponsored the development of the literary, philosophical and scientific societies which, from the 1820s, provided the main contexts for natural history, geological and ethnological collections. This was, in most States, a case of the use of government patronage to facilitate and stimulate processes of class formation through which a 'colonial society' might be marked off and distinguished from a populace still largely marked by the 'convict stain'. The Sydney-based Philosophical Society of Australasia, established in 1821, thus operated through a ballot system which limited membership largely to representatives of the military and the colonial administration, and explicitly excluded emancipists – that is, convicts who had served their term and been given the freedom to settle (Finney, 1984, 1993; Hoare, 1981). The collections assembled in connection with such societies later became the basis of museums that were officially sponsored, regulated and partially funded by State governments in view of the importance that both natural history and geological collections played in the exploration, and exploitation, of the continent. The main change associated with the last third of the century consisted in the changed rationale for government support, based increasingly on the public educational value of museums, and the new organisational forms through which that support was expressed. Sally Gregory Kohlstedt thus notes that Frederic McCoy was initially appointed to the National Museum of Victoria as a part of his capacity as state palaeontologist, so that his salary was paid through the Board of Works and Lands. If the Victorian legislation of 1869, which brought the Museum and Victoria's Public Library and Art Gallery together under the common administrative umbrella of the same committee, portended a new set of priorities, then similar tendencies were also evident in other States. In New South Wales in 1873, the Australian Museum was brought under the jurisdiction of the Minister of Justice and Public Instruction; and in Queensland, in 1884, a few years after its initial establishment under the Minister for Public Works and Mines, the Queensland Museum was made responsible to the Secretary of Public Instruction (Kohlstedt, 1983: 11).

These changes, paralleling the shift in the balance of power from free trade to protectionist liberalism in the political sphere, were also accompanied by a shift in the balance between the different components of the Australian tradition of cultural liberalism that shaped the formation of the intelligentsia during the early years (dating from the 1850s) of the university sector. This tradition, as Melleuish describes it, comprised three wings: (i) a modified version of *civic humanism*, in which education was harnessed to the cause of creating the 'virtuous individual capable of acting dispassionately, free from bias and prejudice'; (ii) the Coleridgean–Arnoldian version of *culture*, oriented to the production of individuals with a higher level of vision, a secular spirituality that was able 'to pierce the illusions of sense and look into the heart of things'; and (iii) an ethos of *scientism* and *utility*, committed to the use of scientific knowledge as the means to human betterment, 'in which scientific principles formed the basis of human action' (Melleuish, 1995: 50). While these traditions were not hermetically separate from one another, the balance of influence between them moved in favour of the last over the last two decades of the nineteenth century and into the twentieth, with Huxley's work playing a significant role in this process. This was also the period in which the new education movement developed a significant momentum in Australia, where the ideas of Johann Friedrich Froebel were particularly influential, reviving the earlier influence of Johann Pestalozzi's anti-textual, object-centred pedagogy while simultaneously criticising the legacy of rote learning bequeathed by the monitorial school in favour of a stress on the self activity of the child.

The effects of the new education movement were readily discernible in the State Schools Exhibition that was held in Melbourne in 1906. In the testimonies and accounts of this offered in the collection edited by Charles Long – an Inspector of Schools, and a leading advocate of the new education – the value of seeing and doing for themselves that children were said to derive from nature study is constantly emphasised. There are also examples of how imaginative pedagogy can relate such study to the new lessons of history arising from the historical sciences whose broader public circulation derived from their associations with evolutionary museums:

> Here, for example, is the attempt of a teacher with a taste for geology to connect his pet subject with the daily life of the children. His school is in a Gippsland dairying district. Starting with the fact that the cow turns the grass into milk, the teacher . . . leads the child to think of the soil in which the grass grows. . . . Then, by means of clear diagrams the process by which the local soil is made is shown; the original strata of the neighbouring highlands, the same strata after upheaval, the strata after denudation, the various soil materials that settled in a lake . . . The earliest forms of plant life on the soil are then shown – lichen, moss, fern – leading up to the grass that now feeds the cow. Thus, the dairy work that goes on daily under the eyes of children is connected, step by step, with the long history of the earth's crust.
>
> (Gillies, 1908: 27)

In the immediately preceding decades, however, such messages are largely absent from Australia's major museums, just as the connections between these and state schooling were, in practice, largely fitful and sporadic. So far as their connections with international museum networks were concerned, the Australian Museum and the National Museum of Victoria remained linked to the anti-evolutionary tendencies in Britain: the latter remained such an 'evolution free zone' that it did not even hold a copy of Darwin's *Origin* in its library until the late 1880s, while the Australian Museum did not hold one either until the late 1870s. The same was true of their initial links with American museums, initiated largely by the latter and establishing connections mainly between Australia's anti-Darwinist curators and the Agassizian tendencies whose influence remained strong in the United States in the 1870s and 1880s (Kohlstedt, 1991b). And, notwithstanding the new jurisdictions to which they were subject, both museums proved able to limit the demands of public instruction that were placed on them while also remaining decidedly on the back foot in terms of their relations to state schooling.[7] The reasons for this have ultimately to do with the distinctive class structure of late-nineteenth-century Australia. While, by this time, heavily urbanised, Australia was not highly industrialised, with a good deal of its economic activity related to the interests of the pastoral sector. This meant a relatively weak industrial middle class and, owing to the relative lack of employment opportunities for new professional groups centred on the growth of science and engineering, a relatively small professional class too, and one mainly centred on the traditional professions, especially law and medicine.[8] It was this balance of class relations – and the strong links of Darwinism with an increasingly unionised working class spanning the urban and rural economies – that was largely responsible for the continuing influence of anti-evolutionary forms of natural history in Australia's public culture until nearly the close of the century.

Vicious circles and rigmaroles: the plan of creation

In *Eight Little Piggies*, Stephen Jay Gould (1993) tells the story of *Trigonia*, a clam that was thought to have become extinct, with the dinosaurs, at the end of the Mesozoic era. In 1802, however, a living trigonian was found in Australia. While this confounded earlier accounts of its extinction, it remained the case that no signs of *Trigonia* had been found in the intervening strata of the Cenozoic era. This key gap in the geological record thus left it open for *Trigonia* to be mobilised against evolutionary accounts of species development. This 'Cenozoic gap', in Agassiz's interpretation, made it possible to drive a wedge into the very core of evolutionary thought, since it provided a basis for denying that species of a genus living in successive, but not connected, geological epochs, were derived from each other. The pre- and post-Cenozoic trigonians were, simply, the products of different creations. Then, in 1865, a trigonian clam was found in Cenozoic strata in – where else? – Australia. But in spite of its obvious implications for the still raging controversies surrounding the publication of Darwin's *Origin*, these were not registered in the public debate except for a two-and-a-half page note by H. M. Jenkins – a little-known British geologist – in an equally obscure journal. The sting in the tail of Gould's account is that this fossil was discovered by Frederick McCoy, a palaeontologist schooled in the Cuverian tradition and an ally of Agassiz, who – although he would have been aware of its significance – did not publish his description of this discovery.

Although Gould warns against interpreting this as a simple case of withholding evidence, the story nicely symbolises the situation at Australia's two major museums – each vying with the other in their claims to national leadership – where nature continued to be laid out in accordance with stoutly pre-evolutionary principles. While there were, as I have suggested, similar reasons for this in terms of the places occupied by these museums within the class dynamics of Australian society, the details of the two cases differed. At the Australian Museum, a key factor was the enduring influence of the Macleay dynasty.[9] Beginning with Alexander Mcleay, who initiated a pattern continued by his son, William Sharp Macleay, and from the 1870s, by William's cousin, William John Mcleay, the Macleays were key figures in an amateur culture of natural history which derived its principal support from the landed classes and the traditional professions. The initial basis for this influence was the collection assembled by Alexander Mcleay who, before emigrating to Australia in 1825 to take up the position of Colonial Secretary, was an influential member of the Linnean Society and a collector of some renown: his entomological collection was considered one of the best in Europe. Using both his administrative and scientific influence, Macleay played a significant role in mobilising support for the establishment of the Australian Museum and served as a member of its Committee of Superintendence. Active in support of the 'exclusivists' versus the emancipists, believing that natural history was properly a matter for gentlemen rather than a concern of government, Macleay's influence was oriented to keeping the Australian Museum disconnected from Sydney's embryonic networks of professional science and to retain it in an ecclesiastical orbit around natural theology.

145

William Sharp Macleay – a key figure in the Museum's administration in the mid-century period – had different theoretical orientations stemming from his commitment to the Quinary system derived mainly from his education in Paris, where he came under the influence of Cuvier, and, later, his susceptibility to German Romantic *Naturphilosophie*. This, as we have seen, resulted in a conception of nature as a divinely governed order in which species were arranged in circular patterns according to their elective affinities: those 'damned circles' and 'rigmaroles' Darwin so disliked. William John Macleay, who, before inheriting the collection that Alexander had passed on to his son, had established his own collection and played a major role in the Entomological Society of New South Wales, was also active politically on behalf of the landed interests in New South Wales. It was this Macleay who played a key role, through the 1870s and into the 1890s, in staving off attempts to reform the Australian Museum – by importing evolutionary thought and stressing the Museum's public educational role – associated with the State administration of Henry Parkes, a free-trade liberal.

'Antiquated squatters and lawyers': these were the terms used by Gerard Krefft to characterise the forces that defeated his attempts to introduce both evolution and reform at the Australian Museum. The logic of events in Melbourne was different, owing less to the power of trustees than to McCoy's own scientific authority, the length of his tenure as Director of the National Museum (42 years), and to his astuteness in bringing the Museum under the administrative umbrella of the University of Melbourne (established in the 1850s). By this latter move, McCoy disconnected the Museum from the pressures of a public educational function associated with its original intended location as an addition to the Public Library, which had been established in the city centre in 1854.[10] For the University and the Library represented different components of a mid-century programme of liberal reform, one modelled fairly closely on mid-century English liberalism, in which state action in the cultural sphere was urged as a means of engaging with the fears of anarchy arising from Victoria's gold rush boom and the rapid urban growth it generated (Melbourne's population trebled between 1851 and 1854). The University, by cultivating the appropriate virtues among an educated elite, was to serve as the incubator through which an enlightened civil society might be developed and transplanted in the colony. While it too was charged with similar functions, the Public Library was also seen as a reforming bridgehead into the working classes, a means for improvement in both morals and manners (Fox, 1988). This was not, to be clear, the programme of the later new liberalism: the debates in Melbourne at this time drew mainly on the arguments that Henry Cole had marshalled in favour of state investment in art and culture in developing the South Kensington Museum in the aftermath of the Great Exhibition. But the Museum's location at the University of Melbourne did mean that it was effectively insulated from the later, more scientific inflection of cultural liberalism prompted by the influence of evolutionary ideas in the broader society, and by the demands for greater public relevance associated with the new liberalism/new education synthesis.

Fashioned, still, on the model of the Enlightenment museum, the National Museum of Victoria did not operate as an instrument of public instruction

146

connected to the new capillary mechanisms of state schooling. Rather, as we saw in chapter 1, it functioned as a rational antithesis to the flashy, showy and corrupting cultures of nature associated with popular circuses and menagerie. Quite the opposite of the American Museum of Natural History, which was very much in the city and engaged with it, McCoy's Museum was located outside the city and opposed to it. It was also located outside of, and opposed to, the progressive ordering of time emerging from the historical sciences. This also involved a different position on the relations between time and space, one that, in contrast to the historicisation of space that was involved in the organisation of colonial time/space relations, made space and time equivalents in ways that nullified the significance of time. This is evident in the account McCoy gave of the order and plan of creation in two public lectures delivered in 1869 and 1870 in which he sought to refute the very principles on which Darwinian thought rested. He had several goes at this. The passage I want to focus on occurs towards the end of the second lecture where he seeks to establish that the differentiation of species by space and time are equivalent and interchangeable, not in the sense that temporal relations are superimposed on spatial ones, but in the sense that both mark separate creations within an overall plan whose coherence derives from its being held together as a unity in a divine intention. It starts as follows:

> You have a whole series of related animals and plants in Australia; another entire series, with all the same relations, in Africa; and another entirely different series, but bearing the same relation to each other, in South America; all under the same conditions, but all different. Here you have the creatures separated by space, and the point I wish to draw attention to is this: If with me you will accept the idea of the whole of the living creation having been conceived as part of a universal plan at the time God gave the first command and first breathed life into any living thing – that all the parts of creation were designed and foreseen and foreknown at once, while, as yet, there were none of them; you will see that, as in our own time, these creatures are separated by space, so in the lowest and former ages they were separated by geological time.[11]

Going on to outline how separate animal and vegetable series can be distinguished by their location in successive rock formations, he instantly checks any tendency to look for signs of progressive development between these. He does so, moreover, through an imagery that establishes an equivalence between the surfaces of colonial peripheries and the depths of the metropolis:

> And if I point out to you the tertiary formation, nearly the last before the creation of man, you will find a condition of things in what is called the London clay – the clay formation which is under London – reminding you strongly at once of these great masses of southern lands of which I have been speaking just now. You find in the London clay – palms, cocoanuts, acacias – a whole series of plants very much resembling those of the Southern Hemisphere, in many instances, yet different in their species. You find serpents, birds, quadrupeds, and insects, the whole establishment so to speak, the whole series of all the different kinds of creatures required either

147

to form food for each other, or to perform all the functions of life, completed almost exactly on the same plan as found in one of those isolated parts of the earth's present surface, Australia, South Africa, or South America to which I drew attention just now.

The forms of interchangeability of space and time that are involved here, however, are not ordered developmentally. The London clay – quite unlike Huxley's piece of chalk – is not represented as a series of accumulating layers; nor are 'the isolated parts of the earth's present surface' seen as containing the survivals of the life forms earlier contained in the London clay. McCoy's point is rather that these are different orders of creation which, he continues, are 'separated by time as well as by space' in the sense that it doesn't really matter which of these is the case. As he goes on to argue, should there be a break, in any particular country, in the continuous chain of being from man and monkeys at the top to the very lowest living creature, it will always prove possible to fill this gap with a specimen from another country, or from an earlier geological layer. And it doesn't matter which since, in either case, what is being completed is not a developmental sequence but a divinely intended order of creation whose variant realisation at different points in time is as devoid of significance as is its variant realisation in different spaces, since it is the unity underlying both that matters. It was for this reason, to go back to the Cenozoic *Trigonia*, that McCoy might, with perfect consistency, have viewed its discovery as of little significance. For this discovery was important only provided that strata were already viewed as being developmentally temporalised in the way Darwinian thought proposed rather than, as McCoy understood them, as another spatial plane within a time which, while it had depth and duration, lacked accumulation.

Shallowing the past

That post-Darwinian evolutionary conceptions had relatively little influence on the ordering and arrangement of natural history exhibits in Australia's major museums – for the tendencies I have discussed in Sydney and Melbourne were generally true also of the other State museums established in the mid- to late nineteenth century (Anderson and Reeves, 1994) – did not mean that evolutionary perspectives lacked influence in the broader culture. On the contrary, if their hold on official science was slight, the works of Darwin, Huxley, Lyell and Lubbock were widely stocked within the libraries of mechanics' institutes; they were also, as Tom Griffiths (1996a: 43–7) notes, of great appeal to the amateur antiquarians who played such an important role in the history of Australian collecting; and their names were invoked in the organisation of public space – the town of Marysville in Victoria named its main streets after Darwin, Lyell, Sedgwick and Murchison, the main representatives of English geology (Fox, 1988: 20). It is also true that, more generally, the place accorded Australia within Eurocentric discourses as the origins of the global time that had been fashioned by the historical sciences – a land of living fossils – had a significant currency in Australia too. This was, indeed, part of a new phase in the colonial settlement of Australia, one in which nature and the landscape were seen in a new light – not as a world turned upside down, nor as one of strange and perverse exceptions to Linnaean classification (Ryan, 1996: 105–11), but as one that had been put 'in place' in its construction as prehistoric and primitive in relation to Europe. This was, however, a positioning in which Australian nature was placed in global time, as its beginning, without becoming fully a part of it, in the sense that this very construction deprived it of any distinctive temporality of its own. Whether viewed, as was the implication of McCoy's position – and an option Darwin had considered when he visited Australia in the 1830s – as a separate creation,[12] or whether seen as the still primitive origins of evolutionary sequences that attained their more developed forms elsewhere, pre-1788 Australia was seen as unaffected by time understood as a global process of progressive accumulation.

The same was true of the human inhabitants of Australia and their material culture which, especially from the mid-century period, was collected on a large scale and exhibited in numerous contexts: in private collections; as parts of colonial displays in international exhibitions in both metropolitan contexts and in the international exhibitions hosted in Sydney, Melbourne and Brisbane; in the developing collections of the major State museums; and in the small town and country museums that also began to be developed in the last quarter of the century. Chris Healy (1997: 93–102) is right to insist on the heterogeneity of the frameworks within which Aboriginal material culture was collected and exhibited. These included trophy collections, such as those of Reynell Eveleigh Johns, the amateur collector whose collection of Aboriginal hunting instruments was sent as Victoria's contribution to the Paris Exhibition of 1878 (Figure 6.2), and the 1890s display of Aboriginal materials at the Western Australian Museum (Figure 6.3); the collections and exhibitions of missionary societies which usually espoused a reforming and civilising orientation to Aborigines, albeit one couched in terms of the Christian time of salvation rather than the developmental time of evolutionary thought; the use of Aboriginal materials as points of anchorage for proto-national identifications seeking a point of connection beyond the hiatus of 1788; and contrapuntal displays in which Aboriginal materials were juxtaposed to imported signifiers of European civilisation – casts of Roman and Greek statues, for example – as evidence of a contrasting primitivism.

The principles underlying this last strategy became increasingly prominent – in museum displays and Australian public culture more generally – as the influence of evolutionary thought increased. The logic that was involved here, however, was quite different from that associated with the use of Aboriginal material culture as the initiating stages in the evolutionary series that characterised the deployment of the typological method in Britain. These, as we have seen, were intended to convey the lesson that in culture, just as much as nature, evolution makes no jumps but progresses step by step, continuously, and at the same pace. The evolution from primitive to developed forms is exhibited in long series in which each stage of development was, ideally, represented as equivalent: the progression from Aboriginal throwing stick to boomerang to bow and arrow to musket, for example, was presented as a continuing process in which each interval of development had the same value. In Australia, by contrast, the abyss of time represented by the colonial frontier operated as a barrier to such continuities. The relation

149

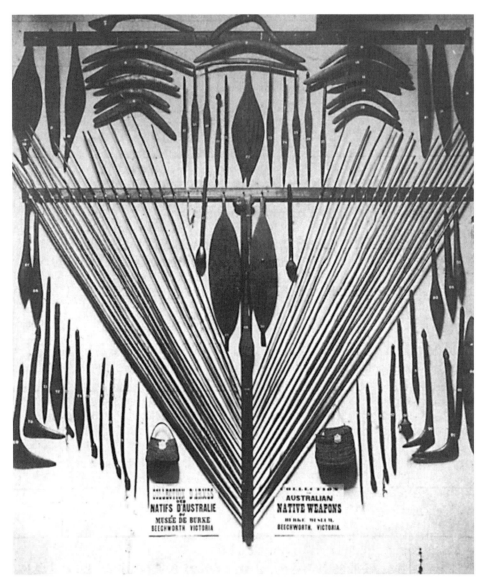

Figure 6.2 Display of Aboriginal hunting weapons based on the collection of R. E. Johns and sent to the Paris Exhibition of 1878.

Source: National Museum of Victoria, Melbourne.

between the time of the colonised and that of the coloniser was not that of time's arrow, a time constantly ascending and accumulating. The two were, rather, separated with the time of the colonised being represented as either a flat time – a time outside of developmental time, running constantly at the same level – or, where degenerationist conceptions prevailed, as a flat time that had become a descending time, time on the way out. There was no common time that connected

Figure 6.3 Collection of Aboriginal material, Western Australian Museum, Perth, c. 1890s.

Source: *Centenary Souvenir: Memoirs of a Museum*, Perth: Western Australian Museum, 1991.

pre-occupation Aboriginal anatomical, social or cultural life to that of the coloniser. Nature, history, culture – everything was required to make an unprecedented historical leap, of a qualitative kind, from one order of time into another, or, if that leap could not be made, to fall by the wayside.

A further reason for this saltational gap consisted in the ways in which, in early colonial history, the dividing line between historical and non-historical materials was drawn. Chris Healy comments usefully on this when taking to task those critics who interpret the shortage of artefacts relating to the post-1788 period of colonial history in late-nineteenth-century Australian museums as evidence of a thin level of interest in the development of a national public historical sphere.[13] What this misses, he suggests, is the significance of the documentary archive that Australian museums acquired in the course of the nineteenth century, as the major figures in public economic, political or cultural life bequeathed an accumulating record of maps, statutes, business records and personal papers as the public signs and legacy of their history making. These 'memorials in paper' (Healy, 1997: 91), Healy argues, served to orchestrate a twofold division. First, they organised a proto-national form of remembering that was distinguished by the stress it placed on written and documented history versus the significance that had been accorded objects within European practices of memory since the antiquarian culture of the eighteenth century. This was, in part, a matter of making a virtue out of a necessity, since the artefactual legacy of early Australian colonial history was, and remains, small. But it was also a way of marking out the division between pre- and post-occupation Australia as one between history, defined in

151

terms of text, writing and documents, and prehistory as the realm of silent and inert objects. And this in turn was an aspect of the construction of Austalia as *terra nullius*, a blank sheet on which history had yet to leave its mark (Ryan, 1996: 125).

This created a distinctive context for the operation of 'pasts beyond memory'. The synthesis of the historical sciences in late-nineteenth-century Britain produced ways of reading the evidence of things themselves that stretched the known and knowable past back beyond the reach of writing. This provided a means of connecting natural history, anthropology, and prehistoric and classical archaeology into object-based accounts of the past that rivalled, and presented a challenge to, the authority of script-based histories. In Australia, by contrast, the script–object distinction was a colonially charged relationship: pre- and postcolonial objects could not be placed on a common interpretative footing of the kind required for their mobilisation against text-based forms of exegesis.

Perhaps the most important factor, however, consisted in the abstraction of Aboriginal material culture from any temporality of its own. The key figure here is Baldwin Spencer who, on becoming Director of the National Museum of Victoria, put into effect a series of changes that reflected his own earlier training at the Pitt Rivers Museum and his connections with the key figures in the post-Darwinian liberal formation of the historical sciences. He was responsible for moving the Museum to join the Library in central Melbourne as a means of stressing its public educational function; for relocating the Museum's holdings of Aboriginal materials to the natural history section; for rearranging these in accordance with evolutionary principles; and for establishing a new network of international connections that linked the Museum to other museums operating in accordance with evolutionary principles. But it was also in his work that the contradictory qualities of evolutionary narratives were pushed into high relief when brought into contact with the 'evolutionary ground zero' which served as their points of origin. These contradictions were evident in the manoeuvres through which Spencer and a whole generation of Australian archaeologists contrived to deny that the stratification of time that had been developed in European prehistoric archaeology through its techniques for equating age with depth of excavation could be applied in Australia.

Mulvaney and Calaby see the guide that Baldwin prepared to the ethnographical collections at the National Museum of Victoria as a key text here in view of the breadth and scope of its influence. The conviction that Aboriginal culture had never had a distinctive temporality of its own is evident in the closing paragraph of Baldwin's introduction:

> The Australian aborigine may be regarded as a relic of the early childhood of mankind left stranded in a part of the world where he has, without the impetus derived from competition, remained in a low condition of savagery; there is not the slightest evidence either in his customs, social organisation, weapons, or implements to show that he has retrograded from a higher state of civilization.
>
> (Spencer, 1901: 12)

Having moved neither up nor down, Aboriginal culture was characterised by a timeless stillness which discounted the need for any stadial excavations since – as a matter of definition – there could be nothing to find. This was not true of colonial archaeology in other contexts. In Near Eastern archaeology, for example, Pitt Rivers's techniques for the excavation of prehistoric sites were used in combination with Galton's anthropometric techniques for reading racial types to construct – via stadial excavations of mound deposits – evolutionary accounts of Near Eastern prehistory as a succession of different phases of racial domination, from palaeolithic bushmen to the Berbers of the pre-dynastic period (Silberman, 1999). That the spade was spared in Australia in favour of the collection of stone implements by archaeologists who 'scoured the land but did not penetrate it' (Griffiths, 1996a: 78) was not, however, a matter simply of Spencer's influence, important though that was. It was an absolute necessity if the colonial fabrication of the Aborigine as the ground zero for Eurocentric narratives of progress were to be maintained while at the same time upholding the 'jump' that was necessary to separate coloniser and colonised. To dig might be to find evidence of development, in which case, as eventually they did, both of these positions would come tumbling down.

The intellectual manoeuvres through which this position was maintained until well into the 1920s were many and varied. They included Spencer's reasoning that stadial cave excavations – which had played a key role in unearthing evidence for human antiquity in Europe – would be unproductive in Australia on the grounds that Aboriginal 'fear of the dark' ruled out cave dwelling as an unlikely option (Mulvaney and Calaby, 1985: 255). They also included denial of the evidence pointing to the antiquity of Aboriginal settlement provided by the sedimented buttock marks at Warrnambool by attributing these to the effects of wind erosion (Horton, 1991). Their effect, however, was, as Griffiths notes, a curious one in which the conjectural paradigm was, so to speak, bent back on itself as a consequence of the odd curvature into which the historical sciences were pressed in Australia. He makes the point in discussing the extent to which stone tool collectors disdained Aboriginal informants, placing themselves as if in the position of finding remnants of long-lost cultures with no living members. By-passing Aboriginal testimony meant that interpreting the meaning of objects became, as one collector put it, 'a major piece of detective work' based on the evidence of the 'stones themselves'. This dual procedure – discounting Aboriginal testimony, and the use of conjectural reasoning in its place – testified to a science that 'was built upon an invention of cultural discontinuity' (Griffiths, 1996a: 82) that both denied Aboriginal memory and, in its place, substituted a fabricated set of 'pasts beyond memory' as a contrived exercise in historical guess work.

More than that, it placed the Aborigine in the same position as his or her material culture. In 1939, A. P. Elkin signalled the need for a shift in the way Australian anthropology viewed its relations to Aborigines, arguing that its treatment of them 'as though they were as their stones' (cited in McGregor, 1997: 214) militated against the need to enlist Aborigines as active agents in the process of their adaptation to Australian society. While the extent to which Elkin was successful in achieving this aim is debatable, the perspective is nonetheless an important one in registering the prospective opening up of a new historical space in which the principles of liberal government might begin to be applied to Aborigines. However, the historical associations between anthropology and the administration of the Aboriginal population in the preceding decades of the twentieth century had been cast in quite a different mould. These were underpinned by the logic of the typological method which, as Steadman notes, formed part of a more general shift in the nineteenth-century understanding of the type (Steadman, 1979: 80–1). This change – broadly speaking, a shift away from the type as an ideal to the type as a statistical average – was evident in the difference between Owen's conception of the species archetype as a purely ideal form underlying its variant manifestations and Darwin's understanding of the genotype, the hereditable component of species, as the statistical effect of a myriad of chance mutations. It was evident, too, in the application of typological reasoning to the artefactual field, in the view that changes from one design type to another are the statistical effect of the countless accidental variations produced by inexact copying across generations of craftsmen. It was through the application of similar principles to Aborigines, treating them as if they were indeed just as much specimen types as their artefacts, that their arrangement in social space was managed via enforced programmes of assimilation that were simultaneously epidermal and cultural.

From 'let die' to 'let live'

When discussing the transition from sovereign power to biopower, Foucault makes it clear that this is not a matter of the complete erasure of the old right – the sovereign's power to kill expressed as the right to take life or let live – so much as its penetration and permeation by a new right, the right to make live and let die as expressed, for example, in eugenic programmes. He also makes it clear that the advent of biopower does not involve the complete suspension of disciplinary power, either, but rather co-exists with it, operating at a different level of the social and using different instruments. 'Unlike discipline,' he says, 'which is addressed to bodies, the new nondisciplinary power is applied not to man-as-body but to the living man, to man-as-living-being; ultimately, if you like, to man-as-species' (Foucault, 2003: 242). Discipline rules a 'multiplicity of men' via an 'anatomo-politics' that dissolves that multiplicity into individual bodies that are kept under surveillance, trained, and, if necessary, punished. In contrast to this individualising orientation, biopolitics deals with the 'multiplicity of man' not as the sum of a number of individual bodies that are to be disciplined separately, but as 'a global mass that is affected by overall processes characteristic of birth, death, production, illness, and so on' (242–3).

These processes affecting aggregate populations are, Foucault continues, 'serial phenomena . . . aleatory events that occur within a population that exists over a period of time' (246). As such, they prompt forms of intervention – like hygienic programmes – which, depending on statistical programmes and forecasts, act on these processes at the level of their generality, regularising life by managing the intersections between social processes and the biological processes of man-as-species. It is in this context that the power to kill transmutes into a new form: that of racism, or more specifically, of scientific racism which functions as 'a way of introducing a break into the domain of life that is under power's control: the break between what must live and what must die' (254). It is here, in the divisions established by evolutionary hierarchies, that evolutionary thought functioned as an integral component of biopower, articulating the power to kill across a set of racialised divisions in a manner that inscribed it within the mechanisms of the modern state. Developed originally in the context of colonial genocides, this power to kill is posed in terms of the need to eliminate the biological threat posed by 'other races', in ways that, Foucault argues, always drew on evolutionary conceptions.

These relations between disciplinary power and biopower assumed a distinctive form in Australia. Its establishment as a penal colony meant that it was initially established as a society that was to be run in accordance with the principles of discipline developed by Enlightenment penology. These were, as John Gascoigne (2002: 133–9) notes, informed by Linnaean principles of classification which provided a means of classifying individual convicts according to the seriousness of their offence and degree of their reform, and distributing them within social space accordingly. This was not, however, as in Europe, solely a matter of the places they occupied within the reformatory apparatus of the penitentiary. Rather, in early colonial Australia, virtually the whole of social space was mapped out in accordance with the disciplinary deployment of the logic of classification. Life outside the penitentiary was thus organised as so many spaces along which the convict's path to rehabilitation could be measured and managed. Van Diemen's Land became 'a kind of open air panopticon' (Ely, in Gascoigne, 2002: 135) where, in the words of its Lieutenant-Governor, George Arthur, 'the facilities afforded . . . for carrying classification into effect are such as could never be attained within the walls of a penitentiary' (in Gascoigne, 2002: 135). Life beyond the walls of the penitentiary at Port Arthur was, for the convict, one of continued surveillance by farmers and householders – everyday gaolers – for whom they provided forced labour. And, moving in the other direction, places of hyper-discipline – Norfolk Island, for example – were established as 'penal colonies beyond the penal colony' for those bodies that proved too refractory for regular forms of discipline.

The construction of separated reformatory spaces, run on a combination of disciplinary and missionary principles, was also an aspect of the early colonial administration of the decimated Aboriginal population that withstood not only the racial wars that were waged across the colonial frontier but also, and deadlier still, the introduction of European diseases (Hughes, 1996: 421–3). These were not at this time, though, historicised spaces. However, they came to be so as Australia came to be regarded as a place where extinct, or soon-to-be extinct, forms of life survived in the separated enclaves of Aboriginal reserves where the race was supposed to live out its last days. Yet this view of Australia as a 'living museum' lasted well into the twentieth century, and certainly beyond the period of 'let die' policies directed at softening the pillow of a dying race to the 'let live' programmes of assimilation in which the goal of biological elimination, however 'passively' pursued, was transformed into one of cultural and epidermal

155

transformation. It was in this context that the historical sciences came out of the enclosed state of the museum which characterised their European incarnation to be applied in a link between ethnography and the state which aimed to speed up the movement of Aborigines through developmental time.

Towards the end of the essay in which he predicted that the antiquities of savages would be found in the surface and drift deposits of Australia, Pitt Rivers admonished the need to respect the saltational logic of the colonial frontier:

> Or two nations in very different stages of civilisation may be brought side by side, as is the case in many of our colonies, but there can be no amalgamation between them. Nothing but the vices and imperfections of the superior culture can coalesce with the inferior culture without break of sequence.
>
> Progress is like a game of dominoes – like fits on to like. In neither case can we tell beforehand what will be the ultimate figure produced by the adhesions; all we know is that the fundamental rule of the game is sequence.
> (Pitt Rivers, 1875: 308)

The key figure around which this rule of the game was worked through in the debates accompanying the shift towards assimilationist policies over the inter-war period was that of the 'half-caste'. While providing a connecting term that could provide for some 'adhesions' between black and white, the savage and the civilised, the key question was: in which direction did the 'half-caste' point? Was it a condition of in-betweenness pointing backwards, a degradation of whiteness portending an inevitable degeneration? Or did it point forward, portending a move through the stages of evolutionary development, a reaching for the light and civilisation?

Baldwin Spencer was a key figure in these debates and their implications for questions of Aboriginal administration in view of his enduring interest in, and influence over, these questions arising from his work as Special Commissioner and Chief Protector of the Aborigines in the Northern Territory. As we have seen, Spencer originally viewed Aboriginal people as having been unmarked by time, and destined to bear its impress only in so far as contact with a superior civilisation entailed their extinction. They would be a part of history only at the point of leaving it. However, his views changed from protectionist and preservationist policies to embrace, albeit hesitatingly, civilising programmes which aimed at bleaching the Aboriginal population while also developing it culturally through a series of successive transformations. The logic of these programmes, and their provenance in the gradualism of post-Darwinian reform liberalism, can be seen from the terms in which the need for them was urged by Elsie Masson, who was a resident at Government House in Darwin at the same time as Spencer, and who later married Bronislaw Malinowski. As a race 'which has not toiled by slow ways to civilisation', Masson argued that if 'the blackfellow attempts to leap at one bound the chasm of ages, he will fall and be annihilated' and therefore urged the white man to 'build a bridge for the black man by which he may cross in safety' (cited in McGregor, 1997: 87). In the early 1920s Spencer lent his support to the construction of one such bridge in the theoretical support he lent to the view that 'half-castes are capable of reaching a higher stage of development than the pure-blood blacks' (Spencer, cited in McGregor, 1997: 145) and the practical support he lent to the development of a 'half-caste' station which, by segregating 'half-castes' from the general Aboriginal population and providing them with special training, would facilitate their absorption into white society – and, through inter-breeding, their progressive disappearance in an epidermal vanishing trick. If, under Arthur, Van Diemen's Land had been an open-air panopticon, this programme for a progressive but still accelerated route through the stages of civilisation entailed the manipulation of bodies in a social space that was mapped out as an open-air museum.

Patrick Wolfe (2000) posits a connection between, on the one hand, Spencer's promulgation of assimilation and his purported discovery of nescience (the failure to realise that conception is the result of sexual intercourse) among the Arunta and, on the other, the historic alliance between ethnography and the state, as represented by assimilationist programmes which aimed at the civic and cultural rather than the physical elimination of Aborigines. This reversal of earlier strategies in which 'half-castes' had been expelled from reserves to occupy the extreme margins of Australian social space in order to set up special staging posts through which they were to be 'incorporated into the settler domain' (Wolfe, 2000: 223) reflected the need to remove the threat their presence embodied to the organisation of the new forms of memory and identity required for the construction of Australia as an imagined nation. The connection Wolfe wishes to establish between the form that such programmes took and Spencer's belief in nescience among the Arunta derives from the role that this belief played, in the conjectures of the historical sciences, in relation to Australia's role as an evolutionary ground zero. For this 'discovery' – reported in 1899 – was presented by Spencer and his co-researcher, Francis James Gillen, as a confirmation of the conjecture of Edwin Sydney Hartland, an amateur English folklorist cast in the Tylorean mode, that such a belief would be found among Australian Aborigines as a survival of prehistoric beliefs. Spencer's and Gillen's apparent empirical and – in the laboratory condi-tions of outback Australia – experimental confirmation of this prediction thus served as one more indicator of the Aborigine's standing as an absolute baseline of primitivism. The effect of this, Wolfe argues, was to establish a point of absolute otherness which made it possible for ethnography and assimilation to come together around a bipolar opposition in which '"part-aborigine" automatically meant "non-aborigine"' (227), so that the transition from 'full-blood' to 'half-caste' could be equated with a transition from prehistory into history.

Wolfe's characterisation of this equation of part-Aboriginal with non-Aboriginal as a 'descending opposition', in which everything that does not entirely coincide with the category of the Aboriginal stands not just outside that category but is opposed to it in relationship of 'p' and 'not p' (226–7), echoes the archaeological structure of the object in a typological display. The racial organisation of 'half-castes' who were placed in staging posts, of whatever kind, was like that of the second, third or fourth – but not the first – object in a typological exhibition: they were both not what they had originally been and not yet at the next stage of what they would become, stalled in a movement that had yet to be completed. For it is only in this light that we can understand the respects in which such assimilationist programmes revived and depended on, while giving a new interpretation to, the 'connective tissue of civilisation' by inscribing this within, in McGregor's telling phrase, a programme of 'civilisation by blood'. Each step towards whiteness involved an accumulating mnemonics through which, by acquiring an increasing archaeological depth with each step away from the entirely flat, a-historical structure of the 'full-blood', epidermal transformation was seen as simultaneously the acquisition of the kind of complexly layered self required for the Aborigine – or, more accurately, the ex-Aborigine – to be freed from the restraint of colonial forms of governmentality and be admitted into liberal forms of self-rule. 'Half-castes' were thus often granted special exemption from the control of the Chief Protectors who were their legal guardians and allowed to assume specific rights and responsibilities – the rights to their own bank accounts, for example – long before this was true for Aborigines more generally.[14]

It is not surprising, given these circumstances, that a good deal of anxiety was invested in devising means of measuring the degree of civilisational advance associated with the dilution of Aboriginal blood. Nor was it surprising that this should also have registered itself as a problem of vision – of seeing evolution happening in changing skin tones. McGregor underlines the importance of these issues for Spencer in his 1923 report on the relative progress of 'half-castes' and Aboriginals in the southern division of the Northern Territory. The photographs accompanying this, Spencer argued, proved more conclusively than words that 'half-castes' were as different from true blacks as octoroons were from 'half-castes'. These self-evident lessons in progress were not, however, quite what they seemed. McGregor notes that the impression of advancement they gave depended on a choice of *mise-en-scène* – domestic settings, with conventional middle-class poses – which stressed approximation to white cultural norms, and what he suspects was a judicious retouching of the images to enhance the fair complexions of those photographic subjects identified as 'half-caste'.[15] Yet, for all that he stressed the power of these images to demonstrate progress more powerfully than any words could, Spencer still felt the need to add a verbal supplement. He thus writes beneath a family portrait (see Figure 6.4):

> Half caste man and woman with their child. The man speaks English well, is most capable in dealing with stock & quite equal to taking his place among white workers. The photograph does not do justice to the half caste woman.

The difficulties here were not unique to Spencer. On the contrary, the vexed issues posed by the difficulty of interpreting the spaces between artefacts, species and races so as to discern the direction and tempo of evolution were shared by evolutionary showmen, both in and outside museums, as part of a distinctive set of problems concerning the relations between words, things and vision.

Figure 6.4 Walter Baldwin Spencer's photograph of 'Half caste man and woman with their child', 1923.

Source: Walter Baldwin Spencer, 'Report on the Half-castes and Aboriginals of the Southern Division of the Northern Territory' (1923), Australian Archives, Canberra, Commonwealth Record Series A1, 30/1542.

7

Words, things and vision
Evolution 'at a glance'

When praising museums for their ability to offer object lessons which appealed to the eye, George Brown Goode drew special attention to the democratic possibilities inherent in their capacity to extend their educational reach beyond the limits attached to writing. The museum was at one with a 'busy, critical and sceptical age' in which the increasing need for 'each man . . . to know all things' meant, given that life was 'too short for many words', that educators in all spheres – in the schoolroom just as much as in the museum – placed a premium on visual instruction. 'The eye is used more and more, the ear less and less,' he argued, 'and in the use of the eye, descriptive writing is set aside for pictures, and pictures in their turn are replaced by actual objects' (Goode, [1889] 1991: 321). Museum curators and directors in Britain were just as convinced of the virtues of an ocular-centric and object-based pedagogy. For F. E. Weiss, the proper task of the botanical museum was to provide 'instruction which is directed to and assimilated by the eye' (Weiss, 1892: 25), a view echoed by Boyd Dawkins who urged that museum displays should aim for a form of 'time arrangement' in which the interconnectedness of human, natural and geological time 'is placed plainly before the eye' (Dawkins, 1890: 42). And Alfred Haddon echoed Goode in stressing the museum's ability to convey information 'visually with accuracy and great rapidity' (cited in Levell, 2001: 254). A similar stress on the primacy of vision was evident in Australia. The trustees of the Melbourne International Exhibition extolled its virtues as 'a national educator, to teach by the eye' (cited in Hoffenberg, 2001: 72). And when, in 1885, an anonymous report from the Mineralogical and Geological Department to the Trustees of the Australian Museum recommended the adoption of a 'comprehensive system of exhibition', this was to pay special attention to the needs of miners as a class of men who wanted 'science to be put before them in a popular light, which speaking to their eyes, spares their time, and remains deeply impressed on their memory'.[1] Its aim, in short, should be to allow the miner to take in the basic principles of the science of mining 'at a glance'.

This stress on the virtues of 'eye-knowledge' arose from the distinctive epistemological concerns of the historical sciences in their claims to be able to decipher the meanings of objects and, thereby, to challenge the text-based narratives of biblical and humanistic scholarship. If these had rested on a hierarchical ordering of the relations between words and things of the kind proposed by Friedrich

August Wolff in his influential division between the first-class disciplines (largely linguistic and grammatical) and the object-based disciplines (such as numismatics and archaeology) (Marchand, 1996: 21–2), the response from within the historical sciences was to reverse this hierarchy. This translated into the belief that no effort should be spared to lay out objects within the museum space in ways that would make the relations between them – relations of temporal succession and development – readily and directly perceptible. That the laws and direction of evolution should be taken in 'at a glance' was a simple given for the evolutionary showman.

The rhetoric of clear and transparent vision that such claims involved reflected the legacy of the Enlightenment museum, where the logic of classification had also aimed to make it possible for the visitor to take in the order of nature 'at a single glance'. Yet the 'glance' of the Enlightenment museum was, in fact, a highly ordered practice of looking, and that of the evolutionary museum no less so. 'How hopeless', Jonathan Hutchinson argued, 'is the vacant gaze of the uninstructed as they wander through galleries in which on every side are accumulated objects which would enchain their interest if only they knew how to understand them' (Hutchinson, 1893: 49). This concern that the visual attentiveness of the uninstructed might not be sufficiently clear and piercing to understand the logic underlying museum arrangements was shared between the two periods, reflecting similarly embattled relationships to the distracting forms of inattention that were attributed to the popular visual entertainments with which museums had to compete. Yet there were also, beneath these common concerns, equally important differences affecting the regulation of vision that the two different types of museum aimed to effect. Their orderings of the relations between words and things were also significantly different, reflecting what were at root, in spite of a shared vocabulary, different regimes of vision. For while the Enlightenment museum ostensibly displayed its logic on the visible surface of things, it was the invisible orders of connection binding things into relations of genealogy and descent that mattered in the evolutionary museum. However much the evolutionary showmen praised the object lessons of things for their ability to strike the eye directly, only an appropriate ordering of the relations between them could make the processes of evolution perceptible. Yet these spaces between things were quite volatile and full of surprising difficulties, generating a distinctive nexus of epistemological and political anxieties.

The spaces in-between: evolution and its blind spots

One of the greatest obstacles that had to be overcome in establishing the public credibility of evolutionary thought was that, as the aggregate effect of a multitude of tiny changes, themselves imperceptible, the *processes* of evolution could not themselves be seen – only their *outcomes*. Darwin understood this clearly:

> It may be said that natural selection is daily and hourly scrutinising, throughout the world, every variation, even the slightest; rejecting that which is bad, preserving and adding up all that is good; . . . We see nothing of these

> slow changes in progress, until the hand of time has marked the long lapse of ages, and then so imperfect is our view . . . that we only see that the forms of life are now different from what they formerly were.
>
> (Darwin, [1859] 1968: 133)

The same was true of the relations between man and his forebears and, within the human species, between different races. In *The Origin of Species*, Darwin accounted for the gaps in the geological record which made it difficult to trace continuous lines of evolutionary development as themselves a necessary result of the ways in which geological processes cover up their own tracks. In the very course of depositing the traces through which their own impact on the earth might be deciphered, large-scale geological transformations obliterate – overwrite, as it were – the evidence laid down by previous stages of development. The earth is thus only a patchy and unreliable palimpsest which, in being periodically wiped clean, functions as an imperfect storage system. Similar conceptions inform *The Descent of Man*, where Darwin notes that the 'great break in the organic chain between man and his nearest allies, which cannot be bridged over by any extinct or living species, has often been advanced as a grave objection to the belief that man is descended from some lower form' (Darwin, [1871] 1981: 201). If viewed correctly, however, Darwin contends that such breaks tend to support rather then refute the perspective of evolution since they merely confirm the general principle that breaks occur, and must occur, at many points in evolutionary series. He then goes on to hypothesise that continuing evolution can only widen the gaps within both natural and cultural evolutionary series as evidence of various intermediate stages of development are wiped out.

> At some future period, not very distant as measured by centuries, the civilised races of man will almost certainly exterminate and replace throughout the world the savage races. At the same time the anthropomorphous apes . . . will no doubt be exterminated. The break will then be rendered wider, for it will intervene between man in a more civilised state, as we may hope, than the Caucasian, and some ape as low as a baboon, instead of as at present between the Negro or Australian and the gorilla.
>
> (Darwin, [1871] 1981: 201)

The application of the 'Darwinian analogy' to the evolution of design and technology posed similar problems. For since, in the early stages of evolution, changes in design were produced gradually as the result of multitudinous tiny and usually unintended changes on the part of countless generations of anonymous potters or builders, this analogy meant that such changes were either too small to see or too large where – in the case of designs separated by significant durations of time – the lack of connecting links made it impossible to trace any relations of historical affiliation between them.

Evolution, in short, could not be seen directly. It could be made evident not in things themselves, but only in a particular narrative ordering of the relations between them through which resemblances were interpreted as descent;[2] and it could not be made evident at all where sequences were interrupted and discontinuous. The spaces between things were, accordingly, invested with a particular and compelling significance as scientific method, across a range of disciplines, came to focus on the task of filling in those spaces in order to provide continuous sequences of lineal descent connecting the past to the present in an unbroken historical order. In seeking to 'verify the existence of forms between forms', as Thomas Richards puts it, Darwinian morphology 'fixed its sights on the grey areas between forms' (Richards, 1993: 55) as the zone where all its distinctive problems of understanding, representation and manipulation clustered. Richards also helps to place these epistemological anxieties into sharper relief by contrasting the implications of evolutionary thought in these regards with those of the tabular order of classification and the redefinition and relocation of monstrosity that was entailed in the transition from the latter to the former.

Within Linnaean classification, he argues, any form that fell outside the logical grid of taxonomy was 'a singularity, a fluke, a freak of nature, and the best that could be done was to place it in a bottomless category for all the deviations from logic traversed by nature, the special category of the monstrous' (47).[3] Once synchronic classification gave way to the task of connecting forms of life to one another within evolutionary sequences of lineal descent, forms that had previously been placed outside scientific order in the realm of the monstrous could now, having been retrieved as ancestors or heirs – that is, as links in evolutionary sequences – be integrated into a scientific ordering of things which posited no limits or exceptions to its reach. The monstrous, for Darwin, becomes merely a trivial, albeit visually striking, departure from species norms.[4] The same was true for the marvellous: the kangaroo, together with other Australian fauna, thus ceased to be the out-of place wonder that it had first appeared to be to European explorers when it was assigned to a stage within mammalian evolution.[5] 'Unusual, deviant, or monstrous forms', as Richards generalises the point, 'can now be fixed on a vast index of change, a book of all changes . . . monsters either disappear forever or mutate themselves into a form which eventually becomes the norm' (56). This was, moreover, an order which, unlike Cuvier's, acknowledged no catastrophic interruptions. In the long, slow evolutionary sequences of Darwinian nature in which change from form to form takes place imperceptibly through the accumulation of innumerable minor adaptations, there is no place for sudden or dramatic mutations.

Yet monstrosity did not so much disappear, Richards suggests, as assume a new form, one that threatened to disrupt the continuous evolutionary ordering of nature from within by playing on its blind spot: the relationships between things. These now took the form of sequences of time marked by fossil, osteological and archaeological remains whose temporal connections to one another depended on conjectural reconstructions of lines of descent which, owing to the nature of geological and archaeological records, were incomplete and destined forever to remain so. 'The order of things', as Richards aptly puts it, was no longer 'the order of ordered things' but 'the order of all things that had ever existed' (48). The spaces between things thus took the form of unknown gaps which morphology had to fill in order to sustain the view of life's evolutionary ordering as the outcome of a multitude of gradual and small-scale mutations. Monstrosity accordingly appeared in the new guise of 'beings that had undergone, or were capable of undergoing, catastrophic mutations of form' (58). For, in passing 'from form to form, moving not one form at a time but skipping many forms in a single jump', these introduced 'chasms of unbridgeable difference' (58) into the reconstructive projects of morphology. Monstrosity, in short, took the form of the mutant. As 'a being without a history', with 'no past, no progenitors, no lineage, no putative position on a reconstructed time-line' (58), the mutant introduced discontinuity into the very midst of the long, slowly unfolding sequences of life that the Darwinian project required.

This was expressed, in the scientific literature, in the heightened interest in the question of hybridity, owing to the degree to which this blurred the relations between forms of life – and, of course, in the human sphere, between races. It was also evident in the concern with mongrelism which, by suggesting the permeability and fluidity of the relationships between forms, also suggested the impossibility of either demonstrating the purity of a lineage or of guaranteeing descent.[6] And in popular exhibitions, the recontextualisation of freaks and monsters as missing links played on the concerns generated by the gaps in the new evolutionary ordering of things.[7] In Victorian culture more generally, however, Richards argues that the figure of Dracula – given a new form and meaning in Bram Stoker's novel[8] – constituted the most worrying and probing expression of this new currency of the monstrous. As 'a creature capable of both *sudden* and *lasting* mutations of form'; as 'the origin of his own species, a human being suddenly transformed into the progenitor of a terrifying new species' (58; emphasis in original); as the lord and master of the Undead, who 'lives in a purgatory of decay instead of just passing through it' (60) to renew life's cycle: in all of these ways, the figure of Dracula haunts the 'blind alleys of Darwinism' (58). In *Dracula*, owing to the speed at which they can mutate and their ability to leap across forms, the dead travel fast; in the Darwinian universe, where nature makes no jumps, the dead toil slowly, and at an even pace, to evolve into the present.

It is not difficult to see why these blind spots of Darwinism should also have been its political hot spots. For there were plenty among the living, too, who wanted to travel fast, and in jumps, by making a revolutionary leap into a new social order. The economic crisis of the 1880s made the dangerous classes of 'outcast London' a ripe ground for political fermentation, and one that was struggled over by different interpretations of socialist thought – all of them deeply influenced by evolutionary theory – in what was to prove a formative period in the longer-term history of the British labour movement. The last two decades of the century were also profoundly important in the early development of feminism which – in the US and Australia just as much as in Britain – was also significantly affected by its engagements with post-Darwinian evolutionary thought. The positions adopted by different branches of the feminist movement differed; but there can be no doubt that the question as to whether nature might not be obliged to take a jump had been placed on the agenda in relation to gender just as much as in relation to class.[9] Between them, these developments portended a series of political mutations which threatened to disturb the sequential ordering of things which – in the reforming programmes of the Lubbock Circle – were intended to apply just as much to the social and political orders as to nature.

164

There was also an evident colonial dimension to the threat of mutation which Dracula represented. His journey from Transylvania to London, from colonial periphery to metropolitan centre, represented an attempt to colonise the centre, in which all the instruments of colonialism are turned back on themselves:

> Dracula brings with him not only an almost unlimited capacity for reproduction but also an association with the traditional carriers of the West's own ecological imperialism – rats, flies, mice, and vermin. He proves a master at using Britain's imperial system of transport to his own advantage. He invades using the very shipping line upon which Britain depended for receiving raw material from the colonial world.
>
> (Richards, 1993: 61–2)

An early version of the theme of 'the empire strikes back', Dracula has constituted the model for the subsequent proliferation of texts in which what is aged and rotting, the primitive and the archaic, returns from the colonial edge to haunt the metropolis. In the case of Dracula's successors, moreover, the threat to the evolutionary ordering of things that such movements of return represent is often worked through directly in relation to the museum. Placed into reverse, colonial relations of collecting provide the routes through which the archaic and the primitive travel back from colony to metropolis where, initially held in the museum's basements and storage areas, they move progressively to the display areas to wreak semiotic havoc among the exhibitions and their visitors: Lincoln Preston's *Relic* (1996), set in New York's thinly disguised American Museum of Natural History, is a recent case in point.

Seeing and knowing

The visual technologies developed for evolutionary museum displays can be understood as, in part, a response to these threats of political and ideological mutation. The museum's task was, so to speak, to batten down a new order of things by reassembling the objects comprising the artefactual domain (bones, fossils, minerals, tools, pottery, etc.) in gradual and continuous lines of evolutionary development. This comprised the central exhibition rhetoric through which the 'evolutionary showmen' sought to display the orders of nature and culture, and the relations between them, in ways that would regulate progress by providing a template for its smooth and uninterrupted advance. Yet there was a problem here, a problem of visibility, which meant that, just as evolutionary morphology fixed its sights on the grey area between forms, so the representational concerns of the evolutionary showmen focused on the spaces between things. How to make the spaces between things represent time, and change through time; how to spread out the spatial distance between things to suggest temporal intervals; how many intervals to have and how then to fill them – these questions were continuously to the forefront of debate in the correspondence and working papers of curators and directors, in the pages of the *Museums Journal*, and in the annual reports of museums.[10] They were evident, for example, in the debates concerning the relative merits of anthropological rotunda versus linear galleries as means of exhibiting the smooth and uninterrupted flow of evolution,[11] while the value of genealogical trees was also widely extolled for their ability to cover both the long reaches of geological and archaeological time as well as the more shallow times of human history (Bouquet, 2000: 178).

The political issues pertinent to the British context were, however, most explicitly worked through in the debates surrounding the development of the typological method. By highlighting the successive differences between apparently similar forms in displays of technologies, weapons and decorative items leading, sequentially, from the simple to the complex, this method offered a means of visualising the invisible laws governing the evolution of human culture. Pitt Rivers was clear in his assessment of the advantages afforded by the exhibition of material objects from this viewpoint. Their virtue, as he put it, was that 'they best seem to illustrate the development that has taken place in the branches of human culture which cannot be so arranged in sequence because the links are lost and the successive ideas through which progress has been effected have never been embodied in material forms' (cited in Chapman, 1981: 480). In his reference to 'the links that are lost', Pitt Rivers echoes the concerns that we find in Darwin regarding the incompleteness of the geological record and, accordingly, the need for an interpretative leap to be made from one phase of development to the next in order to sustain the narrative of an uninterrupted process of natural evolution. However, the incompleteness of the record of cultural development is, for Pitt Rivers, explicitly a political problem to the degree that it suggests that 'the Institutions of Mankind often appear to have developed by greater jumps than has really been the case' (480). Only by 'due search and arrangement', he argues, can the records of progress that are preserved in the material arts 'be placed in their proper sequence' to demonstrate the gradual continuity of the processes through which culture advances. The evolutionary showman was, as a consequence, always driven to fill up the spaces between things by providing more and more things, back-filling the past by providing an ever-more complete record of cultural evolution.

Yet this had some paradoxical – indeed, contradictory – consequences. For one of the guiding principles of evolutionary museums was that things should be so arranged that they might be clearly and distinctly seen if they were to achieve the forms of public legibility to which they aspired. 'There must be no crowding of specimens one behind the other,' Sir William Flower wrote, 'every one being perfectly and distinctly seen, and with a clear space around it' (Flower, 1893: 4). This reflected the rationalising ethos of the evolutionary museum, which drew on the vocabulary the Enlightenment museum had developed in its critique of the cabinet of curiosities to draw up a new set of battle-lines with the unreformed local or provincial museum on one side and the evolutionary expert as showman on the other. If museums were to serve their proper function as 'educational engines' (Lewis, 1989: 3), F. W. Rudler argued, they would have to eschew 'pretty and attractive things, such as are to be found in some museums, heaped together in bower-birdish fashion, where they gratify the senses without nourishing the intellect' and focus instead on 'a limited number of typical specimens' (Rudler, 1876: 4) arranged in clear and distinct relations to one another so as not to confuse or bewilder the visitor. The report that was prepared in 1883 to guide Oxford University as to whether to accept the Pitt Rivers collection similarly went to considerable pains to reassure the University that the collection was no 'miscellaneous jumble of curiosities, but an orderly illustration of human history; and its contents have not been picked up haphazard from dealers' shops, but carefully selected at first hand with rare industry and judgement.'[12]

Yet the tendency to back-fill the past pulled in the opposite direction, undermining the principle of a simple and transparent legibility by cluttering the exhibition space with a confusing profusion of things which, as James Paradis (1997) notes, had already, by the 1880s, become a subject for satirists.[13] And this, in turn, lent added force to the need for a proliferating textual supplement in order to make the messages of evolution clearly readable. One sign of this was the more-or-less universal stress that was placed on the importance of labelling (Forgan, 1994: 149–5). That things should be clearly and distinctly named was widely accepted as a condition of 'best practice' if museums were to serve as effective instruments of popular instruction. So much so that rates of label production were often carefully specified by museum managements eager to discharge their educational responsibilities: the Assistant Keeper at the Liverpool Museum was thus assigned to labelling for three days a week specifically to assist the visitor who could not afford the explanatory guidebook.[14] There was also an eagerness to put the new scientific and professional networks of the internationalised museum world to good use by calling on metropolitan centres to provide authoritative textual supplements which might then be attached to their objects in even the furthest flung colonial locations. In 1889, the Director of the Museum at the University of Otago wrote to Sir William Henry Flower, the Director of the British Museum (Natural History), proposing that a special committee of the British Association for the Advancement of Science be established to produce a representative set of descriptive labels that could then be printed and sold to allow colonial museums an economical way of modernising their displays.[15]

There is an evident contradiction here. Far from being letting off the leash of the written word, the visitor was led into an environment in which the meaning of things – far from standing clearly before the eye – was constantly deferred in being referred to a dense and proliferating web of words.[16] For labels were merely the tip of the textual iceberg in this regard. Witness the following report from the Horniman Museum on the aim of its ongoing programme of reform and rationalisation:

> The work of re-arranging the Museum collections has steadily proceeded during the past year. The object kept in view in the selection and arrangement of specimens for exhibition is that of making the Museum a teaching institution where the general public, students, and school children may be able to obtain information, and widen their outlook, by the inspection of properly labelled specimens exhibited in related series. In addition to identification labels naming and describing each specimen, or group of similar specimens, descriptive labels are constantly being prepared in which are discussed points of wider interest relating to the series to which the individual specimens

belong. As the work of re-arrangement proceeds it is proposed to issue further handbooks, in addition to those already published, giving more connected and detailed accounts of the various series exhibited. By these means it is hoped that in a few years' time the whole of the contents of the Museum may be so displayed and described that instruction may be imparted even to the most casual visitor. The student may pass from the observation of the specimens and the method of arrangement to a study of the descriptive labels, thence to the handbooks, in which references are made to the larger treatises which he may consult in the Library.

(*Annual Report of the Horniman Museum and Library*, 1906: 5–6)

In the cabinet of curiosities, books had been placed alongside other rare and singular objects as sources of visual delight, interacting with the other rarities on display on the same plane rather than serving as a key to their meaning (Jardine, 1997: 176–7). In the later formulations of the Enlightenment, the museum was likened to a book or encyclopaedia, its labels – in supplying the scientific name for each object, usually in Latin – functioning as its index. The labels that proliferated in evolutionary museums differed in two main respects. First, they were in the vernacular, reflecting an agreement with Ruskin on this, if on little else, that Latin and Greek labels served only to 'mystify the illiterate many of their own land' (cited in Ritvo, 1997: 66). Second, as explanatory rather than merely descriptive labels, they articulated a different set of relations between words, things and vision. Alfred Haddon, Advisory Curator to the Horniman Museum and Library and the driving force behind its modernisation in terms of evolutionary principles, summarised the difference succinctly when he argued that 'most of the older museums bear the same relation to modern museums that dictionaries do to textbooks . . . giving the least amount of instruction beyond the bare fact of the existence of given objects' (Haddon, cit. Shelton, 2000: 167). The functioning of explanatory labels in this regard undercut the object-centredness of the evolutionary museum's rhetoric: reading guided looking, just as words became the keys to things.

Haddon's views on this matter reflected the influence of George Brown Goode who, in his advocacy of the 'new museum idea', offered a new assessment of the relations between the museum and the library that effectively undid the Enlightenment conception of the relations between words, things and vision.[17] Goode presented this idea as a revival of the reforming impetus that had been given to the administration of museums by the mid-nineteenth-century mix of liberalism and utilitarianism that had characterised the work of Henry Cole. But he drew his chief inspiration from a later text – William Stanley Jevons's *Methods of Social Reform* (1883) – which provided a crucial bridge from *laissez-faire* liberalism into the new liberalism by providing the case for extending the activities of the state into the cultural sphere with a basis in neo-classical economic theory.[18] This consisted in the principle of the multiplication of utility that Jevons proposed as a means of expressing the added use-value that resulted from the public ownership of cultural resources:[19]

168

The main *raison d'être* of Free Public Libraries, as indeed of public museums, art-galleries, parks, halls, and many other kinds of public works, is the enormous increase of utility which is thereby acquired for the community at trifling cost . . . If a man possesses a library of a few thousand volumes, by far the greater part of them must lie for years untouched upon the shelves; he cannot possibly use more than a fraction of the whole in any one year. But a library of five or ten thousand volumes opened free to the population of a town may be used a thousand times as much. It is a striking case of what I propose to call *the principle of the multiplication of utility*.

(Jevons, 1883: 28–9; emphasis in original)

Goode cites this passage in his 1895 essay 'The principles of museum administration', to support his contention that state action in the cultural sphere would ensure that 'objects which were formerly accessible only to the wealthy, and seen by a very small number of people each year, are now held in common ownership and enjoyed by hundreds of thousands' (Goode, 1895: 72). State provision of public culture can thus multiply culture's effects in ways that can claim both an economic and a moral justification: the first by providing a better distributional rationality; the second by multiplying culture's reforming powers.

In the essays considered so far, Goode places museums alongside libraries in these regards, and makes little attempt to distinguish between them. 'The museum of the future', he argues, must 'co-operate with the public library as one of the principal agencies for the enlightenment of the people' (Goode, [1889] 1991: 322). In his 1888 essay 'Museum-history and museums of history', however, Goode is more particular in his advocacy, placing the museum ahead of the library in terms of its potential to serve as an instrument for public education.[20] Taking his cue from Huxley's definition of the museum as 'a consultative library of objects', Goode argues that this implicit merging of the two institutions overlooks 'differences in the methods of their administration' (Goode, [1888] 1991: 310). He identifies these as follows:

The treasures of the library must be examined one at a time, and by one person at a time. Their use requires long-continued attention, and their removal from their proper places in the system of arrangement. Those of the museum are displayed to public view in groups, in systematic sequence, so that they have a collective as well as an individual significance. Furthermore, much of their meaning may be read at a glance. The museum cultivates the powers of observation, and the casual visitor even makes discoveries for himself, and, under the guidance of labels, forms his own impressions. In the library, one studies the impressions of others.

(Goode, [1888] 1991: 310)

There are two aspects to Goode's advocacy here. One, reflecting Jevons's influence, emphasises the museum's greater distributional capacity when compared to the library: the museum can reach more people; it can address the group as well as the individual; and it can – as he further elaborates the argument – reach all classes through its ability to appeal to the uneducated as well as to the educated.

169

'The influence of the museum upon a community', he argues, 'is not so deep as that of the library, but extends to a much larger number of people' (310). Goode's second argument, however, has to do with the greater capacity of museums to allow those who visit them to learn for themselves because they are able to take in its lessons 'at a glance' and form their own impressions – but only provided that they do so under the 'guidance of labels' (310). Although urging the virtues of the museum's 'object lessons', Goode ultimately subordinates the museum to the library in making looking and seeing dependent on reading and understanding. In Goode's museums, objects prompt questions, but texts provide the answers:

> The specimens must be prepared in the most careful and artistic manner, and arranged attractively in well-designed cases and behind the clearest of glass. Each object must bear a label giving its name and history so fully that all the probable questions of the visitor are answered in advance. Books of reference must be kept in convenient places.
>
> (Goode, [1888] 1991: 308)

The contradiction here is part of a more general one, usefully highlighted by William Ray, who argues that museums of whatever kind are usually character-ised by an incitement to discourse as, in discharging their civic mandate, they aim to ensure that the visitor's visual experience is translated into verbal accounts which can then be exchanged in social discourse outside the museum (Ray, 2001: 125–6). The emphasis the Enlightenment placed on the controlling role of reason in relation to the eye is a case in point. 'Optical demonstration and visualisa-tion', Barbara Stafford argues, 'were central to the processes of enlightening. Yet from a conceptual standpoint, images, paradoxically, were reduced to misleading illusions without the guidance of discourse' (Stafford, 1993: 2). However, while the positions of the Enlightenment and evolutionary museum are formally similar in this respect, they differ with regard to both the specific ways in which their contradictory assessments of the importance of vision were posed as well as in the articulation of the relations between words, things and vision that they effected. To show why this was so, I look first at how the sensory regimes of the Enlightenment museum were forged in the context of its struggle with the earlier culture of curiosity.

Classification and the arrangement of the visible

Cabinets of curiosity assumed new roles during the Renaissance as they came to form nodal points in a network of institutions dedicated to cultivating new forms and relations of urban sociability. This gave rise to a new conception of the museum as a distinctive secular and civic space that had come to be detached, physically and conceptually, from the monastic forms and relations of scholar-ship with which it had earlier been associated. It also involved a change in the ratio of the senses that was involved in the museum space; a shift, as Paula Findlen describes it, from a world of silence and solitude into one of sound and civic sociability. Refashioned into a 'conversable space' where the exhibition of nature's curiosities served as 'a prelude to conversing about natural history' (Findlen, 1994: 100), the cabinet of curiosity became a key locale for ritualised forms of social exchange that were calculated to forge and strengthen bonds of civic solidarity.

This is not to say that the eye was uninvolved in the Renaissance cabinet which, as well as engaging its visitors in conversations, addressed them as spectators: curiosity had, indeed, been chastised in late medieval thought for prying open the secrets of nature to lay them bare before the 'lust of the eyes' (Eamon, 1994: 60). The forms of looking that this involved, however, supposed a wandering rather than a disciplined eye which, rather than functioning in isolation from the other senses or being distanced from the collection, was pulled into it to be caught in a system of side-way glances between objects whose organisation was dialogical.[21] For Stafford, this system of relations functioned to involve sight in, and to subordinate it to, a universe whose governing logic was conversational in which the roles of viewing, speaking and listening mingled complexly with one another. The manifest incompleteness and deliberately perplexing organisation of cabinets of curiosities functioned anamorphically, inviting a practice of vision that would become involved in the scene of the exhibition in order to resolve its puzzling contents. Brought into play in a world whose disorder resembled that of speech, the solutions this practice of seeing worked to effect depended on mechanisms in which relations of sight were modelled on, and inscribed within, relations of spoken language. 'Crammed shelves and drawers, with their capricious jumps in logic and disconcerting omissions', as Stafford puts it, 'resembled the apparent disorganisation of talk' in which a miscellany of objects '"chatted" among themselves and with the spectator' (Stafford, 1994: 238). Bereft of labels, detached from any fixing context, curiosities 'resembled rumours', 'garbled messages' or 'snatches of muttered speech'; as such, they comprised 'unreadable details' belonging to 'a totality forever evading the spectator' (251), who none-theless became involved in an attempt to construct totality by filling in the bits, the spaces, between objects. However, since the relations between objects were not subtended by any classificatory logic, they could be cohered into an order only provisionally through a dialogic social practice whose operational logic was much like that which enables speakers to fill in the missing pieces of each other's speech in order to sustain their conversation.

This, then, was a totality to be made and held, fragilely, in and through conversa-tions in which the side-glancing words of collector and visitor colluded with side-glancing objects to sustain a temporary order. Viewed in this light, Renaissance natural history collections are best seen as parts of a wider communications network in which conversation functioned as the key operator in knitting together gestures and the display of objects as parts of an art of public casuistry, in which truth was demonstrated via an appeal to both the eyes and ears of listeners and seers, who were addressed as participants in that demonstration rather than as detached observers. Within the classifying culture of the Enlightenment, by contrast, the museum aimed to represent a given totality resting on an authoritative knowledge that was 'invisible to the untrained beholder' (251).

The tension between these two principles was resolved largely in favour of the latter as the cabinet of curiosities was transformed into the museum of natural history and, in the process, became charged with the task of public instruction.[22] Stafford singles out two key figures here: Louis-Jean-Marie Daubenton, appointed by Buffon in 1745 as the Chief Curator at the *Cabinet d'histoire naturelle* at the Jardin du Roi, and Joseph-Adrien Le Large de Lignac, Daubenton's more severe and exacting rationalist critic.[23] Daubenton's chief innovation consisted in a system of labelling that aimed to give each object its own label so that it should be clearly and distinctly recognisable, and to arrange the relationships between labelled objects in a manner that would make the order underlying nature intelligible to the visitor. As Daubenton put it in his 1749 description of an ideal cabinet:

> Everything in effect will be instructive; at each glance not only will one gain knowledge of the objects themselves, one will also discover relationships between given objects and those that surround them. Resemblances will define the genus, differences will mark the species; those marks of similarity and difference, taken and compared together, will present to the mind and engrave in the memory the image of nature.
>
> (Daubenton, cited in McClellan, 1994: 80)

In this radical systematisation, the object, no longer a vehicle for civic conversations, functioned as part of a system of directed vision in which – at least in theory – words, losing their side-glancing dialogism, were to relay an authoritative knowledge from the curator to the visitor.[24] The items displayed in the museum were arranged to make visible the structure governing the order of things. However, to the degree that this structure was discernible through the intellect rather than by means of unmediated sense perception, the eye, if it were to see that structure, had to be appropriately directed. Arranged by experts – by 'eyes that know how to see' (Stafford, 1994: 266) – rationally ordered collections were to instruct untutored eyes by placing a filter of words between sight and its objects: a rationalising nomenclature in the form of a system of labels which, since their purpose was simply to nominate the visible that they made transparent, attached themselves to objects like cling-wrap. If the eye here is still centred in comparison with the other senses,[25] it is an eye that has been subjected to reason. No longer able to range freely within the side-glancing relations of words and things that had characterised the Renaissance cabinet, the eye here is disciplined by being allowed access to things only via the mediation of a rationally ordered language.

For Daubenton, however, there were allowable exceptions. Specimens regarded as inherently agreeable to the eye were to be sprinkled through the museum in order to provide some visual respite from the rigours of taxonomy and thus increase the Museum's popularity.[26] Lignac, by contrast, seized on this concession to aesthetic principles of display to elaborate an uncompromising visual didactics in which sight was to be entirely subordinated to the regulation of an ordering mind, just as things were to be placed beneath, and to become accessible only through, a grid of words. It was this that Foucault had in mind when, in his account of the classical *episteme*, he refers to natural history as 'nothing more than the nomination of the visible' (Foucault, 1970: 132), a system in which words and things are so laminated upon one another that seeing and naming are one and the same activity: to see is to name correctly, to name correctly is to see. Stripped of the commentary and cultural detritus that had been attached to them in Renaissance natural history,[27] forms of life are now arranged in systems of visible differences and resemblances in which they are 'the bearers of nothing but their own individual names' (131). While this presents things to the eye in a manner that makes it seem that 'it is the thing itself that appears', the relations between thing and eye are ordered by the purified discourse of classification in which the thing is located within a 'reality that has been patterned from the very outset' by the name it bears and the relations this establishes with other things (130).

This meant, Lee Rust Brown argues, that 'the representative aspect of the thing superseded the thing itself': whether 'stuffed, dried, cultivated, or caged, everything in the Museum was haunted by its own referentiality' within a discipline of seeing in which 'the aim of natural history was to make the living individual point beyond its idiosyncrasies to its place in a system of classes nested within classes like wheels within wheels' (Brown, 1997: 66). Visible things, once inserted within the system of classification, operated as parts of a textual system which 'resembled nothing so much as a library of books' in which the 'contents of nature's hieroglyphic plenitude' were 'selected, abridged, and arranged' (65). Natural objects were thus immanently textually coded so that, 'as part of being themselves', they were 'also diagrammatic signs that "naturally" signified higher-level realities' (123).[28] By doubling the order of nature within themselves, they allowed the visitor to see the hidden order of affinities and resemblances that constituted the divinely ordained intelligibility of the natural world:

> The spectator managed to 'see' the classification not simply by looking at the specimens themselves but by looking, as it were, *through* them to the higher idea that contained them. There was always, in other words, an element of conceptual depth to the page-like exhibition arrangements. The classification was the point: it lay on an invisible plane 'behind' or 'before' examples of its elements.
>
> (Brown, 1997: 78)

Brown's purpose in his discussion of the Muséum National d'Histoire Naturelle under Cuvier's direction is to recover the system of representation associated with pre-Darwinian natural history.

> Time in the Muséum was not the irreversible time of Darwinian evolution . . . The 'history' in natural history described nature as it presently was – and, in doing so, measured nature's fall and recovery (or, more precisely, nature's disintegration and reintegration) by reference to the prospect of a whole structure, a prospect that found initial representation in catalogs, cabinets, and gardens.
>
> (Brown, 1997: 128)

The temporal element here, that is to say, lacked any connection to the principles of irreversible succession characterising evolutionary thought. Rather, time was present as a component of the attempt to reconstruct the order of nature, to cohere the thoughts of God which, although governing the natural order, had become opaque and dispersed, like a ruined book. Yet it was also Cuvier, Foucault argues, who prepared the ground for the later substitution of 'anatomy for classification, organism for structure, internal subordination for visible character, the series for tabulation' that made possible 'the precipitation into the old flat world of animals and plants, engraved in black on white, a whole profound mass of time to which men were willing to give the renewed name of *history*' (Foucault, 1970: 138).

This substitution of the series for the table forms part of a significant shift in the functioning of the visible. If, in the classical *episteme*, naming and seeing were the same within a system of visibility in which the *ratio* of things was attached to their surface, the intelligibility of the evolutionary series consisted in a history of cause, effect and succession which could not itself be seen but simply evoked by the temporally ordered arrangement of objects. In the Muséum, the ruined orders of nature were restored so that they might be taken in 'at a glance' and thereby serve as a counterpoint to the illegibility and disorder of society in the post-revolutionary period (Spray, 1997: 460). This glance was, however, a quite specific one, in which perspectival distance from the particular specimen was achieved by looking more closely into the depth structure of that object arising from its classification. 'The more closely spectators looked into a thing,' Brown argues, 'the further, conceptually, they could see' (Brown, 1997: 70). In the evolutionary museum, by contrast, perspectival distance could be obtained only at the end of evolutionary series as a summation of the direction taken in by the eye as it ranged across the things exhibited and – once tutored to do so – deciphered the meaning of the spaces between them. This was partly a matter of new visual habits in which reading from left to right and from bottom to top came to be understood as tracing changes through time.[29] It was also a matter of a new alignment of the relations between words and things.

Object ventriloquism and evolutionary expertise

The long, slow mechanisms of change operating through *la longue durée* of evolutionary time: these were what the evolutionary showman wanted the visitor to see while, at the same time, being perfectly clear that this was not a message that could be carried on the surface of things. The role of labels, accordingly, was not to cling to things but to narrate the gaps between them. Thus when, at the Science and Art Museum in Dublin, the natural history curators wanted to *show* progress in nature, they had no alternative but to *say* it, for it is only the text of the label prepared to accompany the exhibit on this subject that identifies the relationships between the specimens selected for this purpose as developmental ones:

> The series of Pond-Snails (*Paludina*) shows how a species may be changed into another form in course of time. These shells are taken from beds of rock formed in an ancient lake in Slavonia. No. 1 is from the bottom (oldest) bed, the others successively from newer beds, and the gradual change from a plain to a ribbed shell can be seem to have taken place. We have here in a comparatively short space of geological time the change from one species of a genus into another.
>
> (Carpenter, 1894: 139)

Similar difficulties were evident in ethnological displays governed by the typo-logical method. Although these aimed to visualise the evolution of human culture, this required the interposition of a textual supplement that would interpret successive differences between apparently similar forms as evidence of evolution. Baldwin Spencer was clear regarding the role of labels in providing a grid of intelligibility through which things were to be looked at. 'By means of descriptive labels', he wrote to Edward Tylor, outlining the purpose of his ethnological collection, 'I have tried to make it a kind of record of the Aborigines which the ordinary public can understand and take an interest in. It is quite refreshing to see the visitors reading the labels and examining the specimens.'[30] What this involved is clear from his exhibition of Aboriginal boomerangs (Figure 7.1). Meaningless in itself, this is made intelligible only by the accompanying label which tells the visitor how to read the relationships between the boomerangs as evidence of the evolutionary processes through which differentiation and complexity arise out of an undifferentiated and simple origin:

> The different series exhibited are intended to illustrate the various forms and also the possible development from a straight stick of (1) the ordinary, curved, flat fighting boomerang; (2) the return boomerang; (3) the large double-handed sword; and (4) the club-headed structure called a 'lil-lil'. The possible relationship of these various forms of missiles may be illustrated by the following diagram, the actual specimens illustrating which are shown in Case 4, Series L, and Case 5, Series A:-

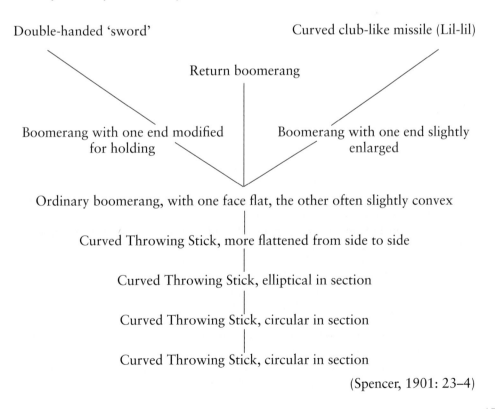

Double-handed 'sword'   Curved club-like missile (Lil-lil)

Return boomerang

Boomerang with one end modified   Boomerang with one end slightly
for holding   enlarged

Ordinary boomerang, with one face flat, the other often slightly convex

Curved Throwing Stick, more flattened from side to side

Curved Throwing Stick, elliptical in section

Curved Throwing Stick, circular in section

Curved Throwing Stick, circular in section

(Spencer, 1901: 23–4)

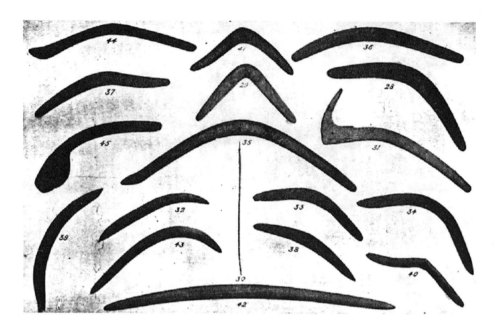

Figure 7.1 Baldwin Spencer's exhibition of the evolution of the Aboriginal boomerang.

Source: Baldwin Spencer (1901) *Guide to the Australian Ethnographical Collection in the National Museum of Victoria*, Melbourne: National Museum of Victoria, plate 3.

In contrast to the cabinet of curiosities, where the eye was left to meander in the spaces between things, and to the Enlightenment museum, where the word is superimposed on things as the recto and verso of an immanently textualised nature, here, through the web of words that is cast over them, the eye is directed in how to read the spaces between things. And not just between things: the relations between bodies and their representations was just as much at issue. This was evident, as we saw in the last chapter, in Baldwin Spencer's administrative practice. It was, however, true more generally of the developing genre of ethnographic photography which, when mobilised in the name of science in contrast to more popular exotic depictions of the colonised, typically sought to capture in the naked bodies of the primitive the 'bare facts' of evolution and to make visible its different stages in photographic series of different bodily types. Yet this anatomical reductionism was never enough. To make them 'speak to the eye', the bare bodies of the colonised were usually accompanied by a proliferating supplement – typically of measuring charts and devices incorporated within the photographic frame – which alone provided the discursive co-ordinates against which the relations of bodies to one another could be assessed.

This was true of attempts to anchor evolution in the supposedly irrefutable authority of the photographic image: Huxley's proposals for securing a 'photo-metric' record of the different stages of racial evolution encompassed within the British Empire, for example (Spencer, 1992). It was equally true of photographic

176

projects designed to disprove evolution by demonstrating unbridgeable differences in the anatomical structures of different races: the purpose of the photographic albums Agassiz produced during his 1855–6 Brazil expedition, for example (Stepan, 2001: 85–111). In both cases, the effect was the same. 'To make the photographic image readable as a type, then', Nancy Leys Stepan writes of scientific ethnographic photography in general, 'it had to be joined to verbal or diagrammatic markers which tacitly called into question its presumed superiority as a direct transcript of reality and the epistemological claims associated with it' (106). It is noticeable, too, that when Eadweard Muybridge sought to illustrate motion through a series of sequential images of a horse, he was able to do so only by incorporating discourse into the frame of each image (Figure 7.2). 'No relations of causal necessity', Crary observes, 'link the positions or sections that are connected in sequence, only an imprecise and disjunct sense of before and after' (Crary, 2001: 140). The problems here are the same as those associated with Spencer's or Pitt Rivers's exhibitions of technological evolution: directional movement through time requires the intervention of discourse in order to become perceptible.

Exhibiting evolution is, in all these instances, similar to the practices of citation which Michel de Certeau attributes to historiographical discourse which generates the effect of reliability by producing a laminated text in which one layer (the historian's narrative) constantly invokes another (in which documents, archives, etc. are cited), subpoening it as 'a referential language that acts therein as reality' and, at the same time, judging it 'in the name of knowledge' (de Certeau, 1988: 94).[31] This results in a 'split structure of discourse' which 'functions like a machinery' for extracting from the citation 'a verisimilitude of narrative and a validation of knowledge' (94). The relations between words and things in the evolutionary museum were characterised by a similar splitting that enabled it to function as a machinery for extracting from the objects on display a verisimilitude for evolutionary narratives and a validation of evolutionary science.

It was within the system of citation established by this set of relations between words and things that the authority of a new form of expertise was installed and exercised as the public eye was subordinated to the evolutionary showman's mediation of the relations between the visible surface of things and the invisible significance of their interconnections. For the split that informs historiographical discourse also produces a hierarchical set of relations between writers and readers in passing off the message of the former as that of 'history itself'. 'It functions', de Certeau argues, 'as a didactic discourse, and does so all the more as it dissimulates the place whence it speaks (it erases the "I" of the author), as it presents in the form of a referential language (it is the "real" that is addressing you), as it narrates more than it reasons (one does not debate a story), and as it takes hold of its readers right where they are (it speaks their language, though otherwise and better than they do)' (de Certeau, 1988: 95). The effect of the relations between words and things, between reading and seeing, in the evolutionary museum was much the same, and all the more so for the fact that its object ventriloquism sought constantly to pass itself off as merely the lesson of things themselves.

177

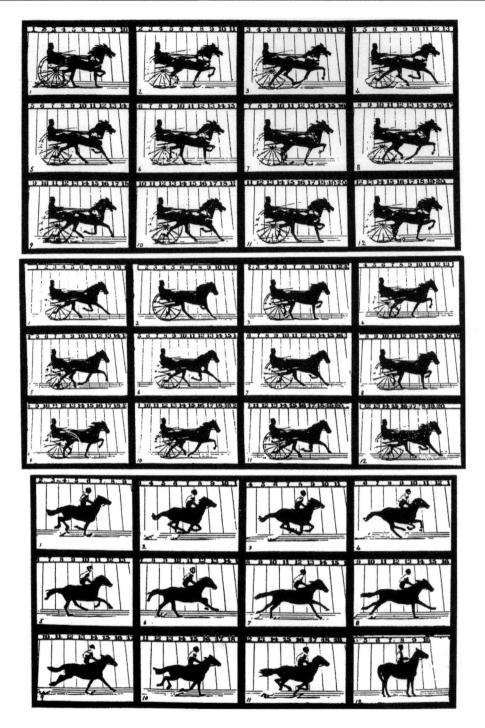

Figure 7.2 Eadweard Muybridge, 'The Horse in Motion'.

Source: 'The Horse in Motion', *La Nature*, 1878.

178

The didactics of evolutionary museums were also different from those of the Enlightenment museum in having a more specific target in view. However much the Enlightenment museum pitted itself against the clouded vision of the popular classes, the eye that was to be placed before the classificatory tables of the Enlightenment museum was, by and large, an undifferentiated one: the museum supplied a rational alternative to the impaired vision of the popular classes, but not a means of connecting with that vision that would prove an effective means of correcting it. Andrew McClellan makes a similar point in relation to the programmes of the Louvre during the revolutionary period, suggesting that the pedagogic strategies which informed these assumed a bourgeois visitor and made no attempt to develop popular forms of instruction directed at the *sans culottes*. By contrast, the visual programmes of late-nineteenth-century museum reformers were directed specifically towards the working classes and aimed both to take account of, and to compensate for, the limitations – perceptual and cognitive – of those classes. Goode's concern that the 'object lessons' of the museum should serve as a means of ensuring that the 'museum of the future in this democratic land should be adapted to the needs of the mechanic, the factory operator, the day labourer, the salesman, and the clerk' (Goode, [1888] 1991: 309) effectively makes the point.

We have already explored some of the issues involved here as exemplified by Pitt Rivers's references to 'those who run' as a code for the working classes (see chapter 4).[32] This phrase, to review the argument and amplify it a little further, had earlier functioned to describe those who, like mechanics and artisans, were regarded as disqualified from citizenship owing to the fact that their occupations, in being 'concerned with things', prevented them from 'exercising a generalising rationality' of the kind necessary to distinguish the interests of civil society as a whole from the egoism of private interests (Barrell, 1986: 8).[33] The economic subservience of those in menial occupations also meant that they lacked that capacity for independent thought, unconstrained by the will of others, that was viewed as necessary for the exercise of civic virtue. It was through this route that the relations between civility and science that had characterised seventeenth-century English thought, in which economic independence – and the lack of subjection to others that this entailed – functioned as a significant measure of the reliability of a person's statements, were carried over into eighteenth-century aesthetic debates. For the connections that these criteria established between civility and credibility entailed, as their correlate, the disqualification of other categories of persons whose conditions of life – whether because they involved subordination to the will of others or because they dulled the senses, destroying their harmony and balance – meant that they could no more be relied on either to speak the truth or to understand it, even when presented to them plainly, than they could be expected to appreciate beauty properly. Unreliable as witnesses and gullible in their susceptibility to the tales circulated within a predominantly oral popular culture, 'children, common people, women and the sick' were, as one contemporary put it, 'most subject to being led by the ears' (Shapin, 1994: 90).

While the term retained these aspects of its earlier usage, then, the references to 'those who run' in the educational programmes of late-nineteenth-century reformers also acknowledged the implications of the extension of male suffrage by recognising the need to develop forms of popular instruction which, aiming to overcome the sensory and intellectual limitations of his occupation, would qualify the working man to exercise his judgement in a manner consistent with his new civic responsibilities. Nor was it just the limitations of occupation that had to be counteracted. There were also rival claims to the scientific direction of the eye and, in the new technologies of vision which characterised the field of popular visual culture, new forms of distracted vision which threatened to offset the disciplinary regulation of the eye that the evolutionary museum aimed to effect. Here, too, the lines of conflict tended to be posed in terms borrowed from earlier Enlightenment debates. The issues involved, however, were significantly different as clear-sighted attentiveness came to be thought of as a capacity that had to be developed against the inherited force of habitual modes of perception rather than as a natural capacity that had only to be set free from the cultural distortions which, in impinging on the field of vision, clouded it. To engage with these issues, however, it will be necessary to go back a step and disentangle two epistemological orientations that, so far, I have implicitly merged: those of wonder and curiosity.

Developing clear-sighted attentiveness

The early eighteenth century marked a turning point in the history of the changing relations between wonder and curiosity over the medieval and early modern periods. These had earlier interacted and had been seen as significant, by both Bacon and Descartes for example, for their role in spurring an interest in natural philosophy. The first half of the eighteenth century, however, saw their paths diverge both epistemologically and socially. Whereas curiosity lost the associations of frivolity that had earlier weakened its epistemological status and took on 'the virtuous trappings of hard work', Lorrain Daston and Katharine Park argue, 'wonder migrated from the pole of awed reverence to that of dull stupor, becoming the ruling passion of the vulgar mob rather than that of the philosophical elite' (Daston and Park, 1998: 305). The dividing line between the two was defined primarily in terms of attentiveness. By the time of the *Encyclopédie*, curiosity was entirely disconnected from its earlier associations of visual lust and greed and was ranked as a noble pursuit demanding continuous hard work and sustained attention that only a few could achieve. Wonder, by contrast, had become a form of gawking, 'a low, bumptious form of pleasure' that 'wallowed in the pleasures of novelty and obstinately refused to remedy the ignorance that aroused it' (328). Gawking wonder was, in short, a passive state of visual inattentiveness.

In accounting for this transition, Darston and Park stress two factors. The first, of crucial importance in the late seventeenth century, arose from the deconfessionalisation of politics and the associated critique of religious-cum-political misuses of prodigies, marvels and miracles for their role in legitimating civic disobedience or mobilising popular support for warring factions within the state. 'After nearly two centuries of prodigy-fuelled strife,' as they put it, 'marvels that bordered on miracles had to be handled like explosives' (338). The second factor concerns the role played by the terms in which curiosity and wonder were contrasted in articulating the distinction between the elite and the vulgar within the developing class dynamics of early capitalism. For these meant that the Enlightenment museum had to wage a struggle on two fronts as it sought, first, to arrange nature clearly before a set of eyes that had been cleansed of the clouding and illusory influence of the oral-visual culture that had sustained the civic conversations of the Renaissance cabinet of curiosities and, second, to counteract the continuing influence of 'gawking wonder' in the rapidly expanding market for commercialised forms of popular visual entertainment. The Enlightenment *savant* was thus pitched into a struggle with the burgeoning popular culture of mechanics, artisans, showmen and prestidigitators, chastising as illusionistic their manipulation of the realm of appearances in order to conjure up a world of the fantastic and grotesque, of popular wonders and oddities. This involved a contrast between the 'invisible quality of mind' that informed the rational instruction of the museum, and the 'visible agility of hand' – the mere mechanical trickery – of the fairground entertainer (Stafford, 1994: 134). Before it could be reliably guided by the former, therefore, the popular eye had to be detached from the distorting influence of the latter:

> The uneducated masses, in a favourite Enlightenment simile, were like the proverbial man born blind who later learned to see. These sudden gainers of vision had to be programmatically weaned away from the disguised manipulations of superstitious priests, the beguilements of oriental despots, and the technical wizardry of optical tricksters. Ever-watchful method and overseeing reason or *Logos* constituted the healing therapy for a spoiled and rotted grasp of reality.
>
> (Stafford, 1994: 9)

The struggles the evolutionary showmen engaged in a century later were similarly waged on a number of different fronts as their endeavours to guide the eye in read-ing the relations between things came up against a multitude of competing forces. There was, as a point of continuity with the Enlightenment, an ongoing struggle with the illusionistic tricks of popular showmen represented, in the late-nineteenth-century context, by, variously: fairground entertainers; the popular shows of the midway zones of the international exhibitions where the visitor's eye was allowed to roam more freely than in the exhibitions themselves (Armstrong, 1982–3); the fakes of popular museum managers like P. T. Barnum and their association with the role of hoaxes in popular theories of knowledge (Harris, 1973); and, related to this, as a part of what Simon During calls the popular enlightenment, the influence of secular magic shows (During, 2002). There was also the con-tinuing, albeit declining, exhibition of freaks and monstrosities which – as befitted the growing power of normalisation – became increasingly medicalised (Gates, 1997a; Ritvo, 1997: 91–4).

There was also a new form of popular showmanship that competed more directly with the evolutionary museum's organisation of the relations between things and vision. I refer here to the exhibition rhetorics that had been developed in association with the phrenology lectures which, in the mid-century period, had played such an important part, in Britain, in developing a working-class culture of self-reform. 'Always', Roger Cooter says of these lectures, 'there were the skulls (often in rows of illustrative of animal and human cerebral progression)' (Cooter, 1984: 173). The difficulty here was that the rhetorics of phrenological and evolutionary displays were essentially similar, as were their objectives and target audiences: both aimed to arrange human crania to make the relations between them readable in ways that would serve as a template for organising action and experience; both aimed to equip their audiences with ways of working on and reforming the self that would allow – by cultural means – a degree of progress or ascent though the natural hierarchies they constructed (Secord, 2000: 70–6); and both were primarily concerned to address the working man, although as Cynthia Russett (1991: 19–21) shows, phrenology also had an active history of use in relation to the reform culture of early feminism in both Britain and the United States. Here, then, was a visual rhetoric that was still doing the circuits of popular fairs in the 1880s and 1890s which ran directly counter to the lessons the evolutionary showmen wanted to impart in their evolutionary displays of human crania. Similar problems were presented by the considerable contemporary success of spiritualism within both popular and scientific circles. For, as Roger Luckhurst (2003: 134) notes in examining the doubts that spiritualism raised in Darwin's own mind, how could his claims regarding the invisible processes and mechanism of evolution be distinguished from those of 'the invisible action of "psychic force" emanating from mediums?'

The burgeoning practice of popular natural history and the countless domestic collections – richly evoked by Asa Briggs (1990) – to which it gave rise were similarly inclined to distract and mislead the eye in the respect that they were still under the sway of the principles of 'curiosity, wonder and close vision' (Merrill, 1989: 5). As 'the apotheosis of singularity' (51), the objects in natural history collections were typically 'unique', 'extraordinary' (60). Although aiming to cultivate the virtues of observation, the weakness of such collections was that they did not offer such observational practices any theoretical guidance or direction; they did not, as Gates puts it in summarising Darwin's objections, 'look beyond the visible and external into the unseen mechanisms of species building' (Gates, 1997a: 182). Worse, they could lead to erroneous interpretations of exhibitions that were arranged for this very purpose: amateur working-class botanists, Ann Secord argues, were more likely to pause before the minute details and arresting features contained in museum displays than they were to abstract from these to absorb the evolutionary lessons inscribed in the relations between things (Secord, 1994).

The discourse of natural history was thus essentially baroque: 'highly coloured, meant to be beautiful and pleasing in itself, a gaudy mosaic' (Merrill, 1989: 93). The popularity of the microscope was linked to this 'gaudy mosaic', its role, like that of the domestic collection, being connected to Romantic notions of the sublime in aspiring to offer a close-up vision of the 'minute infinite . . . a secret world in small compass, which astonishes and awes the eye' (218). It could also be linked to religious discourse. In his influential 1861 text *Common Objects of the Miscroscope*, the Reverend John George Wood argued that the microscope could reveal 'the flashing effulgence of living and ever-changing light with which God wills to imbue even the smallest of his creatures . . . whose wondrous beauty astonishes and delights the eye, and fills the heart with awe and adoration' (cited in Lightman, 1997a: 201). This was accompanied by the challenge that ordinary people with a trained diligence would be able to discern these essential truths in the very midst of the realm of common objects that evolutionary science had claimed as its own.

The most important differences between the conditions in which Enlightenment and evolutionary showmen struggled to master and direct the eye, however, concern the organisation of the discursive field in which questions concerning vision were located. The projects of the Enlightenment in this regard were restorative. Their aim was to counter all those forces which colluded to wrench the eye from its proper position – as figured in the *camera obscura* – of detached and intellectually controlled observation. The observer, in this conception, was a decorporealised entity, an isolated and autonomous individual, detached from the world in an enclosed space within which vision – to achieve the ideal of pure sight – was to be directed by the understanding (Crary, 1996: 25–66). This geometric optics was replaced, in the nineteenth century, by a physiological optics which grounded vision in the body and, thereby, in the array of determinations affecting the sensory economy of the body more generally. This substitution of the 'perceiving body' (Crary, 2001: 23) for disembodied sight had two main consequences. First, it led to a greater stress on the subjective aspects of vision which came to be seen as depending on the composition and functioning of the senses – and the range of factors capable of affecting these, including social and environmental ones – rather than simply registering the stimulus of an external world. Second, this location of vision within the body rendered it amenable to manipulation though a whole new battery of techniques and visual technologies calculated to normalise vision as part of a broader problem of managing attentiveness. These involved, Crary argues, 'arrangements of bodies in space, regulations of activity, and the deployment of individual bodies, which codified and normalised the observer within rigidly defined systems of visual consumption' (Crary, 1996: 18).

If this was the work of new optic devices, like the stereoscope, it was also the work of those new disciplinary institutions – examined by Foucault – in which space is partitioned to regulating the flow of sight between bodies as parts of strategies for regulation behaviour. This, as I have argued elsewhere (Bennett, 1995a: 48–58), was also true of the nineteenth-century museum generally in the development of new architectural forms designed to organise new sets of relationships between perceiving bodies within the museum space. The transition from geometric to physiological optics also entailed a changed orientation towards the problem of ensuring 'correct sight' on the part of the museum visitor. This was, within the project of the Enlightenment museum, essentially a question of countering the influence of irrational factors which, in placing a clouded filter between the disembodied spectator and the world, resulted in occluded vision. However, whereas the *camera obscura* model of vision described 'an ideal relation of self-presence between observer and world', physiological optics made properly attuned perception 'an activity of *exclusion*, of rendering parts of a perceptual field unperceived' (Crary, 2001: 24–5). This meant that, for the evolutionary museum, the organisation of 'correct sight' was conceived as a developmental rather than as a restorative project, and one that needed to take account of the embodied and socially determined nature of the visitor's perceptual capacities.

This is evident in the distinction Pitt Rivers poses between the automaton and the intellectual minds and the way he articulates this to racial and class divisions. This was part of much broader discursive formation in which the distinction between inherited, routine and habitual forms of perception and more conscious forms of attention was mapped on to racialised and classed ways of distinguishing and classifying populations. Pitt Rivers's formulations reflected the influence of Huxley's famous 'automota' essay, first published in 1874, in which consciousness is construed as the mere reflex effect of physiological processes. However, the literature on this subject was extensive and international: Freud, Charcot, Bergson and Tarde are among the figures Crary discusses, while questions concerning automatic forms of perception and behaviour were also central to the American pragmatists' engagements with Darwinism (Menand, 2002: 217–27). The issues that were worked through in this literature related the concerns prompted by physiological optics to those concerning the role of habit and inheritance in social life. And with much the same result in equating a propensity for automated forms of perception with populations exhibiting low levels of evolutionary development while attributing more selective and discriminating forms of attentiveness to those with higher levels of evolutionary development. The working classes, migrants, primitives: it was around these that the distinctive problems of attentiveness posed by physiological optics clustered. Just as they lacked the archaeological depth that could provide the historically stratified self within which an evolutionised version of Smith's 'man within' might be put to work, so also their sensory structure was single-levelled. They were, accordingly, viewed as peculiarly prone to the influence of those hypnotic, trance-like, distracted forms of inattention that were, by the century's close, associated with the development of new visual technologies, especially film, which were believed to diminish any capacity for attentive forms of observation.

The questions concerning the relationships between evolutionary museums, film and early cinema to which these considerations point are complex ones.[34] Mark Sandberg (1995), for example, traces subtle patterns of interaction between early cinema and the development of the folk museum, seeing the latter's ability to distance and freeze the past as a form of cinematic modernity. For the most part, however, film was initially associated with the apprehension that the new forms of urban life characterising the *fin-de-siècle*, and the taste for sensationalist forms of entertainment that accompanied them, had occasioned a disorientating perceptual dislocation in which vision was constantly distracted, led from one object to the next in a relay of illusionistic thrill-seeking without ever being able to settle, to take in the meaning of things (Singer, 1995). Prior to its narrative codification in the second decade of the twentieth century, film was governed mainly by the 'aesthetics of astonishment' (Gunning, 1989) in which the effects of urban shock are heightened through a confronting assault on the spectator's experience. This 'cinema of attractions' (Gunning, 1990) was also associated with places of popular assembly and, thereby, with all of the negative associations that attached to the crowd – the very image of atavistic behaviour – in late-nineteenth-century thought and whose influence museums were meant to counteract. William Uricchio and Roberta Pearson (1998) thus point to the strong association of the nickelodeon (the most popular form of film exhibition in New York at the time) with the fear of dirt, disease and contagion that was attached to the immigrant, who was viewed as especially prone to the risks of vacant and distracted attention (Griffiths, A. 2002: 6).

Although the American Museum of Natural History was one of the first museums to experiment with film, this distrust of the medium was reflected in the fact that there was a delay of fifteen years between the invention of the kinetoscope in 1893 and the first use of film for educational purposes in the Museum (Griffiths, 1998).[35] Even then, it was only admitted on the condition of being subjected to a didactic regime that would bring it into line with the rest of the museum environment: films, when Osborn allowed them to be screened, were accordingly to be used only in lectures where their meaning could be mediated via the scientific authority vested in the lecturer, and where the risk of distracted forms of inattentiveness could be minimised. This was, however, merely the more obvious manifestation of a more general tension. For, in the very process of seeking to make itself more popular, the AMNH also waged a perpetual struggle with the 'circus within' that these endeavours produced. The same was true of the life group:

> The Museum's tactic of luring the spectators' attention via a spectacularised life group in the service of loftier pedagogical goals evokes the figure of the barker announcing the day's performances in travelling circuses or outside storefront movie theatres; this life group thus served a similar hailing function in attempting to attract the wandering gaze of the museum visitor.
>
> (Griffiths, 2002: 28)

The concern always, though, was that attracting the visitor's attention in this way would be at the price of pandering to the distracted gaze of the cinema, the arcade, or the shop window.

Yet there is, in all of this, a paradox. For, in the lengths they went to in order to arrange exhibitions so that progress might be clearly and distinctly seen, and to develop in their visitors the perceptual capacities that would assist this, the evolutionary showmen ultimately opted for methods of visualising that were at odds with the implications of Darwin's account of natural selection. For the series that were constructed in evolutionary museum displays either directly constructed or implied a vantage point which, emerging from those series as their summation, provided a distanced perspective from which their development might be observed. This teleologism is, however, in conflict with what James Krasner calls the 'entangled eye' that emerges from Darwin's own account of vision: entangled because, since it, too, like the natural world it observes, is in directionless flux, the eye can no more be detached from nature to provide a perspective from which its development might be observed than nature itself develops along a unilinear path:

> Darwin thus presents the reader with a vision of the natural world that is both fragmented and fluid. Nature has no clear, monolithic forms, no specially created species, but various biological units that are incessantly flowing, reforming, and rearranging . . . Seeing evolution comes to the same thing as being constantly involved in an empirical illusion, for as the mind flashes between the different orderings of the visual field that constitute species and subspecies, as the various different organic forms crowd, overlap, and mask each other, they seem to blend together like one organic form evolving into another.
>
> (Krasner, 1992: 62)

Paradoxical, then, because this effect of 'visual masking' in which 'the "ghost" or residual image of one form does not have time to clear before the next one is presented' (61) is precisely a method of visualising that was made possible by the varied technical devices, from the phenakistoscope to early film, that had aimed to make motion visible in more dispersed and non-linear forms. And paradoxical too because, as Mary Ann Doane argues, it was precisely pre-narrative cinema that was more in tune than its successor with the Darwinian stress on the role of contingency, of fortuitous variation, versus the standardisation and rationalisation of time that consolidated the 'temporal demand' of modernity (Doane, 2002: 4). Evolutionary museums, as one site for the enunciation of this temporal demand, differed from other cultural technologies of modernity principally in regard to the speed of time they implied.

186

Postscript
Slow modernity

In his biography of Freud, Louis Breger notes that, while his thought was to become central to twentieth-century modernism, the formative years of *fin-de-siècle* Viennese aesthetic modernism by and large passed him by as, instead, he devoted his time to 'science, archaeology and ancient artefacts' (Breger, 2000: 127). Brian Regal (2002) evokes a similar opposition when, in discussing Henry Fairfield Osborn's obsession with the ancestral past of the race plasm, he counterposes the American Museum of Natural History in the early twentieth century to New York's flourishing aesthetic and architectural modernism, including, just up and across Central Park, the emerging jazz scene in Harlem. And Mieke Bal is in the same territory when she notes the contrast between the AMNH and, directly opposite, the Metropolitan Museum of Art, as one between nature and culture and goes on to interpret this as a contrast between two different times. Whereas the story of art's development that the Met tells, she argues, is one of 'ineluctable evolution', that of the AMNH is 'one of fixation, and of the denial of time' (Bal, 1992: 559).

While there is a point to these contrasts, they are, I think, like Anne McClintock's assessment of evolutionary museums as fetish houses of the archaic that I discussed in chapter 1, overdrawn and misleading in their implications for our understanding of the complex relations between museums and modernity. For Bal, the art museum is the paradigm of the museum/modernity relation and the natural history and ethnography museum its other; the one is in and of the time of modernity, the other is its antithesis, belonging either to no time at all or to regressive time. My purpose in the foregoing has been to suggest that, to the contrary, such museums have to be understood as both in and of modernity, belonging to and helping to shape its organisation of the relations between past and present and, moreover, functioning within these to initiate and regulate a 'progressive' movement between past and present. The temporality they organise is, however, a distinctive one, governed by long, unfolding continuities rather than by sharp breaks. The rate of the ongoing forward momentum of social and cultural development they seek to foster can also be characterised in the same terms. These are, then, institutions of 'slow modernity' in which the time series they organise serve as templates for regulated progress and, as such, are just as much institutions of culture as art museums.

William Ray offers the best perspective from which to understand both the similarities between, and distinctiveness of, different kinds of museum in these regards in his discussion of modern culture, in both its public and commercial forms, as a historically specific set of machineries for shaping and directing persons by actively involving them in the processes of their own self-formation. In the case of governmental cultural institutions like museums and libraries, he argues, this has usually involved two contrasting conceptualisations of the citizen as, on the one hand, 'a creature of habit' immersed in pre-reflective routines and customs, and, on the other, as an 'analytical individual', a source of critical autonomy and autonomous judgement. To understand the modern 'logic of culture', Ray argues, means understanding how these two figures of the citizen are constantly in play and call each other forth in the programmes and practices of cultural institutions which strike different balances between these competing tendencies. 'Culture, we now intuitively know,' Ray thus argues, 'mobilises the energy of, and at all moments entertains, two competing ideals: individuality and conformity, semiotic initiative and semiotic uniformity, originality and legibility, self-expression and collective tradition, personal integrity and social solidarity' (Ray, 2001: 74). This has also meant that culture has played a key role in modern processes of social differentiation. As the site of complex overlapping and sometimes contradictory discursive divisions between those who are so ensnared in habit that they need to be governed and those whose capacity for independent judgement vouchsafes a capacity for self-regulation, culture also serves as a social sorting mechanism through which individuals differentiate themselves into the categories it organises, and to do so seemingly on the basis of their 'natural' attributes.

Pierre Bourdieu's account of the part played by the modern art museum in relation to the processes of social distinction characterising developed capitalist societies is a telling example of this 'logic of culture'. The autonomisation and purification of art, its organisation as a disinterested object of aesthetic contemplation, of the 'pure gaze', and its distinction from the vulgarity of the 'popular aesthetic': these have played a key role in the processes of social triage through which bourgeois elites select and differentiate themselves from the popular classes who, in the very process of this charismatic self-selection, are 'othered' as creatures not just of habit but of bad and offensive habit.[1] The question of habit, as we have seen, has been just as much in play in the rhetorics and practices of evolutionary museums, and with equally socially divisive effects in terms of the ways in which such museums have organised the distinction between 'creatures of habit' and 'analytical individuals' and articulated this distinction across relations of class, race, gender and colonial administration. The processes that made this possible are, moreover, ones that need to be understood in terms similar to those proposed by Bourdieu in his account of the autonomy of art. For the practices of distinction that the art museum effects through its role in regulating the social consumption of art products cannot be understood, Bourdieu argues, independently of the process through which a whole set of agents in the art field (artists, curators, private gallery owners, dealers) have historically fashioned art's autonomy. The operations of evolutionary museums are similarly unthinkable without the parts played by distinctive groups of intellectuals working across the historical sciences, as well as those of collectors of and dealers in natural, ethnolological and archae-ological objects, in producing – in the form of 'pasts beyond memory' – a wholly new set of entities within the cultural sphere.

Perhaps a better comparison, however, is with Bruno Latour's account of the 'pasteurisation of France' as a process, symbolised by Pasteur but by no means limited to him, through which a new set of actants – microbes – that were discovered/produced in the laboratory became agents within a significant reorganisation of the constitution of society. 'We cannot form society with the social alone', Latour argues; it is necessary, after Pasteur, 'to add the action of microbes' (Latour, 1988: 35). Or, in a fuller statement:

> There are not only 'social' relations, relations between man and man. Society is not made up just of men, for everywhere microbes intervene and act. We are in the presence not just of an Eskimo and an anthropologist, a father and his child, a midwife and her client, a prostitute and her client, a pilgrim and his God, not forgetting Mohammed and his prophet. In all these relations, these one-on-one confrontations, these duels, these contracts, other agents are present, acting, exchanging their contracts, imposing their aims, and redefining the social bond in a different way.
>
> (Latour, 1988: 35)

There is no single name that can stand in for the processes through which 'pasts beyond memory' were produced. What there is, instead, is a galaxy of names spread across the nineteenth-century development of the historical sciences. It is clear, however, that the processes were essentially similar except that it was the museum and not the laboratory that provided the primary scientific and institutional site for the production of this new object. In their assembly of objects in newly historicised relations of continuity and difference, evolutionary museums not only made new pasts visible; they also enrolled those pasts by mobilising objects – skulls, skeletons, pots, shards, fossils, stuffed birds and animals – for distinctive social and civic purposes. The constitution of late-nineteenth- and early-twentieth-century societies and the colonial relations between them are thus ones in which 'pasts beyond memory' were actively at work, intervening and acting in the relations between classes, races and genders by historicising these in new and distinctive ways which had profound implications for programmes of social development, population management and colonial administration. They reshaped, as Latour puts in relation to the microbe, 'not only society but also nature and the whole caboodle' (38).

Notes

Introduction

1 The term 'prehistoric' was first used in the title of Daniel Wilson's *Prehistoric Annals of Scotland* (see Putnam, 1899: 227) while the term 'dinosaur' was coined by Richard Owen as a collective noun for fossil reptiles. The dinosaur made its first public appearance in the reconstructions of fossil reptiles that Waterhouse Hawkins – following Owen's ideas – prepared for the 1854 Crystal Palace exhibition (see Mitchell, 1998: 95–7, 124–6).

2 I draw here, in the concept of a 'mutation in personhood', on Carlos Novas's and Nikolas Rose's discussion of the changes in the conception of personhood associated with recent advances in the life sciences. See Novas and Rose (2000).

3 There is an ambiguity in the literature regarding the currency of the new liberalism. Sometimes reserved, in its capitalised form, for the social reform orientation that was codified as New Liberalism by L. T. Hobhouse around 1910, the lower-case usage is more elastic in being extended to the closing two to three decades of the nineteenth century to identify the breach with classical liberalism that was marked, philosophically, in the writings of T. H. Green and, practically, in liberal advocacy of an important role for the state in the cultural and moral spheres. This lower-case usage was also common in the USA and Australia. It is, then, this tendency – essentially a bridge between classical liberalism and New Liberalism – that I call the 'new liberalism'.

4 It is worth noting, in passing, the sheer futility of attempts to account for the relations between museums and their visitors which do not take account of the way in which the subjectivities and capacities of those visitors are conceived and, in part, shaped by the broader discursive environment in which museums operate.

5 For Emile Durkheim, Aboriginal totemism thus served as 'the most primitive and simple religion which is actually known' (Durkheim, 1961: 13).

6 Debates about the duration of the frontier period in Australia's colonial history are hotly contested. However, organised racial violence was still common in the mid-nineteenth century, not infrequent in the closing decades of the century and – although diminishing in frequency – carried on well into the twentieth century with, Henry Reynolds records, racial massacres still occurring in the 1920s (Reynolds, 1998: 178–201).

1 Dead circuses: expertise, exhibition, government

1 In praising the advances of scientific anthropology, Frederic Ward Putnam, curator of the Peabody Museum of American Archaeology and Ethnology at Harvard University, remarked that, by the century's end, it was 'no longer considered sacrilegious to exhibit skulls, skeletons and mummies in connection with the works of the same peoples' (Putnam, 1899: 234).

2 See, on nineteenth-century developments in the science of taxidermy which sought to overcome death by perpetuating the impression of life, Bann (1984: chapter 1).

3 The skeleton of Truganini, regarded at the time as the last of the 'full-blooded' Tasmanian Aborigines, was exhumed two years after her death in 1876 and placed in the museum of the Royal Society of Tasmania where, except for periodic loans to other Australian museums, it remained on public display until 1947 (see Ryan, 1981). The National Museum of Victoria exchanged a cast of Truganini's skull for a tyrannosaurus cast with the American Museum of Natural History (see Prescott, 1954: 108).

4 For different perspectives on the connections between hunting and collecting – one centred on a metropolitan context and the other on a colonial context – see MacKenzie (1988) and Griffiths (1996a). Turnbull (1991) also discusses the ways in which the Australian Museum, during the period of Edward Ramsay's curatorship (1874–94), implicitly endorsed hunting expeditions as a means of acquiring Aboriginal remains. The consequences of this continue to reverberate into the present. The British Museum has categorically denied that any of the skeletal remains in its collections were acquired as a consequence of Aborigines being 'shot to order'. While verified instances of this kind are rare, the position of the Foundation for Aboriginal Research and Action (FAIRA) is that the international market for Aboriginal remains provided both an inducement for, and legitimation of, racial killings. (Information gained from FAIRA world-wide web site www.faira.org.au – March 1998.)

5 See Balfour's letter in reply to Alfred Robinson's letter of 10 December 1891: Pitt Rivers Museum Archive, Foundations and Early History, folio 153.

6 The tensions between these different exhibition practices are tellingly discussed in Robert Rydell's account of the Smithsonian Institution's exhibits at the Chicago World's Columbian Exhibition of 1893. See Rydell (1984).

7 An influential pattern was set in the relationships between the menageries – where, in spite of its civic ambitions, the display of animals retained elements of the circus – and the Muséum National d'Histoire Naturelle. On death, the animals were usually transferred to the Muséum as specimens for scientific dissection and, eventually, exhibition (see Burkhardt, 1997).

8 Shari Huhndorf records the case of an eskimo family who, brought to New York to provide a living exhibit at the American Museum of Natural History, fatally contracted pneumonia. After their death, their brains were removed and their bones retained for exhibition in another part of the Museum (Huhndorf, 2000: 123–4).

9 Similarly, Joseph Henry, the Smithsonian Institution's Director, had earlier expressed exception to the deception perpetrated on the public by the unscrupulous showmen responsible for the Cardiff Giant hoax: see Hinsley (1981: 38).

10 O'Hara (1996) suggests that the Quinary system dominated natural systematics until 1840, while Ritvo (1997) shows how it crops up again in the proposals put forward in 1876 by F. W. Rudler for the organisation of natural history museums.

11 Huxley's account of the significance of the horse for evolutionary theory is contained in his 1970 essay 'Palaeontology and the doctrine of evolution', collected in Huxley (1896b). Huxley used the horse to explain the difference between what he called intercalary and linear types, the latter being forms that are intermediate between others in the sense of standing in a direct genetic relationship between them – deriving from an earlier form and begetting a later one – whereas intercalary types are merely intermediate forms whose genetic connections have not been established. Huxley uses the evolution of the horse to illustrate the concept of linear types, the cornerstone of his understanding of evolution.

12 David Oldroyd has applied Latour's perspectives to the social relations of nineteenth-century geology, showing how the British Geological Survey functioned as a centre of calculation in allowing successive generations of geologists to visit distant collecting sites with a better knowledge of regional geological formations than local residents because of the accumulating information system produced by the Survey. See Oldroyd (1990: 340–52). The same was true of palaeontology, where the advantage that Richard Owen derived from his London location and museum positions over fieldworkers like Gideon Mantell has been well documented (Cadbury, 2000: 234–5).

13 I am indebted to John Frow (2001) for drawing my attention to this aspect of de Certeau's work.

14 The reference is to Ruskin, who complained that the 'dreadful Hammers' of geologists –

'I hear the clink of them at the end of every cadence of the bible verses' (cited in Desmond, 1994: 247) – were chipping away at the established structures of time. For a useful survey of the broader influence of geology on Victorian literature, see Dennis Dean (1985).

15 The classic sources are Foucault (1980) and Foucault's essays 'Politics and the study of discourse' and 'Governmentality' in Burchell *et al.* (eds) (1991).

16 This is true, for example, of Nikolas Rose, who aims to desubstantialise the concept of power in preferring to speak of relations of force and of the variable strategies and tactics in and through which such relations are enacted. See Rose (1999: chapter 8).

17 See, in addition to Burchell *et al.* (eds) (1991); Barry *et al.* (eds) (1996); Barry (2001); Meredyth and Minson (2001); vol. 26, no. 2 of *Economy and Society* (1997); and vol. 6, issues 1 and 2 of *Cultural Values* (2002) for useful collections of this literature. I draw here on my own discussion of these issues in Bennett (2003a).

18 Rose does, though, discuss the later, more formally codified New Liberalism (Rose, 2001: 2).

19 For a discussion of the male-centredness of these earlier strategies, see Bennett (1997), republished as chapter 6 of Bennett (1998a).

20 See, for his most developed critique of the regimentary tradition of social contract theory, Huxley (1890a) and, for his critique of the political implications of eugenic conceptions, his essay 'Evolution and ethics' in Paradis and Williams (1989).

21 The classic source on the new education movement is Selleck (1968).

22 I have discussed this tendency elsewhere (Bennett, 1997) on the basis of accounts offered in Coombes (1994) and Kavanagh (1994), and archival evidence from the American Museum of Natural History and the Australian Museum.

23 On the details of Huxley's involvement in adult education, see Desmond (1994: 200–11, 292–310, 346, 361–4), and Bibby (1958). On Darwin's adult education involvements, see Desmond and Moore (1992: 605–6l, 625–8).

24 The membership of this Circle closely overlapped with that of the exclusive scientific dining club, the X-Club, which served as an important vehicle for liberal scientific opinion from the 1860s through to the 1880s.

25 For discussions of the quite different disciplinary ensemble that anthropology belonged to in France in this period, see van Keuren (1982: 13–18), Dias (1998) and Segalen (2001).

26 There are numerous discussions of the relationships between the Ethnological Society and the Anthropological Society, and their eventual merger into the Anthropological Institute of Great Britain and Ireland under the clear hegemony of the liberal scientific intelligentsia. See, for example, van Keuren (1982), Stocking (1987), Rainger (1978) and Hall (1992).

27 The literature on the part played by the structures of colonial science in the development of geology and natural history in Australia is extensive, with the role of the relations between Australian and British museums being especially well treated in this regard. See, on the general relations, Dugan (1987), Inkster and Todd (1988), MacLeod (1982), Stafford (1988) and Moyal (1986). For one of the most thorough and insightful discussions of the consequences of these relationships for museum practices, see Rupke's account of Richard Owen's relations to the Australian Museum and his role in interpreting Australia's extinct fauna (Rupke, 1994). In the field of anthropology, Stocking (1995) provides a magisterial account of the part played by Britain's armchair anthropologists in interpreting ethnographic data supplied by Australian collectors. The work of Baldwin Spencer, as a centre-trained scientist who began to offer independent and authoritative statements from a colonial context, marked the beginnings of a transition from the first to the second stage of Basalla's model, albeit unevenly, as Spencer remained connected to and dependent on both the support and recognition of the British school of anthropology. While Stocking deals with these issues, the more detailed and authoritative account is Mulvaney and Calaby (1985). Mulvaney (1987) relates these issues explicitly to Basalla's model.

28 See, for general discussions, Finney (1993) and Kociumbas (1993). For accounts focusing on specific museums, see Mather (1986), Strahan (1979), Prescott (1954) and Hale (1956).

29 For a detailed account of the progressive disciplinary differentiation of the British Museum

over this period, see Caygill and Cherry (1997) and, for a briefer account, Caygill (1981). Hinsley (1981) provides a similar service for the Smithsonian Institution.

30 Huxley's involvements with museums, from the days of his first position as natural history lecturer at the School of Mines to his later role as a major museum power broker filling both curatorial and director positions with evolutionists in both Britain and its colonies, are admirably detailed in Adrian Desmond's two-volume biography of Huxley: see Desmond (1994 and 1997).

31 The literature on the Pitt Rivers collection is considerable. For the most comprehensive discussion of the typological method, see Chapman (1981).

32 Annie Coombes (1994) offers a peerless discussion of Balfour's work over this period.

33 For discussions of Osborn's contacts with Huxley, Balfour and Darwin and his view of himself as their scientific heir, see Rainger (1991: 37–42, 74) and Desmond (1997: 128).

34 Moyal (1986), Mozley (1967) and Hoare (1981) discuss the role of the Macleay circle in closing the doors of Australia's fledging scientific institutions to the influence of Darwinism until almost the end of the nineteenth century. However, there were other routes through which Darwinian ideas impacted on early scientific culture: Griffiths (1996a) shows how the ideas of the Lubbock Circle influenced Australia's first generation of amateur archaeologists and ethnographers while, although it may have been banned from the official institutions of science, Darwinian literature was, as Laurent (1994) shows, a staple item in the order lists of the mechanics' institutes and schools of art that flourished in this period, playing a significant role in the development of a nationally distinctive socialist culture. For the fullest account of Spencer's period at the National Museum of Victoria, see Mulvaney and Calaby (1985).

35 Sally Gregory Kohlstedt has written convincingly of the extent to which the balance of influence between US and British museums began to shift in the closing decades of the nineteenth century with the US – especially in natural history museums – increasingly being recognised as innovating new practices that Britain would only adopt later. See, for example, her discussion of the role of Goode in this regard (Kohlstedt, 1988, 1991), her discussion of Henry A. Ward (Kohlstedt, 1980), and her more general discussion of these questions across a number of museums (Kohlstedt, 1986). Orozs (1990) develops a similar argument. Kohlstedt (1999) also notes the relative paucity of contact between American and Australian museums before this period, while also emphasising that such contact as there was tended to be between Agassizian tendencies in the US and anti-Darwinist currents in Australia.

36 Key figures in this respect were Boyd Dawkins from the Manchester Museum and F. W. Rudler, initially Professor of Natural Science at the University College of Wales and subsequently Curator of the Museum of Practical Geology in London. Lewis (1989) provides a general account of the role of the Museums Association over this period while Shelton (2000) also comments usefully on the role of the Museums Association in the development of new colonial and international networks suffused with a common reforming orientation to earlier museum practices.

2 The archaeological gaze of the historical sciences

1 Conjectural reasoning has a much longer history in scientific thought; it was, for example, central to the Renaissance concept of *Venatio* as a practice committed to hunting out the secrets of nature (Eamon, 1994: 269–73, 280–5, 291–8). The distinctive contribution of the Scottish Enlightenment was to add a historical dimension to the procedures of conjectural reasoning.

2 For the best account of the relationships between developments in the historical sciences, the diagnostic sciences and the semiotic sciences over this period, and of the role played by art history as a crucial mediator between these different disciplinary ensembles, see Preziosi (1989: 88–93).

3 Most of the literature follows Ginzburg in relating Sherlock Holmes's deductive methods to medical symptomatology. Given Conan Doyle's medical training, there are good grounds

for this. However, as a measure of their contemporary influence, it is worth noting that, in his later years, Conan Doyle became increasingly interested in the intersections between geology, archaeology and palaeontology (Booth, 1997).

4 There is general agreement on this point in most of the available accounts. Donald Grayson traces the emerging dominance of prehistoric archaeology to the establishment of human antiquity, and sees the institutional expression of this in the publication, commencing in 1864, of the first journal of prehistoric archaeology and the organisation, in 1865, of the first in a series of international conferences on prehistoric anthropology and archaeology (Grayson, 1983: 2–4). Bowdein van Riper echoes this assessment, tracing in detail the relative fortunes of historical and prehistoric archaeology. The first, peaking in the 1840s and 1850s, was dedicated mainly to the Romantic quest to discover a national past rooted in an indigenous folk culture and was largely indifferent to developments in geology and palaeontology, scorning even Thomsen's three-age system. Prehistoric archaeology, by contrast, rose to prominence in the 1860s when it carried all before it in its new, active relationship with both geology and anthropology, while historical achaeology entered into a phase of relative inactivity and disciplinary isolation (van Riper, 1993: 1–11, 15–16, 28–35, 39–43, 184–204, 214–21). Philippa Levine concurs, adding an interesting discussion of the respects in which the late-nineteenth-century disciplinary synthesis of archaeology and anthropology was to revolutionise classical archaeology (Levine, 1986: 170).

5 See Rudwick (1976a) for a more extensive discussion of the 'pre-fossil' careers of fossils.

6 I draw here on my discussion in Bennett (2002)

7 Thomsen was the first Curator of the National Museum in Copenhagen. He began to arrange the Museum's collections in accordance with the three-age system in 1816, but it was not until 1836 that he published a definitive statement of the system and its underlying principles in an issue of the Museum's guide (Freeland, 1983).

8 See, for the most detailed accounts of these developments, Grayson (1983), van Ripper (1993) and Rupke (1983).

9 A surveyor with the Geological Survey of Great Britain at the time of publishing *The Story of a Boulder*, Geikie was to become its Director General in 1882, partly as a consequence of the role he had played in the so-called Highlands controversy, which consolidated the hegemony of London-based geology over more local and regional forms of knowledge. For details of his career and its significance, see Oldroyd (1990).

10 See, for a related account of the relations between developments in mineralogy and geology, Rudwick (1996).

11 Cuvier linked a critique of conjectural reasoning to his critique of presentism in geology, arguing that the view that causes that were currently active in the present should be sufficient to account for past revolutions of the globe – a view he disputed – merely increased the speculative, almost novelistic, strand within geology as guesswork stood in for observation in conjectural accounts as to how causes discernible within the present might have operated in the past (Rudwick, 1997: 40, 175–6, 182, 220, 252).

12 For a more extended discussion of Balzac's novel and the place it accords Cuvier's work, see Maleuvre (1999: chapter 3). See also Bennett (2003b) for an earlier discussion of these issues.

13 These limitations are apparent in Cuvier's controversies with Geoffrey Saint-Hilaire. For a useful account of these, see Bourdier (1969).

14 There are many accounts of the Werner/Hutton controversies. Here, I rely mainly on those offered in Chitnis (1970), Gould (1987), Grayson (1983) and Porter (1977).

15 See Rudwick (1985) for a discussion of the extent to which the major controversies in nineteenth-century British geology revolved around how to read the correct sequence of the rocks.

16 Rupke distinguishes the English school of historical geology from both the Scottish and continental traditions, where secular philosophies provided the main intellectual contexts in which the implications of geological inquiries were debated. Rupke attributes its reconciliation with Paleyism to a combination of its exponents' political conservatism and the need, deriving from Buckland's position at Oxford, to establish a place for geology within an educational programme that was still directed mainly at training a gentry clergy.

This resulted, among other things, in considerable pressure to locate geology as part of a universal history in which the study of biblical and other literary texts had to be taken into account in curriculum design. 'To those who were steeped in the classical tradition,' as Rupke puts it, 'it seemed inappropriate to transfer the authority of primary sources from textual and testimonial evidence to what seemed to be broken bits of muddy rock and fossils crowding some small museum or a don's room' (Rupke, 1983: 56).

17 Rudwick suggests that there were some exceptions to this in the depictions of human development in geology textbooks of the 1830s and 1840s, but notes that these had made no impact on the terms in which the past was popularly represented in the public domain. Here, as he puts it, the deep past constituted a 'single undifferentiated otherness' (Rudwick, 1992: 97) in relation to the human present.

18 Desmond (1982) recounts how, in the 1850s, Owen developed a theory of progressive development which, in pushing fishes and reptiles closer together to provide for continuity in the fossil record as well as in its branch-like structure, in which some lines of lateral specialisation became defunct, helped prepare the way for the anti-teleological impetus of Darwin's theory of natural selection. By this time, the only significant anti-evolutionist was Louis Agassiz (Lurie, 1960).

19 Huxley's position through most of the 1850s offered less scope for theorising long evolutionary sequences than Owen's and was significantly at odds with Darwin in its insistence on the existence of persistent types: that is, of fossils that remained unchanged though long periods of evolutionary time. This resulted in an interrupted, discontinuous account of life on earth, in which all major evolutionary developments were held to have taken place in deep time to be followed by relative stability in the more recent geological periods covered by the stratified rocks (Desmond, 1982: 85–94).

20 Not that Owen took this lying down: he refashioned his earlier version of the dinosaurs over the period 1872–8 in order to refute Huxley's dinosaur–bird line of descent (Desmond, 1982: 121–9). The semiotic currency of the dinosaur has remained unstable over the subsequent period, having been endlessly redesigned in order to envisage the prehistoric past in forms aligned to changing social, political and cultural concerns (Mitchell, 1998).

21 The narrative implications of objects placed in series arranged to be read from left to right are foregrounded when such conventions are unexpectedly disrupted. For a telling discussion, see W. J. T. Mitchell's account of Rudolph Zallinger's mural *The Age of Reptiles* at the Peabody Museum of Natural History, in which the conventions of evolutionary narratives are suspended by, first, arranging dinosaurs in a left–right sequence which runs backwards in time and, second, having dinosaurs from different epochs face one another rather than follow on after the other (Mitchell, 1998: 187–98).

22 The Australian prehistorian D. J. Mulvaney views the influence of Huxley's work in this respect as crucial. See his discussion of the significance of Huxley's reading of Aboriginal skulls from the Hunterian Museum in 'Fact, fancy and Aboriginal ethnic origins', originally published in 1966 and reprinted in Mulvaney (1990).

23 Philip Steadman (1979), on whose work I draw here, shows how the Darwinian analogy informing these procedures was widely applied across the fields of architecture and the applied arts as well as in the practices of prehistoric archaeology and anthropology.

24 The fullest account of this aspect of early Australian archaeology is given by Tom Griffiths (1996a). For a discussion of related concerns in South Africa, see Dubow (1995) and, for the USA, Hinsley (1981).

3 Reassembling the museum

1 See, for a fuller elaboration of this point, Annie Coombes's discussion of Henry Balfour's interpretation of the typological method (Coombes, 1994: 118–19).

2 These principles were first systematically introduced at the Museum of Practical Geology, opened in 1851 (see Forgan, 1999; Yanni, 1999: 58–60).

3 I draw here on Jan Golinski's formulation of the properties of 'black-boxes' (Golinski, 1998: 140).

4 See, for example, Hetherington (1999).

5 The armchair phase of anthropology and its status as a historical science remained formally ascendant until a 1909 meeting of anthropologists from Oxford, Cambridge and London universities agreed on the need to break with what A. R. Radcliffe-Brown described as the 'hypothetical reconstruction of the "history" of non-literate peoples' (cited in K. Thompson, 1980: 256) to establish, in its stead, social anthropology as a comparative study of the institutions of primitive societies based on a sound fieldwork basis.

6 There is an extensive literature on this subject, contrasting the effects of regional and typological displays, and discussing varied ways of combining them. The most favoured of these was the anthropological rotunda which combined evolutionary sequences running from the centre to the periphery with regionalised 'slices'. See, for a sample of the debates, Pitt Rivers (1891), Rudler (1876) and, for an earlier discussion of their significance, Bennett (1995a: 182–3). It is also worth noting that the articulation of typological and regional principles proposed by the anthropological rotunda echoed Gottfried Semper's earlier proposal for an ideal museum (Steadman, 1979: 95) and was reactivated, in the 1960s, in proposals for reconstructing the Pitt Rivers Museum (Stocking, 1999).

7 For a discussion of Waterhouse's architectural conceptions and their application to the Museum, see Girouard (1981). See Rupke (1994: 341–2) for a discussion of the role of religious belief in Owen's views of the Museum's purpose.

8 Although Dawkins was a Huxley protégé (he had worked with Huxley at the Geological Survey and had drawn on his support in securing the position of Curator at the Manchester Museum), he placed a different interpretation on the moral and religious significance of Darwinism (Desmond, 1982: 181).

9 For two detailed discussions of the development of the US National Museum and its internal divisions, see Hinsley (1981, chapter 4) and Kulik (1989).

10 See Stearn (1981) for what remains the most detailed and authoritative account of the establishment of the British Museum (Natural History), although Rupke (1994) is more insightful. The best accounts of the late-nineteenth-century developments affecting the British Museum's holdings in ethnology and prehistoric archaeology are Caygill (1997), Mack (1997) and King (1997).

11 For a thorough stock-taking of the degree to which evolutionary principles were implemented within British local and provincial museums, see the two collections edited by Shelton (2001a, 2001b).

12 The Horniman was the first museum to be managed by the London County Council which demonstrated an altogether admirable reforming zeal, quickly appointing Alfred Haddon as Advisory Curator to make up for the lack of evolutionary expertise among the Museum's existing staff. The Museum also commissioned Patrick Geddes to submit a scheme for a botanical garden to illustrate the botanical orders and their evolution in ways that would replicate the lessons of the museum (Levell, 2001: 257). This followed on a distinctive nineteenth-century tradition of seeking to produce a 'reforming nature' that would act directly on civic morals (Drayton, 2000).

13 For the fullest account of this long, complicated and acrimonious episode in the Museum's history, see Strahan (1979).

14 See, for a discussion of such collections in the Pacific, Thomas (1991: 163–7); and, for a discussion of a collection connected to a colonial administrative project which sought to graft colonial relations of power on to those of traditional Fijian chieftainship, Thomas (1988).

15 This was chiefly due to the influence of Louis Agassiz, whose neo-Cuverian principles continued to inform the Museum's arrangements after his death. See Lurie (1960) and Winson (1991).

16 See, for example, the discussion of the South Kensington Museum in Barringer (1998).

17 For discussions of the role of aesthetic modernism in this regard, see Clifford (1988); Marcus and Myers (eds) (1995); Torgovnick (1990); and Hiller (ed.) (1991).

18 See, for revealing discussions of the varied exhibition strategies of the museums of missionary societies, Coombes (1994: 161–86) and Thomas (1991: 152–8).

19 David van Keuren (1982) details how the liberal intelligentsia connected to the Ethnological

Society developed a co-ordinated approach to securing positions for its protégés in museums as well as dominating the affairs of scientific associations, particularly the British Association for the Advancement of Science. He sees this strategy as having played a major role in marginalising and discrediting the rival Anthropological Society.

20 I have argued this point more fully in Bennett (2000).

21 For detailed discussions of this aspects of the US National Museum's influence, see Hinsley (1981) and Rydell (1984).

22 The key institution in the US was the American Museum of Natural History whose public lecture programme aimed, as Henry M. Leipziger put it, to 'carry the treasures of the institution to every corner of this great city', thereby transforming the museum from a 'repository' into 'a great living teacher' (Leipziger, 1911: 220). Haddon, who visited the American Museum of Natural History (Levell, 2001: 268), initiated a programme of carefully planned lectures which Coombes has rightly assessed as 'one of the most consistent and developed uses of the museum context for educational purposes' (Coombes, 1994: 154). In Australia, the lack of appropriate facilities often delayed the introduction of public lectures as a part of the standard repertoire of museum activities. It was thus not until 1910 that the construction of a lecture theatre allowed the Australian Museum to introduce a programme of Popular Science Lectures, although it had earlier (from 1905) offered a programme of scientific demonstrations intended mainly for teachers (McDonald, 1979: 151).

23 In Britain, the Day School Code of 1894 counted instruction in a museum as school attendance, although it initially limited the size of school parties to 15 children per group. The Code had more or less immediate effects on the operating procedures of museums: by the late 1880s, the Liverpool Museum, like most provincial museums, observed the requirements of the Code in logging the number of children visiting each year as well as the number of specimen boxes sent to schools. By the turn of the century, William E. Hoyle argued, the Code had made museums 'an integral part of the national apparatus for elementary instruction. These are now no longer merely store houses of material for investigation by specialists, nor means for teaching budding MBs and BSCs in university classes, but they come into intimate relation with the children learning the three Royal Rs in the elementary schools. I rejoice to think also that they occupy a neutral territory, where private school, Board school, and Voluntary school may meet upon a common ground' (Hoyle, 1902: 229). For more detailed discussions of the Code and its effects, see Lewis (1989), Coombes (1994) and Kavanagh (1994).

24 H. Coates gives a good sense of the distinctive forms of regulation that were judged necessary to make the child's visit to the museum useful and instructive. The real issue, he argued, was not an increased attendance on the part of juveniles 'but an increased stimulus to systematic study on the part of the children' (Coates, 1899: 45). He then approvingly notes the consequence of an experiment, based on the example of the Carnegie Museum, which translated school visits to the Perthshire Natural History Museum into an occasion for an essay competition, resulting in a 'number of boys and girls who visited the museum with pencil and note-book in hand, going carefully around the cases in serial order and noting the chief features in each. This was very different from the aimless way – familiar, doubtless, to you all – in which the children had previously been accustomed to wander from case to case or from room to room' (46).

25 The critic here is Henry Higgins (cited in Chard, 1890: 60) who took issue with Huxley's programme of teaching by means of common things, arguing instead the need for specimen boxes to be based on the principles of wonder and curiosity if the interest of the child were to be effectively awakened. W. Hewitt, the Science Instructor for the Liverpool Board of Schools, understood the principles of specimen boxes more clearly in a letter he wrote arguing against the inclusion of objects of mere curiosity in school collections and urging instead the need for 'some really good specimens of common objects'. See Hewitt's letter of 31 December, Minutes of Museum Subcommitee, Liverpool Museum, vol. 2, April 1879–July1889.

26 This practice was widespread – see, for example, Denny (1898) on the use of cabinets of teaching specimens in the elementary schools of Sheffield, and Chard (1890) on their use in Liverpool. In colonial Queensland, geological specimens were circulated to state schools

by the Queensland Museum as early as 1888. It was, however, Dr Talmage of Utah who perhaps most clearly identified the nature of the relations between museums and schools that such specimen boxes developed by attaching the museum to a capillary mechanism for the distribution of knowledge. For Talmage, according to a Mrs Tubbs, the curator was 'a scientific specialist' with the teacher 'standing between the curator and the children, acting as a distributor of knowledge' (cited in Tubbs, 1897: 72).

27 One of the issues considered by the 1850 Select Committee on the National Gallery, for example, was whether the rules excluding young children from the British Museum might be extended to the National Gallery.

28 Lewis notes that the Museums Association included a number of overseas museums from as early as 1891 and that, by 1897, the Association had changed its rules in order to regularise the membership of overseas institutions which, by this time, included museums from the United States, South Africa, New Zealand, Canada, Australia and Jamaica. When the *Museums Journal* was established in 1901, it included an overseas editorial board from the outset and had contributions from overseas museums in the first issues. See Lewis (1989: 10–11).

29 Gerard Krefft exemplified this reverse flow of knowledge and techniques when, in presenting a paper to the Royal Society of New South Wales, he justified reading page after page from Edward Gray's classic essay advocating the separation of research and exhibition collections on the grounds that Gray was someone 'whose opinion should be well considered' by those involved in establishing museums in 'these colonies' in view of his experience, as a curator of the British Museum, in 'the largest and most important Museum in the world' (Krefft, 1868: 16).

30 A good example is the 1841 Report of the Select Committee on National Monuments. Although this was extremely thorough in its approach to the reform of museums alongside that of other national cultural institutions located in London, it exhibited little sense of those museums as the organising centres of national networks.

31 At its third meeting in 1891, the Committee of the Australian Association for the Advancement of Science appointed to consider the Improvement of Museums as a Means of Popular Education proposed a set of recommendations that closely resembled key aspects of the Museums Association's 1889 proposals.

32 The roots of the American Museums Association – which was established in 1906 as a joint organisation for the staff of natural history and art museums – were in the Association of American Naturalists that was established in 1883 as an offshoot of the American Association for the Advancement of Science (Kohlstedt, 1986: 168–9).

33 See, for further developments of her argument, Marchand (1994, 1996 and 1997).

4 The connective tissue of civilisation

1 Maleuvre develops this view in critique of those negative assessments of museums – initiated by Quatremère de Quincy (1898), and echoed by Adorno (1967) and Crimp (1993) – in which the art museum is taken to task for wrenching works of art from their original contexts and thus severing their ties with the more natural and organic links of tradition and 'true memory'. See, for a fuller discussion, Bennett (2003b).

2 The added cultural weight lent to degenerationist conceptions in the emerging genre of science fiction is also important here. See Fayter (1997).

3 Darwin, who had a copy of *Physics and Politics* in his study, draws explicitly on Bagehot in his own account, in *The Descent of Man*, of the role of the moral faculties in social development (see Darwin, 1981: 162). The value Bagehot placed on the benefits to be derived from the principle of variability played a considerable role in Darwin's criticisms of the eugenic conceptions of Francis Galton (see Greene, 1981: 104–11; Jones, 1980: 21–4). Bagehot's influence on Huxley is discussed by Paradis and Williams (1989: 16–24). His influence on Pitt Rivers's account of the difference between the 'intellectual mind' and the 'automaton mind' is readily discernible, although not explicitly acknowledged (see Pitt Rivers, 1875).

4 See Greene (1981: 101–2) for a discussion of the influence of this aspect of Spencer's thought on the general intellectual climate of late-nineteenth-century debate, including Darwin's own views.

5 It is, of course, the subtlety of Bagehot's materialism that is the problem, distinguishing it sharply, in its trans-generational metaphysics, from the idea of the body as a 'memory pad' which Pierre Bourdieu proposes to identify the bodily aspects of learning, practice and cognition associated with the concept of habitus (Bourdieu, 2000: 141).

6 This is not to deny important differences between Lamarck's account and the later Spencerian tradition. As Mike Hawkins usefully points out, the role of the law of the survival of the fittest in Spencer's work 'entailed the continuous purging of the unfit; he had no vision of these latter improving their position and moving up the evolutionary ladder' (Hawkins, 1997: 88).

7 See Hawkins (1997: 90–1) for a useful account of the role of this distinction in Spencer's thought.

8 There are clear links with Freudian accounts here. However, rather than treating these as providing a means of understanding colonial discourse as the product of a psycho-analytically grounded process of splitting (see Bhabha, 1994), the approach taken here would account for the structure of the Freudian psyche as a product of the deployment of techniques of self-examination within the context of archaeological topologies derived from the historical sciences.

9 The quoted passages here are from Tiffany and Adams (1985).

10 See Barrell (1986) for the classic account of the discourse of civic humanism.

11 I draw here on earlier discussions of related issues: see Bennett (1996; 1998b).

12 See, for a range of contemporary texts, Ritchie (1891), Stephens (1893) and Dewey (1898). For secondary discussions of Huxley's text, see Noland (1964) and Helfand (1977). For overviews of the ethics and evolution literature and its relations to the debates between the various schools of eugenic thought, different strands of liberalism, theories of mutuality and emergent socialist thought, see Semmel (1960), Searle (1976), Jones (1980), Hawkins (1997) and Fichman (1997).

13 See Huxley (1890a, 1890b) for examples of his earlier skirmishes with social contract theory.

14 See Pick (1989: 220–1) for details of Huxley's assessments of Booth.

15 This is not, though, to deny interactions between them: Linda Dowling notes the influence of Darwinism on Walter Pater's aesthetics (Dowling, 1996: 80–1).

16 I am indebted here and in what follows to Ian Hunter's discussion of Arnold (Hunter, 1988) while also drawing on my own earlier elaboration of that discussion (Bennett, 1990: 176–81).

17 See the essays collected in Jardine, Secord and Sparry (1996) for a representative coverage of this earlier history.

18 See Bynum (1974) for an extended discussion of the chequered political career of this concept from its interpretation in the context of late-eighteenth-century variants of the great chain of being, through the anthropologies of Johann Blumenbach and Thomas Jerrold, both of whom allowed, as Bynum puts it, that with 'man, at least, nature made a jump' (57), to its reinstatement in the context of post-Darwinian evolutionary thought.

19 See Desmond (1982: 58–9, 69–70, 74–5) for an account of the defeat of catastrophism and the implications of this for Owen's subsequent evolutionary formulations. Desmond also discusses Huxley's theory of persistent types and its consequences – in Huxley's early work – for his account of evolution which was considerably less smooth and gradualist than that of either Owen or Darwin (85–94).

20 Stedman Jones (1984) remains the classic account here.

21 This is the view that informs Anne Coombes's assessment of the role of museums in this period: see Coombes (1988).

22 Typological principles were not, however, the only principles of display evident in the Wellcome Museum. These were most evident in the Hall of Primitive Medicine. Elsewhere – in the Anatomy Room and Portrait Gallery – quite different principles of exhibition obtained. The address of the Museum overall, moreover, was clearly to the medical

profession. Entry was restricted to qualified practitioners and medical students, and the Museum was used to host receptions for international learned associations of doctors, anatomists, medical historians and anthropologists. For accounts of the Museum, see Daukes (1944), Haggis (1942), MacCallum (1911), MacDonald (1980), Sizer (1970) and Skinner (1986).

23 There is a considerable literature on the historical development and changing formation of these interrelations: see Duffin (1978), Fee (1976, 1979), Gilman (1985), Hall (1992), Mosedale (1978), Russett (1989), Sayers (1982) and Schiebinger (1993).

24 It is important to distinguish the position of museums from that of international exhibitions in this regard, as the latter frequently comprised more open and, if not dialogic spaces, ones in which the colonised occasionally co-mingled with other visitors and thereby, according to Peter Hoffenberg, rendered the imperial gaze more interactive than usual (Hoffenberg, 2001: 16–17).

25 It is worth noting that Huxley occasionally feminised nature when it suited his purpose. His 1868 essay 'A liberal education; and where to find it' is instructive in this respect. While, in its raw state, nature's lessons are simply brutal ('Nature's discipline is not even a word and a blow, and the blow first; but the blow without the word. It is left to you to find out why your ears are boxed' (370). This pugnacious nature, however, is altogether transformed for the man who has received a liberal education: 'He will make the best of her, and she of him. They will get on together rarely; she as his ever beneficent mother; he as her mouthpiece, her conscious self, her minister and interpreter' (371).

26 There is a vast literature on this subject, but Gascoigne (2002) offers a useful account of the Enlightenment roots of this tradition and its application in both metropolitan and colonial contexts.

27 These formulations have had a long reach into the twentieth century, with, surprisingly, a discernible influence on the theories of everyday life developed by Henri Lefebvre and Michel de Certeau (see Bennett, 2004).

28 The passage is excerpted from an 1865 essay 'Education – black and white'.

29 David Allen's arguments concerning the declining involvement of women in the organisation of natural history societies in the mid-century period tend in the same direction (see Allen, 1994: 143–53), as do James Secord's on the processes through which women's moral authority in the sphere of reading was challenged by the rise of a new male scientific clerisy (Secord, 2000: 43–6).

30 For examples of this literature, and recent assessments of it, see Gamble (1894), Gates (1997a, 1997b), Jann (1997) and Shteir (1997). Evelleen Richards (1997) discusses the involvement of women in anti-vivisection campaigns.

5 Selective memory: racial recall and civic renewal at the American Museum of Natural History

1 I could only find one issue of this news-sheet – issue 7 – suggesting that it had only been running for a few months at the time of its publication in 1937, and that it failed to establish itself as a regular publication.

2 Osborn's racial descriptors proved quite varied. The pseudo-scientism of the Latinate label used here derives from Osborn (1927a).

3 This is especially true of Osborn (1916), in which he attempts a synthesis of palaeontology and archaeology.

4 The building of the AMNH and its collections were privately owned. However, it was built on land regulated by the Park Commissioners which, in its original terms, specified that the AMNH was to provide free public entry on Wednesdays, Thursdays, Fridays and Saturdays. It was also stipulated that on the other days when the Museum was reserved for the use of paying visitors or card-holding members, 'all professors and teachers of public schools of the City of New York, or other institutions of learning in said city, in which instruction is given free of charge' were also to be allowed access to the library and collections 'for study, research and investigation' (*9th Annual Report*, 1877: 23). The

Museum's trustees proved determined to limit the extent to which the Park Commissioners could intrude into its affairs, initially with notable success. However, the Commissioners were an important force in the 1890s in further liberalising the extent to which the Museum offered free public access.

5 Agassiz was a key figure in the Florentine Academy, later called the Lazzaroni, which, in 1848, took control of the Association of American Geologists and Naturalists and renamed it the American Association for the Advancement of Science (Menand, 2002: 157–8).

6 I draw here on both Menand (2002: 217–27) and Rorty (1999: 26–9, 265–71) for their assessments of the relations between Darwinism and pragmatism.

7 The contrast with Britain here is instructive. Following Adler's example, parallel organisations were established in Britain in the late 1870s where they urged the need for the state to promote secular forms of ethical training that would replace religious instruction. In 1897, the Union of Ethical Societies set up the Moral Instruction League which aimed to substitute systematic, non-theological moral instruction for religious teaching in state schools. See Selleck (1968).

8 See *Nature*, vol. 15, 7 December 1876: 129.

9 The situation of natural history museums in this regard contrasted with that of art museums which, as was the case with the Metropolitan Museum Art in New York and of the Museum of Fine Arts in Boston (see Tomkins (1989) and Conforti (1997) respectively), explicitly modelled themselves on the South Kensington Museum. The influence enjoyed by the South Kensington Museum, however, derived as much from its cultural authority as European as from its substantive innovations, many of which had been trialled earlier in America, allowing Orosz to write, with some justice, that 'the South Kensington was an American-style museum which happened to reside in England' (Orosz, 1990: 234).

10 In total, 8,795,386 immigrants to the US were recorded between 1901 and 1911, with a further 5,735,811 by 1920 (Menand, 2002: 381).

11 Douglas Sloan (1980) views the period between 1870 and 1900 as one characterised by a decline in the AMNH's public education function. However, both Dallett (1988) and Kennedy (1968) provide a more balanced assessment of this question.

12 Bickmore relinquished the role of Director to become the first Curator of the Department of Public Instruction.

13 Sally Gregory Kohlstedt's work is invaluable for the service it has performed in relation to this aspect of American museum history. See, for example, Kohlstedt (1979, 1980). The Field Museum followed the example of the AMNH in developing, in 1911, its own system for circulating specimen collections to Chicago's public schools through its N. W. Harris Public School Extension programme (Simms, 1928). Ramsey (1938) – a member of the Department of Public Education at the AMNH – also provides a useful survey of the educational activities of the Buffalo Society of Natural Sciences, and the Milwaukee Public Museum – which began circulating specimen boxes to schools in 1889, with the Carnegie Museum following suit in 1900.

14 The text cited here is excerpted from the opening address given by the State Governor on the occasion of a lecture given by Alfred Bickmore to the Teachers of the Common Schools in 1893.

15 I paraphrase here from the lecture notes Bickmore included in his autobiographical sketch and account of the AMNH.

16 Osborn was, however, unsympathetic to the Greensward conception of Central Park as insufficiently wild (Osborn, 1899). This sometimes occasioned difficulties in his relations with the Park Commissioners and was one of the factors which prompted the active role he played in the establishment of the New York Zoological Society Park (Regal, 2002: 112).

17 See Rainger (1991: 108) for an account of Osborn's familiarity with the Pestalozzian system.

18 Rainger discusses Knight's work at some length, as does Mitchell (1998), but with the added advantage of placing it in the context of a longer history of visual representations of scenes of prehistoric life.

19 This was also a more general aspect of American evolutionary thought in this period: Regal

shows how Osborn's arguments drew on the earlier formulations of a number of his mentors, especially those of Edward Drinker Cope (Regal, 2002: 37–40, 51–4, 60–5).

20 See, for more detailed accounts of these tendencies, Kennedy (1994) and Thomas (2000).
21 Boas, Louis Menand notes, 'was the first social scientist to refer to "cultures," in the plural' (Menand, 2002: 384).
22 My account of Boas's work here draws on several sources, including Hinsley (1981), Jacknis (1985) and Stocking (1999) but, most especially, on Bunzl (1996).
23 Mason viewed anthropology as a sub-branch of natural history, and saw its task in relation to ways of life and customs as an objectifying one, treating these as things to be measured, counted and dissected like natural specimens (Mason, 1890).
24 Indeed, and much worse from Osborn's perspective, a 1908 study conducted by Boas showed that children born in the US of immigrant parents had different bodily characteristics from children born in Europe of the same parents, thus establishing the cultural plasticity of human types (Menand, 2000: 385).

6 Evolutionary ground zero: colonialism and the fold of memory

1 I draw here also on Griffiths (1996b), Attwood (1996a, 1996b), Mulvaney (1981) and Horton (1991).
2 While Aboriginal claims to a 40,000 or 60,000 year old history have often been couched, in the public domain, in terms of the language of deep time, there is real tension between this, and the linear concept of time it embodies, and the cyclical, self-renewing time of the dreamtime (Griffiths, 2000).
3 The reference to Australia as a 'palaeontological penal colony' is common in the contemporary secondary literature, but, as Newland (1991: 55) makes clear, the term was also current in the mid-nineteenth century. However, I have not been able to track down examples of such usage.
4 This perspective is developed by Nicholas Thomas (1991: 163–7) in relation to colonial collections in the Pacific, and by Hoffenberg (2001: 143–4).
5 There are many accounts of these episodes. Here, however, I have relied mainly on Finney (1993).
6 I draw here mainly on Mulvaney and Calaby (1985).
7 The Curator's Reports to the Trustees for the period 1881–7, and the Australian Museum's correspondence with the Department of Public Instruction over the period 1895–1904, are instructive in this respect. While these record a number of cases in which the Museum had responded to isolated requests for loans of specimens from schools and colleges, there were no concerted efforts in this area except for the decision, in 1889, to make the collection open for teaching purposes on Monday afternoons when it was closed to the public. The overall emphasis of these documents, moreover, is on the Museum's scientific role. Where possible, public access was limited as an unwarranted interference with this primary role: from 1891, children under 12 years were not admitted unless accompanied by an adult, and, in the same year, permission was sought to close the Museum after 5.00 pm over the summer months.
8 I draw here on Melleuish (1995) and on Connell and Irving (1992).
9 I draw here on Finney (1984, 1993), Stanbury and Holland (1988) and Strahan (1979).
10 In the areas outside that of his scientific authority, however, McCoy's sphere of influence was progressively whittled away in the 1880s and 1890s: see Rasmussen (2001).
11 I am unsure of the published location of this text. The version I have worked from, obtained from the archives of the Macleay Museum at the University of Sydney, is a set of galley proofs titled 'The order and plan of creation: the substance of two lectures delivered in connection with the Early Closing Association by Professor McCoy'. It advises that the lectures were delivered without notes, and that the text has been derived from shorthand written reports, revised by McCoy.
12 So much so that his arrangement presented Australian natural history in the form of a different assembly for each of Australia's colonies (Mulvaney and Calaby, 1985: 246).

13 Although neither of them singles me out for criticism in this regard, they well might have for this is a view that informs my discussion of the development of Australian museums in Bennett (1995a).

14 This relation of legal dependency was open to abuse, with monies that should have been paid to Aborigines as wages or benefits often being siphoned off for other purposes, or for their own benefit, by the administrators appointed for these purposes. Queensland is the best documented case: see Kidd (1997).

15 These photographs are in marked contrast, in subject matter and style, to Spencer's earlier photographs – from his period in Tennant Creek and Barrow Creek, for example, during his 1901–2 expedition to the Northern Territories (Spencer, 1987). These focus on ceremonial and economic activities, body decorations, and are imbued with elements of romanticism – and, occasionally, eroticism – but are quite free of any concern with how to register progress photographically.

7 Words, things and vision: evolution 'at a glance'

1 Australian Museum Archives, Series 24: 5.

2 This was the basis for Rudolf Virchow's dissent from evolutionary theory: namely, that it presupposed its own conclusions – for resemblance could be interpreted as descent only on the basis of a prior assumption that resemblances could and should be read as parts of a connected narrative (Zimmerman, 2001: 71).

3 It should be noted, however, that the Enlightenment also placed considerably less epistemological weight on the category of the monstrous than had been the case within the *Wunderkammern* of the early modern period. Lorraine Daston and Katharine Park (1998: 350–5) thus note that Buffon only dedicated three pages to monsters in his *Histoire Naturelle*. Since they did not form a part of nature's ordinary phenomena and were not governed by its laws, they were of interest only as exceptions.

4 For a discussion of this point, see Ritvo (1997: 91–4).

5 The classic source on early perceptions of Australian flora and fauna remains Smith (1969). The transforming influence of evolutionary thought is discussed by Moyal (1986).

6 Ritvo (1997) discusses the concerns clustered around hybridity and mongrelism; Young (1995) offers a challenging discussion of the currency of hybridity in nineteenth-century cultural theory.

7 This was, again, a step not taken in Germany where Virchow and others contested such temporal re-interpretations of, for example, excessive hairiness as 'signs pointing beyond themselves to an animal past', seeing in them, rather, 'signs of individual pathologies, signs pointing merely to themselves' (Zimmerman, 2001: 83).

8 See Gelder (1994) for a discussion of the refashioning of the figure of Dracula in nineteenth-century literature. For a discussion of Dracula tending in the same direction as that of Richards, see Marsh (1995), and for a discussion of the contrastive, pre-evolutionary logic of the racialised brutishness represented by the figure of Frankenstein, see Malchow (1993).

9 See Love (1983), Jones (1980), Richards (1989, 1997) and Walkowitz (1992) for discussions of these matters.

10 These difficulties associated with making change visible had a more general provenance in the natural and physical sciences: see, for example, Flint (2000) for a discussion of contemporary debates concerning how best to make the mechanisms of glacial movement visible.

11 I have discussed elsewhere contemporary debates regarding the relative merits of different ways of making evolution perceptible in ethnology exhibition contexts, and especially with a view to teaching the gradualness of progress: see Bennett (1995a: 179–86).

12 Pitt Rivers Museum Archive, Foundations and Early History, folios 3–4.

13 See also Petch (2001) for an interesting discussion of this tendency in the Pitt Rivers Museum.

14 See 30 July 1884 memorandum from Henry Higgins, Minutes of Museum Subcommittees, Liverpool Museum, vol. 2, April 1879–July 1889.

15 Correspondence of Sir William Henry Flower, British Museum of Natural History.

16 Not just words, of course, although these do seem to have been to the fore in Anglophone contexts. Nélia Dias's work on anthropology museums in late-nineteenth-century France suggests that a different economy of the visible was organised through the use of display techniques which, in aiming to ward off the tendency towards relativism that was associated with the *fin-de-siècle* subjectivication of vision, relied increasingly on statistics, charts and tables rather than words to regulate the visitors' vision: see Dias (1998).

17 Haddon had come into contact with Goode through both the Museums Association and his extensive connections with American museums (Levell, 2001: 269).

18 Jevons also played an important role as a mediating figure in the relationships between Australian and British debates on these matters. See Davison (1997/8).

19 I draw here on my discussion in an earlier essay: see Bennett (1995b).

20 In some contemporary British formulations, however, the museum was conceived as an aid and supplement to the library. The Committee on Museums established by the British Association for the Advancement of Science thus recommended in 1887 that the museum should be regarded as 'a book of plates close at hand to illustrate the volumes in the library' (cited in Forgan, 1999: 192).

21 In describing this system of glances as dialogical, I am drawing on the work of Mikhail Bakhtin (1981).

22 Although I draw mainly on Stafford's account of the differences between curiosity and the Enlightenment in these regards, Kevin Hetherington (1999, 2002) has also written perceptive accounts of these issues even though he somewhat confusingly collides the visual practices of curiosity with those of classification and takes no account of the specific problems of vision associated with evolutionary thought.

23 Daubenton was something of a go-between in the debates and struggles between Buffon's approach to natural history as still centrally concerning the story of life on earth and Condorcet's campaign to reform natural history displays in accordance with the principles of a tabular rationalism. See Corsi (1988).

24 Ritvo (1997) notes, however, that the endeavour of binomial classification to overcome the nomenclatural chaos that had characterised Renaissance natural history always fell short of its aims.

25 This aspect of museum practice echoed the stress placed on the languages of painting and gesture in view of their ability to 'speak to the eyes'. See Mirzoeff (1995) for a recent discussion of this aspect of Enlightenment thought.

26 This was also true of the Museum's menagerie, which retained aspects of the circus in its exhibition of animals: see Burkhardt (1997). It is also worth remarking the reappearance of similar arguments in Balfour's attitude to evolutionary displays (see chapter 3, p. 78).

27 This often also involved the loss of forms of knowledge associated specifically with women and in colonial contexts, indigenous peoples: see Schiebinger (1998).

28 This textual coding of objects is made clear in Frederick McCoy's assessment that a botanical garden in which the classes, families and genera are clearly labelled 'will teach the principles of botanical classification, even if but poorly furnished with plants' (McCoy, 1857: 8). For it shows that classification still works even if there are no objects to perform the textual functions assigned to them.

29 Ann Blum (1993) makes it clear that there is nothing natural about such practices of looking. Indeed, it was not until the 1880s that they made any significant headway in pictorial forms of zoological illustration.

30 Letter to Edward Tylor (1 September 1900) *Tylor Papers*, Box 13A, Folio S16, Pitt Rivers Museum.

31 I am indebted here to Frow (2001) for drawing this aspect of de Certeau's discussion to my attention.

32 Huxley also used the term in the same way when summarising – in a lecture for working men – the lessons that can be learned from a piece of chalk (see chapter 2, p. 37), and it recurs in his 1865 essay 'On the methods and results of ethnology' (see Huxley, 1968: 248).

33 This distinction has a longer history rooted in the medieval revival of the classical distinction between the *artes liberales* and the *artes serviles* and the association of these, respectively,

with the subjects of the *trivium* and *quadrivium* and with the mechanical arts: see Eamon (1994: 82).

34 The position of photography in relation to the museum was quite different. The indexical quality of the photograph meant that both natural history and ethnographic photographs could be used in museums alongside specimens and artefacts as if they had the same degree of referentiality. The meaning of photographs could also be stabilised by the use of captions. This was not possible with film which, owing to the split between filmic representation and pro-filmic event effected by the editorial processes of cutting, lacked the photograph's indexical quality (Griffiths, A., 2002: 88–100, 113, 122–4, 168–70).

35 Notably, however, it was introduced into the Musée Grévin almost immediately it was invented: see Schwartz (1995). This was a hybrid institution which, modelled on Madame Tussauds, asserted an anti-museum ethos of modernity in extolling the virtues of the fabricated objects it displayed while also drawing on the associations between museums and classicism to distance itself from low-brow, semi-pornographic wax anatomy collections popular on the fair circuit.

Postscript

1 Nick Prior's work adds valuably to Pierre Bourdieu's own researches on the role of art museums within the socio-cultural dynamics of modernity: see Prior (2002).

References

Abrams, Philip (1968) *The Origins of British Sociology, 1834–1914*, Chicago and London: University of Chicago Press.

Adorno, Theodor W. (1967) 'Valéry Proust Museum' in *Prisms*, trans. Samuel and Shierry Weber, London: Neville Spearman.

AMNH (1911) *American Museum Journal*, New York: AMNH.

Albury, W. R. and D. R. Oldroyd (1977) 'From Renaissance mineral studies to historical geology, in the light of Michel Foucault's *The Order of Things*', *British Journal for the History of Science*, vol. X, part 3, no. 36.

Allen, David Elliston (1994) *The Naturalist in Britain – A Social History*, Princeton, NJ: Princeton University Press.

Anderson, Margaret and Andrew Reeves (1994) 'Contested identities: museums and the nation in Australia' in Flora S. Kaplan (ed.) *Museums and the Making of 'Ourselves': The Role of Objects in National Identity*, London: Leicester University Press.

Armstrong, Meg (1992–3) '"A jumble of foreignness": the sublime musayums of nineteenth-century fairs and expositions', *Cultural Critique*, winter.

Attwood, Bain (ed.) (1996a) *In the Age of Mabo: History, Aborigines, and Australia*, Sydney: Allen & Unwin.

Attwood, Bain (1996b) 'Making history, imagining Aborigines and Australia' in Tim Bonyhady and Tom Griffiths (eds) *Prehistory to Politics: John Mulvaney, the Humanities and the Public Intellectual*, Melbourne: Melbourne University Press.

Australian Museum Archives, Series 24: Curators Reports to the Trustees, Box 1, 1881–87.

Bagehot, Walter (1873) *Physics and Politics: Or Thoughts on the Application of the Principles of 'Natural Selection' and 'Inheritance' to Political Society*, London: Henry S. King & Co.

Bagehot, Walter [1896] (1963) *The English Constitution*, London: Collins/Fontana.

Bakhtin, Mikhail (1981) *The Dialogic Imagination*, Austin, TX: University of Texas Press.

Bal, Mieke (1992) 'Telling, showing, showing off', *Critical Inquiry*, vol. 18, no. 3.

Balfour, Henry (1893) *The Evolution of Decorative Art: An Essay upon its Origin and Development as Illustrated by the Art of Modern Races of Mankind*, London: Rivington, Percival & Co.

Balfour, Henry (1904a) 'The relationship of museums to the study of anthropology', *The Museums Journal*, vol. III.

Balfour, Henry (1904b) 'Presidential address to section H. – Anthropology', *Report of the British Association for the Advancement of Science*, pp. 689–700.

Balzac, Honoré de (1977) *The Wild Ass's Skin* [*La peau de chagrin*; 1st edition 1831], Harmondsworth: Penguin Books.

Bann, Stephen (1984) *The Clothing of Clio: A Study of the Representation of History in Nineteenth-Century Britain and France*, Cambridge: Cambridge University Press.

Bannister, Robert C. (1979) *Social Darwinism: Science and Myth in Anglo-American Social Thought*, Philadelphia, PA: Temple University Press.

Barrell, John (1986) *The Political Theory of Painting from Reynolds to Hazlitt: 'The Body of the Public'*, New Haven, CT, and London: Yale University Press.

Barringer, Tim (1998) 'The South Kensington Museum and the colonial project' in Barringer and Tom Flynn (eds) *Colonialism and the Object: Empire, Material Culture and the Museum*, London and New York: Routledge.

Barringer, Tim and Tom Flynn (eds) (1998) *Colonialism and the Object: Empire, Material Culture and the Museum*, London and New York: Routledge.

Barry, Andrew (2001) *Political Machines: Governing a Technological Society*, London and New York: Athlone Press.

Barry, Andrew, Thomas Osborne and Nikolas Rose (eds) (1996) *Foucault and Political Reason: Liberalism, Neo-Liberalism and Rationalities of Government*, London: UCL Press.

Barthelemy-Maudaule, M. (1982) *Lamarck the Mythical Precursor: A Study of the Relations between Science and Ideology*, Cambridge, MA: MIT Press.

Basalla, G. (1967) 'The spread of Western science', *Science*, no. 156.

Bennett, Tony (1990) *Outside Literature*, London: Routledge.

Bennett, Tony (1995a) *The Birth of the Museum: History, Theory, Politics*, London: Routledge.

Bennett, Tony (1995b) 'The multiplication of culture's utility', *Critical Inquiry*, vol. 21, no. 4 (republished in Bennett, 1998a).

Bennett, Tony (1996) 'That those who run may read: museums and barriers to access', *Evaluation and Visitor Research in Museums: Towards 2000*, Sydney: Powerhouse Museum.

Bennett, Tony (1997) 'Regulated restlessness: museums, liberal government and the historical sciences', *Economy and Society*, vol. 26, no. 2.

Bennett, Tony (1998a) *Culture: A Reformer's Science*, Sydney: Allen & Unwin; London and New York: Sage.

Bennett, Tony (1998b) 'Speaking to the eyes: museums, legibility and the social order' in Sharon MacDonald (ed.) *Politics of Display: Museums, Science, Culture*, London and New York: Routledge.

Bennett, Tony (1999) 'Pedagogic objects, clean eyes and popular instruction: on sensory regimes and museum didactics', *Configurations. A Journal of Literature, Science and Technology*, vol. 6, no. 3.

Bennett, Tony (2000) *Intellectuals, Culture, Policy: The Technical, the Critical and the Practical*, The Open University, Milton Keynes: Pavis Papers in Social and Cultural Research.

Bennett, Tony (2002) 'Archaeological autopsy: objectifying time and cultural governance', *Cultural Values*, vol. 6, nos 1–2.

Bennett, Tony (2003a) 'Culture and governmentality' in Jack Bratich, Jeremy Packer and Cameron McCarthy (eds) *Foucault, Cultural Studies and Governmentality*, New York: SUNY Press.

Bennett, Tony (2003b) 'Stored virtue: memory, the body and the evolutionary museum' in Suzannah Radstone and Katharine Hodgkin (eds) *Regimes of Memory*, London: Routledge.

Bennett, Tony (2004) 'The invention of the modern cultural fact: toward a critique of the critique of everyday life' in Elizabeth Silva and Tony Bennett (eds) *Contemporary Culture and Everyday Life*, Durham: Sociologypress.

Bentham, Jeremy (1843) *Works, vol. IV*, London: Tait.

Bernal, Martin (1991) *Black Athena: The Afroasiatic Roots of Classical Civilisation*, London: Vintage.

Betts, John Rickards (1959) 'P. T. Barnum and the popularisation of natural history', *Journal of the History of Ideas*, no. 20.

Bhabha, Homi K. (1994) *The Location of Culture*, London and New York: Routledge.

Bibby, Cyril (1958) 'Thomas Henry Huxley and university development', *Victorian Studies*, vol. 2, no. 2.

Bickmore, Albert S. (n.d.) 'Autobiography with a historical sketch of the founding and early development of the American Museum of Natural History', unpublished ms.

Blanckaert, Claude, Claudine Cohen, Pietro Corsi and Jean-Louis Fischer (eds) (1997) *Le Muséum au premier siècle de son histoire*, Paris: Éditions de Muséum National d'Histoire Naturelle.

Blum, Ann Shelby (1993) *Picturing Nature: American Nineteenth-Century Zoological Illustration*, Princeton, NJ: Princeton University Press.

207

Bohrer, Frederick N. (1994) 'The times and spaces of history: representation, Assyria and the British Museum' in Daniel J. Sherman and Irit Rogoff (eds) *Museum Culture: Histories, Discourses, Spectacles*, Minneapolis: University of Minnesota Press.

Booth, Martin (1997) *The Doctor, the Detective and Arthur Conan Doyle: A Biography of Arthur Conan Doyle*, London: Hodder & Stoughton.

Bouquet, Mary (2000) 'Figures of relations: reconnecting kinship studies and museum collections' in Janet Carsten (ed.) *Cultures of Relatedness: New Approaches to the Study of Kinship*, Cambridge: Cambridge University Press.

Bourdier, Frank (1969) 'Geoffroy Saint-Hilaire versus Cuvier: the campaign for palaeontological evolution' in Carl J. Schneer (ed.) *Toward a History of Geology*, Cambridge, MA: MIT Press.

Bourdieu, Pierre (1984) *Distinction: A Social Critique of the Judgement of Taste*, London: Routledge & Kegan Paul.

Bourdieu, Pierre (2000) *Pascalian Meditations*, Cambridge: Polity Press.

Bravo, Michael T. (1996) 'Ethnological encounters' in Nicholas Jardine, James A. Secord and Emma C. Spray (eds) *Cultures of Natural History*, Cambridge: Cambridge University Press.

Bredekamp, Horst (1995) *The Lure of Antiquity and the Cult of the Machine: The Kunstkammer and the Evolution of Nature, Art and Technology*, Princeton, NJ: Markus Wiener.

Breger, Louis (2000) *Freud: Darkness in the Midst of Vision*, New York: John Wiley & Sons.

Brewer, John (1995) '"The most polite age and the most vicious." Attitudes towards culture as a commodity, 1660–1800' in Ann Bermingham and John Brewer (eds) *The Consumption of Culture, 1600–1800: Image, Object, Text*, London: Routledge.

Briggs, Asa (1990) *Victorian Things*, Harmondsworth: Penguin Books.

British Museum (Natural History) (1893) *The Association of Women Pioneer Lecturers: The Work and the Method*, London: British Museum (Natural History).

Brown, Lee Rust (1997) *The Emerson Museum: Practical Romanticism and the Pursuit of the Whole*, Cambridge, MA: Harvard University Press.

Bunzl, Matti (1996) 'Franz Boas and the Humboldtian tradition: from *Volksgeist* and *Nationalcharakter* to an anthropological concept of culture' in George W. Stocking Jr. (ed.) *Volksgeist as Method and Ethic: Essays on Boasian Ethnography and the German Anthropological Tradition*, Madison, WI: University of Wisconsin Press.

Burchell, Graham, Colin Gordon and Peter Miller (eds) (1991) *The Foucault Effect: Studies in Governmentality*, London: Harvester Wheatsheaf.

Burkhardt, Richard W. (1997) 'La Ménagerie et la vie du Muséum' in Claude Blanckaert, Claudine Cohen, Pietro Corsi and Jean-Louis Fischer (eds) *Le Muséum au premier siècle de son histoire*, Paris: Éditions de Muséum National D'Histoire Naturelle.

Bynum, William Frederick (1974) 'Time's noblest offspring: the problem of Man in the British Natural Historical Sciences, 1800–1863', PhD dissertation, University of Cambridge.

Cadbury, Deborah (2000) *The Dinosaur Hunters: A True Story of Scientific Rivalry and the Discovery of the Prehistoric World*, London: Fourth Estate.

Cameron, R. P. (1890) 'The best means of making museums attractive to the public', *Museums Journal*.

Canghuilhem, Georges (1988) *Ideology and Rationality in the History of the Life Sciences*, Cambridge, Mass: MIT Press.

Carpenter, George H. (1894) 'On collections to illustrate the evolution and geographical distribution of animals', *Museums Journal*.

Caygill, Marjorie (1981) *The Story of the British Museum*, London: British Museum.

Caygill, Marjorie (1997) 'Franks and the British Museum – the cuckoo in the nest' in Majorie Caygill and John Cherry (eds) *A. W. Franks: Nineteenth Century Collecting and the British Museum*, London: British Museum.

Caygill, Marjorie and John Cherry (eds) (1997) *A. W. Franks: Nineteenth Century Collecting and the British Museum*, London: British Museum.

Chapman, William Ryan (1981) 'Ethnology in the museum: AHLF Pitt Rivers (1827–1900) and the institutional foundations of British anthropology', D. Phil. thesis, Oxford University.

208

Chard, John (1890) 'On circulating museum cabinets for schools and other educational purposes', *Journal of the Museums Association.*

Chitnis, A. and C. Chitnis (1970) 'The University of Edinburgh's Natural History Museum and the Huttonian-Wernian debate', *Annals of Science*, vol. 26, no. 2.

Clifford, James (1988) 'On collecting art and culture' in *The Predicament of Culture. Twentieth-Century Ethnography, Literature and Art*, Cambridge, MA and London: Harvard University Press.

Coates, H. (1899) 'School children and museums', *Museums Association Proceedings.*

Collini, Stefan (1979) *Liberalism and Sociology: L. T. Hobhouse and Political Argument in England, 1880–1914*, Cambridge: Cambridge University Press.

Collini, Stefan (1991) *Public Moralists: Political Thought and Intellectual Life in Britain, 1850–1930*, Oxford: Clarendon Press.

Collins, Hugh (1985) 'Political ideology in Australia: the distinctiveness of a Benthamite society', *Daedelus*, vol. 114, no. 1.

Conforti, Michael (1997) 'The idealist enterprise and the applied arts' in Malcolm Baker and Brenda Richardson (eds) *A Grand Design: The Art of the Victoria and Albert Museum*, New York and Baltimore: Harry N. Abrams Inc. and the Baltimore Museum of Art.

Connell, Robert and Terence H. Irving (1992) *Class Structure in Australian History: Poverty and Progress*, Melbourne: Longman Cheshire.

Conrad, Joseph [1902] (1995) *Heart of Darkness*, London: Penguin Books.

Cook, Jill (1997) 'A curators' curator: Franks and the Stone Age collection' in Marjorie Caygill and John Cherry (eds) *A. W. Franks: Nineteenth Century Collecting and the British Museum*, London: British Museum.

Coombes, Anne E. (1988) 'Museums and the formation of national and cultural identities', *Oxford Art Journal*, vol. 11, no. 2.

Coombes, Anne (1994) *Reinventing Africa: Museums, Material Culture and Popular Imagination in Late Victorian and Edwardian England*, New Haven, CT, and London: Harvard University Press.

Cooter, Roger (1984) *The Cultural Meaning of Popular Science: Phrenology and the Organisation of Popular Consent in Nineteenth Century Britain*, Cambridge: Cambridge University Press.

Corsi, Pietro (1988) *The Age of Lamarck: Evolutionary Theories in France*, Berkeley, CA: University of California Press.

Crary, Jonathan (1996) *Techniques of the Observer: On Vision and Modernity in the Nineteenth Century*, Cambridge, MA: MIT Press.

Crary, Jonathan (2001) *Suspensions of Perception: Attention, Spectacle, and Modern Culture*, Cambridge, MA: MIT Press.

Crimp, Douglas (1993) *On the Museum's Ruins*, Cambridge, MA: MIT Press.

Dallett, Nancy (1988) 'Science for citizens: The American Museum of Natural History, 1869–1936', unpublished MA dissertation.

Darwin, Charles [1859] (1968) *The Origin of Species by means of Natural Selection or The Preservation of Favoured Races in the Struggle for Life*, Harmondsworth: Penguin Books.

Darwin, Charles [1871] (1981) *The Descent of Man, and Selection in Relation to Sex*, Princeton, NJ: Princeton University Press.

Daston, Lorraine and Katharine Park (1998) *Wonders and the Order of Nature, 1150–1750*, New York: Zone Books.

Daukes, S. H. (1944) 'The historical medical museum: its future and possibilities', *Museums Journal*, no. 44.

Davison, Graeme (1993) *The Unforgiving Minute: How Australians Learned to Tell the Time*, Melbourne: Oxford University Press.

Davison, Graeme (1997/8) 'The unsociable sociologist – W. S. Jevons and his survey of Sydney, 1856–8', *Australian Cultural History*, no. 16.

Dawkins, W. Boyd (1877) 'The need for museum reform', *Nature*, vol. 16, May 31.

Dawkins, W. Boyd (1890) 'On museum organisation and arrangement', *Museums Association Proceedings.*

Dawkins, W. Boyd (1892) 'The museum question', *Museums Association Proceedings*.

Dean, Dennis R. (1985) '"Through science to despair": geology and the Victorians' in J. G. Paradis and T. Postlewait (eds) *Victorian Science and Victorian Values: Literary Perspectives*, Piscataway, NJ: Rutgers University Press.

Dean, Mitchell (1999) *Governmentality: Power and Rule in Modern Society*, London: Sage.

Dean, Mitchell (2002) 'Powers of life and death beyond governmentality', *Cultural Values*, vol. 6, nos 1–2.

De Certeau, Michel (1988) *The Writing of History*, New York: Columbia University Press.

Deleuze, Gilles (1999) *Foucault*, London: Athlone Press.

Denny, A. (1898) 'The relation of museums to elementary teaching', *Museums Journal*.

Desmond, Adrian (1982) *Archetypes and Ancestors: Palaeontology in Victorian London*, Chicago and London: University of Chicago Press.

Desmond, Adrian (1989) *The Politics of Evolution: Morphology, Medicine, and Reform in Radical London*, Chicago and London: University of Chicago Press.

Desmond, Adrian (1994) *Huxley: The Devil's Disciple*, London: Michael Joseph.

Desmond, Adrian (1997) *Huxley: Evolution's High Priest*, London: Michael Joseph.

Desmond, Adrian and James Moore (1992) *Darwin*, Harmondsworth: Penguin Books.

Dewey, John (1898) 'Evolution and ethics', *The Monist*, vol. 8, no. 3.

Dias, Nélia (1994) 'Looking at objects: memory, knowledge in nineteenth-century ethnographic displays' in George Robertson, Melinda Mash, Lisa Tickner, Jon Bird, Barry Curtis and Tim Putnam (eds) *Travellers' Tales: Narratives of Home and Displacement*, London and New York: Routledge.

Dias, Nélia (1998) 'The visibility of difference: nineteenth-century French anthropological collections' in Sharon MacDonald (ed.) *The Politics of Display: Museums, Science, Culture*, London and New York: Routledge.

Dirks, Nicholas B. (2000) 'The crimes of colonialism: anthropology and the textualisation of India' in Peter Pels and Oscar Salemink (eds) *Colonial Subjects: Essays on the Practical History of Anthropology*, Ann Arbor, MI: University of Michigan Press.

Dirks, Nicholas B. (2001) *Castes of Mind: Colonialism and the Making of Modern India*, Princeton, NJ: Princeton University Press.

Doane, Mary Ann (2002) *The Emergence of Cinematic Time: Modernity, Contingency, The Archive*, Cambridge, MA: Harvard University Press.

Dowling, Linda (1996) *The Vulgarisation of Art: The Victorians and Aesthetic Democracy*, Charlottesville and London: University Press of Virginia.

Drayton, Richard (2000) *Nature's Government: Science, Imperial Britain and the 'Improvement' of the World*, New Haven, CT, and London: Yale University Press.

Dubow, Saul (1995) *Scientific Racism in Modern South Africa*, Cambridge: Cambridge University Press.

Duffin, Lorna (1978) 'Prisoners of progress: women and evolution' in Sara Delamont and Lorna Duffin (eds) *The Nineteenth-Century Woman: Her Cultural and Physical World*, London: Croom Helm.

Dugan, Kathleen (1987) 'The zoological exploration of the Australian region and its impact on biological theory' in Nathan Reingold and Marc Rothenberg (eds) *Scientific Colonialism: A Cross-Cultural Comparison*, Washington DC: Smithsonian Institution Press.

During, Simon (2002) *Modern Enchantments: The Cultural Power of Secular Magic*, Cambridge, MA: Harvard University Press.

Durkheim, Emile (1961) *The Elementary Forms of Religious Life*, New York: Collier.

Eamon, William (1994) *Science and the Secrets of Nature: Books of Secrets in Medieval and Early Modern Culture*, Princeton, NJ: Princeton University Press.

Elias, Norbert (1987) *Time: An Essay*, Oxford: Blackwell.

Fabian, Johannes (1983) *Time and the Other: How Anthropology Makes Its Object*, New York: Columbia University Press.

Fayter, Paul (1997) 'Strange new worlds of space and time: late Victorian science and science fiction' in Bernard Lightman (1997) *Victorian Science in Context*, Chicago and London: University of Chicago Press.

Fee, Elizabeth (1976) 'The sexual politics of Victorian anthropology' in Mary S. Hartman and

Lois Banner (eds) *Clio's Consciousness Raised: New Perspectives on the History of Women*, New York: Octagon Books.

Fee, Elizabeth (1979) 'Nineteenth-century craniology: the study of the female skull', *Bulletin of the History of Medicine*, vol. 53.

Felski, R. (1999–2000) 'The invention of everyday life', *New Formations*, no. 39, pp. 13–31.

Fichman, Martin (1997) 'Biology and politics: defining the boundaries' in Bernard Lightman (ed.) *Victorian Science in Context*, Chicago and London: University of Chicago Press.

Findlen, Paula (1994) *Possessing Nature: Museums, Collecting, and Scientific Culture in Early Modern Italy*, Berkeley, Los Angeles and London: University of California Press.

Findlen, Paula (2000) 'The modern muses: Renaissance collecting and the cult of remembrance' in Susan A. Crane (ed.) *Museums and Memory*, Stanford: Stanford University Press.

Finney, Colin (1984) *To Sail beyond the Sunset: Natural History in Australia 1699–1829*, Adelaide: Rigby.

Finney, Colin (1993) *Paradise Revealed: Natural History in Nineteenth-Century Australia*, Melbourne: Museum of Victoria.

Fletcher, J. J. (1920) 'The Society's heritage from the Macleays', presidential address in commemoration of the centenary of the birth of Sir William Macleay, *Proceedings of the Linnean Society of New South Wales*.

Flint, Kate (2000) *The Victorians and the Visual Imagination*, Cambridge: Cambridge University Press.

Flower, W. H. (1888) *A General Guide to the British Museum (Natural History)*, London: British Museum (Natural History).

Flower, Sir William H. (1893) 'Modern museums', *Museums Association Proceedings*.

Flower, Sir William Henry (1898) *Essays on Museums and Other Subjects Connected with Natural History*, London: Macmillan & Co.

Forbes, Henry O. (1901) *Report of the Director of Museums Relative to the Re-arrangement of, and the Cases for, the Collections in the Free Public Museums*, Liverpool: City of Liverpool.

Forgan, Sophie (1994) 'The architecture of display', *History of Science*, vol. 32, part 2, no. 96.

Forgan, Sophie (1999) 'Bricks and bones: architecture and science in Victorian Britain' in Peter Galison and Emily Thompson (eds) *The Architecture of Science*, Cambridge, MA: MIT Press.

Foucault, Michel (1970) *The Order of Things: An Archaeology of the Human Sciences*, London: Tavistock.

Foucault, Michel (1972) *The Archaeology of Knowledge*, London: Tavistock.

Foucault, Michel (1978) *History of Sexuality*, New York: Pantheon

Foucault, Michel (1980) *Power/Knowledge: Selected Interviews and other Writings, 1972–1977*, ed. Colin Gordon, New York: Pantheon Books.

Foucault, Michel (1985) *The Use of Pleasure: The History of Sexuality, Vol. 2*, New York: Random House.

Foucault, Michel (1991) 'Governmentality' in Graham Burchell, Colin Gordon and Peter Miller (eds) *The Foucault Effect: Studies in Governmentality*, London: Harvester Wheatsheaf.

Foucault, Michel (1997) *Ethics: Subjectivity and Truth*, London: Allen Lane.

Foucault, Michel (2003) *Society Must Be Defended*, New York: Picador.

Fox, Paul (1988) 'The State Library of Victoria: science and civilisation', *Transition*, no. 26.

Freeland, Guy (1983) 'Evolutionism and arch(a)eology' in D. Oldroyd and I. Langham (eds) *The Wider Domain of Evolutionary Thought*, Dordrecht: D. Reidel Publishing Co.

Freud, Sigmund (1969) *Civilisation and its Discontents*, London: Hogarth Press and the Institute of Psycho-analysis.

Frow, John (2001) 'A politics of stolen time' in Jon May and Nigel Thrift (eds) *Timespace: Geographies of Temporality*, London and New York: Routledge.

Fullerton, John (ed.) (1998) *Celebrating 1895: The Centenary of Cinema*, London: John Libby.

Gamble, Eliza Burt (1894) *The Evolution of Woman: An Inquiry into the Dogma of her Inferiority to Man*, London and New York: Knickerbocker Press.

Gascoigne, John (1994) *Joseph Banks and the English Enlightenment: Useful Knowledge and Polite Culture*, Cambridge: Cambridge University Press.

211

Gascoigne, John (2002) *The Enlightenment and the Origins of European Australia*, Cambridge: Cambridge University Press.

Gates, Barbara T. (1997a) 'Ordering nature: revisioning Victorian science culture' in Bernard Lightman (ed.) *Victorian Science in Context*, Chicago and London: University of Chicago Press.

Gates, Barbara T (1997b) 'Revisioning Darwin with sympathy: Arabella Buckley' in Barbara T. Gates and Ann B. Shteir (eds) *Natural Eloquence: Women Reinscribe Science*, Madison, WI: University of Wisconsin Press.

Gates, Barbara T. and Ann B. Shteir (eds) (1997) *Natural Eloquence: Women Reinscribe Science*, Madison, WI: University of Wisconsin Press.

Geddes, Patrick (1905) *Syllabus of a Course of Ten Lectures on Great Cities: Their Place in Geography, and their Relation to Human Development*, London: Horniman Museum.

Geikie, Archibald (1858) *The Story of a Boulder, or Gleanings from the Note-Book of a Field Geologist*, Edinburgh: Thomas Constable & Co.

Gelder, Ken (1994) *Reading the Vampire*, London: Routledge.

Gillies, William (1908) 'A visitor's impression' in Charles A. Long (ed.) *Record and Review of the State Schools Exhibition*, Melbourne: Ministry of Public Instruction.

Gilman, Sander L. (1985) *Difference and Pathology: Stereotypes of Sexuality, Race, and Madness*, Ithaca, NY, and London: Cornell University Press.

Gilroy, Paul (2000) *Against Race: Imagining Political Culture beyond the Color Line*, Cambridge, MA: Belknap Press of Harvard University Press.

Ginzburg, Carlo (1980) 'Morelli, Freud and Sherlock Holmes: clues and scientific method', *History Workshop*, no. 9.

Girouard, Mark (1981) *Alfred Waterhouse and the Natural History Museum*, New Haven, CT, and London: Yale University Press in association with the British Museum (Natural History).

Golinski, Jan (1998) *Making Natural Knowledge: Constructivism and the History of Science*, Cambridge: Cambridge University Press.

Goode, George Brown [1888] (1991) 'Museum-history and museums of history' in Sally Gregory Kohlstedt (ed.) (1991) *The Origins of Natural Science in America: The Essays of George Brown Goode*, Washington, DC: Smithsonian Institution Press.

Goode, George Brown [1889] (1991) 'The museums of the future' in Sally Gregory Kohlstedt (ed.) (1991) *The Origins of Natural Science in America: The Essays of George Brown Goode*, Washington, DC: Smithsonian Institution Press.

Goode, George Brown (1895) *The Principles of Museum Administration*, York: Coultas and Volans.

Goode, George Brown (ed.) (1897) *The Smithsonian Institution, 1846–1896: The History of its First Half Century*, Washington, DC: Smithsonian Institution Press.

Goodman, David (1990) 'Fear of circuses: founding the National Museum of Victoria', *Continuum: An Australian Journal of the Media*, vol. 3, no. 1.

Gould, Stephen Jay (1987) *Time's Arrow, Time's Cycle: Myth and Metaphor in the Discovery of Geological Time*, Cambridge, MA: Harvard University Press.

Gould, Stephen Jay (1993) *Eight Little Piggies*, London: Penguin Books.

Grayson, Donald (1983) *The Establishment of Human Antiquity*, New York, London, Sydney: Academic Press.

Greene, John C. (1981) *Science, Ideology, and World View: Essays in the History of Evolutionary Ideas*, Berkeley and Los Angeles: University of California Press.

Griffiths, Alison (1998) '"Animated Geography": early cinema at the American Museum of Natural History' in Fullerton (ed.) *Celebrating 1895: The Centenary of Cinema*, London: John Libby.

Griffiths, Alison (2002) *Wondrous Differences: Cinema, Anthropology, and Turn-of-the-Century Visual Culture*, New York: Columbia University Press.

Griffiths, Tom (1996a) *Hunters and Collectors: The Antiquarian Imagination in Australia*, Melbourne: Cambridge University Press.

Griffiths, Tom (1996b) 'In search of Australian antiquity' in Tim Bonyhady and Tom Griffiths (eds) *Prehistory to Politics: John Mulvaney, the Humanities and the Public Intellectual*, Melbourne: Melbourne University Press.

Griffiths, Tom (2000) 'Social history and deep time', *Public History Review*, no. 8.

Gunning, Tom (1989) 'An aesthetic of astonishment: early film and the (in)credulous spectator', *Art and Text*, no. 34.

Gunning, Tom (1990) 'The cinema of attractions: early film, its spectator and the avant-garde', in Thomas Elsaesser (ed.) *Early Cinema: Space, Frame, Narrative*, London: British Film Institute.

Haddon, Alfred C. (1895) *Evolution in Art as Illustrated by the Life-Histories of Designs*, London: Walter Scott Ltd.

Haggis, A. W. J. (1942) 'The life and work of Sir Henry Wellcome', typescript, 4 vols.

Hale, H. M. (1956) 'The first hundred years of the museum, 1856–1956', *Records of the South Australian Museum*, vol. 12.

Hall, Catherine (1992) *White, Male and Middle-Class: Explorations in Feminism and History*, Cambridge: Polity Press.

Hannah, Matthew G. (2000) *Governmentality and the Mastery of Territory in Nineteenth-Century America*, Cambridge: Cambridge University Press.

Haraway, Donna (1992) 'Teddy bear patriarchy: taxidermy in the Garden of Eden, New York City, 1908–1936' in *Primate Visions: Gender, Race and Nature in the World of Modern Science*, London: Verso.

Harris, Neil (1973) *Humbug: The Art of P. T. Barnum*, Boston: Little Brown & Co.

Hawkins, Mike (1997) *Social Darwinism in European and American Thought, 1860–1945*, Cambridge: Cambridge University Press.

Hayden, Dolores (1981) *The Great Domestic Revolution: A History of Feminist Designs for American Homes, Neighbourhoods and Cities*, Cambridge, MA: MIT Press.

Healy, Chris (1997) *From the Ruins of Colonialism: History as Social Memory*, Melbourne: Cambridge University Press.

Hedley, Charles (1913) *Report on a Visit to Certain American Museums in 1912*, Australian Museum, Sydney, Miscellaneous Series VIII.

Helfand, Michael S. (1977) 'T. H. Huxley's "Evolution and Ethics": The politics of evolution and the evolution of politics', *Victorian Studies*, vol. 20, no. 2.

Helliwell, Christine and Barry Hindess (2002) 'The "empire of uniformity" and the government of subject peoples', *Cultural Values*, vol. 6, nos 1–2.

Hetherington, Kevin (1999) 'From blindness to blindness: museums, heterogeneity and the subject' in John Law and John Hassard (eds) *Actor Network Theory and After*, Oxford: Blackwell/The Sociological Review.

Hetherington, Kevin (2002) 'The unsightly: touching the Parthenon frieze', *Theory, Culture and Society*, vol. 19, nos 5/6, pp. 187–205.

Higgins, Rev. H. H. (1892) 'On the cultivation of special features in museums', *Museums Association Proceedings*.

Hiller, Susan (ed.) (1991) *The Myth of Primitivism: Perspectives on Art*, London and New York: Routledge.

Hinsley, Curtis M. (1981) *Savages and Scientists: The Smithsonian Institution and the Development of American Anthropology, 1846–1910*, Washington, DC: Smithsonian Institution Press.

Hoare, Michael (1981) 'Botany and society in eastern Australia' in D. J. and S. G. M. Carr (eds) *People and Plants in Australia*, Sydney: Academic Press.

Hoffenberg, Peter (2001) *An Empire on Display: English, Indian, and Australian Exhibitions from the Crystal Palace to the Great War*, Berkeley, Los Angeles and London: University of California Press.

Home, R. W. and Sally Gregory Kohlstedt (eds) (1991) *International Science and National Scientific Identity: Australia between Britain and America*, Dordrecht: Kluwer Academic Publishers.

Horton, David (1991) *Recovering the Tracks: The Story of Australian Archaeology*, Canberra: Aboriginal Studies Press.

Hoyle, William E. (1902) 'The use of museums in teaching', *The Museums Journal*, February.

Hudson, Kenneth (1982) *A Social History of Archaeology: The British Experience*, London: Macmillan.

Hughes, Robert (1996) *The Fatal Shore*, London: Collins Harvill.

Huhndorf, Shari M. (2000) 'Nanook and his contemporaries: imagining Eskimos in American culture, 1897–1922', *Critical Inquiry*, no. 27.

Hunter, Ian (1988) *Culture and Government: The Emergence of Literary Education*, London: Macmillan.

Hutchinson, Jonathan (1893) 'On educational museums', *Museums Association Proceedings*.

Huxley, Thomas H. [1865] 'On the method and results of ethnology' in T. H. Huxley (1896b) *Discourses: Biological and Geological: Essays*, London: Macmillan.

Huxley, Thomas H. (1868) 'A liberal education; and where to find it', *Macmillan's Magazine*, March.

Huxley, Thomas H. (1882) *Science and Culture and Other Essays*, London: Macmillan & Co.

Huxley, Thomas H. (1890a) 'Government: anarchy or regimentation', *The Nineteenth Century*, no. 159.

Huxley, Thomas H. (1890b) 'On the natural inequality of men', *The Nineteenth Century*, no. 155.

Huxley, Thomas H. (1893) *Methods and Results: Collected Essays, Vol. 1*, London: Macmillan & Co.

Huxley, Thomas H. (1894) 'Evolution and ethics' in J. Paradis and G. C. Williams (1989) *T. H. Huxley's Evolution and Ethics with New Essays on Its Victorian and SocioBiological Context*, Princeton, NJ: Princeton University Press.

Huxley, Thomas H. (1896a) 'Suggestions for a proposed natural history museum in Manchester', Report of the Museums Association.

Huxley, Thomas H. (1896b) *Discourses: Biological and Geological: Essays*, London: Macmillan.

Huxley, Thomas H. [1896c] (1968) *Man's Place in Nature and Other Anthropological Essays*, New York: Greenwood Press.

Inkster, Ian (1985) 'Scientific enterprise and the colonial "model": observations on the Australian experience in historical context', *Social Studies of Science*, no. 15.

Inkster, Ian and Jan Todd (1988) 'Support for the scientific enterprise, 1850–1900', in R. W. Home (ed.) *Australian Science in the Making*, Sydney: Cambridge University Press in association with the Australian Academy of Science.

Jacknis, Ira (1985) 'Franz Boas and exhibits: on the limitations of the museum method of anthropology' in George Stocking Jr (ed.) *Objects and Others: Essays on Museums and Material Culture*, Madison, WI: University of Wisconsin Press.

Jann, Rosemary (1997) 'Revising the descent of women: Eliza Burt Gamble' in Barbara T. Gates and Ann B. Shteir (eds) *Natural Eloquence: Women Reinscribe Science*, Madison, WI: University of Wisconsin Press.

Jardine, Lisa (1997) *Worldly Goods*, London: Basingstoke.

Jardine, Nicholas, James A. Secord and Emma C. Spray (eds) (1996) *Cultures of Natural History*, Cambridge: Cambridge University Press.

Jay, Martin (1994) *Downcast Eyes: The Denigration of Vision in Twentieth-Century Thought*, Berkeley and Los Angeles, CA: University of California Press.

Jenkins, David (1994) 'Object lessons and ethnographic displays: museum exhibitions and the making of American anthropology', *Comparative Studies in Society and History*, vol. 36, no. 1.

Jenkins, Ian (1992) *Archaeologists and Aesthetes in the Sculpture Galleries of the British Museum 1800–1939*, London: British Museum Press.

Jevons, W. Stanley (1883) *Methods of Social Reform*, New York: Augustus M. Kelley.

Jones, Caroline A. and Peter Galison (eds) (1998) *Picturing Science, Producing Art*, London and New York: Routledge.

Jones, Greta (1980) *Social Darwinism and English Social Thought: The Interaction between Biological and Social Theory*, Brighton: Harvester Press.

Jordanova, Ludmilla (1985) 'Gender, generation and science: William Hunter's obstetrical atlas' in William Frederick Bynum and Roy Porter (eds) *William Hunter and the Eighteenth Century Medical World*, Cambridge: Cambridge University Press.

214

Joyce, Patrick (2003) *The Rule of Freedom: Liberalism and the Modern City*, London: Verso.

Kahn, Joel S. (2001) *Modernity and Exclusion*, London: Sage.

Kavanagh, Gaynor (1994) *Museums and the First World War: A Social History*, London and New York: Leicester University Press.

Kehoe, Alice Beck (1998) *The Land of Prehistory: A Critical History of American Archaeology*, New York and London: Routledge.

Keith, Sir Arthur (1913) 'What should museums do for us?' reprinted in the 1927 edition of *The Wellcome Historical Medical Museum Handbook*, London: Wellcome Historical Medical Museum.

Kennedy, J.M. (1968) 'Philanthropy and science in New York City: the American Museum of Natural History, 1868–1968', Yale University PhD dissertation.

Kennedy, Roger G. (1994) *Hidden Cities: The Discovery and Loss of Ancient North American Civilisation*, New York: The Free Press.

Kidd, Rosalind (1997) *The Way We Civilise*, St Lucia: University of Queensland Press.

King, J. C. H. (1997) 'Franks and ethnography' in Marjorie Caygill and John Cherry (eds) *A.W. Franks: Nineteenth Century Collecting and the British Museum*, London: British Museum.

Kingston, Beverley (1988) *The Oxford History of Australia. Vol. 3: 1860–1900, Glad, Confident Morning*, Melbourne: Oxford University Press.

Knell, Simon (1996) 'The roller-coaster of museum geology' in Susan Pearce (ed.) *Exploring Science in Museums*, London: Athlone Press.

Knox, Margaret (1927) 'Nature on the lower East Side', *Natural History*, vol. 27, no. 4.

Kociumbas, Jan (1993) 'Science as cultural ideology: museums and mechanics' institutes in early NSW and Van Diemen's Land', *Labour History*, no. 64.

Koerner, Lisbet (1996) 'Carl Linnaeus in his time and place' in Nicholas Jardine, James A. Secord and Emma C. Spray (eds) *Cultures of Natural History*, Cambridge: Cambridge University Press.

Kohlstedt, Sally Gregory (1979) 'From learned society to public museum: the Boston Society of Natural History' in A. Oleson and J. Voss (eds) *The Organisation of Knowledge in Modern America*, Baltimore, OH, and London: Johns Hopkins University Press.

Kohlstedt, Sally Gregory (1980) 'Henry A. Ward: the merchant naturalist and American museum development', *Journal of the Society for the Bibliography of Natural History*, vol. 9, no. 4.

Kohlstedt, Sally Gregory (1983) 'Australian museums of natural history: public practices and scientific initiatives in the 19th century', *Historical Records of Australian Science*, vol. 5.

Kohlstedt, Sally Gregory (1986) 'International exchange and national style: a view of natural history museums in the United States 1850–1900' in Nathan Reingold and Marc Rothenberg (eds) *Scientific Colonialism: A Cross-Cultural Comparison*, Washington, DC: Smithsonian Institute.

Kohlstedt, Sally Gregory (1988) 'History in a Natural History Museum: George Brown Goode and the Smithsonian Institution', *The Public Historian: A Journal of Public History*, vol. 10, no. 2.

Kohlstedt, Sally Gregory (ed.) (1991a) *The Origins of Natural Science in America: The Essays of George Brown Goode*, Washington, DC: Smithsonian Institution Press.

Kohlstedt, Sally Gregory (1991b) 'International exchange in the natural history enterprise: museums in Australia and the United States' in R. W. Home and Sally Gregory Kohlstedt (eds) *International Science and National Scientific Identity: Australia between Britain and America*, Dordrecht: Kluwer Academic Publishers.

Krasner, James (1992) *The Entangled Eye: Visual Perception and the Representation of Nature in Post-Darwinian Narrative*, Oxford: Oxford University Press.

Krefft, Gerard (1868) 'The improvements effected in modern museums in Europe and Australia', *Royal Society of New South Wales*, vol. 2.

Kuklick, Henrika (1991) *The Savage Within. The Social History of British Anthropology, 1885–1945*, Cambridge: Cambridge University Press.

Kulik, Gary (1989) 'Designing the past: history-museum exhibitions from Peale to the present' in Warren Leon and Roy Rosenzweig (eds) *History Museums in the United States: A Critical Assessment*, Urbana, IL, and Chicago: University of Illinois Press.

Lankester, Ray E. (1880) *Degeneration: A Chapter in Darwinism*, London: Macmillan & Co.

Latour, Bruno (1987) *Science in Action*, Cambridge, MA: Harvard University Press.

Latour, Bruno (1988) *The Pasteurisation of France*, Cambridge, MA: Harvard University Press.

Latour, Bruno (1993) *We Have Never Been Modern*, Cambridge, MA: Harvard University Press.

Latour, Bruno (1999) *Pandora's Hope: Essays on the Reality of Science Studies*, Cambridge, MA: Harvard University Press.

Laurent, John (1994) 'Some aspects of the role of institutes in technical education in New South Wales, 1878–1916' and '"This meeting is now closed": the social significance of the institutes in retrospect' in Philip C. Candy and John Laurent (eds) *Pioneering Culture: Mechanics' Institutes and Schools of Arts in Australia*, Adelaide: Auslib Press.

Law, John (1999) 'After ANT: complexity, naming and topology' in John Law and John Hassard (eds) *Actor Network Theory and After*, Oxford: Blackwell and The Sociological Review.

Legassick, Martin and Ciraj Rassool (2000) *Skeletons in the Cupboard: South African Museums and the Trade in Human Remains 1907–1917*, Cape Town: South African Museum.

Leipziger, Henry M. (1911) 'The museum and the public lecture', *The American Museum Journal*, vol. XI, no. 7.

Levell, Nicky (1997) *The Collectors' Gallery: A Textual and Visual Summary*, London: Horniman Museum.

Levell, Nicky (2001) 'Illustrating evolution: Alfred Cort Haddon and the Horniman Museum, 1901–15' in Anthony Shelton (ed.) *Collectors: Individuals and Institutions*, London: Horniman Museum and Gardens and Museu Antropológico da Universidade de Coimbra.

Levine, Philippa (1986) *The Amateur and the Professional: Antiquarians, Historians and Archaeologists in Victorian England, 1838–1886*, Cambridge: Cambridge University Press.

Lewis, Geoffrey (1989) *For Instruction and Recreation – A Centenary History of the Museums Association*, London: Quiller Press.

Lightman, Bernard (1997a) *Victorian Science in Context*, Chicago, IL, and London: University of Chicago Press.

Lightman, Bernard (1997b) '"The voices of nature": popularising Victorian science' in Lightman, *Victorian Science in Context*, Chicago, IL, and London: University of Chicago Press.

Long, Charles R. (1909) *The Aim and Method in History and Civics*, Melbourne: Macmillan & Co.

Love, Rosaleen (1983) 'Darwinism and feminism: the "woman question" in the life and work of Olive Schreiner and Charlotte Perkins Gilman' in D. Oldroyd and I. Langham (eds) *The Wider Domain of Evolutionary Thought*, Dordrecht: D. Reidel Publishing Co.

Lubbock, John [1870] (1865) *Pre-Historic Times as Illustrated by Ancient Remains and the Manners and Customs of Modern Savages*, London: Williams and Norgate.

Lubbock, John (1978) *The Origin of Civilisation and the Primitive Condition of Man*, Chicago, IL, and London: University of Chicago Press.

Luckhurst, Roger (2003) 'Demon-haunted Darwinism', *New Formations*, no. 49.

Lurie, Edward (1960) *Louis Agassiz: A Life in Science*, Chicago, IL, and London: University of Chicago Press.

MacCallum, W. G. (1911) 'On the value of public medical museums, and on the possibility of establising such a museum in each of the larger cities', *The International Association of Medical Museums Bulletin*, no. 3.

McClellan, Andrew (1994) *Inventing the Louvre: Art, Politics, and the Origins of the Modern Museum in Eighteenth-Century Paris*, Cambridge: Cambridge University Press.

McClintock, Anne (1995) *Imperial Leather: Race, Gender and Sexuality in the Colonial Contest*, London and New York: Routledge.

McCoy, Frederic (1857) *On the Formation of Museums in Victoria*, Melbourne: Goodhugh and Hough.

McDonagh, Josephine (1987) 'Writings on the mind: Thomas De Quincey and the importance of the palimpsest in nineteenth century thought', *Prose Studies*, no. 10.

MacDonald, Gilbert (1980) *One Hundred Years Wellcome: In Pursuit of Excellence*, London: Wellcome Foundation.

McDonald, P. M. (1979) 'Education' in R. Strahan (ed.) *Rare and Curious Specimens: An Illustrated History of The Australian Museum*, Sydney: The Australian Museum.

McGrane, Bernard (1989) *Beyond Anthropology: Society and the Other*, New York: Columbia University Press.

McGregor, Russell (1997) *Imagined Destinies: Aboriginal Australians and the Doomed Race Theory, 1880–1939*, Melbourne: Melbourne University Press.

MacIntyre, Stuart (1991) *A Colonial Liberalism: The Lost World of Three Victorian Visionaries*, Melbourne: Oxford University Press.

Mack, John (1997) 'Antiquities and the public: the expanding Museum, 1851–96' in M. Caygill and John Cherry (eds) *A. W. Franks: Nineteenth Century Collecting and the British Museum*, London: British Museum.

MacKenzie, John M. (1988) *The Empire of Nature: Hunting, Conservation and British Imperialism*, Manchester: Manchester University Press.

MacLeod, Roy (1982) 'On visiting the "moving metropolis": reflections on the architecture of imperial science', *Historical Records of Australian Science*, vol. 5, no. 3.

Malchow, H. L. (1993) 'Frankenstein's monster and images of race in nineteenth-century Britain', *Past and Present*, no. 139.

Maleuvre, Didier (1999) *Museum Memories: History, Technology, Art*, Stanford, CA: Stanford University Press.

Marchand, Suzanne L. (1994) 'The rhetoric of artefacts and the decline of classical humanism: the case of Josef Strzygowski', *History and Theory*, no. 33.

Marchand, Suzanne L. (1996) *Down from Olympus: Archaeology and Philhellenism in Germany, 1759–1970*, Princeton, NJ: Princeton University Press.

Marchand, Suzanne L. (1997) 'Leo Frobenius and the revolt against the west', *Journal of Contemporary History*, vol. 32, no. 2.

Marchand, Suzanne L. (2000) 'The quarrels of the ancients and moderns in the German museums' in Susan A. Crane (ed.) *Museums and Memory*, Stanford, CA: Stanford University Press.

Marcus, George E. and Fred R. Myers (eds) (1995) *The Traffic in Culture: Refiguring Art and Anthropology*, Berkeley and Los Angeles, CA: University of California Press.

Marsh, Joss Lutz (1995) 'In a glass darkly: photography, the premodern, and Victorian horror' in Elazar Barkan and Ronald Bush (eds) *Prehistories of the Future: The Primitivist Project and the Culture of Modernism*, Stanford, CA: University of Stanford Press.

Mason, Otis T. (1890) 'The educational aspect of the United States National Museum', *Notes Supplementary to the Johns Hopkins University Studies in Historical and Political Science*, no. 4.

Mather, Patricia (1986) *A Time for a Museum: The History of the Queensland Museum, 1862–1986*, Brisbane: Queensland Museum (published as vol. 24 of the *Memoirs of the Queensland Museum*).

Maxwell, William H. (1911) 'Cooperation in education', *The American Museum Journal*, vol. XI, no. 7.

Meller, Helen (1990) *Patrick Geddes: Social Evolutionist and City Planner*, London: Routledge.

Melleuish, Gregory (1995) *Cultural Liberalism in Australia: A Study in Intellectual and Cultural History*, Melbourne: Cambridge University Press.

Menand, Louis (2002) *The Metaphysical Club*, London: Flamingo.

Mercer, Colin (1997) 'Geographies for the present: Patrick Geddes, urban planning and the human sciences', *Economy and Society*, vol. 26, no. 2.

Meredyth, Denise and Jeffrey Minson (eds) (2001) *Citizenship and Cultural Policy*, London: Sage.

Merrill, Lynn L. (1989) *The Romance of Victorian Natural History*, Oxford: Oxford University Press.

217

Miller, David Philip and Peter Hanns Reill (eds) (1996) *Visions of Empire: Voyages, Botany, and Representations of Nature*, Cambridge: Cambridge University Press.

Mirzoeff, Nicholas (1995) 'Signs and citizens. Sign language and visual sign in the French Revolution' in Ann Bermingham and John Brewer (eds) *The Consumption of Culture, 1600–1800: Image, Object, Text*, London and New York: Routledge.

Mitchell, Timothy (1988) *Colonising Egypt*, Cambridge: Cambridge University Press.

Mitchell, W. J. T. (1998) *The Last Dinosaur Book: The Life and Times of a Cultural Icon*, Chicago and London: University of Chicago Press.

Molella, Arthur P. (1984) 'Joseph Henry, "visionary theorisers", and the Smithsonian Institution', *Annals of Science*, no. 41.

Mosedale, Susan Sleeth (1978) 'Science corrupted: Victorian biologists consider "the woman question"', *Journal of the History of Biology*, vol. 11, no. 1.

Moyal, Ann (1986) *A Bright and Savage Land*, Ringwood, Victoria: Penguin Books.

Mozley, Ann (1967) 'Evolution and the climate of opinion in Australia, 1840–76', *Victorian Studies*, vol. X, no. 4.

Mulvaney, D. J. (1981) 'Gum leaves on the Golden Bough: Australia's palaeolithic survivals discovered' in John D. Evans, Barry Cunliffe and Colin Renfrew (eds) *Antiquity and Man: Essays in Honour of Glyn Daniel*, London: Thames & Hudson.

Mulvaney, D. J. (1987) 'Patron and client: the web of intellectual kinship in Australian anthropology' in Nathan Reingold and Marc Rothenberg (eds) *Scientific Colonialism: A Cross-cultural Comparison*. Papers from a conference at Melbourne, 25–30 May, 1981, Washington, DC: Smithsonian Institution Press.

Mulvaney, D. J. (1990) *Prehistory and Heritage: The Writings of John Mulvaney*, Canberra: Department of Prehistory, Research School of Pacific Studies, Australian National University.

Mulvaney, D. J. and Calaby, J. H. (1985) *'So Much That Is New': Baldwin Spencer, 1860–1929: A Biography*, Melbourne: Melbourne University Press.

Murray, David (1904) *Museums: Their History and their Use*, Glasgow: James MacLehose and Sons.

Newland, Elizabeth Dalton (1991) 'Dr George Bennett and Sir Richard Owen: A case study of the colonisation of early Australian science' in R. W. Home and Sally Gregory Kohlstedt (eds) *International Science and National Scientific Identity: Australia between Britain and America*, Dordrecht: Kluwer Academic Publishers.

Noland, Richard W. (1964) 'T. H. Huxley on culture', *Personalist*, vol. 45.

Novas, Carlos and Nikolas Rose (2000) 'Uncertain subjects: risk, liberation and contract', *Economy and Society*, vol. 29, no. 1.

O'Hara, Robert J. (1996) 'Representations of the natural system in the nineteenth century' in Brian S. Baigrie (ed.) *Picturing Knowledge: Historical and Philosophical Problems Concerning the Use of Art in Science*, Toronto, Buffalo and London: University of Toronto Press.

Oldroyd, David R. (1990) *The Highlands Controversy: Constructing Geological Knowledge through Fieldwork in Nineteenth Century Britain*, Chicago, IL: University of Chicago Press.

Orosz, Joel J. (1990) *Curators and Culture: The Museum Movement in America, 1740–1870*, Tuscaloosa and London: University of Alabama Press.

Osborn, Henry Fairfield (1895) 'The hereditary mechanism and the search for the unknown factors of evolution', *Biological Lectures delivered at the Marine Biological Laboratory of Wood's Hall in the Summer Session of 1894*, Boston and London: Ginn and Company.

Osborn, Henry Fairfield (1896) 'A student's reminiscences of Huxley', *Biological Lectures delivered at the Marine Biological Laboratory of Wood's Hall in the Summer Session of 1895*, Boston and London: Ginn and Company, Athenaeum Press.

Osborn, Henry Fairfield (1899) 'The New York Zoological Park', *Science*, no. 7.

Osborn, Henry Fairfield (1911) 'The museum of the future', *The American Museum Journal*, vol. XI, no. 7.

Osborn, Henry Fairfield (1916) *Men of the Old Stone Age: Their Environment, Life and Art*, London: G. Bell & Sons.

Osborn, Henry Fairfield (1923) *The American Museum and Citizenship*. Annual Report of the American Museum of Natural History, no. 54.

Osborn, Henry Fairfield (1924) 'Race progress in relation to social progress', *Journal of the National Institute of Social Science*, no. 9.

Osborn, Henry Fairfield (1927a) *Creative Education in School, College, University, and Museum: Personal Observation and Experience of the Half-Century 1877–1927*, New York: C. Scribner & Sons.

Osborn, Henry Fairfield (1927b) *Man Rises to Parnassus: Critical Epochs in the Prehistory of Man*, NJ: Princeton University Press.

Osborn, Henry Fairfield and George H. Sherwood (1913) *The Museum and Nature Study in the Public Schools*, New York: Miscellaneous Publications of the American Museum of Natural History, no. 3.

Osborne, Thomas (1998) *Aspects of Enlightenment: Social Theory and the Ethics of the Truth*, London: UCL Press.

Otis, Laura (1994) *Organic Memory: History and Body in the Late Nineteenth and Early Twentieth Centuries*, Lincoln and London: University of Nebraska Press.

Outram, Dorinda (1984) *Georges Cuvier: Vocation, Science and Authority in Post-Revolutionary France*, Manchester: Manchester University Press.

Outram, Dorinda (1996) 'New spaces in natural history' in Nicholas Jardine, James A. Secord and Emma C. Spray (eds) *Cultures of Natural History*, Cambridge: Cambridge University Press.

Owen, Richard (1862) *On the Extent and Aims of a National Museum of Natural History*, London: Saunders, Otley & Co.

Paradis, James G. (1989) 'Evolution and ethics in its Victorian context' in James Paradis and George C. Williams (eds) *T. H. Huxley's Evolution and Ethics with New Essays on Its Victorian and SocioBiological Context*, Princeton, NJ: Princeton University Press.

Paradis, James G. (1997) 'Satire and science in Victorian culture' in Bernard Lightman (ed.) *Victorian Science in Context*, Chicago, IL, and London: University of Chicago Press.

Paradis, James and George C. Williams (1989) *T. H. Huxley's 'Evolution and Ethics' with New Essays on Its Victorian and SocioBiological Context*, Princeton, NJ: Princeton University Press.

Parr, A.E. (1959) 'The habitat group', *The Curator*, vol. 2, no. 2.

Parr, A. E. (1961) 'Dimensions, backgrounds, and uses of habitat groups', *The Curator*, vol. 4, no. 3.

Pearson, Charles (1894) *National Life and Character: A Forecast*, London: Macmillan.

Pels, Peter (2000) 'The rise and fall of the Indian Aborgines: Orientalism, Anglicism, and the emergence of an ethnology of India, 1833–1869' in Peter Pels and Oscar Salemink (eds) *Colonial Subjects: Essays on the Practical History of Anthropology*, Ann Arbor: University of Michigan Press.

Petch, Alison (2001) 'Assembling and arranging: The Pitt Rivers' collections, 1850–2000' in Anthony Shelton (ed.) *Collectors: Individuals and Institutions*, London: Horniman Museum and Gardens and Museu Antropológico da Universidade de Coimbra.

Pick, Daniel (1989) *Faces of Degeneration: A European Disorder, c. 1848 – c. 1918*, Cambridge: Cambridge University Press.

Pickstone, John V. (1994) 'Museological science?', *History of Science*, vol. 32, part 2.

Pigott, Ann and Ronald Strahan (1979) 'Administrators of rank (1836–60)' in Ronald Strahan, *Rare and Curious Specimens: An Illustrated History of the Australian Museum*, Sydney: The Australian Museum.

Pitt Rivers, A. H. Lane Fox (all titles through 1880 published under Lane Fox) (1875) 'On the principles of classification adopted in the arrangement of his anthropological collection, now exhibited in the Bethnal Green Museum', *The Journal of the Anthropological Institute of Great Britain and Ireland*, vol. 4.

Pitt Rivers, A. H. Lane-Fox (1891) 'Typological museums, as exemplified by the Pitt Rivers Museum at Oxford, and his Provincial Museum at Farnham', *Journal of the Society of Arts*, no. 40.

219

Pitt Rivers, A. H. Lane-Fox (1906) *The Evolution of Culture, and Other Essays*, Oxford: Clarendon Press.

Poovey, Mary (1995) *Making a Social Body: British Cultural Formation, 1830–1864*, Chicago, IL, and London: University of Chicago Press.

Poovey, Mary (1998) *A History of the Modern Fact: Problems of Knowledge in the Sciences of Wealth and Society*, Chicago: University of Chicago Press.

Porter, Roy (1976) 'Charles Lyell and the principles of the history of geology', *British Journal for the History of Science*, no. 9.

Porter, Roy (1977) *The Making of Geology: Earth Science in Britain*, Cambridge: Cambridge University Press.

Poulot, Dominique (1997) *Musée, Nation, Patrimonie: 1789–1815*, Paris: Gallimard.

Poulter, Clare E. (1980) 'The proper study of mankind: anthropology in its social context in England in the 1860s', PhD dissertation, University of Cambridge.

Prakash, Gyan (1999) *Another Reason: Science and the Imagination of Modern India*, Princeton, NJ: Princeton University Press.

Pratt, Mary Louise (1992) *Imperial Eyes: Travel Writing and Transculturation*, London and New York: Routledge.

Prescott, R. T.M. (1954) *Collections of a Century: The History of the First Hundred Years of the National Museum of Victoria*, Melbourne: National Museum of Victoria.

Preston, Lincoln (1996) *Relic*, New York: Bantam.

Preziosi, Donald (1989) *Rethinking Art History. Meditations on a Coy Science*, New Haven, CT, and London: Yale University Press.

Prior, Nick (2002) *Museums and Modernity: Art Galleries and the Making of Modern Culture*, Oxford: Berg.

Prosler, Martin (1996) 'Museums and globalisation' in Sharon MacDonald and Gordon Fyfe (eds) *Theorising Museums*, Oxford: Blackwell/The Sociological Review.

Putnam, Fredric Ward (1899) 'A problem in American anthropology', *Science*, vol. X, no. 243.

Quatremère de Quincy [1815] (1989) *Considérations morales sur la destination des ouvrages de l'art*, Paris: Fayard.

Rainger, Ronald (1978) 'Race, politics, and science: the Anthropological Society of London in the 1860s', *Victorian Studies*, vol. 22, no. 1.

Rainger, Ronald (1991) *An Agenda for Antiquity – Henry Fairfield Osborn and Vertebrate Palaeontology at the American Museum of Natural History 1890–1935*, Tuscaloosa and London: University of Alabama Press.

Ramsey, Crace Fisher (1938) *Educational Work in Museums of the United States: Development, Methods, and Trends*, New York: H.W. Wilson & Co.

Rasmussen, Carolyn (2001) *A Museum for the People: A History of the Museum Victoria and its Predecessors, 1854–2000*, Melbourne: Scribe Publications.

Ray, William (2001) *The Logic of Culture: Authority and Identity in the Modern Era*, Oxford: Blackwell.

Regal, Brian (2002) *Henry Fairfield Osborn: Race, and the Search for the Origins of Man*, Aldershot: Ashgate.

Reigel, Henrietta (1996) 'Into the heart of irony: ethnographic exhibitions and the politics of difference' in Sharon Macdoland and Gordon Fyfe (eds) *Theorizing Museums*, Oxford: Blackwell/The Sociological Review.

Reynolds, Henry (1998) *This Whispering in Our Hearts*, Sydney: Allen & Unwin.

Richards, Evelleen (1983) 'Darwin and the descent of woman' in D. Oldroyd and I. Langham (eds) *The Wider Domain of Evolutionary Though*, Dordrecht: D. Reidel Publishing Company.

Richards, Evelleen (1989) 'Huxley and woman's place in science: the "woman question" and the control of Victorian anthropology' in J. R. Moore (ed.) *History, Humanity and Evolution*, Cambridge: Cambridge University Press.

Richards, Evelleen (1997) 'Redrawing the boundaries: Darwinian science and Victorian women intellectuals' in Bernard Lightman (ed.) *Victorian Science in Context*, Chicago and London: University of Chicago Press.

Richards, Thomas (1993) *The Imperial Archive: Knowledge and the Fantasy of Empire*, London: Verso.

Richter, Melvin (1964) *The Politics of Conscience: T. H. Green and His Age*, London: Weidenfeld & Nicholson.

Ritchie, David G. (1891) *Darwinism and Politics*, London: Swan Sonnenschein & Co.

Ritvo, Harriet (1987) *The Animal Estate: The English and Other Creatures in the Victorian Age*, Cambridge, MA: Harvard University Press.

Ritvo, Harriet (1997) *The Platypus and the Mermaid and Other Figments of the Classifying Imagination*, Cambridge, MA: Harvard University Press.

Rorty, Richard (1999) *Philosophy and Social Hope*, London: Penguin Books.

Rose, Nikolas (1996) 'The death of the social? Re-figuring the territory of government', *Economy and Society*, vol. 25, no. 3.

Rose, Nikolas (1998) *Inventing Our Selves: Psychology, Power, and Personhood*, Cambridge: Cambridge University Press.

Rose, Nikolas (1999) *Powers of Freedom: Reframing Political Thought*, Cambridge: Cambridge University Press.

Rose, Nikolas (2001) 'Community, citizenship and the third way' in Denise Meredyth and Jeffrey Minson (eds) *Citizenship and Cultural Policy*, London: Sage.

Rosenzweig, Roy and Elizabeth Blackmar (1992) *The Park and the People: A History of Central Park*, New York: Henry Holt & Co.

Rowse, Tim (1978) *Australian Liberalism and National Character*, Melbourne: Kibble Books.

Rudler, F. W. (1876) *On Natural History Museums, with suggestions for the formation of a Central Museum in Wales*, London.

Rudler, F. W. (1897) 'On the arrangement of ethnographical collections', *Museums Journal*.

Rudwick, Martin J. S. (1976a) *The Meaning of Fossils: Episodes in the History of Palaeontology*, Chicago, IL, and London: University of Chicago Press.

Rudwick, Martin J. S. (1976b) 'The emergence of a visual language for geological science', *History of Science*, vol. XIV.

Rudwick, Martin J. S. (1979) 'Transposed concepts from the human sciences in the early work of Charles Lyell' in Ludmilla Jordanova and Roy S. Porter (eds) *Images of the Earth: Essays in the History of the Environmental Sciences*, Chalfont St Giles: British Society for the History of Science.

Rudwick, Martin J. S. (1985) *The Great Devonian Controversy: The Shaping of Scientific Knowledge among Gentleman Specialists*, Chicago, IL: University of Chicago Press.

Rudwick, Martin J. S. (1992) *Scenes from Deep Time: Early Pictorial Representations of the Prehistoric World*, Chicago, IL, and London: University of Chicago Press.

Rudwick, Martin J. S. (1996) 'Minerals, strata and fossils' in Nicholas Jardine, James A. Secord and Emma C. Spray (eds) *Cultures of Natural History*, Cambridge: Cambridge University Press.

Rudwick, Martin J. S. (1997) *Georges Cuvier, Fossil Bones, and Geological Catastrophes*, Chicago, IL: University of Chicago Press.

Rupke, Nicolaas A. (1983) *The Great Chain of History: William Buckland and the English School of Geology*, Oxford: Clarendon Press.

Rupke, Nicolaas A. (1994) *Richard Owen: Victorian Naturalist*, New Haven, CT, and London: Yale University Press.

Russett, Cynthia Eagle (1991) *Sexual Science: The Victorian Construction of Womanhood*, Cambridge, MA: Harvard University Press.

Ryan, Lyndall (1981) *The Aboriginal Tasmanians*, St Lucia: University of Queensland Press.

Ryan, Simon (1996) *The Cartographic Eye: How Explorers Saw Australia*, Melbourne: Cambridge University Press.

Rydell, Robert W. (1984) *All the World's a Fair: Visions of Empire at American International Expositions, 1876–1916*, Chicago, IL, and London: University of Chicago Press.

Sandberg, Mark B. (1995) 'Effigy and narrative: looking into the nineteenth-century folk museum' in Leo Charney and Vanessa Schwartz (eds) *Cinema and the Invention of Modern Life*, Berkeley, Los Angeles and London: University of London Press.

221

Saunders, John R. (1956) 'Development of educational services, 1869–1956', *Annual Report of the American Museum of Natural History*.

Sayers, Janet (1982) *Biological Politics: Feminist and Anti-Feminist Perspectives*, London and New York: Tavistock.

Schiebinger, Londa (1993) *Nature's Body: Sexual Politics and the Making of Modern Science*, London: Pandora.

Schiebinger, Londa (1998) 'Lost knowledges, bodies of ignorance, and the poverty of taxonomy as illustrated by the curious fate of *Flos Pavonis*, an abortifacient' in C. A. Jones and P. Galison (eds) *Picturing Science, Producing Art*, London and New York: Routledge.

Schmitt, Peter J. (1969) *Back to Nature: The Arcadian Myth in Urban America*, New York: Oxford University Press.

Schnapp, Alain (1996) *The Discovery of the Past: The Origins of Archaeology*, London: British Museum Press.

Schudson, Michael (1997) 'Paper tigers', *Lingua Franca*, August.

Schuyler, David (1986) *The New Urban Landscape: The Redefinition of the City Form in Nineteenth-Century America*, Baltimore: Johns Hopkins University Press.

Schwartz, Vanessa R. (1995) 'Cinematic spectatorship before the apparatus: the public taste for reality in *fin-de-siècle* Paris' in Leo Charney and Vanessa Schwartz (eds) *Cinema and the Invention of Modern Life*, Berkeley, Los Angeles and London: University of London Press.

Searle, G. R. (1976) *Eugenics and Politics in Britain, 1900–1914*, Leyden: Noordhoff International Publishing.

Secord, Anne (1994) 'Science in the pub: artisan botanists in early nineteenth-century Lancashire', *History of Science*, no. 32.

Secord, James A. (1997) 'Introduction' to Charles Lyell, *Principles of Geology*, London: Penguin Books.

Secord, James A. (2000) *Victorian Sensation: The Extraordinary Publication, Reception, and Secret Authorship of 'Vestiges of the Natural History of Creation'*, Chicago, IL, and London: University of Chicago Press.

Segalen, Martine (2001) 'Anthropology at home in the museum: the case of the Musée National des Arts et Traditions Populaires in Paris' in Mary Bouquet (ed.) *Academic Anthropology and the Museum: Back to the Future*, New York and Oxford: Berghahn Books.

Selleck, R. J. W. (1968) *The New Education: The English Background, 1870–1914*, Melbourne: Pitman.

Sellers, Charles Coleman (1980) *Mr Peale's Museum: Charles Willson Peale and the First Popular Museum of Natural Science and Art*, New York: W. W. Norton & Co.

Semmel, Bernard (1960) *Imperialism and Social Reform: English Social-Imperial Thought, 1895–1914*, Cambridge, MA: Harvard University Press.

Shapin, Steven (1994) *A Social History of the Truth: Civility and Science in Seventeenth-Century England*, Chicago, IL, and London: University of Chicago Press.

Shapin, Steven (1998) *The Scientific Revolution*, Chicago, IL: University of Chicago Press.

Shapin, Steven and Simon Schaffer (1985) *Leviathan and the Air-Pump: Hobbes, Boyle, and the Experimental Life*, Princeton, NJ: Princeton University Press.

Sheets-Pyenson, Susan (1987) 'Civilising by nature's example: the development of colonial museums of natural history 1850–1900', in N. Reingold and M. Rothenberg (eds) *Scientific Colonialism: A Cross-Cultural Comparison*, Washington, DC: Smithsonian Institution Press.

Shelton, Anthony (2000) 'Museum ethnography: an imperial science' in Elizabeth Hallam and Brian V. Street (eds) *Cultural Encounters: Representing 'Otherness'*, London and New York: Routledge.

Shelton, Anthony (ed.) (2001a) *Collectors: Individuals and Institutions*, London: Horniman Museum and Gardens and Museu Antropológico da Universidade de Coimbra.

Shelton, Anthony (ed.) (2001b) *Collectors: Expressions of Self and Other*, London: Horniman Museum and Gardens and Museu Antropológico da Universidade de Coimbra.

Sherwood, George H. (1927) 'The story of the Museum's service to the schools: methods and experiences of the American Museum of Natural History', *Natural History*, vol. 27, no. 4.

Shteir, Ann B. (1996) *Cultivating Women, Cultivating Science: Flora's Daughters in England, 1760–1860*, Baltimore, OH, and London: Johns Hopkins University Press.

Shteir, Ann B. (1997) 'Elegant recreations? Configuring science writing for women' in Bernard Lightman (ed.) *Victorian Science in Context*, Chicago, IL, and London: University of Chicago Press.

Silberman, Neil Asher (1999) 'Petrie's head: eugenics and Near Eastern archaeology' in Alice B. Kehoe and Mary Beth Emmerichs (eds) *Assembling the Past: Studies in the Professionalisation of Archaeology*, Albuquerque: University of New Mexico Press.

Simms, Stephen C. (1928) *Field Museum and the Child – An Outline of the Work Carried on by Field Museum of Natural History among School Children of Chicago through the N.W. Harris Public School Extension and the James Nelson and Anna Louise Raymond Public School and Children's Lectures*, Chicago, IL: Field Museum of Natural History.

Singer, Ben (1995) 'Modernity, hyperstimulus, and the rise of popular sensationalism' in Leo Charney and Vanessa Schwartz (eds) *Cinema and the Invention of Modern Life*, Berkeley, Los Angeles and London: University of London Press.

Sizer, C. A. (1970) 'The Museum of the Wellcome Institute of the History of Medicine', *Museums Journal*, no. 70.

Skinner, Ghislaine (1986) 'Sir Henry Wellcome's Museum for the Science of History', *Medical History*, no. 30.

Sloan, Douglas (1980) 'Science in New York City, 1867–1907', *Isis*, vol. 71, no. 256.

Sloan, Phillip R. (1997) 'Le Muséum de Paris vient à Londres' in Claude Blanckaert, Claudine Cohen, Pietro Corsi and Jean-Louis Fischer (eds) *Le muséum au premier siècle de son histoire*, Paris: Éditions de Muséum National d'Histoire Naturelle.

Smith, Bernard (1969) *European Vision and the South Pacific, 1768–1850*, London: Oxford University Press.

Spencer, Baldwin (1901) *Guide to the Australian Ethnographical Collection in the National Museum of Victoria*, Melbourne: Government Printer.

Spencer, Baldwin (1987) *The Aboriginal Photographs of Baldwin Spencer* (selected and annotated by Geoffrey Walker, edited by Ron Vanderwal), Ringwood, Vic.: Viking O'Neil.

Spencer, Frank (1992) 'Some notes on the attempt to apply photography to anthropometry during the second half of the nineteenth century' in Elizabeth Edwards (ed.) *Anthropology and Photography, 1860–1920*, New Haven and London: Yale University Press/The Royal Anthropological Institution.

Spray, Emma (1997) 'Le spectâcle de la nature: contrôle du public et vision républicaine dans le Muséum jacobin' in Claude Blanckaert, Claudine Cohen, Pietro Corsi and Jean-Louis Fischer (eds) *Le Muséum au premier siècle de son histoire*, Paris: Éditions de Muséum National d'Histoire Naturelle.

Stafford, Barbara Maria (1993) *Body Criticism: Imaging the Unseen in Enlightenment Art and Medicine*, Cambridge, MA: MIT Press.

Stafford, Barbara (1994) *Artful Science: Enlightenment Entertainment and the Eclipse of Visual Education*, Cambridge, MA: MIT Press.

Stafford, Robert A. (1988) 'The long arm of London: Sir Roderick Murchison and imperial science in Australia' in R.W. Home (ed.) *Australian Science in the Making*, Sydney: Cambridge University Press/Australian Academy of Science.

Staiff, Russell (1997) 'History and the painted landscape in nineteenth century South Australia' in Clare O'Farrell (ed.) *Foucault: The Legacy*, Queensland: Queensland University of Technology.

Stanbury, Peter and Julian Holland (eds) (1988) *Mr Macleay's Celebrated Cabinet*, Sydney: Macleay Museum.

Steadman, Philip (1979) *The Evolution of Designs: Biological Analogy in Architecture and the Applied Arts*, Cambridge: Cambridge University Press.

Stearn, W. T. (1981) *The Natural History Museum at South Kensington: A History of the British Museum (Natural History)*, London: Heinemann.

Stedman Jones, Gareth (1984) *Outcast London: A Study in the Relationship between Classes in Victorian Society*, Harmondsworth: Penguin Books.

Stepan, Nancy Leys (2001) *Picturing Tropical Nature*, London: Reaktion Books.

Stephens, Leslie (1893) 'Ethics and the struggle for existence', *The Contemporary Review*, no. 64.

Stewart, Susan (1995) 'Death and life, in that order, in the works of Charles Wilson Peale' in Lyne Cooke and Peter Wollen (eds) *Visual Display: Culture Beyond Appearances* (1995) Seattle: Bay Press.

Stocking, George W. Jr. (1968) *Race, Culture and Evolution: Essays in the History of Anthropology*, New York: Free Press.

Stocking, George W. Jr (ed.) (1985) *Objects and Others: Essays on Museums and Material Culture*, Madison, WI: University of Wisconsin Press.

Stocking, George W. Jr (1987) *Victorian Anthropology*, New York: Free Press.

Stocking, George W. Jr (1992) *The Ethnographer's Magic and Other Essays in the History of Anthropology*, Madison, WI: University of Wisconsin Press.

Stocking, George W. Jr (1995) *After Tylor: British Social Anthropology, 1888–1951*, London: Athlone.

Stocking, George W. Jr. (1999) 'The spaces of cultural representation, circa 1887 and 1969: reflections on museum arrangement and anthropological theory in the Boasian and evolutionary traditions' in Peter Galison and Emily Thompson (eds) *The Architecture of Science*, Cambridge, MA: MIT Press.

Stoler, Laura Ann (1995) *Race and the Education of Desire: Foucault's History of Sexuality and the Colonial Order of Things*, Durham and London: Duke University Press.

Strahan, Ronald (1979) *Rare and Curious Specimens: An Illustrated History of the Australian Museum*, Sydney: The Australian Museum.

Thomas, David Hurst (2000) *Skull Wars: Kenwick Man, Archaeology, and the Battle for Native American Identity*, New York: Basic Books.

Thomas, Nicholas (1988) 'Material culture and colonial power: Ethnological collections and the establishment of colonial rule in Fiji', *Man*, vol. 24.

Thomas, Nicholas (1991) *Entangled Objects: Exchange, Material Culture, and Colonialism in the Pacific*, Cambridge, MA: Harvard University Press.

Thomas, Nicholas (1994) *Colonialism's Culture: Anthropology, Travel, Government*, Cambridge: Polity Press.

Thompson, Edward P. (1967) 'Time, work-discipline and industrial capitalism', *Past and Present*, no. 38.

Thompson, Kenneth (1980) 'Folklore and sociology', *Sociological Review*, vol. 28, no. 2.

Thompson, M. W. (1977) *General Pitt-Rivers: Evolution and Archaeology in the Nineteenth Century*, Bradford-on-Avon: Moonraker Press.

Tiffany, Sharon and Kathleen Adams (1985) *The Wild Woman: An Inquiry into the Anthropology of an Idea*, Cambridge: Schenkman.

Tomkins, Calvin (1989) *Merchants and Masterpieces: The Story of the Metropolitan Museum of Fine Art*, New York: Henry Holt & Company.

Torgovnick, Marianna (1990) *Gone Primitive: Savage Intellects, Modern Lives*, Chicago, IL, and London: University of Chicago Press.

Toulmin, Stephen and June Goodfield (1977) *The Discovery of Time*, Chicago, IL, and London: University of Chicago Press.

Trigger, Bruce (1989) *A History of Archaeological Thought*, Cambridge: Cambridge University Press.

Tubbs, Mrs (1897) 'The relation of museums to elementary education', *Museums Journal*.

Turnbull, Paul (1991) '"Ramsay's regime": the Australian Museum and the procurement of Aboriginal bodies, c. 1874–1900', *Aboriginal History*, vol. 15, no. 2.

Tylor, Edward (1871) *Primitive Culture*, 2 vols, London: John Murray.

Uricchio, William and Roberta E. Pearson (1998) 'Corruption, criminality and the nickleodeon' in John Fullerton (ed.) *Celebrating 1895: The Centenary of Cinema*, London: John Libbey.

Valverde, Mariana (1996) '"Despotism" and ethical liberal governance', *Economy and Society*, vol. 25, no. 3.

van Keuren, David Keith (1982) 'Human sciences in Victorian Britain: anthropology in institutional and disciplinary formation, 1863–1908', PhD thesis, University of Pennsylvania.

van Riper, A. Bowdein (1993) *Men among the Mammoths: Victorian Science and the Discovery of Human Prehistory*, London and Chicago: University of Chicago Press.

Walkowitz, Judith R. (1992) *City of Dreadful Delight: Narratives of Sexual Danger in Late-Victorian London*, Chicago, IL: University of Chicago Press.

Weimann, Jeanne Madeline (1981) *The Fair Women: The Story of the Women's Building, World's Columbian Exhibition. Chicago 1893*, Chicago, IL: Academy Chicago.

Weindling, Paul (1989) *Health, Race and German Politics between National Unification and Nazism, 1870–1945*, Cambridge: Cambridge University Press.

Weiss, F. E. (1892) 'The organisation of a botanical museum', *Museums Association Proceedings*.

Whewell, William M.A. (1837) *History of the Inductive Sciences: From the Earliest to the Present Times*, London: John W. Parker, vol. 3.

Williams, Raymond (1976) *Keywords: A Vocabulary of Culture and Society*, London: Fontana/Croom Helm.

Winson, Mary P. (1991) *Reading the Shape of Nature: Comparative Zoology at the Agassiz Museum*, Chicago, IL, and London: University of Chicago Press.

Wolfe, Patrick (2000) 'White man's flour: the politics and poetics of an anthropological discovery' in Peter Pels and Oscar Salemink (eds) *Colonial Subjects: Essays on the Practical History of Anthropology*, Ann Arbor: University of Michigan Press.

Yanni, Carla (1999) *Nature's Museums: Victorian Science and the Architecture of Display*, London: Athlone Press.

Young, Robert J. C. (1995) *Colonial Desire: Hybridity in Theory, Culture and Race*, London and New York: Routledge.

Zimmerman, Andrew (2001) *Anthropology and Antihumanism in Imperial Germany*, Chicago, IL, and London: University of Chicago Press.

Index

226

Uricchio, William 184
US National Museum 75, 79,
132, 196–7(n)

Valverde, Mariana 89
van Keuren, David 33, 196(n)
van Riper, Bowdein 59, 194(n)
Vaux, Calvert 125, 201(n)
Victorian Public Library 141,
146, 152
Virchhow, Rudolf 203(n)
Vogt, Carl 111

Walker, Francis Amasa 124
Ward, Lester Frank 119
Waterhouse, Alfred 73, 196(n)

Weismann, August 121, 128,
130
Weiss, F. E. 160
Wellcome Historical Medical
Museum 65, 107,
199–200(n)
Werner, A.G. 48
Western Australian Museum
149, 151
western civilisation, models of
60
Whewell, William 36–7
Williams, G. C. 90
Williams, Raymond 100
Wilson, Daniel 44, 131–2,
190(n)

Winckelmann, Johann 24, 39,
75
Wolfe, Patrick 157
Wolff, Friedrich August 161–2
wonder, culture of 125–6, 163,
180–2, 187(n)
Wood, John George 183
Wunderkammern 203(n)

Yanni, Carla 74
Young, Robert J. C. 203(n)

Zallinger, Rudolph 195(n)
Zadig, method of 56
Zimmerman, Andrew 15,
82–4